The Lost Key

Dr Robert Lomas gained a first class honours degree in Electrical Engineering before being awarded a PhD for his research into solid state physics and crystalline structures. He later worked on electronic weapons systems and emergency services command and control systems. He has established himself as one of the worlds leading authorities on the history of science and lectures on Information Systems at Bradford University's School of Management, one of the UK's leading business schools. He is a regular speaker on the Masonic lecture circuit as well as a strong supporter of the Orkney Science Festival. He has co-authored the best-selling *The Hiram Key*, *The Second Messiah*, *Uriel's Machine* and *The Book of Hiram* and written *The Invisble College*, *Freemasonry and the Birth of Modern Science* and *The Man who Invented the Twentieth Century*.

The Lost Key

The Supranatural Secrets of the Freemasons

ROBERT LOMAS

CORONET

First published in Great Britain in 2011 by Coronet
An imprint of Hodder & Stoughton
An Hachette UK company

First published in paperback in 2012

1

Copyright © Robert Lomas, 2011

A CIP catalogue record for this title is available from the British Library

ISBN 978 1 444 71061 8

Typeset in Garamond 3 by Hewer Text UK Ltd, Edinburgh

Printed and bound by CPI Group (UK) Ltd, Croydon, CR0 4YY

Hodder & Stoughton policy is to use papers that are natural, renewable and recyclable products
and made from wood grown in sustainable forests. The logging and manufacturing processes are expected to conform to the environmental regulations of the country of origin.

Hodder & Stoughton Ltd
338 Euston Road
London NW1 3BH

www.hodder.co.uk

Dedicated to
My Brethren of the Lodge of Living Stones
No. 4957

ACKNOWLEDGMENTS

IT WAS MARK BOOTH, my old friend and mentor, who encouraged me to tackle this book. The ideas in it have haunted me for many years, but I have always hesitated to get started on a project I thought too ambitious for me. Over many years Mark has motivated me to draft it, guided my approach to the more difficult parts and helped me arrange and articulate my ideas into a structure that I hope enables me to share them with other seekers. He is an inspirational editor, a joy to work with, and I thank him for making this book possible.

John Wheelwright, my trusted copy-editor and second pair of eyes for many years, has once more proved his worth as a guardian of clarity of expression. I appreciate his help with standardising my spelling and improving my grammar, and for his cheerful encouragement and clear appraisal whenever I became confused and muddled.

Charlotte Haycock has been a staunch bulwark of common sense in dealing with all issues of production, and I am grateful to her for smoothing so many paths.

My agents Bill Hamilton and Charles Brotherstone of A.M. Heath & Co. have been consistently supportive, and I am indebted to them for their continuing encouragement and professional skills.

Not least I would like to thank my brethren of the Lodge of Living Stones. In particular I would like to thank Bro. Douglas Inglesent for introducing me to the lodge; Bros. Hew Gill, Tony Baker and Martin Jackson for their stimulating discussions; and those Past Masters of the lodge who asked not to be named but who have consistently acted as trustworthy guides and mentors on my somewhat stony path towards the Centre.

Finally I would like to thank my wife, children and grandchildren for their loving support.

CONTENTS

CONTENTS

CONTENTS

INTRODUCTION

A Heinous Confession

I WAS INTRODUCED to the social and spiritual joys of Freemasonry by women. My first, extremely positive, experience of Masonry occurred in Chester at the exquisitely manicured hands of a lodge of lady Masons, the Lodge of the East Gate. As a male Freemason, this is a heinous confession to have to make.

I was but a youth of seventeen when the daughter of a senior lady Freemason invited me to her mother's Gentlemen's Night. It was an evening of firsts. For the first time I wore a (hired) dinner suit and black tie. For the first time I escorted a charming young lady, elegant in long dress, bare shoulders and swept up hair, to a formal dinner and dance. And for the first time I experienced the spiritual warmth and sparkle that the group mind of a well-integrated lodge can offer – although then I did not know the cause, only the effect. I knew nothing of the Masonic teaching that members of a lodge should strive to meld their souls together by group effort, so that the lodge becomes capable of greater mental feats than any individual member. Had anybody suggested such an idea to me on that first evening I would have dismissed it, but I went away with a deep sense of the specialness of Freemasonry which remains with me.

During that and many later social evenings spent with the ladies of the East Gate I came to enjoy the ceremonial, the formality of the three separate and distinct gavels knocking in a single room-circling echo to call for silence, and I noted the respect the lady brothers expressed towards each other. And to their male guests. At the time I put my impressions down to what I felt must be the benefits of a matriarchal society.

Perhaps I should explain. My childhood world was dominated by three sisters, children of Caroline Blackwell née Griffiths. Annie was the eldest,

Jenny the most adventurous, and Sophia, the youngest, was my maternal grandmother. These three were born towards the end of the nineteenth century in the Welsh border town of Mold and brought up speaking only Welsh. (The Welsh word for grandmother, *Nain*, is the only name I ever used for Sophia.) Jenny and Sophia moved to Manchester, married, had daughters of their own and were widowed young; Annie also married but stayed near Mold and, although she loved children, was never able to have any of her own. These hardy, self-reliant women, who struggled through two world wars, shaped my childhood.

In many ways I was properly prepared not only to survive but to thrive on the fringes of the matriarchal hierarchy that is women's Freemasonry. The Lodge of the East Gate drew much of its membership from the extended female branches of the Blackwell and Griffiths families of the greater Mold area, the tribal donors of my own mitochondrial DNA. This could only have made me feel more at home, for the senior lady brethren who supplied my formative experiences of Freemasonry were the sisters, cousins and nieces of my *Nain* and maternal great-aunts. I joined male Freemasonry because of this early positive experience, and, when I later met resistance to my curiosity about The Craft's origins, I persevered because I had already formed a positive picture of the benefits which Freemasonry can bestow.

So my secret is out. When I joined Freemasonry, just over twenty years after that first Gentlemen's Night, I was hoping to re-experience the social warmth and fellowship I had felt as a boy in the motherly embrace of the Lodge of the East Gate. But I soon began to wonder if male Freemasonry had lost the spark which animated the ladies.

Masculine Masonry offered social programmes with exactly the same objectives as the Gentlemen's Nights of the East Gate, and over the years I supped at and enjoyed them; I was no stranger to the jolly Pickwickian side of male Masonry, which I affectionately nicknamed 'the Belly Club'. For a knife-and-fork Mason this is the club *par excellence.* This kind of Freemasonry is simple. It provides congenial male dining companions, good food, deferential table service and a chance to be praised for visiting, eating and being a solid trencherman. The ritual work in this type of Freemasonry is a bit of fun whose purpose is to work up the brethren's appetite for the serious business of dining.

This style of Masonry is found in many large cities and is character-ised by lodges which meet in restaurants and gentlemen's clubs. In more provincial Masonic centres, where budgets may be tighter, the level of gourmet attainment may fall below the standard of the late, lamented Café Royal, but, by concentrating on good red meat and puddings with custard, the main calorific aim of the Belly Club can still be achieved. Dedicated members can be recognised by their distinctive regalia, including extra-large trouser waistbands and soup-stained ties. This style of Masonry is congenial, relaxing and minimises the demands on the weary brain, although overindulging in its charms can in later life lead to a need to buy apron-string extensions. However, it rarely creates the spiritual tingle of group alertness I sensed at that lodge of lady Masons.

During my early flirtation with the male side of The Craft I began to wonder if eating was all there was to it. I suspected that the spiritual warmth I had sensed in the lady brethren of the Lodge of the East Gate was a function not of Freemasonry but of female society. Perhaps the men Masons met for reasons other than the ones that motivated the ladies. I even wondered if there might be some truth in the idea that the men only met to form a networking club.

This idea is a common one and arouses suspicion and fear among the excluded 'profane' (as the ritual calls non-Masons). It had been the subject of whole shelves of literature, which I decided I ought to read. The genre started with William Hannah's *Darkness Visible* (1952)[1], which claimed that Masonic networking takes place with Satan himself. Hannah thought that Satan awarded the brethren occult powers, which is a quite startlingly superstitious suggestion and probably says more about Hannah than it does about Freemasonry. By comparison, the claims of Steven Knight in *The Brotherhood* (1984)[2] were much milder, although almost as paranoid. He put forward the suggestion that Freemasonry secretly rules the world by preferring, and appointing, incompetent Freemasons over better-qualified non-Masons. This genre climaxed in the claims of Martin Short, whose *Inside The Brotherhood* (1989)[3] hinted that Freemasonry might control the police, the under-world, the armed forces and all charities, for the purpose of making or breaking the careers of its followers. As any member of The Craft knows, this mythical secret network of arch-manipulators is an urban myth; there is no such inner cadre. Freemasonry does not offer material preferment, but at its best teaches a deep spiritual knowledge of yourself and the world you live in. However, as I will show, this knowledge has to be worked for and earned. It is not an automatic entitlement of the newly entered Apprentice Freemason. And not every Freemason finds the lost key to this secret.

When I joined Freemasonry, nearly a quarter of a century ago, I was searching for an elusive something I had seen at the Lodge of the East Gate. I was not sure what it was, but I did know that it was not small-minded networking. Had social or professional climbing been my purpose I would have done far better by attending academic conferences and public science and literature festivals in order to meet people who could make common cause with me in the matters that concerned my professional interests. In my experience, any imaginary inner cadre has proved incapable of wreaking the destruction attributed to it by Hannah, Knight and Short. And I suspect the ability of senior Freemasons to promote professional careers is as limited as their ability to destroy mine proved to be.

For me, the attraction of Freemasonry was not an opportunity to network with its hierarchy but to relive a fond memory of the spiritual sparkle and shared purpose I had seen at the Lodge of the East Gate. I wanted to understand an Order that can cause this effect and to become a part of it. It was the covert offer of spiritual rewards which attracted me. At first this prize eluded me, although the early aspiration remained in my heart. Eventually I would discover that it was not to be found in the pomp and pageantry of Grand Lodges, but had to be sought in the dark silence of a lodge of contemplation.

Our childhood dreams are not easy to set aside, and they often drive us in ways we do not recognise. My bookshelf holds a battered and much-thumbed copy of *How to Drive a Steam Train*, and, if I looked closely in the deeper recesses of my filing cabinets, I suspect I could also unearth several notebooks containing long lists of numbers for railway engines long since scrapped. My ambition to be a train driver suffered a severe blow in 1960, when steam train production ceased – I was forced to seek solace in the study of physics instead. But . . . probe deep into the inner layers of my cold physicist's heart, and you will find an anorak-wearing nerd who rejoices in long lists of obscure facts that can be produced on a whim to stun (or more likely bore) the unlearned into worshipful awe. In short I have a curiosity about obscure and little-known facts. One facet of Freemasonry offered endless opportunities for indulging my secret train-spotter in the company of the fellow oddballs I like to call the degree-collecting club.

This entity knows that inside many an outwardly sensible and respectable grown man lurks a pimply juvenile show-off. The Masonic degree-collecting club provides a presentable front for indulging this inner nerd. It tempts you with promises of increasingly obscure secret knowledge, the prospect of participating in new and intriguing rituals, and a chance to raid the dressing-up box and wear ever wilder and more extreme finery in the privacy of a well-tyled lodge. The vistas set before a degree-collector are wide. To offer just a few possibilities: you can be lowered into the Secret Vault under Solomon's Temple, sail on the Ark with Noah, stand alongside the Empress Helena as she discovers the True Cross, meet and converse with the mysterious Melchizedek, learn how to survive the red-hot torments of the grid-iron, carry a sword and wear the red cross and white mantle of Holy Violence, and even fear having your hand chopped off by a mad axeman – all in the safety of your own lodge room. I firmly identify with the aspirations of the degree-collectors. I have indulged in many of their amusing side-adventures, and may yet try more. My support for this rather odd path through Freemasonry can perhaps be most clearly seen in the collection of side-degree rituals I have preserved on the Masonic collection website at the University of Bradford (www.bradford.ac.uk/webofhiram/).

The average Masonic degree-collector may be able to bore for Britain, but his fascination and indulgence do no harm. He lives out his fantasies in the company of consenting adults. The bottom line is that side degrees preserve many fascinating traditions of Freemasonry, so I hope my brother collectors will continue to expand their eccentric glory. But degree-collecting is not the true purpose of Freemasonry. Indeed it turns out that it is often just an amusing sideshow.

* * *

So what is Masonry's true purpose? Perhaps you might think it is Charity, but again I would disagree. The charity show-off response is a relatively new addition to Freemasonry: spawned in response to the hostile reaction to The Craft as portrayed by Hannah, Knight and Short. I was taught by my Antient Sistren of Freemasonry, that charity should be one of the best-kept secrets of The Craft. If people need help that does not mean that they also need their noses rubbed in the fact that they are being forced to accept a handout. Charity should be undertaken by stealth. It should be a source of help and comfort for the recipient but a matter of the deepest secrecy for the donor. At all costs it should avoid damaging the self-esteem of the recipient. The practice of public alms-giving, followed by the equally public humiliation of the recipient, brought about by the need to praise the donor for their generosity before the cash is handed over, is not in the spirit of The Craft that I was taught. Masons should give to charity because they feel empathy with the suffering of their fellow human beings and wish to relieve their distress. They should never add to that distress by demanding publicity for what is no more than a natural act of humanity. (In such cases the epithet 'whited sepulchre' springs to mind.)

If men want to indulge in public charity then Round Table and the Lions exist for just that. They set out to seek publicity in order to raise their organisations' profiles as fund-raisers. They do, though, have the justification that they need publicity for their fund-raising ventures in order to encourage the general public to support them and donate to their chosen causes. Freemasonry cannot use this argument, because it raises its charitable funds from its members. It does not need to publicise itself outside The Craft to seek extra donations; there is no Masonic reason to publicise charitable giving other than self-aggrandisement. I am in favour of donating to charity, but believe donations must be strictly anonymous. The public parading of charity seems to me demeaning to the recipients and to undermine what I have come to believe is the real purpose of Freemasonry.

But what is that purpose? The founder of my current lodge, Walter Wilmshurst, wrote in June 1908:

> The body of a human is the greatest marvel of creation, and can be made
> the most delicate instrument in the world. It is the God-given instrument

of living science, and its perfecting is an integral part of Masonic training. I believe there is a science of sciences, and this I hold to be the science of Masonic Initiation. There are perfected men, who in varying degrees possess this science, and are therefore kin with the living intelligences of the universe, who are the natural modes of the divine mind.

This book is the story of my struggle to discover for myself this 'science of sciences' and to strive towards communication with the 'living intelligences of the universe'. I will describe my progress through various layers of Masonic activities, seeking to discover the secrets hidden at its centre. As I search for knowledge of myself I will set out the questions I asked and reveal insights The Craft had to offer.

I warn you, though, the quest will be confusing and irrational at times. The Craft did not yield its secrets easily. Its past is like the ever-changing skin of a chameleon, and its many possible histories showed themselves in different guises as I strove to understand it. It forced me to rethink my views on many aspects of my education and past experience.

Since I first decided to knock on the closed door of the lodge and seek entry, Freemasonry has rewarded me with a series of increasingly intriguing conundrums. Each time I have lifted the top off the latest Russian doll of mystery I have found another closed container nestling within. As a result I have been encouraged to reflect, to grow and to learn how to approach the next level. Each time I find myself asking 'But what is the purpose?' . . . and each time I get a richer answer. The Craft encourages its followers to make a daily advancement in Masonic knowledge and it does so by gently denying too easy an approach to its mysteries.

Ultimately you will have to reach your own conclusions about The Craft's teachings. But, if you will suspend your scepticism for a while, I will share with you what I have learned about Freemasonry over four decades of study.

We will start with a brief summary of where, when and by whose hand did Freemasonry begin.

I

Whence Come You?

What is Freemasonry?

ASK A FREEMASON this question, and you can expect an answer quoted directly from Freemasonry's book of ritual: 'A peculiar system of morality veiled in allegory and illuminated by symbols.' To me, though, Freemasonry is something more.

It is something that can make three mature, professional men – a psychologist, a surgeon and a physicist – stand in a dark, cold car park on a wet and foggy September evening and talk for an hour and a half about their deepest spiritual urges. That meeting of three Masons, students respectively of the human mind, the human body and the workings of the world humans inhabit, prompted me to write this book. What is the nature of the force which can bring together such a disparate collection of individuals to share their innermost feelings?

In part it is their shared search for the truth about the human condition.

But it is the way they have been taught to set aside differences, concentrate on shared values and become a scintillating group mind which represents a hope for a solution to a modern dilemma, the conflict between religion and science. In fact they have adopted a model of behaviour which may help resolve many difficulties in modern society.

Let me explain. Western civilisation is founded on two pillars: one of secular science, the other of supernatural religion, but, unlike the priestly and kingly pillars of mutual Masonic support, the two are often in conflict. The outlooks these pillars symbolise are the scientific spirit of curiosity – observation of the hidden mysteries of nature and science, the attitude that anything and everything may be questioned and that all assertions should be tested – and the religious ethics of Christianity

9

– the brotherhood of all men, the value of the individual and the importance of love in motivating actions. I do not believe it is possible for
theology to discover a set of metaphysical ideas that can be guaranteed
not to conflict with the ever-advancing and always changing ideas of
science. Hence, a scientific education tends to make religion seem like
superstitious nonsense.

Take the three men in the car park I mentioned above – the psychologist (Bro. Hew), the surgeon (Bro. Tony) and the physicist (me). We are
all Masons, and if asked 'What are the three grand principles on which
Freemasonry is founded?' we have all been ritually trained to answer,
'Brotherly Love, Relief and Truth'. But try probing a little deeper and
asking, 'And which of these principles first attracted you to want to learn
more about The Craft?' The psychologist will give you one answer,
'Brotherly Love'; the surgeon will give another, 'Relief', and the physicist will provide a third, 'Truth'. And indeed when we three meet to
discuss the nature of life, Bro. Hew champions Love as the power which
makes people work together, Bro. Tony speaks of the satisfaction which
comes from Relieving suffering and helping patients function once more
in society, while I am always obsessed with 'Why is this True?'

This is where Freemasonry offers a way to reconcile the demands of
science and religion. To become a Freemason you need only express a
belief in the existence of an order at the centre of creation. This is metaphorically expressed as a belief in a Supreme Being. Masonry leaves me
free to believe in the immutable but statistically uncertain laws that
govern the interactions of atoms without forcing me to project human
characteristics onto the Grand Geometrician of the Universe. It leaves
Bro. Hew free to imagine the Great Architect as the ultimate fount of
human Love, offering hope for a better future, and it leaves Bro. Tony
free to pray to the Most High that his surgical interventions may
succeed in relieving distress. My Great Architect is a fair but disinter-
ested guardian of ultimate Truth and offers the hope of a great unified
theory of everything. Bro. Hew's Great Architect inspires people to
work together with love towards the greater good, and Bro. Tony's
inspires him to perform 'miracles' of healing. Yet we three can all meet
and use the religiously neutral and politically unbiased language and
symbols of The Craft to help us work together to understand the world
we live in.

Freemasonry is the force that can bring together such a disparate collection of individuals to share their innermost feelings. Bro. Hew, Bro. Tony and I all agreed that the experience of the lodge meeting and the participation in working the ritual with individuals who share a hunger for spiritual truth creates something bigger than our individual egos. But, knowing the human imperfections of the lodge, how does it achieve this? That has engaged me ever since I first encountered the deeper aspects of Masonry, and my answers have changed as I have learned more about the workings of The Craft.

Freemasonry has spread throughout the world to become its second largest spiritual organisation in numbers and extent, exceeded only by the Roman Catholic Church. It has spread because it has worked – not for everyone, but for a significant proportion of individuals – for at least thirty generations. (I have estimated the number as between seven and three per thousand of males 'free-born and over the age of twenty-one'.[4] This 'market share' of males that Freemasonry attracts as members has not dropped below 0.3 percent of the adult male population in the last 300 years.)

The Various Origins of Freemasonry

Over the years, as my knowledge of Freemasonry's past has grown, I have come to realise that The Craft has more than one history. It has a mundane sequence of real, documented events, and it also has a series of mysterious mythical creations, which have grown over years of ritual telling and retelling. Each of these histories is important. The mundane history took me some time to uncover, mainly because it was deeply intertwined with the mythical histories (and has been covered in depth in my other books). But there were vested interests in Freemasonry who didn't like this true history and tried their best to divert me from discovering it. Similarly, there will be many Masons who will be disturbed by my latest attempts to unravel the mythical history and its effect on the purpose and development of The Craft.

When I first joined Freemasonry I was told that it began in London in 1717, in four public houses where a crowd of local gentlemen and minor lords met to drink. Apparently, whilst wandering around local building sites these grand gentlemen were struck by the high moral standards of the workmen they saw and immediately asked to be admitted to their trade guilds so that they might learn how to become better individuals. Within ten years much of the minor nobility of London joined, and soon afterwards Freemasonry became a popular pastime of all the royal families of Europe. As I learned more about the inner teachings and ritual of Freemasonry this official explanation became less and less credible. Eventually I started to research the origins myself. My present view has developed slowly over the years. As a scientist, I am always prepared to change my opinion as and when I discover more facts. I believe that three of these alternative histories are significant to understanding The Craft. The first is the set of mythical histories which are told within the various rituals, degrees and side-orders which make up the Order; the second is the official history, promoted by the United Grand Lodge of England (UGLE), which is told to all newly made Masons under the English Constitution and rigorously promoted worldwide by UGLE; and the third is the real historical facts of where, when and how Freemasonry began. These three types of history were somewaht difficult to separate out when I encountered them.

The mythical histories – or traditional histories as Masons call them – are intended to carry a ritual message and have a spiritual, or esoteric, subtext.

The official UGLE history is a political construct, created soon after the Jacobite rebellion of 1715, with the purpose of distancing London Freemasons from their Stuart roots and the threat of being suspected of treason against the newly installed Hanoverian monarchy. It is whimsical, politically motivated and amusingly unbelievable.

The real history of Freemasonry is less romantic and more commonplace. It is only lifted above banality by the far-reaching and unexpected consequences of the self-help actions of a small group of redundant stonemasons in fifteenth-century Aberdeen.

Once I had dismissed the imaginary 'official' London story – of bored gentlemen wandering around local building sites and asking common workmen for instruction on how to improve their morals – as too incredible to accept, I found the story of the first Masonic lodge in the records of Aberdeen Burgh Council. There I read about Bros David Menzies and Alexander Stuart, the first speculative Freemasons. Their lodge rebuilt St Nicholas Kirk in Aberdeen in 1476. And this inspired group of working stonemasons first used the strange symbols and rituals that are the defining feature of modern Freemasonry.

Myth and Reality – The St Clairs of Roslin

There is a strand in the popular history of Freemasonry which says that it was created by Sir William St Clair during the building of Roslin Chapel in West Lothian in the mid-fifteenth century. It is a story which has a great following and some element of truth to it. Roslin Chapel *was* involved in the beginnings of Freemasonry, but when I came to undertake a closer investigation of Sir William St Clair, the 12th Baron Roslin and the man who built the chapel, I found it highly unlikely that he could be capable of coming up with the important ideas which became such an integral part of Freemasonry.

Unlike their over-hyped public image, the St Clair family were not a group of high-minded thinkers and patrons of the arts. They were political opportunists, pirates, rogues and failed usurpers. From 1066 until 1484 the St Clairs amassed lands and titles in the northern parts of the Isles of Britain, until by the early fifteenth century William the 12th Baron was also 11th Baron Pentland, 9th Baron Cousland, 3rd Earl of Orkney, 1st Earl of Caithness, 1st Baron Dysart and 1st Lord Sinclair. He owned more of Scotland than the Stuart kings, and he also controlled the Norse lands of Caithness, Orkney and Shetland which then were not part of Scotland.

Public veneration of the True Cross at the Abbey of the Holy Rood, built to house the fragment of the True Cross brought by Queen Margaret as her dowry when she married Malcolm III of Scotland, had given the Stuart kings a powerful spiritual focus for their Divine Right to rule. David I, Margaret's eldest son, saw the advantage of capitalising on the power of his mother's famous relic and claimed to have experienced a popular miracle when the True Cross saved his life by appearing between him and a raging stag. (What better sign could a king want that he was destined by God to do exactly as he chose?) David built the Abbey of the Holy Rood conveniently close to Edinburgh Castle and then moved the miraculous splinter to it (and hence to his political capital) from the site of his mother's tomb in Dunfermline Abbey. By their continuing use of the relic the kings of Scotland demonstrated how to harness religious myths to drive political objectives. This lesson was not lost on the ambitious St Clair family.

William (1410–1484), the 12th Baron Roslin, was a Norse noble holding lands from the King of Norway, as well as the most powerful landowner in Scotland, not excluding King James II. William built Roslin Chapel because he had seen, from the way the fragment of the True Cross had demonstrated to the king's subjects that God was on the side of their temporal lord, how holy relics could reinforce the will of a ruler. He, like the Stuart kings, wanted streams of pilgrims eager to venerate a holy relic that was part of a self-reinforcing system of political value.

William wanted a powerful political and religious symbol of power, but he did not own any relics. He was, though, astute enough to harness folk myths to aid his cause. In medieval times the central focus of the spiritual world was the Temple of Jerusalem (contemporary maps showed it as the physical centre of the world). His decision to build a replica of the ruins of Temple Mount in Roslin was a move of inspired political cunning. Churches are repositories of myth, and the Temple of Jerusalem was the greatest mythical influence in the medieval world.

Building a church was a way of demonstrating power and influence, and the political influence of the Barons of Roslin, in terms of the titles and lands they held, peaked under William the 12th Baron. He became the most powerful noble in Scotland at a time when the succession to the Crown of Scotland was distinctly wobbly. He married three times, each time increasing his land holdings. William's first wife, Elizabeth (40 and twice widowed), was the daughter of Archibald, 4th Earl of Douglas and Lord Warden of the Marches, and Archibald's second wife Margaret Stewart, daughter of King Robert III. William had known that if Elizabeth had sons they could be serious contenders for the Scottish Crown. And she did manage to bear him a daughter and a son, before dying during the second childbirth around 1451. William now had a son with a potential claim to the Scottish throne and was in control of large swathes of Scotland at the time he began to build Roslin Chapel in 1456.[5]

But William St Clair was not capable of creating a vision of the Temple of Solomon in Scotland. He liked the idea of a shrine as a spiritual focus for his leadership, but he needed to employ people far more skilful at deploying myth to design the chapel and carve its rich symbolism. The stonework of Roslin speaks to people today as clearly and as powerfully as it did when it was first cut. This political concept of an inspirational shrine to showcase the best features of the St Clair heritage, and inspire new layers of legend to enhance the mythical reputation of the family, worked when it was built and continues to work in areas its builders never imagined. (The success of Dan Brown's *Da Vinci Code* shows this clearly.)

The chief architect of Roslin Chapel was Sir Gilbert Hay. He originated the ornate and complex symbolism of the building, employed stonemasons to work on it and supervised and showed them the power of myth, metaphor and symbolism. Hay was a scholar of the political manipulation of power, with practical experience of creating new myths to support political positions and win control of kingdoms. When William invited him to work 'in his castell of Rosselyn' in 1456[6] Hay came from serving at a French court seeped in the myths of the Holy Grail and the ideas of Chrétien de Troyes. He had personally translated into the Scots language three classic French works of knightly chivalry: *The Buke of the Ordre of Knychthede* (a chivalric manual), *The Buke of the Law of Armys* (a treatise on the principles of warfare) and *The Buke of the Gouernaunce of Princis* (a manual on how to take and retain control of a kingdom).[7]

William's interest in Gilbert Hay was driven by a yearning to understand political control – he had an eye on the crown. William, the strongest noble in Scotland, had used his marriage to a daughter of the Douglas family to position himself well up the Scottish pecking order, had seized control of Orkney, Shetland and Caithness, was Chancellor of Scotland and was setting up a power base at the burgh of Roslin. He planned a focus for spiritual power to rival the Abbey of the Holy Rood to supply sacred support for his secular ambitions.

When work started on Roslin Chapel there was no resident workforce. Gilbert Hay recruited operative masons to create the ornate stonework of the chapel, and the village of Roslin was built to house them. By housing immigrants in Roslin for a job that lasted for forty years William created an indigenous workforce of skilled masons. But when William's estates were forcibly split up *c.* 1484, as his plot to take the crown failed, the masons of Roslin were made redundant.

They moved on and took with them a basic training in the application of myth, metaphor and symbolism to create inspirational public buildings. The evidence of the scope and depth of this training remains today, cut into the intricately carved stones of Gilbert Hay's architectural masterpiece of Roslin Chapel. And one group of itinerant craftsmen from Roslin went on to create the beautiful and enduring Craft I have come to love.

Out of Work – Freemasonry's Mundane Beginnings

Many of the redundant masons preferred to seek work elsewhere in Scotland, rather than return to wherever their fathers, or even grandfathers, had come from forty years before. And, if they wanted work in Scotland, Aberdeen was where the action was.

In 1157 CE the seaside citizens of Aberdeen had built a small kirk dedicated to St Nicholas, the patron saint of distressed sailors. In the fifteenth century new waves of plague sweeping across the land, the increase in the Burgh's population and the people's urgent fear of dying all gave the town powerful motives to enlarge its kirk. The work began in 1477, just around the time William St Clair was being forced to break up his estates and cease his building work, and many highly skilled stonemasons were unemployed and available. This was fortunate for Aberdeen, because there were not enough local masons to undertake the work required. The redundant masons of Roslin moved to Aberdeen to become part of its fifty-year building project.

The Burgh Council had a good track record of working with stonemasons, as its first volume of records in 1399 shows. It tells of an early contract between the 'comownys of Ab'den [the commoners of Aberdeen]' on the one part, and two 'masonys [masons]' on the other part, which was agreed on the Feast of St Michael the Archangel. The work contracted for was for 'xii durris and xii wyndowys, in fre tailly [12 doors and 12 windows, free of customs duty]' to be delivered in good order at any quay in Aberdeen.[8]

When the Council decided to extend the Kirk of St Nicholas it helped the masons organise themselves into a lodge, under a Master of Kirk Works, and so the winding down of building work at Roslin coincided with the growth of a permanent lodge, attached to St Nicholas's Kirk in Aberdeen. On 27 June 1483 the Council records say (in the Scots language).

> It was rehersit be Dauid Menzes, master of the kirk wark, that it was appoyntit betuix the masownys of the luge efter that thai war accordit vpon certane controuersy betuix thaime that gif ony tym tocum ony of thaim offendit til vther for the first faute he suld gif xx s. to Sanct Nicholace wark and, gif thai fautit the thrid tym, to be excludit out of the luge as a common forfautour.[9]

This translates as:

> The council decided that David Menzies, the master of the church works, was appointed to rule of the masons of the lodge [consisting of six members], whose names are duly recorded at the end of the minute, they were to be fined 20 shillings and 20 shillings, to be paid to the parish church [Saint Nicholas Kirk] for the first and second offenses respectively, in the event of any of them raising any debate or controversy. It was also written that if they forfeit for the third time they were to be excluded from the lodge as a common wrongdoer.

This by-law was approved by the aldermen and Council, the masons being obligated to obedience 'be the faith of thare bodiis [by the faith of their bodies]'. Two in particular were labelled as offenders and cautioned that, should either of them break the rules they had agreed to, if they '*beis fundyn in the faute thairof salbe expellit the luge fra that tyme furtht* [were found at fault would thereby be expelled from the lodge from that time forward]'.[10]

This is the first recorded example of a group of masons being formed into a lodge with a Master set to rule over it and control its actions. This was to have far-reaching consequences, as it formed the basis for modern Freemasonry.

On 15 November 1493 the relationship between the masons, the Master of the Lodge and the Burgh Council were formalised when three extra masons were hired for a year by the aldermen and Council, 'to abide in thar service, batht in the luge and vtenche, and pass to Cowe, than to hewe and wirk one thar aone expensis, for the stuf and bigyne of thar kirk werke [to abide in the service of the council, both in the lodge and in public, and go to the village of Cowe to cut and work at their own expense the stones and blocks of the church work]'.

A previously unnoticed minute from 1493 shows how the lodge was changing from a simple group of contracted stoneworkers to a more important social force. It read, 'Alexander Stute, masonis, hirit be the aldirman for ane yer to remane and abide in thar seruice, batht in the luge and vtenche [Alexander Stuart, a mason, is named here to serve as an alderman for one year, both in the lodge and elsewhere].'[11]

By 1493 the Master of the Lodge was also a member of the Burgh Council. In addition there is a minute of 22 November 1498, which tells how a mason named David Wricht (one of the masons mentioned in the extended 1483 entry) took an oath of loyalty to continue with the work of the lodge:

> Be his hand ophaldin, to make gude seruice in the luge [by token of holding up his hand to make good service in the lodge] the said day that Nichol Masone and Dauid Wricht oblist thame be the fathis of thar bodiis, the gret aithe sworne, to remane at Sand Nicholes werk in the luge . . . to be leile trew in all pontis [and the said day that Nicholas Mason and David Wright obligated themselves to be faithful with their bodies, the great oath being sworn, to continue the work of St Nicholas in the lodge and to be loyal and true in all points].[12]

In 1498 the newly enlarged St Nicholas Kirk was formally opened and dedicated by Bishop Elphinstone, but building work, supervised by the 'masownys of the luge' continued until 1520, by which time the building had 32 altars, each in its own chapel.

The formal beginnings of that first lodge of Freemasons was in June 1483, when Bro. David Menzies, Master of the Kirk Work, was appointed Master of the newly formed lodge and made responsible for carrying out the building tasks under the direction of the Council. Ten years later the Master of the Lodge of Aberdeen was an Alderman of the Burgh Council. Within another ten years the Masons of the Lodge were honoured to stand alongside the king to perform the ceremony of laying the foundation stone of a new college of learning. The

Masons of the Lodge of Aberdeen had become an important social power in the Burgh, so much so that they are mentioned along with the king in the Latin inscription on the front of King's College. It translates as: 'By the grace of the most serene, illustrious and ever-victorious King James IV: On the fourth before the nones of April in the year one-thousand five-hundred the Masons began to build this excellent college.'[13]

This April date is significant for Freemasons, as it is traditionally accepted as when the building of Solomon's Temple started.[14] Historian David Stevenson of St Andrews University points out that the choice of date, coupled with the highly unusual mention of the stone-working masons along with the king, shows that the mythical traditions of kings leading the efforts of masons to build important national structures (such as Solomon's Temple) were already in place.[15]

When the Grand Lodge of Scotland granted the Lodge of Aberdeen a warrant, on 30 November 1743, it incorrectly named 1541 as the year of its formation. It was only much later that investigation of the Council minutes proved that the lodge had existed since 1483. The lodge charter, issued at the formation of the Grand Lodge of Scotland in 1736, said 'that the records had by accident been burned, but that since December 26, 1670, they have kept a regular lodge, and authentic records of their proceedings'. The Lodge of Aberdeen could have claimed existence from 1483 if somebody had checked the Council minutes, but nobody did. As a result the lodge was only officially acknowledged as 'before 1670' when the Grand Lodge of Scotland was formed.

The written Masonic records of the Lodge of Aberdeen from 1670 are in the form of an old minute book measuring 12 inches by 8 inches. It contains the 'Lawes and Statutes' of 1670 preserved along with the 'Measson Charter' which outlines the general laws, the roll of members and apprentices and the register of their successors, and a volume of diagrams of Masons' Marks known as the Aberdeen Mark Book. It was put together by Bro. James Anderson who describes himself as 'Glazier and Mason and Writer of the Book'.

By 1670 only 12 of the 37 lodge members worked stone. The rest were known as speculative masons, as they were taught rituals and symbolism, not stone-working. These speculative, or philosophical, masons were four noblemen, three church ministers, an advocate, nine merchants, two surgeons, two glaziers, a blacksmith, three slaters, a professor of mathematics, two wig-makers, an armourer, four carpenters and several gentlemen.[16]

Personal Reflections

Freemasonry, as we know it today, began in Aberdeen in the late fifteenth century.[17] The first recorded Master of a Lodge is Bro. David Menzies, Master of the Kirk Work in the Lodge of Aberdeen. His lodge was structured and employed by Aberdeen Burgh Council to rebuild and extend the Kirk of St Nicholas. This fifty-year building project started around the time a large contingent of masons were made redundant by the political downfall of William St Clair, the 12th Baron Roslin, who for the previous thirty years had provided the best-paid stone-cutting work in Scotland. At Roslin the most skilful masons of the day had worked under the guidance of Sir Gilbert Hay.

When the Burgh Council of Aberdeen decided to create a new Kirk to reflect the increase in wealth and population of the city, they had a pool of unemployed but excellent craftsmen to draw upon. The lodge into which the craftsmen were formed invented, or discovered, Freemasonry.

To understand what happened I now need to move on from the historical events and think about the mythical history of Freemasonry, which grew up alongside its practical reality. Like a caterpillar metamorphosing into a butterfly, these first spiritual pioneers developed from a band of operative masons into a brotherhood of speculative Masons. (Whilst operative masons work, cut, shape and build real temples out of stone, speculative Masons use the Masonic art of temple-building as a metaphor for building souls. Whereas an operative uses the tools of a stoneworker to cut and shape rock, the speculative uses metaphysical tools to cut and shape a soul.)

When I first joined Freemasonry I was unaware of the immense power of these metaphysical tools, but as I progressed I discovered it was the knowledge and use of these tools which lies at the heart of Freemasonry's long-term success. Some ideas go back thousands of years, but the peculiar package of myth, metaphor and symbolism that is Freemasonry began in Aberdeen.

The real history of Freemasonry's origins at Roslin might seem like the fruit of expediency, even cynicism – something that will delight enemies of The Craft – but when William St Clair employed Gilbert Hay to be architect of his chapel, he brushed up against a genuine spiritual impulse, a craft with a spiritual dimension. I will show how this spiritual force was nurtured by the redundant itinerant masons of Aberdeen to blossom in strange and unexpected places. However, to illuminate how this happened I must discuss how the mythical history of Freemasonry originated with the stone-cutters of the Lodge of Aberdeen, and how from such an early date this Masonic lodge adopted and extended a pre-existing tradition of speculative teaching.

2

The Mysterious Genesis of The Craft

Surely It's Older Than That?

A S A GUEST of the Lodge of the East Gate I had been told that Freemasonry began with the masons who built King Solomon's Temple, and that modern-day lodges carried on traditions begun by those ancient brethren. When I joined Ryburn Lodge I learned little more about the origins of The Craft. However, I was impressed by the ceremony, the ornate symbolism and the ritual which surrounded my Initiation, all of them suggesting great age and tradition. So I did not expect to find later on that Freemasonry had begun with a group of redundant stonemasons employed by Aberdeen Council to restore and extend the local church.

For my first couple of years after being 'made a Mason' I had no real idea of what I had joined. Even after taking my first degree I couldn't explain what Masonry was, or if it had a purpose. I had been told during the ceremony that 'Freemasonry is a system of morality veiled in allegory and illustrated by symbols,' but that explanation, straight from the ritual book, meant nothing to me. My early impression was that I had inadvertently joined a bit of a mongrel organisation – a sort of cross between an old-fashioned gentleman's club and an informal benefit society.

I was confused by conflicting statements. I recognised religious elements in the ritual, and yet I was told that religious discussion is forbidden within the lodge. It was made clear that Masonry is not a religion, and its teachings should enhance any religious beliefs I might already hold. Brethren, who obviously believed they spoke the truth, assured me that Masonry was a system of extreme antiquity, that it was practised by the ancient Egyptians and had been passed down to my lodge from early Hebrew masters.

I had the vaguest notions of the origin and history of The Craft. Its present purpose and future possibilities remained one of Freemasonry's great secrets. Senior brethren told me that I needed to work at my ritual – if I did, all would become clear. But it didn't.

I took degrees, I progressed through the offices of the lodge, I attended practices, and learned great chunks of ritual by rote; I listened to catechismal instruction-lectures and formal explanations of the symbolic tracing boards night after lodge night. It only served to confuse me. The ritual said that the role of the lodge Master was to 'employ and instruct his brethren in Freemasonry', but he didn't instruct me. He just kept telling me to 'keep working at it and it will all become clear'. It still didn't. I began to suspect that, although my brethren paid lip service to the ritual claim that the lodge meetings were for 'expatiating on the mysteries of The Craft', most of them were not sure what those mysteries were, let alone how to expatiate them.

Out of desperation to understand what I had joined, I decided to undertake my own research. At first I accepted the popular perception that Masonry is a system of immemorial antiquity, started among the primitive builders of the East and perpetuated in the West, for strange mystical purposes which had passed down the generations. As I accumulated more information I tried to make sense of what was starting to seem like a massive conspiracy theory. I discovered many variations on the history of Masonry and so found myself exploring and investigating different explanations to aid my own understanding.

As I became more knowledgeable I was asked to give lectures, first in my own lodge, and later to other lodges round and about Halifax. I joined different degrees, such as the Royal Arch, and what Masons call side-orders, such as the Mark Mason Degree, and collected historical data about the actions of individual Freemasons. I accumulated many versions of the traditional histories from various strands of Masonic practice and I built timelines of key events. The more I asked about the conflicting evidence, the more myths I was told, and the more this led me to think about historical realities. Now, as I look back, with the benefit of far more information, I see that in my early attempts to understand Masonry I was accumulating a mixture of different origin myths, interspersed with historical facts, and was not always able to distinguish between them.

During this information-collection period I bumped into another guy who was also interested in where Freemasonry had come from. His name was Chris Knight. Neither of us knew the other was a Freemason initially, but our wives knew each other through the local playgroup, and we met socially. Once we realised we were both Masons, though, we ended up pooling our information and spent hours talking about where Freemasonry had come from. The upshot was that Chris suggested we should write a book about our thoughts and findings. I was doubtful that they would be of much interest to the wider world, but Chris persuaded me that we should have a go, and for the next few years we spent enormous amounts of time trying to piece all the disparate and strange things we found together into a sensible story. The end of this process was a book we called *The Hiram Key*, which proved to be success-ful, although it generated a lot of hostility towards us from the then officers of the United Grand Lodge of England. Over the next four years we wrote three other books together before our writing interests moved in different directions. (I became more interested in the links between the formative ideas of Freemasonry and their effects on the beginnings of modern science, and in scientific biography, and began writing on my own.)

Just before we finished our final book together (*The Book of Hiram*) the hostility of UGLE finally became too much for Chris and drove him out of The Craft. The pressure almost had the same effect on me, but I was lucky enough to be invited to visit a lodge which was so different that it inspired me to rethink everything I thought I knew about Freemasonry, including whether it was worth remaining within it. In this lodge I rediscovered the spiritual warmth I had experienced at the ladies' Lodge of the East Gate. Just as I was beginning to think I had been totally mistaken about Freemasonry's spiritual depths, I found a lodge that not only understood the esoteric way of The Craft but was working to pass on that understanding to its members.

My interest in The Craft revived and I again began to deliver Masonic lectures, on science and the teaching of Freemasonry. My interest in writing about the history of Freemasonry was also renewed. As I dug deeper I recognised that if I wanted to understand the genuine spiritual impulses which had inspired Bro. David Menzies' little band of Masons to create The Craft, I had to study the spiritual force that motivated them.

A First Clue to the Ancient Mysteries of The Craft

I knew from the records of the Burgh Council that the first recorded lodge was set up in Aberdeen around 1483. When I first said this in public the apologists for the United Grand Lodge of England's 'Monty Python' theory of Masonic origins countered that 'that first lodge in Aberdeen was a purely operative lodge'. This had been the official position of UGLE since at least 1886, when Robert Freke Gould published his *History of Freemasonry*, taken as authoritative by UGLE. Yet the work of Scottish historian David Stevenson showed that from the early sixteenth century Freemasonry had a mystical element, connected with the 'art of memory' and the strange, secret 'Mason word'. Then, some four years after the publication of *The Hiram Key*, evidence emerged from dated artefacts that there was definite use of symbology in Freemasonry in the late fifteenth century.

On 21 July 2000 an article appeared in both *The Times* and the *Daily Telegraph* by Orkney journalist Kath Gourlay. She reported the results of scientific tests carried out on an artefact belonging to Lodge Kirkwall Kilwinning known as the Kirkwall Scroll. She wrote:

> The results of radiocarbon dating carried out on a rare wall hanging have shocked members of a Masonic lodge in the Orkney Islands, who have been told that their document is a medieval treasure worth several million pounds . . . radiocarbon dating of the scroll points to the huge 18-ft sailcloth hanging as being fifteenth-century.[18]

Here the mystery deepened. There were two radiocarbon dates for the scroll: one for the centre section, and a quite different one for the outer sections. Gourlay continued:

> Contact with the University of Oxford Research laboratory, which did the radiocarbon dating, adds to the mystery by supporting both dates.
>
> 'We analysed material from the Kirkwall Scroll on two separate occasions,' says a spokesman from the Archaeology and History of Art department which carried out the work. 'You have to allow a certain margin of error in calibrating carbon content, and the first sample, taken from the outside edge of the material, was possibly eighteenth- or early

nineteenth-century (1780–1840). The second piece, which came from the central panel, produced a much older date – fifteenth- or early sixteenth-century (1400–1530).'[19]

I had seen the scroll a year before, in September 1999, in the company of Professor Karl Pribram, the noted brain scientist (we had both been speaking at the Orkney Science Festival). Karl is an Emeritus Professor of Stanford University and the Director of the Center for Brain Research and Informational Sciences at Radford University in Virginia. Late one Sunday evening we were invited to a private viewing at Lodge Kirkwall Kilwinning, whose lodge rooms are in the street opposite St Magnus's Cathedral, and we walked together from the Harbour Hotel up the narrow, winding High Street, entering by a side door. We were escorted up the stairs to the Temple and shown what looked like a large roll of carpet hung on a spindle high on the west wall of the lodge. Once it was unrolled I could see it was a sheet of canvas almost 20ft long and 6ft wide and completely covered with the hand-painted Masonic symbols I had learned in my own lodge. This canvas carpet gave me my first clue to the important role of symbolism in the development of Freemasonry.

The Early Symbols of Freemasonry

The Kirkwall Scroll is made of three pieces of strong linen (probably sailcloth) sewn together and hand-painted. It consists of a centre strip, 4ft wide and 18ft 6in long, painted with hundreds of Masonic symbols. The two outer strips, each about 9 inches wide and 18ft 6in long, appear to be maps. When you examine the back of the scroll, behind its hessian backing, you can see that the outer strips have been cut from a single, 18-inch-wide strip of material before being sewn to the outer edges of the centre strip.

When I researched the Kirkwall Scroll I came to the conclusion that it is an early tracing board in the form of a floorcloth that could be unrolled, section by section. In Masonic ritual a tracing board is described thus:

> The Tracing Board is for the Master to lay lines and draw designs on, the
> better to enable the Brethren to carry on the intended structure with

regularity and propriety. The Volume of the Sacred Law may justly be deemed the spiritual Tracing Board of the great Architect of the Universe, in which are laid down such Divine laws and moral plans that, were we conversant therein and adherent thereto, would bring us to an ethereal mansion not made with hands, eternal in the Heavens.

The Kirkwall Scroll is big. It is meant to be unrolled, section by section, as the relevant rituals are being worked. (For the benefit of non-Masons I should perhaps explain that when Freemasons get together they often act out the story of a myth, which they call 'working the ritual'.)

Masonic writer Walter Wilmshurst, founder Master of the Lodge of Living Stones, describes the purpose of a tracing board:

> In earlier days, when the Craft was a serious discipline in a philosophic and sacred science, the tracing board was the most revered symbol in the lodge; it was a diagram which every Brother was taught to draw for himself, so that both his hand and his understanding might be trained in Masonic work. At each Lodge-meeting the board of the degree about to be worked was drawn from memory with chalk and charcoal on the floor by the Master, who from previous practice was able to do this quickly and accurately. During the ceremony, the Candidate took the steps of the degree over the diagram (as is still done to-day where floor-cloths are used). The diagram was explained to him during the ceremony, and he then expunged it with a mop and pail of water so that uninitiated eyes might not see it and to learn a lesson in humility and secrecy. It was to convey to every Mason's mind matters of deep import and secret instruction. It is designed to reveal an ancient doctrine from heavenly sources for the spiritual uplift of man.[20]

The Kirkwall Scroll was created in the fifteenth century, in the earliest days of The Craft, and it showed all the esoteric aspects of Masonry Wilmshurst alludes to. Moreover, the carbon dating showed it to be older than Lodge Kirkwall Kilwinning, and it had never been possible to fully extend the scroll on the floor of any of the rooms the lodge has ever owned. It arrived at the lodge in 1786.

Over the last hundred years many theories have been put forward to explain the scroll's purpose and meaning, but most have come from groups that would prefer it not to have esoteric overtones. Its radiocarbon dating in the twenty-first century, and the revelation that there is a 280-year difference in age between the central strip and the two side panels, pushes the proved use of Masonic symbols back before any previously known speculative Masonic lodge.[21]

Bro. Wilmshurst, the founder of my lodge, left extensive notes in its library about the function of floorcloths and tracing boards. He links them to a deep spiritual secret. Writing in 1929 he said:

> The drawing of the tracing board diagram from memory upon the ground was eventually superseded by the use of painted floor-cloths, which could be unrolled a section at a time, and wooden boards resting on trestles, which could be uncovered one by one. On these permanent diagrams would be painted.
>
> The boards are cryptic prescriptions of a world-old science, taught and practised in secret in all ages by the few spiritually ripe and courageous enough for following a higher path of life than is possible as yet to the popular world. The detailed interpretation of their symbolism is necessarily difficult, for symbols always comprise so much more than can be verbally explained, and so few Masons have been educated in the language of ancient esoteric symbolism.[22]

Nevertheless, somebody in the fifteenth century was educated in ancient esoteric symbolism and had applied their knowledge to The Craft of Masonry and to the Kirkwall Scroll.

The radiocarbon dating places the scroll and its Masonic symbols between 1400 and 1530, with a best-guess estimate of around 1470. There are only two lodges known to have been in existence between 1400 and 1530. One was the Masonic lodge which flourished in Aberdeen in the 1480s; the other was the Lodge of Edinburgh, which has continuous minutes back only to 1599, but is mentioned in minutes of the Corporation of Edinburgh in 1475. Historian David Stevenson, of St Andrews University, notes:

> The seal of cause of the Incorporation of Masons and Wrights of Edinburgh was granted in 1475 . . . These seals should not, however, be taken to mark the beginnings of organisation by the crafts concerned; rather it would usually be the case that craft organisation had existed and evolved for generations, with the granting of a seal representing the

culmination of the process, even though it is often the first point at which the organisation becomes visible to the historian.[23]

It seemed to me that the only conceivable pool of Masons trained in the persuasive power of symbols would have been the redundant stone-cutters of Rosslyn, and some of them might have managed to get work in nearby Edinburgh and become part of the lodge there. However, I have no strong evidence of the *speculative* importance of the early Lodge of Edinburgh, such as the Master becoming a member of the Council, as I found for the Lodge of Aberdeen.

But let us ignore for the moment which of these two early lodges (both of which now carry the No 1 on the roll of the Grand Lodge of Scotland) might have created the Kirkwall Scroll. There is still the question of how the scroll got to Kirkwall from either of them. And how could the spiritual tradition of symbolic teaching predate the earliest known speculative lodges? To answer these questions I've had to look at the history of Lodge Kirkwall Kilwinning.

Bro. William Graham, Accidental Saviour of the Kirkwall Scroll

Lodge Kirkwall Kilwinning was established on Monday 1 October 1736, two hundred and fifty years after the scroll was painted. It was the earliest lodge in Orkney and became a popular meeting place for influential Orcadians. James Baikie, the Provost of Kirkwall, followed his brother Alexander into the chair of the lodge, becoming its second Master. Mastership of the lodge soon became a mark of honour among the minor gentry of Kirkwall, and membership a badge of social distinction.

The social role of the lodge mattered in Orkney society. When William Graham, who donated the Scroll to the lodge, came to Kirkwall in 1785 it was the main social networking site of the town. William was ambitious. He had been born in Stromness on the mainland of Orkney but had moved to London for a period. Having secured a job as customs officer for Kirkwall he now intended to make his mark on the social scene. His father, Alexander Graham, was a rich trader in kelp-slag (the calcined ashes of a brown seaweed called kelp, used to manufacture alum).

In 1760 a cluster of alum producers set up factories near Edinburgh. The value of kelp increased, and the Edinburgh producers needed reliable sources of kelp-slag. A boom ensued, which lasted from 1770 to 1830. In the late 1700s Alexander Graham was shipping 60,000 tons of kelp-slag per annum and getting £20 per ton for it in Edinburgh. He ran a fleet of cargo ships, based in the port of Stromness, which carried the kelp-slag down the east coast of Scotland to the Firth of Forth, unloaded the slag at Leith and then collected a cargo of coal for Aberdeen before sailing back up to Orkney. The ships stopped over at Aberdeen to unload the coal and take on small luxuries – typically items like gloves, paper, sealing wax and sugar.[24]

The port of Stromness, situated at the top of the Hamnavoe sound, has direct access to the Atlantic, and its traders were doing business with the Hudson's Bay Company and North Atlantic whaling ships. However, Kirkwall's lairds claimed the right to tax any trade which passed through this thriving port, including Alexander Graham's kelp, coal and small luxuries. Graham took it on himself to challenge this ruling and succeeded.

In 1785 William decided to go back to Orkney, where he had been offered the job of Customs Officer for the burgh of Kirkwall (which, considering his father's legal success in freeing Stromness from Kirkwall customs duty, seems rather ironic). Soon after his arrival he applied to become a joining member of Lodge Kirkwall Kilwinning. A month later he presented the Master of the Lodge, Robert Baikie, with the scroll. The minutes for 27 January 1786 say:

> The Master presented to the Lodge a floorcloth, gifted to the Brethren by Bro. William Graham of 128 of the Ancient Constitution of England.[25]

When William gave the scroll to the lodge it had already been disguised by adding outer panels. The reason for the disguise is simple enough to explain. Orcadians, being only recently separated from Norway, could not have failed to notice that the scroll contains symbols that could be interpreted as referring to the Norse goddess Freyja. By adding the outer panels, showing the travels of the tribes of Israel in the desert under Moses, these esoteric references to the pre-Christian heritage of northern Scotland could be hidden from the Kirk.

William Graham added the side panels to Christianise this old Masonic floorcloth, but where did he get the central panel from? I believe it was a gift from his father. For years Alexander Graham had traded with both Edinburgh and Aberdeen, and so had every chance to acquire a Masonic floorcloth from either of these long-established Masonic centres (Masonic relics often pass into the hands of non-Mason relatives and end up being sold). Both places had lodges of Freemasons in the late 1400s, so it might have been created at either – but I think that the central scene of the top panel, with its Norse overtones, makes it far more likely that it came from Aberdeen, as the lands around there had historically been Norse.

The Kirkwall Scroll dates from the earliest days of Freemasonry, and it uses the symbolism of a path towards what is known today in Freemasonry as 'the Centre'. This is a state of being where the Mason becomes at one with creation. And in this, the oldest symbolic document of Masonic ritual, the metaphor of a Norse deity, Freyja, is used as a symbol of the 'God experience', which, as I will show, became the focus of Freemasonry.

The Kirkwall Scroll shows the symbolic spiritual journey of Freemasonry and has been radiocarbon dated to the time when Freemasonry was established in Aberdeen by masons made redundant after working for William St Clair of Roslin. Those masons, who had worked at Roslin under the guidance of Gilbert Hay, had been exposed to a range of powerful spiritual symbols, and all the symbols we now call Masonic can be found on the Kirkwall Scroll. I believe they created it to display those symbols during their meetings and to transmit the symbolic knowledge they had learned from Gilbert Hay.

Anderson's Constitutions – *Starting the Myth*

The Grand Lodge of London was formed in 1717, just two years after the 1715 Jacobite rising, to allow members of the London lodges to distance themselves from earlier Masonic lodges which had been supporters of the Stuart kings. I explained the politics of this period in *The Invisible College* and showed the reasons that the London Masons of 1717 had to deny their Scottish roots:[26] if they hadn't they would have been accused of treason against George I. The four lodges came together to form a Grand Lodge, which took on itself the power to warrant the creation of new lodges, although the existing lodges retained the traditional right of seven Master Masons to form a new lodge. This new Grand Lodge publicly expressed its loyalty to the new Hanoverian monarchy and encouraged Hanoverian nobility to become patrons in place of the Stuart monarchs.

This is when the 'Monty Python' theory of Masonic origins arose (the idea that a group of gentlemen meeting in a London pub came up with the idea of asking the guys on their local building site to give them some guidance on how to improve their morals). It was invented to cover up the Jacobite roots of The Craft. The ploy was successful, and within six years of forming a new Grand Lodge under the Grand Mastership of Bro. Anthony Sayer the London Masons took the Duke of Montagu as a noble Grand Master and ever since have had some minor lord or other (and occasionally a prince or even a king) as Grand Master. When this disingenuous distancing was first planned the main players probably did not envisage that their new 'Grand Lodge' would extend its scope much beyond Westminster and the City of London. But they were successful far beyond these simple ambitions for reasons which are strangely ironic.

They had set out to make clear that they had no loyalty, nor even links, to the Scottish Masonic Lodge system, which largely supported the Stuart kings. (This can be seen in the circumstances of the foundation of The Royal Order of Scotland which was set up to tacitly proclaim James VII of Scotland as their absent Grand Master.)[27] By separating itself from its Scottish roots London Masonry rebuilt the social popularity of The Craft within London's Hanoverian society, but it had to pay a high price. It was forced to disown its real history, marked by a series of ancient constitutions and statutes, which stretched back over two hundred years. Although it was an Order whose practices had been refined by ten generations of selective reinforcement, it proclaimed itself to be new-born.

This meant it could not draw on tradition to provide authority. It needed something to replace this lost mundane history, and the man who stepped forward with a solution was a Mason made in the Lodge of Aberdeen: Bro. the Rev. James Anderson, Presbyterian Minister to

Swallow Street Chapel in London and personal Chaplain to the Earl of Buchan (who was also a member of the Lodge of Aberdeen) and a confidant of his patron. Anderson was steeped in the most powerful mythical history of Freemasonry, which he had learned from his mother lodge.

The then Grand Master, John Theophilus Desaguliers, had a hand in refining the regulations but Anderson wrote down the mythical history of The Craft he had learned from the Lodge of Aberdeen and established the foundation for the widespread spiritual substrate to UGLE Freemasonry which ensured its long-term success. It was published in a book now popularly known as either *The Constitutions* or *Anderson's Constitutions*.

What Anderson did was reconnect The Craft to a great spiritual tradition which was in danger of being lost.

Anderson's Mythical History of The Craft

Anderson's opus is partly a set of rules of how to govern the new system of Grand Lodge Freemasonry and partly a mythical history of The Craft which begins with Adam as the first Freemason and traces Freemasonry down to the early eighteenth century. The frontispiece of *The Constitutions of the Free-Masons* shows Desaguliers' successor Grand Master Montagu and his Wardens coming from the North, the traditional place of sacred knowledge, to hand over to his own successor, Grand Master Wharton and his Wardens, the treasured history of The Craft. The ceremony takes place in a vast pillared temple which supports in its roof an image of the Greek sun god Helios riding his chariot from East to West. But what great sacred knowledge is contained within that history?

When Anderson was writing *The Constitutions* he began his book with a history of Freemasonry, which he says is to be read at the admission of every new brother, with the obvious intent of making sure that all newly made Masons know where The Craft began.

Anderson starts his history with this bold statement:

Adam, our first parent, created after the image of God, the great Architect of the Universe, must have had the Liberal Sciences, particularly Geometry, written on his Heart; for ever since the Fall, we find the principles of it in the Hearts of his Offspring, and, which, in process of time, have been drawn forth into a convenient Method of Propositions, by observing Laws of Proportion taken from Mechanism: So that as the Mechanical Arts gave occasion to the learned to reduce the Elements of Geometry into Method, this noble Science thus reduced, is the Foundation of all those Arts (particularly of Masonry, and Architecture) and the Rule by which they are conducted and performed.[28]

He thus makes the claim that Masonry, as a system of knowledge, existed before the world was created and draws on a transcendental repository of knowledge created by the Great Architect. He says that the Great Architect of the Universe, when he made the first man in His Own Image, imparted this Knowledge into Adam's heart. This makes Adam the first Freemason.

Anderson went on to claim that Jesus Christ was a Mason, saying, 'Nay, that holy Branch of Shem (of whom, as concerning the Flesh, Christ came) could not be unskilful in the learned Arts.' And he maintains that Freemasonry was invented in heaven and given as a gift to mankind, saying that at the time of the building of Solomon's Temple:

> The wise King Solomon was Grand Master of the Lodge at Jerusalem, and the learned King Hiram was Grand Master of the Lodge at Tyre, and the inspired Hiram Abif was Master of Work, and Masonry was under the immediate care and direction of Heaven.[29]

Anderson set out a mythical pedigree for The Craft that made it attractive to the Hanoverian nobility – and before the end of the century the Grand Lodge of London had the Prince of Wales as its Grand Master. As the noble gentlemen of London learned of the secret history of The Craft, how it was ordained by God as a gift of knowledge to men and was the root of all power and Truth, they flocked to join. The Craft expanded rapidly. When it was formed in 1717 the Grand Lodge of London had mustered just over a hundred members, and not a single nobleman amongst them. After the exile of James II (VII), the formation of the overtly Jacobite Royal Order of Scotland and the Jacobite uprising of 1715, none of the London-based nobility wanted to be part of what had become an Order with close links to the alternative British monarchy. Once it was clear that the Grand Lodge of London's support for the Hanoverian monarchy had been accepted, then the nobility began to get involved, and Freemasonry was set to take over the world.

Personal Reflections

Everything I had been told as a Freemason confused a series of mythical histories with the actual provable facts. Over time I have come to realise that to understand the basis of Freemasonry's spiritual appeal – and hence the origins of its supranatural secrets of spiritual self-development – I needed to untangle the romance from the facts, the myth from the mundane. By looking at early records of bodies outside Freemasonry I had discovered that a quite large group of stonemasons had worked on the building of Roslin Chapel, a myth-inspired political icon, under the early spin doctor Sir Gilbert Hay. The masons who worked under his guidance, even though they were being used for a political purpose, were taught extremely important ideas:

1. Symbols can be understood without words and can be used to change people's attitudes and emotions.
2. A myth can be just as much a religious relic as a piece of the True Cross.

When William St Clair's plot to take the crown of Scotland failed, his lands and titles were broken up and the masons dispersed. One group, led first by Bro. David Menzies and later by Bro. Alexander Stuart, learned how to use these ideas from Roslin to improve the skills and the importance of their lodge members. They began to take in other trades and local gentry to learn the skills of self-development which they had mastered.

I have found two pieces of evidence which shed light on what they did in the privacy of their lodge room.

- I have traced one of the symbolic floorcloths they used in their ceremonies and discovered that it contains all the major Masonic symbols which are now a key part of Freemasonry's spiritual teaching.
- I have revisited a neglected but powerful and coherent mythical history,

which has been written down by a member of the Lodge of Aberdeen in order to give to London Freemasonry an alternative traditional heritage to replace the one it had had to abandon in order to avoid suspicion of treason.

Both these clues indicate that the early lodge in Aberdeen developed many of the spiritual hallmarks of today's Craft and that these practices of spiritual self-help have been honed and refined by many generations of Freemasons studying, teaching and applying them.

These simple stonemasons stumbled upon an understanding of the supranatural secrets which I have found to be such an inspirational part of the present-day Craft. But, as a scientist, I did not find it an easy transition to enter an Order which acknowledges the existence of God, as I shall explain in the next chapter. However, my research alerted me to the fact that speculative Freemasonry played a role in the development of modern science, and many of my scientific heroes were Freemasons. Those results have shown me that spiritual and mystical teaching was a part of Freemasonry in both its real history and official origins. However, before I could follow their lead and learn the study of symbols and the mysterious way in which they encode truths about nature, I found to my horror I had to confront God directly.

But how?

3

Facing Up To The Darkness

In Whom Do You Put Your Trust?

WHILE TRAINING TO be a scientist I put behind me any need to think about God. Then – when I felt I could safely relax in the knowledge that God's existence or non-existence was a non-question – Freemasonry chose to make me remember how Job challenged God to explain Himself, and God roared down upon him in the shape of a whirlwind demanding to know, 'Who is this who darkens my counsel by words without knowledge?' Years of scientific training had not completely eradicated my urge to cringe.

I had brought it upon myself by asking to join my local lodge. Having been invited to visit the lodge rooms to meet some of the members, I had liked what I saw and made a formal request to be considered for membership. Only afterwards did it dawn on me what I had done. The first question The Craft put to me forced me to reach deep down through my childhood fears and review my adult thinking.

After I had asked my old friend Bro. Mike Astell if I could join Ryburn Lodge, he took me to one side as I prepared to fill in my application form. 'Before you hand that in, I need to talk to you. There's an important question in it that you'll have to answer before we'll decide to accept the form.'

'What's that?'

'You'll be asked if you believe in a Supreme Being.'

I felt a cold, deep fear in the pit of my stomach. I was going to have to think long and hard about my answer, for my relationship with God had not been a comfortable one. One of the first questions I would be asked during my Initiation into Freemasonry was 'In all times of danger and difficulties, in whom do you put your trust?'

When this was asked I knew I would be standing in open lodge, stripped of all valuables, vulnerably dressed in a flimsy and revealing white suit, and completely blindfolded. The ritual answer I would be expected to give would be, 'In God'. As a scientist I was disturbed both by the question and by the answer I would need to give.

I was forewarned, and so had plenty of time to think my position through. Unlike Job, I was not going to be intimidated. I was not going to be excluded by a technicality from an Order which I felt, from my earlier experience of the Lodge of the East Gate, had useful knowledge to pass on. However, I also had no intention of recanting my scientific ways and confessing them erroneous. But, since I was serious about joining Freemasonry, I had to decide what sort of Supreme Being, if any, I was prepared to believe in. So long as I did believe in one, The Craft didn't care . . . but I did.

Hellfire and Discipline

One thing at least was certain. I didn't believe in the Presbyterian God who haunted my childhood memories. He was a horrible, small-minded, jealous God, who concentrated on forbidding anything which might be the least pleasurable. For all that, my inner child had been shaped by this stern, miracle-working, all-knowing and all-punishing God, who bristled with a vast range of prejudices.

As a child I attended Sunday School every Sabbath afternoon at Singleton Mission in Tulley Street, Salford. The Mission Hall was a big building containing a maze of rooms that had seemed randomly tacked together. There was a hall with a stage where the Sunday School prizes were presented, and at the other end of the building was a smaller hall without a stage, where we played games at the Christmas party. Beyond the small hall was a chapel where the grown-ups sat for God to talk to them, and where children were never allowed. Between the halls were two smaller rooms, one a kitchen and the other what my Sunday School teacher called the vestry. That was where we little ones sat round in a circle while she told us all about God and occasionally mentioned his son Jesus. There was a big fireplace at the end of the vestry. On the walls hung two pictures of Jesus. One showed him with a candle lantern in his hand, knocking on a door in a dark street. I liked to look at the picture as we sang 'In this world of darkness so we must shine, you in your small corner and I in mine.'

The Jesus of this childhood picture had a black moustache and beard, with long hair like a girl. But I knew that Jesus lived in Palestine millions of year ago, and I guessed they probably didn't have barbers in the Stone Age, when he was alive, so he wouldn't have been able to have a short back and sides. I tried to imagine my dad with long hair, like my mum, and it made me laugh out loud.

My teacher heard. 'Don't you laugh at Jesus,' she said, 'or he'll punish you. Gentle Jesus only likes well-behaved little boys.' She sounded very angry. 'So you behave yourself, Master Lomas, or you'll go to hell to suffer and burn for ever.'

She showed me a picture of hell in an illustrated version of the Bible, to make sure I knew what to expect.

'Hell is hotter than the fire in the grate and it's filled with red and yellow flames,' she said with relish. 'And lots of devils with pitchforks who keep poking you.'

I didn't want to go to hell so I stopped laughing and sat up straight. (God can tell if you're paying attention by watching if you're sitting up straight.)

At the other end of the vestry there was a different picture of Jesus. He was sitting on a rock, dressed in a white sheet and with a white towel on his head. It was easy to recognise Jesus because I could see his moustache, his beard and his long girl's hair under the towel. I wondered if he'd just washed his hair, because my mum wrapped a towel round her head when she washed hers every Thursday night. Jesus had lots of little children sitting round him in a circle, just like we sat around our Sunday School teacher when she told us all about God. Under the picture it said 'Suffer the little children to come unto me.' (I couldn't read it, but Miss read it out for us, and I remembered it.)

I wondered if it was just the children who didn't behave well who had to suffer. If they'd sat up straight and paid attention then perhaps Jesus wouldn't have made them suffer in hell. I was quite curious about this, but I didn't want to ask Teacher, as she didn't like being asked questions.

'Don't you be impertinent, young Master Lomas,' she'd said, 'or you'll go straight to hell. You mark my words.'

There were all sorts of children in that picture, and they were all sitting up straight and paying attention so as not to upset God, whose job it was to make sure the children had to listen to what His son Jesus told them.

I was left at Sunday School for the first time at 2 p.m. on the seventh of January, when I was four years old. I don't remember that first session, but I've been told that I cried. However, I soon got used to staying and must have stopped snivelling. As I write I have my first attendance card in front of me. It has spaces for attendance marks for every week of the year, and they have all been filled.

I had to take this 'Scholar's Attendance Card' with me every Sunday to get those marks. It is printed on blue card, about 7cm by 6cm and folded in the middle. On the front it says 'The Single Session STAR ATTENDANCE CARD' with spaces below for the Name of the Scholar (Robert Lomas), my class (Class B1), the number in the class (46), the name of the teacher, and the time the school opened (2 p.m.). Beneath this is a space for the name of the Sunday School, which says 'Singleton Mission Hall, Tully Street, Salford 7'. The Superintendent of the school was Miss Johnstone. She marked and signed the card for each child as they arrived. I got two marks if I arrived on time, one mark for arriving late and no marks for not turning up. I always had two marks – my parents made sure I was always first there.

At the end of the year the marks were totalled up, and if you had a good attendance you got a prize. I always won a prize. Looking at that card I can see that for the last two Sundays in July Miss Johnstone has marked the square with 2H, the H standing for holiday. Those four marks were awarded because I still had to go and visit God even when I was away on holiday – and it was during such visits to other churches that I discovered that God wasn't the same for everyone.

I was about six years old when I realised that some people worshipped a less stern and frightening God than I did. That summer my parents took me for a fortnight's holiday to stay with my mother's auntie Annie (she lived with Uncle Joe in the old family home in Wales). To make sure I didn't miss any marks for Sunday School I had to go to Bistre

Church, Buckley, my nearest church, on the holiday Sunday and get a letter from the vicar. There I met a different God.

My uncle Joe was a very important man at Bistre Church. He was in the choir and knew the vicar. And the vicar was a man, not a lady like Superintendent Johnstone at Singleton Mission. Uncle Joe took me to church three times each Sunday, although I still only got one lot of Sunday School marks. The first service was at eight o'clock. I could hear the bell ringing as we walked up the path to the side gate. Uncle Joe held my hand, and I took two steps for every one of his, just to keep up. Even dressed in his Sunday-best suit and highly polished boots, he smelt of Woodbines with a strange, pungent, metallic overtone from his flint-and-petrol cigarette-lighter. Uncle Joe smoked all the time, except in church.

At Bistre Church I first saw a service called Holy Communion that was different from anything I'd ever seen in Sunday School. I was allowed into the main church with the adults. The vicar wore a white dress, a bit like the one Jesus wore in the picture in Singleton vestry. (Miss Johnstone always wore a normal lady's dress.) The vicar had brought some food, which he put on the big stone altar at the front of the church. He had a little bottle of wine and some funny crumbly biscuits. There was lots of singing, and I sat with Uncle Joe by the side of the choir in special seats right near the front of the church. The vicar waved the bottle and biscuits about and prayed a bit and waved his arms in the air, while all the people lined up to be given a biscuit and sip of the wine, which the vicar had poured into a big silver cup.

'Is it a party?' I remember whispering to Uncle Joe. I was more than a little nervous that God wouldn't approve of us having a picnic in church, and I didn't want to be sent to hell for it.

'No,' he said. 'We are eating the body and blood of Jesus as his disciples did at the Last Supper.'

I thought it was a really odd idea to eat bits of God's son and I was rather upset by the idea, but regular Sunday School had taught me not to question the way things were. Just to accept it and do as I was told.

But even my intensive training in acceptance was not enough to stop me asking Uncle Joe about the wine. One thing I was *quite* sure of was that drink is evil.

'My Sunday School teacher told me that God doesn't like you to drink,' I said. 'She says I should join the Band of Hope and take the pledge never to touch strong drink.'

'It's different when the Vicar has blessed the wine,' Uncle Joe explained. 'God likes you to drink some wine to help you remember His Son.'

That sounded fair enough, so when Uncle Joe went up to the vicar and held out his hand for a biscuit, I followed him and held out my hand too. The vicar smiled at me and put his hand on my head and said, 'Bless you in the name of the Father, the Son and the Holy Ghost' – but he didn't give me a biscuit or offer me a sip of wine.

As we were walking home after the service I asked Uncle Joe why the vicar wouldn't give me a biscuit. 'Because you haven't been confirmed yet,' he said.

'What does confirmed mean?'

'It means that you've learned your catechism, promised Jesus that you will renounce sin, and stood up before the whole church to proclaim that you are a Christian.'

'Can I do it today?' I asked.

'No,' he said, 'you'll need to be much older before the bishop will confirm you.'

'I don't think we have bishops in my Sunday School. Will Miss Johnstone confirm me?'

Uncle Joe smiled. 'No, she can't because she's only a woman, not a bishop.'

Looking back I think this was when it first began to dawn on me that there are many different Gods, and each one has been fashioned in the image of the people who worship Him. (One of the great virtues of Freemasonry is that it doesn't force any particular type of God onto you.)

My Sunday School attendance cards show, and my bookshelf confirms, that I won a prize for full attendance every year until I was ten years old. All in all, I attended over 300 basic sessions to convince me of the all-knowing oversight of a God who saw, recorded and punished every misdeed of action or thought. That was why, when Mike Astell asked me if I believed in a Supreme Being, my first thought was that I was quite sure I didn't believe in the mean, vindictive, small-minded God who had tormented me through Sunday School. But would this exclude me from Freemasonry?

I certainly wasn't anti-church. I have always enjoyed singing hymns and chanting the plainsong of Matins and Psalms. Indeed Mike already knew that for many years I had played the organ in my village church, although I would never take Communion. I had long since adopted the advice of physicist Feynman to see Nature, and by implication God, as basically absurd. It had freed my sense of mystery to enjoy the ritual whilst ignoring any strange assumptions the church made about reality.

Ultimately my scientific view of creation had left me in a state of awe and wonder when I contemplated the vast expanse of the Universe, or the nature of the subatomic zoo that emerged when I tried to shake the quarks out of atomic nuclei. At each end of the scale, in the dark reaches of intergalactic space, or in the tiny interactions of subatomic physics, my science had gently melded into an uncertainty that is deep and impressive. But I found it impossible to accept that all this wonder of creation has simply been arranged by a personal God to allow Him to preside over humanity's struggle with good and evil and make sure everyone sits up straight and listens carefully to Sunday School teachers.

I had been fortunate enough to fail the 11-plus exam and had been allocated a place at a local secondary modern, where they weren't interested in religion. Heys Boys' Secondary Modern School, Prestwich, allowed me to wander off the Presbyterian path and become an indifferent agnostic.

A New Approach to Religion

God receded from my consciousness during my time at secondary school. Instead of being the whole focus of every Sunday, He became a benign but indifferent subject of morning assemblies. Each morning the whole school joined together to sing about God and then forgot about Him until the next morning, when we'd sing about some other worthy aspect of the creditable life.

The only other time God was mentioned was during the weekly religious instruction lesson. I thoroughly enjoyed listening to exciting retellings of the outrageous acts of the Old Testament kings of Israel and how God rewarded and punished them. Jesus hardly seemed to figure in those lessons, and I suppose it was through listening to that historical treatment of the tales of Samuel, Saul, David and Solomon that I first became intrigued by the wonderful myths of the Old Testament. I remain grateful to the long-suffering Mr Clarkson who ploughed through the Old Testament, picking out the most exciting battles and acts of treachery to keep us boys entertained, and in the process gave me a sound grounding in the life and times of King Solomon.

So the vindictive God of my Sunday School mellowed into a king-maker and political dabbler whose aim had been to ensure His favoured people prospered – as long as they did what He told them. Instead of a living threat, God became an historical oddity with little relevance to my daily life.

Sunday School had left in my mind the impression that Jesus was a rather unimportant wimp who wore a tea-towel on his head and wandered around in sandals performing miracles using powers borrowed from his all-powerful Dad. The real force always seemed to be controlled by the mysterious Yaweh (as Mr Clarkson always referred to Him). Yaweh appeared in burning bushes and whirlwinds to speak directly to His favoured kings and prophets. He could part the Red Sea or make the sun stand still in the sky if He wanted to. This power to perform miracles didn't become a particular problem for me until I started to study science seriously, at which point I realised that Yahweh, with His supernatural powers, could never have been real. He was only a wonderful myth. And by the time I asked to join Freemasonry I certainly couldn't believe in Him.

All the same, simply running through the list of what I no longer believed in wasn't helping me focus on what I *did* believe in. I needed a viable concept of a Supreme Being which I could accept if I was to become a Mason.

The View from Physics

I thought deeply about the nature of reality whilst researching my PhD in solid-state physics. During this period I studied quantum electro-dynamics in great detail, and the more theory I understood, the less I knew of the search for reality. There are things in quantum theory that have no logical cause, and trying to attribute one to them results in total confusion or mathematical inconsistencies.

These personal issues with the Supreme Being were inadvertently resolved for me by physicist Richard Feynman. In his Alix G. Mautner Memorial Lectures on quantum electrodynamics he pointed out that the fearsome and arbitrary God of my childhood was quite absurd, if viewed in the right light. This is what he said:

> There is the possibility that after I tell you something you just can't believe it. You can't accept it. You don't like it. A little screen comes down and you don't listen anymore. I'm going to describe to you how Nature is – and if you don't like it, that's going to get in the way of your understanding it. It's a problem that physicists have learned to deal with. They've learned to realise that whether they like a theory or they don't like a theory is *not* the essential question. It's not a question of whether a theory is philosophically delightful, or easy to understand, or perfectly reasonable from a point of view of common sense. The theory of quantum electrodynamics describes Nature as absurd from the point of view of common sense. And it agrees fully with experiment. So I hope you can accept Nature as it is – absurd.[30]

I took Feynman's use of Nature, with a capital N, to be a codeword for the physicist's forbidden word, God. If Nature was absurd, then so was God. I gratefully accepted his viewpoint and simply applied my knowledge of physics to practical problems without worrying about why things are as they are. Richard Feynman helped me overcome my childish nightly need to offer a prayer of appeasement to the vindictive and vengeful Presbyterian God who lurked in the dark depths of my psyche, ready to punish me with eternal hellfire for any blasphemous thought.

I did not object to my new freedom and didn't miss God at all. If my ethical and moral views had remained rooted in the religious teaching I received in Sunday School, then the insights science gave me would have posed irreconcilable problems. If my morality had stayed based only on the instructions of a personal God, and I had also to believe that such a limited and parochial God was totally responsible for the vast scope of creation, then I would have faced severe doubts

about the value of any ethical teaching that this restricted and parochial God might promote. The fact that every religious believer I met
seemed to have a different idea of what God was only added to my
uncertainty. But fortunately science carried me to a more reasoned
philosophical position.

The God of my childhood had been arbitrary, unforgiving and
omnipotent. The practice of quantum physics was exactly the same –
which might be why I took to its uncertainty so readily. It wasn't
difficult for me to move quantum physics into the mental role recently
vacated by my Sunday School God. Its formulas were arbitrary, its
experimental verdict was unforgiving and its effects omnipotent.
Feynman's rationalisation of how the exact value of the quantum
coupling constant (which takes a value of 137.03597) arises summed
up my position.

> Nobody knows. It's one of the greatest damn mysteries of physics. You
> might say the 'hand of God' wrote that number and 'we don't know how
> He pushed His pencil'.[31]

The wilful God of my childhood never explained and never apologised,
so I was quite content to accept that He made up the number for the
quantum coupling constant on a whim one morning. The fact of not
knowing didn't affect the outcomes.

But this wasn't a good answer for the lodge. I could hardly define
God as the author of the arbitrary constant of quantum coupling. I
needed a better answer, but for my own peace of mind that answer had
to come from among the ranks of respectable physicists, and who could
be more respectable than Einstein? Reading his thoughts on religion for
inspiration I found this.

> You will hardly find one among the profounder sort of scientific minds
> without a peculiar religious feeling of his own. But it is different from
> the religion of the naive man. For the latter, God is a being from whose
> care one hopes to benefit and whose punishment one fears; a sublimation
> of a feeling similar to that of a child for its father, a being to whom one
> stands to some extent in a personal relation, however deeply it may be
> tinged with awe. But the scientist is possessed by the sense of universal
> causation. The future, to him, is every whit as necessary and determined

as the past. There is nothing divine about morality, it is a purely human affair. His religious feeling takes the form of a rapturous amazement at the harmony of natural law, which reveals an intelligence of such superiority that, compared with it, all the systematic thinking and acting of human beings is an utterly insignificant reflection. This feeling is the guiding principle of his life and work, in so far as he succeeds in keeping himself from the shackles of selfish desire. It is beyond question closely akin to that which has possessed the religious geniuses of all ages.[32]

Einstein had condemned my Presbyterian God as the God of a naive man. I was no longer naive. I had been educated in the ways of science, so a God with the virtue of not being personally interested in me, but who retained the power to fix the value of the quantum coupling constant, perhaps had promise after all. I could easily accept Einstein's definition of a Supreme Being as the Guardian of the Laws of Physics.

Isaac Newton, the father of all modern physics, had been inspired by Masonic ideas to formalise the laws of physics.[33] As Newton first discovered the laws of physics, I decided that I ought to consider his views on a Supreme Being, which he had put forward in *Principia Mathematica*:

The most beautiful system of the sun, planets and comets, could only proceed from the counsel and dominion of an intelligent and powerful being. And if the fixed stars are the centres of like systems, these, being formed by the like wise counsel, must be all subject to the dominion of one; especially since the light of the fixed stars is of the same nature with the light of the sun, and from every system light passes into all the other systems; and lest the systems of fixed stars should, by their gravity, fall on each other, he hath placed those systems at immense distances from one another.

This being governs all things, not as the soul of the world, but as Lord over all; and on account of his dominion he is wont to be called the Lord God or Universal Ruler, for God is a relative word, and has a respect to servants; and Deity is the dominion of God not over his own body, as those imagine who fancy God to be the soul of the world, but over servants. The Supreme Being is eternal, infinite, absolutely perfect,

omnipotent and omniscient . . . We know him only by his most wise
and excellent contrivances of things and final causes.[34]

Newton had provided another description which did not conflict
with my views of what a God could be – eternal, infinite, absolutely
perfect, omnipotent and omniscient, yet refraining from miraculous
meddling with the laws of physics. My Supreme Being was confirmed
as Guardian of the Laws of Physics.

I felt that I could trust this Guardian God, described by Newton and
Einstein, and when asked, 'In all times of danger and difficulties, in
whom do you put your trust?' I was able to answer with full conviction,
'In God.'

To my mind this definition of God was acceptable and reasonable.
And I would see, once I had been initiated, how my Guardian compared
with Freemasonry's concept of God. I didn't have to wait long. Soon
after my Initiation I met a God very different from the one of my
childhood.

A First Audience with the Great Architect

I was about to undergo my Initiation and was ambitious to become a
Master Mason. I had no idea of what an extraordinary progression of
mind-developing stages I was to go through. I didn't know it that
evening, but there were would be two basic degrees to take before I
became a Master Mason, and then there would be a choice of further
degrees which only a Master Mason could apply to join.

I was about to be initiated into the lowest grade, that of an Entered
Apprentice. I would be trained and tested in the art of memory before I
could progress to become a Fellowcraft, and then there would be further
training and examination before I could become a Master Mason.
Because Freemasons talked about degrees I expected something like
the process of taking a degree that I knew from university. The university system begins by sharing knowledge, proceeds by giving
opportunities to apply this knowledge before finally testing the candidate to prove that knowledge has been transferred and understood.
Only then is the degree conferred. It takes years. But I was to receive my

first Masonic degree in less than an hour. The teaching process was to be completely different, and it would be years after the award of the degree before the extent of the knowledge entailed in it would become apparent. Fortunately I did not realise just how long a process I was embarking on when I was instructed to undress in the Ladies toilet outside the closed door of the lodge.

Although I tried not to show it, I was nervous as I was taken to a side room (which served as the Ladies toilet when the lodge had female visitors) and told to strip. I was given a skimpy suit of flimsy white pyjamas to cover myself; there was no way to fasten the jacket, and one of the trouser legs was long and the other short. It's difficult to look composed and sophisticated in such a ridiculous costume. Not only were my props of self-confidence and professional assurance being taken away, but I was blindfolded, so that I couldn't judge the attitude of the brethren who were conducting the ritual.

'How will I know where to go?' I protested. 'I can't see a thing.'

'Don't worry,' replied the Tyler, who was helping me prepare myself. 'There are two officers of the lodge, called the Junior and Senior Deacons, who will guide you round the lodge.'

That was all very well, but I would have no way of knowing if they were deadly serious, or laughing behind my back. I was being forced to trust in their goodwill – and this was the first lesson of the Degree of Entered Apprentice: learn to face up to your fear of failure and be prepared to trust the goodwill of your lodge brothers to help you.

I now heard myself described, as I stood, blindfolded and stripped of all valuables at the door of the lodge, as:

A poor candidate in a state of darkness, who has been well and worthily recommended, regularly proposed and approved of in open Lodge and who now comes forward of his own free will and accord humbly soliciting to be admitted to a part of the Mysteries and privileges of Freemasonry for which ceremony he comes properly prepared.

I had wanted to join The Craft because I had seen the positive effects that membership of Freemasonry had on the members of the Lodge of the East Gate, and I felt that there was a spiritual warmth to Freemasonry that made it attractive to join. But during the ritual of Initiation I was confused and uncertain. Only later, when I watched the ceremony and eventually acted it out as an officer of a lodge, did I begin to understand its intent. With that hindsight I know that during my Initiation Masonry introduced me to three key lessons: to face my fears, to know myself and to recognise that I am a microcosm of the universe. I realise now that I needed to face my fears so that I would be prepared to face down my fear of being taught to know myself. But I had to know myself before I could learn about my place in the cosmos and my part in the immutable laws which run it. To know myself I had to think about 'life, the universe and everything'.

Freemasonry taught me to think of the task of improving myself as akin to the job of building King Solomon's Temple. The various building materials were prepared at a distance. They were taken to Jerusalem and put together silently and reverently, without the sound of axe or hammer. The aim of the architect was to build a perfect structure for which every part is properly prepared and ready to fit in with the rest.

This beautiful myth makes King Solomon's Temple a metaphor for extending the human spirit. It was the superstructure of my spirit that Freemasonry wanted me to engage in raising. On being made an Entered Apprentice, the lowest grade of Freemason, I had been enlisted into the building of a temple not made with hands or subject to decay. I was being taught that my every thought, word and deed contributed new material to this invisible construct that is my soul. In the metaphor of Masonry I was told to strive to contribute stones and timber of a quality and finish worthy of the Great Architect's design.

But the Masonic Great Architect was a different entity from the God of my childhood. Now that my initial crisis with the issue of the Supreme Being had been overcome I was free to explore the Masonic philosophy of God. And once I was an insider a lot more material was available to me. I quickly found that in 1985 the United Grand Lodge of England had issued a statement about its understanding of the nature of the Great Architect of the Universe. It includes these four statements.

- Freemasonry is not a religion.
- There is no separate Masonic God.
- Masons share a common respect for the Supreme Being.
- Freemasonry is open to individuals of all beliefs.[35]

This was a world view refreshingly different from that of my Presbyterian upbringing. I was pleased to discover how well my idea of God as an impersonal, incorruptible yet capricious Guardian of the Laws of Physics fitted with Freemasonry's official statements about the Great Architect of the Universe. As I entered the lodge I was asked, 'At all times of trouble and danger in whom do you put your trust?' and had been prompted to reply, 'In God'. But I knew the God I trusted was the causative force which guaranteed the integrity of the laws of physics, so it was not a problem for me when I was then asked to kneel to join the lodge in a prayer for the success of my Initiation. Indeed my trust in the laws of physics was so deeply ingrained that I knew any prayer to those laws could only be a comforting form of words for the supplicant and was not going to change anything except my feelings. It could do no harm to share in a common form of words with the lodge to express a shared hope for a successful outcome.

References to the Great Architect were scattered throughout the ritual I went through during my Initiation, which is known as Taking the First Degree. But the Masonic Great Architect is not a tyrant who unreasonably interferes in the affairs of men. For example the Great Architect figured in the first working tool I was given as an Entered Apprentice: the 24-inch gauge, which was described as an implement made use of in architecture to measure the work. For me as a Freemason, it was a tool to help me manage my time. I was told that the 24-inch gauge represents the twenty-four hours of the day – part to be spent in prayer and praise to Almighty God, part in labour and refreshment, and part in relieving a brother in distress. At first sight this is a recipe for a balanced life. If I substituted reflection on my physicist's sense of universal causation in place of prayer, this tool broke down to time spent thinking about the laws of physics, time spent earning a living, time spent relaxing, whilst still leaving some time for good works. But the Great Architect has other roles to play in the First Degree.

He is mentioned in connection with what are called the important landmarks of Freemasonry. (Landmarks are fixed points in the landscape which help you find your way about, and the ritual landmarks of Freemasonry serve just such a purpose. They are a means to help you find your way through a metaphorical landscape towards the mystical

Centre, where the lost secrets of Freemasonry are to be found.) In the First Degree I was introduced to a landmark that caught my physicist's imagination: the Volume of the Sacred Law. This is what I was told about it by the Worshipful Master:

> As a Mason, I would first recommend to your most serious contemplation the Volume of the Sacred Law, charging you to consider it as the unerring standard of truth and justice, and to regulate your actions by the Divine precepts it contains. Therein you will be taught the important duties you owe to God, to your neighbour and to yourself.
>
> To God, by never mentioning His Name but with that awe and reverence which are due from the creature to his Creator; by imploring His aid on all your lawful undertakings and by looking up to Him, in every emergency, for comfort and support.
>
> To your neighbour, by acting with him upon the square; by rendering him every kind of office which justice or mercy may require; by relieving his distresses and soothing his afflictions, and by doing to him as, in similar cases, you would wish he should do to you.
>
> And to Yourself, by such prudent and well-regulated course of discipline as may best conduce to the preservation of your corporeal and mental faculties in their fullest energy, thereby enabling you to exert the talents wherewith God has blessed you; as well as to His glory as to the welfare of your fellow creatures.

When I was initiated the book which was open on the pedestal of the lodge was the Bible. At first I had assumed that the term Volume of the Sacred Law was simply a name for the Bible, but as I learned more about The Craft I found that the situation was not so simple.

When I checked with the 1985 UGLE statement about Freemasonry and Religion I also found the following statement: 'Freemasonry, by forbidding religious discussion at its meetings will not allow a Masonic theological doctrine to develop.' I found this an important statement, as it goes well beyond simply forbidding the discussion of religion and politics, which had been in force since the adoption of Anderson's Constitutions. It shows an awareness of Masonic dogma being inadvertently created if points of religious agreement were discussed in lodge. My personal experience of dogma, at the hands of various Sunday School teachers, had left me highly sensitive to the danger of it. Here I now found a strong statement of the religious tolerance at the heart of Masonic regulation.

The more I thought about the issue of tolerance of different belief systems, the more I came to appreciate the wisdom of the question 'Do you believe in a Supreme Being?' It can be answered positively by members of all religious faiths and also by those, such as me, who might not accept any specific supernatural belief but have a sense of universal causation from the study of physics. This question checks for the minimal condition for becoming a Freemason, without either including or excluding the possibility of an individual's concept of a Supreme Being coinciding with the divinity as it is understood in a specific religious faith, such as the faiths associated with the Bible.

A new understanding of the tolerant and benevolent nature of the Great Architect, as described by Masonry, had begun to take root within my mind as the ceremony of my First Degree unfolded. I was particularly taken by the beautiful ritual description of the symbolism of the Masonic Temple. To me it represented the wonder and awe I had experienced from my study of physics. Here's how the Worshipful Master explained what Einstein had described as a physicist's 'rapturous amazement at the harmony of natural law':

> The Universe is the Temple of the Deity whom we serve; Wisdom, Strength and Beauty are about His throne as pillars of His works, for His Wisdom is infinite, His Strength omnipotent, and Beauty shines through the whole of the creation in symmetry and order. The Heavens He has stretched forth as a canopy; the earth He has planted as a footstool; He crowns His Temple with Stars as with a diadem, and with His hand He extends the power and glory. The Sun and Moon are messengers of His will, and all His law is concord.

Later, when Bro. Mike took me to hear the lecture on the First Degree Tracing Board at Rokeby Lodge in Halifax, I learned more about how the symbolism of the Great Architect is interlinked with the Masonic concept of the Volume of the Sacred Law. (A Masonic tracing board is a symbolic drawing designed to encode within an image the main teaching points of a degree.)

> As the Tracing Board is for the Master to lay lines and draw designs on, the better to enable the Brethren to carry on the intended structure

with regularity and propriety, so the Volume of the Sacred Law may justly be deemed the spiritual Tracing Board of the Great Architect of the Universe, in which are laid down such Divine laws and moral plans, that were we conversant therein, and adherent thereto, would bring us to an ethereal mansion not made with hands, eternal in the Heavens. The Rough Ashlar is a stone, rough and unhewn as taken from the quarry, until, by the industry and ingenuity of the workman, it is modelled, wrought into due form, and rendered fit for the intended structure. This represents man in his infant or primitive state rough and unpolished as that stone, until by the kind care and attention of his parent or guardians, in giving him a liberal and virtuous education, his mind becomes cultivated, and he is thereby rendered a fit member of civilised society. The Perfect Ashlar is a stone of a true die or square, fit only to be tried by the Square and Compasses. This represents man in the decline of years, after a regular well-spent life in acts of piety and virtue, which cannot otherwise be tried and approved than by the Square of God's Word, and the Compass of his own self-convincing conscience.

A liberal scientific education had changed my attitudes and hopefully developed my intellect, so turning me into a fit member of civilised society. But it had also made me take a far more sceptical attitude to the Bible. Having been forced to study it as a child, I reread it as an adult and came to the conclusion it was the best attempt of people without the benefit of scientific knowledge to make sense of the world they lived in and explain how that world had come about. Although I had by now resolved my position about the nature of the Great Architect, my inner Presbyterian-trained child was uncomfortable with the open Bible which stood at the centre of the lodge.

On my travels I saw that lodges with members who were of different religious faiths opened other books on the pedestal alongside the Bible. I saw the Torah opened in lodges with Jewish members and the Koran in lodges with Muslim brothers. I have even seen copies of all three holy books open on the same pedestal.[36]

I discussed the matter with Bro. Mike, and he drew my attention to another statement in *Freemasonry and Religion* which explained the open Bible and the nature of the Oath of Initiation that I had taken over the

Volume of the Sacred Law in Ryburn Lodge. 'The obligations taken by Freemasons are sworn on or involve the Volume of the Sacred Law, or the book held sacred by those concerned.' This is a clear statement of tolerance towards any belief system, which accepts there is a non-exclusive regulative force to be discovered behind creation. All physicists, even those who claim to be agnostic, accept this view. I began to realise that the term 'Volume of the Sacred Law' was a symbol of the religious tolerance of The Craft.

Having given careful thought to the matter I decided that the best book in which to find my conception of the divine laws and moral plans of the Great Architect was Newton's *Principia Mathematica*. That book inspired my development as a scientist, and I have studied, revered and respected it over many years. I had spent two solid years as a teenager studying the methodology contained in this book so that I could use it to understand and predict the movements of any physical object. The mathematical apprenticeship I had served under Newton had filled me with respect for his insight. And by the time I was passed to the Second Degree The Craft would show me just how much it reflected the system of belief laid out in that book and just how much Masonic philosophy had inspired Newton in his scientific work.

My first inkling of this insight came as my First Degree ceremony drew to its close. That was my biggest surprise about the nature of The Craft so far.

Once I had been allowed to take my seat in lodge I was told that I would have to commit to memory certain questions and answers which I would be tested on before I could be passed to the Second Degree. Alternate questions were put to each of the two wardens by the Master. As I listened one question jumped out. It concerned a major issue in the history of science. I was amazed to discover that before I would be allowed to learn anything more about Freemasonry I would have to stand up in open lodge and recite an item of scientific faith, a topic once known as the heresy of Galileo.

Here is part of the sequence of questions and answers that I was told to learn.

Q.: Where were you made a Mason?
A.: In the body of a Lodge, just, perfect, and regular.

Q.: And when?

A.: When the sun was at its meridian.

Q.: As in this country Freemasons' Lodges are usually held and Candidates Initiated in the evening, how do you reconcile that which at first sight appears a paradox?

A.: The sun being a fixed body and the earth continually revolving around the same, on its own axis, and Freemasonry being a universal science, diffused throughout the whole of the inhabited globe, it necessarily follows that the sun must always be at its meridian with respect to Freemasonry.

Before I could proceed to the next stage of Masonic teaching I had to publicly affirm that that the Earth was in orbit around the Sun. As a physicist this was easy.

Personal Reflections

I had been taken by surprise at the depth of emotion that the first question The Craft put to me had stirred up in my heart, rather than my head. I had long since dismissed as a non-issue the tyrannical nature of the Presbyterian God I had been forced to worship as a child. But before I could even hope to learn more about the secrets of The Craft I had to acknowledge a Supreme Being in which I could put my trust. It was pointed out that this did not have to be the God of any particular established religion (and certainly not the sadistic mythical tyrant who made the Sunday afternoons of my childhood such a burden), but there was a minimum requirement, if I wanted to become a Mason, to acknowledge that I believed there was a force which regulated the order of the universe. As a fully qualified solid-state physicist I placed a deep and sacred trust in the laws of physics and, after much thought, I was able to finally discard the last remnants of the jealous and irrational Presbyterian God and replace them with the calm reliability of a Guardian of the Laws of Physics.

One of the things which impressed me deeply during my First Degree ceremony was the tolerance of different viewpoints which was embedded in the ritual, but I was also surprised to discover that I would have to affirm in open lodge that I fully accepted the Galilean heresy before I could be passed to the Second Degree. My first steps into Freemasonry had not uncovered anything controversial, so far.

4

The Hidden Mysteries of Nature and Science

Becoming a Fellowcraft

TO BECOME A Fellowcraft Freemason I now needed to memorise a long obligation and a full set of questions, but more importantly I was going to have to make a semi-public affirmation that I fully accepted the Galilean heresy. No flat-Earther or believer in an Earth-centred universe was going to be allowed into the Second Degree of Freemasonry.

During my First Degree, Worshipful Master Paul had told me, 'Masonry consists of several degrees with peculiar secrets restricted to each. These secrets, however, are not bestowed upon Candidates indiscriminately but according to merit and ability.' I had been told a little more around the dinner table after the ceremony and now knew that there were three degrees in Freemasonry: Entered Apprentice, Fellowcraft and Master Mason.[37]

I had been told during my First Degree that 'Freemasonry is a peculiar system of morality, veiled in allegory and illustrated by symbols,' but I was only just beginning to understand how important symbols were in the way The Craft transferred its knowledge. The first clue came when I was taken to see the lecture on the First Tracing Board. That board was a glorious, complicated mix of images. It had sky and ground, pillars and altar, tools and stars, all laid out within the directions of the four corners of the world. As the basic ideas of the degree were explained the lecturer had pointed to the images on the board which showed these meanings symbolically. This was much more like the type of scientific instruction I had received as an undergraduate, where complicated situations were often represented by the graphs and sketches the lecturer would draw on the blackboard and refer to as he explained the science. I had been somewhat disappointed about the unstructured way my

Initiation had been carried out, as nothing was explained. Now I was beginning to realise that the tracing boards were the instructional diagrams of the degrees of The Craft. But to understand them I would need to have experienced the drama and emotion of the rituals. It would be quite some time before I understood just how successfully Freemasonry had managed to tap into the power of these symbols.

All the symbols for all the degrees of the present-day Craft can be found in the Kirkwall Scroll, and that has been reliably carbon dated to the time of the first lodge in Aberdeen. After years of research I have become quite certain that modern Freemasonry developed from this group of operative masons. Their first Masters, having worked under Sir Gilbert Hay at Roslin, had realised the power symbols have to convey deep spiritual messages, and the scroll shows how they arranged a whole lexicon of symbols into a series of steps which an Apprentice would be encouraged to take as he learned to use and carve the symbols. It is significant that those first Freemasons used symbols to encode their thoughts because they could not write down their ideas. It would be many years before all the members of any lodge would be literate, and so the power of symbols was used to instruct all thought fit to learn. In this way, that first lodge discovered and encoded what have become fundamental Masonic ideas about the power of symbols.

Some of the symbols used in Freemasonry date back over 70,000 years to the very first carvings known to be made by the human race.[38] Since their first discovery symbols have had an important impact on human thinking. And Freemasonry, by encouraging their formal study, inspired its followers to express the most abstract ideas. Freemasons have known for hundreds of years that symbols speak to us at a level far deeper than writing, and that, while writing is not actually needed to understand The Craft, symbols can illuminate it. My own research has confirmed that all humans have deep-rooted emotional reactions to symbols in general, and many Masonic symbols evoke positive emotional responses in most individuals.[39]

For over five hundred years the crude Masonic symbols on the Kirkwall Scroll have been drawn and redrawn on the floors of Freemasons' lodges to sensitise the brethren to their power. Other early lodges have similar floorcloths, and over the years I have been invited to view many of them; they all incorporate the same basic set of symbols. But Freemasonry did not create these symbols. It feels as if the symbols have an independent transcendental reality which Freemasonry responds to and benefits from. And the rituals and lectures have grown as formal ways to display and teach the meaning of these symbols to Apprentices.

The Craft has used symbols to communicate its ideas via a traditional system that transcends language. An idea formulated in symbols can be transmitted without corruption and guarantees a continuity of tradition. As a modern Mason I have been taught to carry out my symbol work in exactly the same way a mason of five hundred years ago did. I face the same problems in my search for Truth that the Mason of 1490 had to face, and the symbols provide the same answers.

Now as I stood before the closed door of the lodge, mentally repeating the password I had been given to allow me to enter the lodge in the Second Degree, I was about to be advanced to the Degree of a Fellowcraft. And I was properly prepared in the ludicrous flimsy white suit which revealed odd parts of my body to the scrutiny of the brethren. But this time I was not blindfolded. I would be able to see the faces of those who were to instruct me.

Bro. David, the Tyler, had knocked on the door of Ryburn Lodge.

'Who comes there?' called the Inner Guard, Bro. Colin.

Bro. David replied on my behalf. 'Bro. Robert Lomas who has been regularly initiated into Freemasonry and who now comes forward, of his own free will and accord, humbly soliciting to be passed to the Second Degree for which ceremony he comes properly prepared.'

After I gave the password and demonstrated the appropriate grips I was allowed into the Temple. As I moved into the lodge room a set square was held against my naked breast by the Inner Guard, who said, 'Enter this Fellowcraft Lodge on the square.'

The Worshipful Master, Bro. Paul Powell, spoke to the Lodge. 'Let the Candidate kneel whilst the blessing of heaven is invoked on what we are about to do.'

I was by now quite comfortable with idea of displaying due reverence to the laws of physics and using that display of awe and wonder to share aspirations with the brethren of the lodge.

The Master gestured towards the Lodge Chaplain, Bro. Stanley, who said, 'We make humble, earnest petition for guidance, O Great Geometrician of the Universe, on behalf of this Lodge of Fellowcraft Freemasons and this Candidate who kneels before us. Grant that his good work, begun in studies of the liberal arts, may be continued to lead to a fuller understanding of the glory of Thy works.'

This was the first time I had heard God referred to as the Great Geometrician and to enhance this knowledge a geometrical metaphor would be used. Once I had proved myself a worthy apprentice, by reciting my responses to each of the Wardens, I stood in the West of the lodge and the Senior Warden took my hand, holding it outwards the Master, who sat in the East.

'Allow me to introduce to you Brother Lomas,' he said. 'Who has been regularly initiated into Freemasonry and who now comes forward of his own free will and accord, humbly soliciting to be passed to the degree of a Fellowcraft, for which ceremony he is properly prepared.'

I felt rather silly standing in my flimsy white rags clutching the white-gloved hand of the impressively dressed Senior Warden and wondering what on earth was going to happen next. The Master replied;

'Brother Senior Warden. I will attend to your introduction and, for that purpose you will now instruct the Senior Deacon to advance the Candidate to the East in due form.'

The Senior Warden gave the First-Degree sign to signal he was about to carry out the instruction and turned to the deacon who was escorting me.

'By command of the Worshipful Master, you will now advance Brother Lomas to the Pedestal by the proper steps, there to take his Obligation.'

The two Deacons led me to the North side of the lodge and turned me to face the South. The Senior Deacon then spoke directly to me. 'Brother Lomas. The method of advancing from West to East in this Degree is by five or more steps, the first three emblematical of ascending a spiral staircase, the rest bold ones.'

He turned to face me. 'I will first go through them myself.' He proceeded to walk in a circle, lifting his feet high off the ground in an exaggerated fashion, mimicking the process of climbing up a winding staircase. Having completed a full circle he next strode boldly towards the Master's pedestal.

'You will now copy my example,' he said. The Junior Deacon, who stood beside me, guided me as I made the same exaggerated movements. This left me facing the Master's pedestal, ready to take my oath as a Fellowcraft Freemason.

That done, I was instructed in the grips, postures and passwords of the degree, and my knowledge tested first by the Junior Warden and then by the Senior. But there was one more shock in store for me in the final stage of my Second-Degree ceremony.

I was standing in the West of the lodge. The Senior Warden had turned me to face the Worshipful Master and once again was holding out my right hand towards him. He said, 'Allow me to present to you Bro. Lomas on his passing for some further mark of your favour.'

Master Paul ordered that I was to be dressed in a Fellowcraft apron, which had two blue rosettes on it. A period of concentrated fumbling followed as the Warden, wearing the traditional white gloves of a Master Mason, tied two slender tie-cords which held the apron in place around my waist. Finally, with my apron now precariously positioned, I again turned to face the Worshipful Master, who announced:

> The Fellowcraft apron, with which you have just been invested, points out that as a Craftsman you are expected to make the liberal arts and sciences your future study; that you may be the better enabled to discharge your duty as Mason and to estimate the wonderful works of the Almighty.

As a scientist, I believed my vocation was to estimate the wonderful works of nature and express them in the symbols of mathematics. Many years later, I discovered that much of the mathematics that I used to investigate questions in physics had evolved out of Masonic teaching about symbols. The algebra of equations was discovered by a Freemason by the name of John Wallis, who became a founder of the Royal Society, and he in turn inspired Isaac Newton to apply the science of equations to study the laws of nature; only when I understood the Royal Society did I realise I had come full circle at that moment. I had recently gone to the writings of Isaac Newton to find a definition of a Supreme Being which I could accept as a scientist. If I hadn't found such a definition I would never have become a Freemason. Then, after being made a Mason, I was told it was my duty to follow in the footsteps of Newton and study the hidden mysteries of nature and science. This would be my first inkling that the teachings of Freemasonry might have played a more important role in my training as a physicist than I had ever realised.

Once upon a time the Lodge of Aberdeen had an operative tradition of working only two ceremonies. This remained the norm for the next few hundred years. The lodge trained Apprentices in the symbology of The Craft, after which they would be given the Mason word and be freed from their Apprenticeship and become Fellowcrafts. Many Craftsmen moved away to get work and joined other Incorporations of Masons. In time they formed their own lodges (it remains true today that any seven Master Masons can decide to form a lodge to pass on their knowledge), each with their own interpretation of the basic lessons, to pass on the symbolic teaching they had found so inspiring. In this way Freemasonry spread southwards through Scotland and eventually into England, first taking root in York.[40]

By that time Freemasonry, with its knowledge of 'the Mason Word', 'Mystic Symbols' and the 'Art of Memory', had become widely established in Scotland. The fact that a Master of the Lodge of Aberdeen became an alderman of the Burgh (rather than simply being taken on as an employee of the Council) showed that the practice of intermingling patrons and craftsmen began early in the recorded history of Freemasonry. By the seventeenth century the Lodge of Aberdeen was regularly taking in members who were not working Masons but important players in Aberdeen society.

By the late sixteenth century it had become common practice for men who were interested in the esoteric knowledge of symbols which Freemasonry taught to join lodges to receive instruction in the power of the mystic signs and the art of memory. Once they had proved themselves proficient in their ritual knowledge of symbols they were given the 'Mason word', which allowed them to identify themselves as Craftsmen in the mental science of symbolic thinking.

Because of the way symbols can be used to communicate without using words Masons soon got a reputation for being able to recognise one of their own, and to confer without anyone noticing the exchange. This power of 'second sight' was widely thought to be imparted to those who had been given the 'Mason word',[41] which encouraged non-Masons to want this mysterious skill. Those who had the Mason word were able to see meanings in symbols that others could not. It is perhaps in some ways not dissimilar to the way in which physicists share knowledge, in ways impenetrable to non-scientists, using mathematical symbols. In a similar manner medieval operative masons could draw and understand diagrams, even though they might be literally unlettered and unable to read.

The speculative Masons were 'accepted' into the lodge to learn the ritual knowledge of symbolism, rather than the practice of stoneworking. In a world of declining trade guilds (often called Incorporations in Scotland) it was the means by which The Craft was transformed from a meeting place for artisans and operative stoneworkers into the groups of spiritual and speculative Freemasons that exist today. By the time *Anderson's Constitutions* were published, in 1723, this tradition was so firmly established that most Masons were Free and Accepted, rather than operative. This mundane history had been summarised within the First-Degree Ceremony of Initiation.

I first heard it from Bro. Dennis Oldthwaite, a red-faced, jolly man whose family had farmed lands around the Ryburn Valley since the compilation of the Domesday Book. Towards the end of my Initiation he had trundled across the chessboard carpet to present me with the working tools. At the time I was too taken by his mannerisms to reflect on what he was telling me. Dennis was an impressive presence. He fitted into his dark suit like a badly wrapped side of beef but his face always split into an enormous grin, and his good humour was infectious. His broad Yorkshire voice boomed out as he explained the practical uses a stone-cutter would make of the 24-inch gauge, the common-gavel and the chisel.

Then came the reference to the origins in the ritual, when he said, 'But as we are not all operative, but Free and Accepted, or Speculative Masons, we apply these tools to our morals.'

My first thought was what does it mean to apply the physical tools I hold in my hands to the immaterial emotional responses I call my morals?[42] Now I understand that I was being given early instruction in the use of symbols to convey ideas that are impossible to put into language. I was being introduced to the idea that my own mind and intellect were something I could build for myself, and that symbols were tools for thinking.

Gradually, as this teaching spread southwards, operative activity took second place to the symbolic work of constructing a spiritual and invisible Temple of the spirit. The shaping of minds became the main aim of the Free and Accepted Masons. In the process the mundane history of Freemasonry became less important than the mythical history. The mundane history dealt only with the material aspects of the world, the practical problems of building and the trade-guild politics. But the mythical history offered a way of approaching the transcendental centre of human awareness and tapping into the wisdom of timeless symbols. And, from the evidence of the earliest symbols in the Kirkwall Scroll, I can now see that Freemasons were open to any ideas about the nature of transcendental divinity which could help them develop understanding. The use of the symbol of the Norse Goddess Freyja on the seventh panel of the Kirkwall Scroll[43] shows a remarkable flexibility and open-mindedness about the nature of the Great Architect.

My proposer, Bro. Michael Astell, took me to Lightcliffe Lodge to hear Bro. Allen Atkins give the ritual account of the Second Tracing Board. The significance of Euclid in the mythical history of Freemasonry was spelled out in the ritual description Allen delivered.

> The River Nile, annually overflowing its banks, caused the inhabitants to retire to the high and mountainous parts of the country. When the waters subsided they returned to their former habitations; but the floods frequently washing away their landmarks caused grievous disputes among them, which often terminated in a civil war. They hearing of a Fellowcraft's Lodge being held at Alexandria, the capital of their country, where Euclid presided, a deputation of the inhabitants repaired thither, and laid their grievances before him. He with the assistance of his Wardens and the rest of the Brethren, gathered together the scattered elements of Geometry, digested, arranged, and brought them into a regular system, such as was practised by most nations in those days, but is bettered in the present by the use of fluxions, conic sections, and other improvements. By the science of Geometry he taught the Egyptians to measure and ascertain the different districts of land; by that means put an end to their quarrels: and amicably terminated their differences.

I realised that a new side of God was being revealed to me through geometry. Euclid seemed a fine Masonic role model for a physicist. I remembered that this new aspect of Supreme Being had already been introduced during the ceremony of my Second Degree. Deeper memories of the power of geometry began to stir as I stood listening to Bro. Allen explaining its role in the degree.

> Geometry, the first and noblest of sciences, is the basis on which the superstructure of Masonry is erected. By Geometry we may curiously trace nature through her various windings to her most concealed recesses. By it we may discover the power, wisdom, and goodness of the Great Geometrician of the Universe, and view with amazing delight the beautiful proportions which connect and grace this vast machine. By it we may discover how the planets move in their different orbits, and mathematically demonstrate their various revolutions. By it we may rationally account for the return of seasons, and the mixed variety of scenes which each season produces to the discerning eye. Numberless worlds are around us, all formed by the same Divine artist, which roll through the vast expanse, and are conducted by the same unerring law of nature. While such objects engage our attention, how must we improve, and with what grand ideas must such knowledge fill our minds! It was a survey of nature, and an observation of her beautiful proportions, which first induced men to imitate the Divine Plan, and study symmetry and order. This gave rise to society, and birth to every useful art. The architect began to design, and the plans which he laid down, having been improved by time and experience, have produced some of those excellent works which have been the admiration of every age.

Before I took my Second Degree I had been wondering why Freemasonry insisted that I affirm the Galilean heresy that the Earth orbits around the Sun, before I could be made a Fellowcraft. Now I understood. The knowledge that the Earth orbits the Sun arises purely from the study of geometry and is an area of research where I was fully at home, as I had decided to study science at the age of seventeen. I have never regretted that choice.

The Hidden Mysteries of Reading and Writing

I have already said I was fortunate enough to fail the 11-plus exam and so went to a secondary modern school. I consider this good fortune because it relieved me of any urge to worry about the need to achieve. I was free to enjoy learning for its own sake, because nobody expected much from an 11-plus failure. If I showed interest the hard-pressed teachers often responded by offering tremendous help. One teacher in particular, John Hywel Roberts, took pity on me and helped me grow wiser.

When I started at Heys Road he was newly qualified, a teacher in his first year of professional practice. He was a native Welsh speaker and has since told me that he struggled with English spelling. He inspired me to take an interest in history, encouraged my music and helped me improve my Welsh. But let me tell you about our first meeting.

It was in a North Manchester secondary modern school. I was sitting at a hard wooden double desk in a poky south-facing classroom. The sun was low in the afternoon sky, and its beams were full of the dancing motes of chalk dust where it cut through the shadows cast by the cramped rows of desks.

This was my first history lesson as an 11-plus failure. In front of the class stood a young teacher, red-faced, red-haired and nervous, who spoke with an impenetrable North Wales accent. His grey Burton suit, white shirt and red tie marked him out from the new intake of blue-blazered, white-shirted, blue-tied first-year boys of class 1B.

'Hello,' he said. 'I'm Mr Roberts and I am going to teach you history.'

John Roberts was away from home in a hostile, alien environment where thoughtless young boys mocked his Welsh accent by nicknaming him Paddy. Hungry for a degree in history, he had only been able to get into the University of Aberystwyth if he enrolled for a teaching certificate. I didn't know it then, but he was spending all his spare time studying for the qualifications he really wanted and a way out of a dead-end career as a secondary modern teacher in alien England. I was part of the burden he dreamed of escaping from.

My report from my Salford primary school said it all: 'could do better'; 'must work harder and concentrate on his spelling'; 'presentation poor';

'inclined to daydream'. Despite my hours of hard work, trying to construct meaning from text books and exam crib sheets, I had not been on the list of children considered intelligent enough to be offered a place at grammar school.

My parents had recently moved from Salford to a house in Prestwich. My equally thick childhood friends, also deemed unfit for grammar school, were going *en masse* to Leicester Road Secondary Modern; they were starting in a new school, but they were starting with friends they had known throughout primary school. When I walked into the playground of Heys Road Secondary Modern School, Prestwich, I knew no one.

Then I suffered a further humiliation. When the new intake was sorted into classes I was placed well down the second stream of what I had already been told was a second-stream school. I wasn't just unfit for grammar school I was barely fit for any education at all. The 'better' teachers, with more influence, taught the top, alpha stream. They encouraged the boys (it was a segregated, boys-only school) who were going to make something of themselves to become carpenters, apprentice fitters or even toolmakers at Trafford Park (still a massive conglomerate of engineering companies in those days). Potential artisans were pushed by the teaching hierarchy of Heys Road and considered the best classes to teach. The lower streams were thrown upon the questionable mercy of the old and cynical, or the young and inexperienced. It was such a young and inexperienced Mr Roberts who taught me. Looking back, I find it hard to believe just how lucky I was.

We were well matched. We had both shown early promise. He had gone to Aberystwyth to study history and had been forced by circumstances to take a teaching certificate. (He would eventually take that history degree at his own expense.) I had been told by my primary teacher that I had a vivid imagination and daydreamed too much, but if I worked hard and concentrated on my writing and spelling then I could do well. So, when I didn't learn to spell, and my writing didn't improve, it was obviously my own fault for not working hard enough. All my teachers, except Mr Roberts, thought I deserved to fail through lack of effort. (I knew I had worked as hard as I was able to for the 11-plus exam, but my best wasn't good enough – which meant *I* wasn't good enough either.)

So two misfits in the fifties educational system met in a small suburban classroom and faced up to our disappointments in our own ways.

I had failed the 11-plus because I could not read. When I look at my primary school reports they all comment that I tended to daydream and did not pay attention or concentrate on my spelling. I did well at learning my times tables and doing mental arithmetic but, apart from that, I was written off as too lazy to pay attention. In mitigation, perhaps I should point out that much of the teaching in the top primary classes was intended to prepare us children for the academic rigour of a grammar-school education. I found sums easy to do in my head but struggled to write down answers in a form that my teachers could read; I tended just to put down numbers, with none of the words which were called the 'working out'. The reason for this was not recognised at the time; it was not until much later that I found out I was dyslexic.

I left primary school barely able to read out loud, and most of the time quite unable to follow what was written on the blackboard. Fortunately I was blessed with a good memory, and if a teacher spoke out loud as he wrote on the blackboard I remembered it. But when I was confronted with reading, spelling and comprehension tests my inability to make sense of the odd shapes on paper was obvious.

A few years ago I presented a paper at the Orkney Science Festival, which I called 'The Shared Secret'. It was a description of the problem that reading presents to a dyslexic child. I calculated that it is 55,000 times more difficult for a dyslexic child to learn to read than for a non-dyslexic, and it is only those dyslexic children who have an excellent memory for shapes who manage to crack the secret of reading.

To my dyslexic mind each word is a separate and unique shape, similar to the pictograms used in Chinese and Japanese scripts, and each shape has to be learned separately. Unless somebody tells me how to say the word which the shape represents, then I have no idea how it sounds. I am totally unable to relate the letters of the alphabet to the shapes of words or to build a word from a sequence of letters. To learn how to read I had to memorise every single word-shape in my vocabulary and learn its sound before I could read it. But there is a further layer of complication. When I see each word-shape in context, it looks different. If the word is on its own in the middle of a page, then it has a different context shape than it has if it is embedded within a paragraph.

If it is at the beginning of a line it looks different from the way it looks when at the end of a line, or in the middle. Each individual word-shape has ten different positions where it can appear in written text – and each of those context shapes has to be memorised for every single word. Until my illiterate mind could link every word/sound to its multiple context shapes I could not interpret it as a word or read it out loud.

During their first attempts at teaching me to read, my primary school teachers used books which showed separate words, set in a blank page. The writer of the textbook assumed that if I learned the word once I would recognise it wherever else it appeared. So did my teachers. But I didn't. As the word reappeared in each of the nine other possible positions where it could be used in sentences I had to relearn it. And each time I saw it in a new position I had to ask what the word was, so that I could learn what was (to me) a new shape – even though for my teachers it was the same word. Small wonder they wrote in my school reports that I did not pay attention to reading and seemed unable to concentrate; a simple task for my teachers and schoolmates was utterly baffling for me. I started school in the 1950s, which was long before dyslexia was 'discovered', so I was written off as inattentive and thick.

Not until I started to make progress with piano lessons did I develop a way of overcoming my failure to read. It was another stroke of good fortune for me that my father was a frustrated pianist and decided I should learn the piano. For that I will always be grateful to him, as he made me get up early on Saturday mornings to sit for half an hour at the grand piano of Mr David Rudofsky. I laboriously learned to translate the odd shapes of the musical notation into hand shapes on the keyboard and eventually into beautiful musical phrases. I quickly saw that there was a mechanical linkage between shapes on paper and sounds. I could turn the unique shapes of the musical chords into hand shapes which I pressed on the keyboard. When I played notes on the keyboard, in the sequence indicated by the shapes, then the music sang out from the piano. Magically the score turned into music.

As I progressed to playing popular songs I added the shapes of the lyrics into the music. I would play the notes on the keyboard and sing the words along. As I was doing this it dawned on me that both systems worked in the same way – so for the first time I had a way of making sense of reading. As it turned out, reading words was much harder than reading music, because music is always written along a stave, and each note is separately written on that stave. Reading books was more complex because of the ten different word positions which had to be learned. Lyrics, though, were written between the stave, like music notes, and so I began to understand how it worked. I started to pay more attention to the minute similarities between the same word in different positions, and to ignore the massive differences. I started to look at the top of each line of text, as if it was a stave of music, and to ignore the confusing shapes which emerged when the word was set within a paragraph. Suddenly I found I could read. Using this technique I could learn, memorise and verbalise words, once I knew the sound they made. But I didn't know how to guess from their shape what that sound might be, so I got better at devising tricks to get people to speak out loud any new words I came across.

I soon discovered that any teacher would say the word I was pointing at and then tell me its meaning if I said, 'I'm not quite sure what that means.' It worked well enough for me to build up a basic vocabulary. Sometimes, though, the trick earned me an old-fashioned look. I remember asking Mr Roberts the meaning of 'frog'.

'You mean you don't know what a frog is?' he asked in his rich North Wales accent. 'You've never seen a little hopping and croaking green amphibian sitting on a lily pad.' When he put it like that I had the grace to blush.

Mr Roberts saw this.

'It couldn't be that you're having trouble reading it, is it, boy? You find the reading hard. Don't you?'

I admitted I did and told him it was easier when someone told me what the word said, so I could memorise it. From then on he was sympathetic to my difficulties and would always tell me any word I asked – but he would also insist I repeat it back to him whilst I looked at its shape.[44]

Once I had made the connection between music page and piano keyboard it was a simple step to move from a piano keyboard to a typewriter keyboard. At the age of twelve I saved up my pocket money and bought an old portable typewriter. My cousin had been to typing school, and she showed me where to put my hands on the keyboard and which keys to use with each finger. She gave me lots of exercises to play on the QWERTY keyboard, and I compared the shapes which appeared on the paper with shapes I was copy-typing until I could reproduce the text.

Even today if you ask me how to spell a word I have no idea, but I know the shape it makes on the keyboard and can play the equivalent of the musical phrase on the typing keyboard to make the word-shapes I need to write. I can also spell if I look down at my fingers and see the letters marked on the keys I am pressing to make the word-shape. In this way I learned how to write and to fake the ability to spell.

The combined result of John Roberts' encouragement, my improved music-reading ability and my new-found dexterity as a typist was that I appeared to blossom. Suddenly I could read.

I didn't read as other people do, though, and I still don't. I am still quite unable to make sense of the alphabet, and I can't use a printed dictionary. Again perhaps I can explain just how different this makes the world seem by giving an example.

When I'm searching a telephone directory, I do it by flipping through it from the back to the front whilst simultaneously hoping for a name similar to the one I want to skip across my line of vision. If somebody is watching me, they often start a conversation that goes something like this:

Helpful Observer: 'Why don't you start at the front and then turn to the section you want?'

Me: 'How do I know which section I want until I see it?'

Helpful Observer: 'It's arranged alphabetically.'

Me: 'So how does that help me find it?'

Helpful Observer: 'Well you turn to the section of names which start with the letter you want.'

Me: 'That's what I'm doing now, when I see any name which starts like the one I'm looking for, I'll stop and search around that bit of the directory.'

Helpful Observer: 'Why don't you just turn to the alphabetic section you want?'

Me, pointing out the obvious: 'Because I don't know where it is until I find it.'

Helpful Observer: 'It's alphabetical.'

Me: 'You said that already but it doesn't tell me where to find the name I want.'

Helpful Observer: 'You just turn to the part of the alphabet you want to use.'

Me: 'That's what I'm doing. I'll stop when I find it.'

Helpful Observer: 'Do you mean you don't know the order of the letters in the alphabet?'

Me: 'That's right.'

Helpful Observer: 'But why don't you learn it?'

Me: 'Well thanks so much for that helpful suggestion. What a wonderful idea. For the last fifty years it's never crossed my mind that if I bothered to learn the alphabet I could use it find things in directories and dictionaries and lists. What a great idea! Why didn't I think of it for myself? Thank you, thank you! Your suggestion will transform my whole life!'

To me the alphabetic sequence is an arbitrary and illogical whim that I am congenitally incapable of remembering. And spelling remains a mystery to me, particularly when I hand-write, as I can fill in the unimportant parts in the centre of words with almost any letters.

So only the shapes matter to me. But that ability to see shapes turned me towards the study of science. I was already inclined towards the use of symbols, long before I became a Mason; the shapes numbers and letters make when they are used in equations have always been far simpler to understand than the odd, arbitrary combinations for spelling words.[45] I find the symbols of mathematics beautiful and understandable, while words are slippery and ambiguous. Unlike most of my contemporaries, therefore, I had no difficulty with algebra. I loved the way equations could be shaped and manipulated to yield up answers to interesting questions. Here was a way to reveal things I didn't know.

I quickly learned that mathematics held the key to understanding how the world worked. The symbols and shapes were a natural language which my dyslexic mind took to as a pig takes to a fresh mud wallow.

When I first met numbers, by chanting times tables at primary school, I was fascinated by the way they fitted together. I quickly discovered for myself the series of ten's complements which enabled me to make rapid estimates in mental arithmetic.

In my third year at Heys Road I met another inspirational teacher, who introduced me to the joy of geometry. His name was Mr Ernest Sussman, and he, too, was young and newly qualified. Like John Roberts he was a musician. But more importantly he had a flair for making geometry come alive. He showed me all the wonderful ways I could deduce facts about the world from simple knowledge of points, lines and shapes. He would sprinkle his lessons with stories of Euclid, the mathematician who had written the first textbook about this wonderful deductive geometry. And one thing Mr Sussman said has always remained in my mind, because it involved the God I was trying to escape from. He claimed that Euclid said, 'The laws of nature are but the mathematical thoughts of God.'

By that time God's tyrannical presence had happily receded from my life, so, although I liked the drama of the quote well enough for it to stick in my mind, I didn't take it seriously. Now the Second Degree of Freemasonry was revealing to me a new and interesting aspect of God. With God the Masonic Supreme Being appearing in the guise of the Great Geometrician of the Universe, Mr Sussman's quote resurfaced and challenged me to rethink my position.

As part of the ritual lecture of the Second Degree I memorised the following series of questions and answers:

Q: Why were you passed to the degree of a Fellowcraft?

A: For the sake of Geometry, the science on which Masonry is founded.

Q: What is Geometry?

A: A science whereby we find out the contents of bodies unmeasured by comparing them with those already measured.

Q: Its proper subjects?

A: Magnitude and Extension, or a regular progression of science from a point to a line, from a line to a superficies, and from a superficies to a solid.

Q: What is a point?

A: The beginning of geometrical matter.

Q: A line?

A: The continuation of the same.

Q: A superficies?

A: Length and breadth without a given thickness.

Q: A solid?

A: Length and breadth with a given thickness, which forms a cube, and comprehends a whole.

When I first heard this I was transported back to Mr Sussman's classroom. I could smell the chalk and hear it scraping on the blackboard as the hidden mysteries of shape and interrelation were laid out in front of me. That enthusiastic introduction to mathematics which I received at the hands of Mr Sussman had a profound effect on my future career.

Heys Road School did not have a sixth form and no pupils had ever taken General Certificate of Education (GCE) exams. When I reached the fifth year I was entered for ten ULCI (Union of Lancashire and Cheshire Institutes) exams, which were a lower level than the GCE.

By then I had developed handling techniques to overcome my oddities with reading and writing. Because I only looked at the upper envelope of the typed word, which defined its shape, I had accidentally discovered how to speed-read, and was devouring large numbers of books. I did not have to decode the letters which made up the word, as I could not even see them. To me, words look like a musical score that encodes speech rather than musical notes and can be quickly scanned for meaning. The intense effort I had put into memorising the shapes of all the basic words in all the contexts where I might meet them had developed my memory, and I had little trouble in recalling the contents of these books even if I did appear to be scanning, rather than absorbing each page carefully as I read it. In those days, when much examination content consisted of reproducing facts, this was a highly practical skill.

I had partially solved the problem of writing by learning to touch-type but all my teachers complained my handwriting was illegible. Heys Road Boys County Secondary School taught copperplate handwriting. It was in effect a continuous loopy line which had little shape to it. I found it extremely hard to read, as all the landmark shapes I could see in typeset words were smoothed into loopy nothingness when hand-written. By learning to type I now knew which letter keys to hit and in which order to hit them so as to write words I used regularly. But I needed some way of making unique word-shapes in handwriting. Copperplate, though, was not the sort of script I could either read or write with any precision.

Then by yet another stroke of good fortune I received a letter from a close friend of the family, whom I knew as 'Uncle' Harold. It was hand-written but with each letter contributing a clear-cut and distinct outline to the word-shapes. When I saw him next I asked him about the writing style he used and he told me it was called Italic. Soon afterwards he gave me a book which showed how to form each letter. Now I had a way forward. The italic letters were not connected by meaningless loops and swirls but stood out as individual shapes, just as the letters on a type-writer did. Once I had learned to draw the shape of the individual italic letter I could look in my visual memory and see where it was on the keyboard and then draw it. Italic script enabled me to write as if I was typing. It slowed my writing down, and I made far more mistakes than I did with a typewriter, but this method had the advantage that other people could read it. It worked because each of the individual italic letters could be drawn quite separately, unlike copperplate script, which had to be created in a single flowing scribble.

I was pleased when most of my teachers commented how much easier it was to read my writing and in my naïve way I was quietly proud of solving the problem. But I was about to meet an example of mindless prejudice which still makes me angry fifty years later.

I was about six months into my experiment in italic hand-writing when I moved form. That meant a new teacher. At the time I thought her old, although, looking back, she must have been only middle-aged. However she was so firmly set in her ways that she was unable to accept any sort of individuality in her pupils. She also taught religious studies, and – as I knew to my cost from my time at Sunday School – teachers of religious ideas can often be control freaks. She took a dislike to my italic writing and set out to force me to revert to the unusable copperplate that the rest of the class, and the school, favoured. In front of the class she berated my written work. She poked fun at the highly angular shapes of my writing, calling it uncultured and barbarian. I don't think she went as far as telling me my handwriting was an offence against God, but I'm sure she must have thought it. When I told her it was a far better way to write, because I could read it myself, she really lost her rag and sent me to the Headmaster to be caned for insolence.

After refusing a chance to apologise I duly received two strokes on each hand but refused to change my way of writing. Instead I appealed over her head to my new English teacher, a Mr Drewery, to whom I explained why I had decided to change my writing style. I told him I was tired of being told how bad my handwriting and spelling were. I wrote him an essay about the importance of clear handwriting, and he spoke to the woman, and her attacks ceased. But her hostility simmered on: instead of being attacked I was ignored. However, as her subject was religious instruction it made little difference. I already knew the Bible far better than she did – six solid years of Singleton Mission Sunday School had made sure of that. I went on to score a Grade 1 pass in RI (religious instruction) in the ULCI exam.

It has never ceased to amaze me that some of the most fervent followers of what they claim to be a God of Love have also been among the most bigoted and aggressive people I have encountered. But this last attack on my developing scientific mindset by a dedicated follower of the vicious, spiteful and tyrannical God of my childhood finally showed me that I need no longer fear the bitter reprisals of this dreadful Lord. Now I knew I could fight back and win. I was beginning to develop the mind of a scientist.

Climbing on the Shoulders of Masonic Giants

I scored top grades in all ten ULCI exams, to both my own and my teachers' great surprise. Having failed the 11-plus, and been consistently taken to task for erratic spelling, I decided that I wanted to do something practical. I was interested in the new discipline of electronics, so I applied to the General Post Office to become an apprentice telephone engineer. The GPO offered me a place to start in September. But when the school learned of my success in ULCI they asked if I, and four other students, would like to stay on an extra year and take O level GCEs. For the very first time in my life I saw the possibility of going to college, studying science and becoming a technician in a lab, rather than a wireman who climbed telegraph poles. I got myself a Saturday job, selling shoes at a large shop in Market Street, Manchester, so I could afford to contribute to my keep, and settled down to another year's study for eight O levels.

The most exciting memory from my GCE studies was being shown calculus. Mr Sussman couldn't resist adding a layer of exciting stories about the life and times of Isaac Newton, who soon became a hero for me. I did just as well at O level as I had the previous year and so became a minor celebrity at Heys Road; I got the best grades in the school's history. College became a possibility, not a remote dream, and I changed my Saturday job from selling shoes to pumping petrol and worked Friday evenings, Saturday afternoons and evenings and all day Sundays at a local filling station. I was earning almost as much from that part-time job as I would have earned working full-time as a GPO apprentice, and I had weekdays free to study science. I passed my driving test before I left Heys Road and bought a cheap car (a Ford Prefect 100E), and on my last day I drove my own car to school, parked in the staff car park and achieved another Heys Road first.

I wanted to study science and I was sure the only way to understand it was to learn mathematics. I loved the patterns numbers created and found the manipulation of equations sheer delight. My struggle to learn to read had developed my ability to see patterns and proved a useful skill for an aspiring scientist. I signed up at Salford Technical College to take three A level GCEs, in Applied Mathematics, Pure Mathematics and Physics. I spent the next two years wallowing in Newton's Laws, the mystery of the calculus and the basics of atomic theory.

All these memories flooded through my mind as I stood in Ryburn Lodge, listening to Worshipful Master Paul explain my duties as a newly passed Fellowcraft. All the delights of discovering the inherent power of Newton's Laws of Motion to explain the world came back to me.

The highlight of that Second Degree was being charged with a duty to study the hidden mysteries of nature and science. I was made to stand in the South East corner of the Lodge. This represents the direction of the shadow cast by the rising Sun on the shortest day of the year. Symbolically I stood in line with the dawn of the day of least light. I received these final instructions whose message was clear: I was still in darkness but I was being offered a way of thinking to help me move towards the light of Truth. This is what the Master said:

> Bro. Lomas. When you were made an Entered Apprentice, you were placed in the North East Corner of the Lodge showing that you were newly admitted. In this Degree you are placed in the South East Corner to mark the progress you have made in the science.
>
> And, as I trust, the import of the former charge, neither is, nor ever will be, effaced from your memory, I shall content myself on this occasion by observing that, as in the former Degree you made yourself acquainted with the principles of moral truth and virtue, in this Degree you are permitted to extend your researches into the more hidden mysteries of nature and science.

With my newly acquired status as a Fellowcraft I was now not only free to study the more hidden mysteries of nature and science, it had become my Masonic duty. My two years studying the diverse manifestations of Newton's Laws of Motion had prepared me to take full advantage of this new freedom. But it was a while before I realised just how important this particular interest of Freemasonry had been in the formation of the modern scientific society of which I was a product.

As I have said, Mr Sussman, the teacher who showed me the ways of the calculus, was an enthusiastic fan of Sir Isaac Newton, and he sprinkled his maths lessons with tales of the great man. He was fond of quoting a statement of Newton's: 'If I have seen further it is only by standing on the shoulders of giants.' It was nearly forty years before I found that Newton had stood on the shoulders of *Masonic* giants, many of them founder members of the Royal Society.

The men who founded the Royal Society had trained as Masons, and, just as I was being taught the power of symbols through the degrees of The Craft, so had they been. The common interest shared by the ragbag collection of poverty-stricken out-of-work Parliamentarian academics and newly enfranchised royalist fat cats was their interest in Freemasonry.[46] After the death of Oliver Cromwell when Britain tottered on the brink of fresh conflict, the controversial decision to invite the king to return was taken. In this chaotic Restoration London the Royal Society began.

The moving spirit during the creation of the Royal Society was a Freemason, Sir Robert Moray. He was a member of the Lodge of Edinburgh, and his motive was political. Moray, who in part at least had been spying for Charles II, brought the news that the Dutch were planning war with England and had a far superior navy. Charles had no money and little expertise to call on. He had a great enthusiasm for naval matters but no resources. Moray had an inspired solution. He took up Masonic contacts in and around London, knowing they were involved in studying 'the hidden mysteries of nature and science'.

He quickly discovered that the main centre for Freemasonry in Restoration London was Gresham College, a public college that Sir Thomas Gresham had set up to support his Masonic ideals of study. Here Moray found the answer to Charles's dilemma. When the king had returned to England he had thrown many of the Parliamentarian scientists out of their university posts in a knee-jerk response, and they were struggling financially; an important group was based at Gresham College, surviving on the stipends the college paid to them or to their friends. Here was a pool of expertise in naval technology that could be tapped into.

These 'scientists' were all politically out of favour as well as extremely short of money. True, Charles could not afford to pay them, but he could bring them back into public favour. And Moray was resourceful. He knew many wealthy gentlemen Masons who were interested in the study of science. He harnessed the two groups by persuading them to work together for the good of their king and country, using Masons and Masonic ideas to solve the problems of Charles's navy.

This bringing together of Royalist Freemasons with money and Parliamentarian Freemasons with scientific skills into a self-funding group to tackle a crisis touched the imagination of the newly restored kingdom, and Moray used their shared interest in science as a basis for a new society to focus the application of science on the problems of defence.

Moray won the confidence of the Parliamentary Masons when he made their deposed leader, John Wilkins, take the chair of their first meeting. Wilkins had been married to Oliver Cromwell's sister Robina.

By rehabilitating Cromwell's brother-in-law with the king, Moray showed the other Parliamentary scientists that they were all equal in his Masonically inspired scientific body. He laid his ground carefully, and, despite the king's busy schedule, within a week of that first meeting, Moray had gained a Royal Charter for the group.

Bro. Robert Moray created something far greater than he ever dreamed. The Society developed, it took on a life of its own and soon separated from its Masonic roots, taking in many others who were not Masons. Nonetheless, the new Society was built on Masonic philosophy, and this inspired it to nurture the most important scientific developments of all time. The problems faced by Charles's navy were the problems of understanding the Universe, and by developing techniques to aid navigation the founders of the Royal Society created techniques that enabled their members to study the stars. A policy of carrying out flamboyant demonstrations spread the ideas of science to the more influential layers of society. Using the microscope to investigate minute creatures for the amusement of the nobility led to the science of biology being discovered. Finally the policy of publishing the results of studies and experiments increased the rate of innovation. In less than twenty years the study of the stars had moved on from the arcana of astrology to using Newton's Laws to predict the return of Halley's Comet.

The newly formed Royal Society was a potent package which took a lively group of thinkers and gave them funding, encouragement and a means of sharing knowledge. Without the change in attitude to the study of the skies which the Royal Society achieved, Newton's work on gravitation would never have been published. It is important to remember that, less than a generation earlier, Galileo had been persecuted by the Church for daring to suggest the Earth might revolve around the Sun.

The ritual injunction to recite the formal statement of the Galilean heresy in the test questions of the Fellowcraft Degree remains as a permanent memorial to Bro. Sir Robert Moray and his action in promoting the Fellowcraft duty to 'study the hidden secrets of Nature and Science in Order to better know his Maker'. I don't believe that on 28 November 1660 Sir Robert set out to create the world's premier scientific society; he probably only expected the group to solve the military problems Charles could not afford to tackle. However, the Masonic principles of equality and the study of the hidden mysteries of science he applied created a tremendous living force. His group was free from the shackles of religious dogma and had a uniquely democratic structure for its time. Either by accident or design, he took three of the most powerful ideas of Freemasonry and applied them to the development of technology.

These ideas were:

1. That studying the works of nature can lead to an understanding of God's underlying plan: i.e. that there is an underlying order in the laws of nature that can be determined by observation and experiment. (This idea led directly to the work of Newton.)
2. That all men are equal. If they come together to discuss learning and eschew discussion of religion and politics they will be able to co-operate. This exclusive focus on experimental science helped the Royal Society become a major force in creating the modern scientific age.
3. That for Officers and Presidents to have true power, they must be elected by, and have the support of, the members they rule. William Schaw, the First Grand Warden of Freemasonry, had decreed this sixty years earlier, and Moray ensured that the Charters of the Society included the Fellows electing their own leaders, so that they were loyal to them.

These principles proved a sound foundation for building a scientific institution. Moray's fourth principle, the application of Masonic charity to aid a brother in distress, brought wealthy amateurs into the society and encouraged scientists, who had been strong supporters of Parliament, to sit down and work with wealthy Royalists, who funded their work and assisted their rehabilitation into Restoration society.

The men that Moray brought together to found this Society had all been trained, as I was being trained, in the Masonic art of understanding and interpreting symbols. The Masonic idea that symbols carry deep meaning, combined with the Masonic ideal of equality, became the key to uncovering the secrets of the heavens.

Freemason Dr John Wallis was one member of this group. A friend of John Wilkins and a brilliant mathematician, he had been Savilian Professor of Geometry at Oxford during Cromwell's rule and developed the theory of equations and algebraic notation that Isaac Newton was taught. Before Wallis nobody had realised the power inherent in the Masonic symbol of equality (the two pillars) and the Masonic philosophy of balance and harmony which it symbolised. He used this insight to create the modern mathematical method of equations.

Wallis recognised the incredible mystery hidden within simple equations. They enable mathematicians to access the core ideas that make a universe work and keep it working. Why this should be, nobody knows, but all physicists accept the mystery that enables us to write down and understand the laws of nature. As Professor of Physics Graham Farmelo explains:

> An equation is fundamentally an expression of perfect balance . . . It is perfectly possible to imagine a universe in which mathematical equations have nothing to do with reality. Yet the marvellous thing is that they do. Scientists routinely cast their laws in the form of equations featuring symbols that each represent a quantity experimenters can measure. It is through this symbolic representation that the mathematical equation has become one of the most powerful weapons in the scientist's armoury.[47]

Wallis's method of equations was a new way to reveal how things that might appear different are really exactly the same. It was a major step forward in knowledge to discover that, by working out something on one side of an equation, you can discover a truth about something on its other side. Wallis's *Treatise of Algebra* (1683) explained how the formal manipulation of symbols reveals matters which are otherwise inaccessible to human understanding and that symbolic equations can uncover the hidden mysteries of nature. This book inspired Isaac Newton, the man whose Laws of Motion I spent two years studying at Salford Technical College.

Newton was fascinated by the Masonic teaching about the geometry of King Solomon's Temple, and it became a lifelong obsession for him. He was introduced to the power of geometry by reading Freemason William Lilly's book *Christian Astrology* (1647), and this pushed him to study the writings of Lilly's fellow Mason Wallis, who became an early inspiration for him ('About the beginning of my mathematical studies, the works of our celebrated countryman, Dr Wallis, fell into my hands . . .'[48]).

Wallis introduced Newton to the Masonic hero Euclid and to the works of another Freemason, William Oughtred, the inventor of the slide rule and author of a book on the power of symbolic reasoning, *Clavis Mathematicae* (1631). When Newton joined the Royal Society in 1671 it was dominated by speculative Freemasons, and Newton's notes show that his interest in symbolic thinking grew rapidly around this time.

Newton wrote three times as many words about the sacred geometry of King Solomon's Temple as he did about physics, but his work in physics dominated the world of science for three hundred years after his death.[49] Even when Einstein improved the theory, it didn't stop scientists using Newton's Laws for most practical purposes. (The whole of the syllabus of my A level in Applied Mathematics consisted of learning how to apply Newton's Laws of Motion to a vast range of practical engineering problems.) Newton applied Wallis's idea that the Masonic symbol of equality (the equals sign, '=', is the two pillars rotated by 'an angle of ninety degrees, or the fourth part of a circle') was the key to uncovering the secrets of the heavens. This insight from Masonic philosophy enabled Newton to solve the mystery of how the heavens moved.

Whenever I sit in lodge and see the symbol of the two pillars on the tracing board, reminding me of a vertical '=' sign, I can't help reflecting on the incredible mystery hidden within the simple equations that I studied at Salford Technical College. There I learned to access ideas that make a universe work and keep it working. Nobody knows why this should be, but as a student I was taught to accept the mystery and simply calculate the laws of nature.

Mr Sussman's maxim that 'the laws of nature are but the mathematical thoughts of God' now took on a new force for me as I stood in Ryburn Lodge. Isaac Newton – the scientist whose discoveries underpinned the entire object of study of two out of my three A levels – had been as inspired by the mystical geometry of Solomon's Temple to discover fluxions and vanishingly small increments. Freemasonry was increasingly forcing me to rethink my attitude to the Great Architect.

Personal Reflections

My Second Degree confirmed my belief that rational observation of nature and science is a more certain way to understand the Great Architect than to accept the revelations of others, but Freemasonry had not yet done anything to make its teaching stand out from other systems of social and scientific education. You might think that so far the knowledge I had met did not seem to be anything more than the fossilised remains of the sources of inspiration for my mathematical and scientific heroes.

Surely there was more to Freemasonry than that?

It turned out there *was* much more to The Craft. It does have secrets, but before I could learn them I had to face up to the reality of death.

5

Into the Valley of Death

Another Leading Question

I TOOK MY First Degree the last Wednesday of one month, and the last Wednesday of the following month I took my Second. At the time I accepted the general view of lodge members that it was important to wear the highest-ranking apron you could.

As a fully accredited 11-plus reject I was fully attuned to emblems of failure. When I met the Masonic system of pinnies as badges of rank I remembered my first day at Heys Road and being placed in a lower stream of a lower-level school. This made the pure white apron of an Entered Apprentice seem like a badge of low achievement which marked me out from the blue-edged pinnies of my superiors. I was being sucked into a hierarchical system which I soon realised had no educational purpose – although I have since recognised that it is a means of motivating older members, who have been through all the offices of the lodge, but still want to collect badges. (It would be many years yet before I found the lodge which showed me that the rewards of Freemasonry come as benefits to the mind and spirit, not as badges of rank, and explained the real purpose of the rank system that is found within the offices of a lodge.)

The first two degrees had pleasantly surprised me. I had been intrigued by the idea of the benign Great Architect of the Universe – such an agreeable contrast to the jealous God inflicted on me when I was a child. And I had been delighted by the confirmation that studying the hidden mysteries of nature and science would lead to an understanding of the ways of the Great Architect, also known as the Grand Geometrician of the Universe. My love of geometry made this a welcome concept. So far my Initiation into Freemasonry had been tranquil, quick and interesting.

It had challenged me to some rethinking but hadn't fundamentally disturbed my world view. That was about to change.

Before the lodge was ready to raise me to the Third Degree it had another Candidate to bring in. At the time I wondered why they didn't simply finish off my Third before bringing in the new Entered Apprentice. It wasn't until I held office in the lodge that I realised that each ceremony involves a considerable effort for all the brethren taking part: they have to learn their parts, word-perfectly, to know where to stand and how to move, and they all work together to make the experience as good as it can possibly be for the Candidate. Naturally, having recently rehearsed and carried out a First and a Second, the lodge team were keen to do further examples, before they had to work at delivering a Third.

I had been in for such a short time that I hadn't realised that all the officers of the lodge changed jobs at the end of the Masonic year and moved onto another role. This is called the Ladder of Progression and is followed by all Master Masons. Each year they move up to the next office. They begin as a Steward, moving up through Head Steward, Tyler, Inner Guard, Junior Deacon, Senior Deacon, Junior Warden, Senior Warden until they become Master. Then they become a Past Master. As a Past Master they may become Director of Ceremonies, Chaplain, Secretary or Treasurer. (There is one other office, which is voluntary and depends on skill, that of Organist.) As a result of this ladder, once a team has learned, practised and delivered a ceremony they all move into another role at the year's end and start the learning process all over again. When I first heard of this system it struck me as an inefficient use of resources, a sort of 'Buggins's Turn' to ensure all had prizes. I still feel this way about the system of Provincial and Grand Offices, but eventually I found a lodge which explained that, at least at lodge level, this system has a real purpose. This slow upward movement through the hierarchical offices of the lodges is an essential part of the Masonic teaching about a process known as the 'The Art of Memory'. By the time a Mason has held every office in the lodge, in the correct order, he has memorised all the words of every ritual for every degree. If put forward as an objective, this involves learning 17,000 words of ritual, word-perfectly, which would seem impossible to achieve. However the Masonic system makes it seem almost simple, as, piece by small piece, each component of the jigsaw is memorised and then fitted into the complete picture. And when a ceremony is worked the whole piece is heard as one whole recitation.

The team who initiated and passed me wanted to avoid having to learn the Third Degree before they all moved upwards at the end of the Masonic year. They initiated and raised Keith, the new Candidate, so that we could both take our Third Degree the following Masonic year. This meant the newly promoted team could then learn their parts in the Third Degree and do two ceremonies in quick succession. As a result I enjoyed my few months as a Fellowcraft to watch Bro. Keith's progress and reflect on the good impression I had received of the first two degrees. I became settled and complacent.

It came as a shock when Mike Astell, my proposer and mentor, told me that I would be doing my Third after the Installation of the new Master and his Officers. I now had to make sure I was word-perfect in another set of test questions and the similar but annoyingly different obligation of the Fellowcraft that I would have to recite to the lodge to prove I had made sufficient progress in The Craft's 'Art of Memory'.

I have already mentioned that one of the questions I had to commit to memory stood out: 'What are the peculiar objects of research in this Degree?' To which I must answer, 'The hidden mysteries of nature and science.' The idea of joining in an investigation of the deeper problems of nature and science excited me. Ever since I had realised that mathematics could enable me to understand the behaviour of the world I had been hooked on the emotional highs to be found in solving problems and understanding reality. Now it seemed that The Craft was offering an opportunity to develop that knowledge. But there was a warning bell sounding amid this joy and excitement. I had spent many years in the company of skilled scientists, and few of my lodge brethren at Ryburn seemed to be of the curious and enquiring mindset I associated with scientists who studied nature and science as a vocation. I wondered if I was being prepared for the revelation of some deeper secrets about science. Were the deepest secrets of Masonry special insights into the mysteries of nature and science? I have often read that in moments of deep crisis, when they think they are about to die, people have reported that their whole life flashes before them. As I waited for my Raising to begin I found my mind conducting a similar review of my life as a student of the hidden mysteries of science.

Apprenticed to the Mysteries of Nature and Science

My time at Salford Technical College provided me with a solid ground-ing in mathematics and physics. With three GCE A levels, in Applied Mathematics, Pure Mathematics and Physics, I wanted to go to university.

I had gone to Tech hoping I might get a few A levels and be able to apply for a technician apprenticeship in electronics somewhere in Manchester. But at the Tech I mixed with a different type of student from those at Heys Road. No one at Heys Road had considered going to university. It wasn't something that secondary modern boys did; they left school at fifteen and went on to be labourers, to work in shops and warehouses, or, if they were highly ambitious, applied to be appren-tice fitters for the Gas Board.

My difficulties with English and spelling had pushed me towards studying maths, where my dyslexic grasp of symbols and patterns proved a positive advantage but it also opened a new world to me. And I had finally developed enough skill at italic letter-shaping and inten-sive word-shape recognition to disguise my lack of skill in spelling, so I was no longer the oddity who was a careless speller and couldn't use a dictionary. I did not need a large vocabulary of hard-to-spell words for mathematics: I used a small and specialised range of words, which I was able to reproduce quickly and accurately, and a large array of symbols that I loved manipulating. In physics I was not only allowed to draw pictures, instead of explaining in words – I was encouraged to do so. I soon found I could master optics by drawing light rays and lenses on squared graph paper. For the problems of applied mathematics I sketched out vector diagrams of the forces so I could see the geometry of the situation and use the elegant conventions of trigonometry to calculate the resultant forces.

The God of my childhood, having receded into a vague presence at morning assembly at Heys Road, now disappeared completely. At tech-nical college we didn't have morning assemblies. We didn't even have regular lessons. There were about twenty of us studying Double Maths and Physics. We had lectures and tutorials together, but did not have a lesson every hour on the hour as at Heys Road. We had to find different rooms in different buildings scattered around the campus where we met different lecturers for different topics. Nobody told us how to get there or made sure we went. At the lecture we were set problems and encouraged to go to the library to work on our own and bring solutions along to the tutorials. If I chose to slip off into Manchester Central Reference Library (only a half an hour's walk down the crescent) to work quietly, nobody would bother me. All that mattered was to turn up with correctly worked out answers to the problems I had been set.

So there wasn't any need to bunk off! We never had more than three or fours hours a day when we had to attend teaching sessions, and sometimes it was only a couple of hours in the morning and the rest of day was our own. I didn't realise it until much later, but I could not have had a better introduction to university study. Had I passed the 11-plus and gone to the local grammar school I would never have gone to university, because it did not encourage its pupils to go on to study science or engineering. A few of its highest flyers went to Oxbridge to study Arts subjects, but the bulk of its pupils went on to work in banks and offices. That would not have interested me, for I had fallen deeply in love with the power of mathematics to explain anything and everything about the world.

Salford Tech was based in a splendid red-brick Victorian pile, opened in 1896, with a magnificent entrance which gave easy access to its Great Hall. There were four floors, labelled upwards from A to D. (There was a sign displayed prominently on the wall facing the bottom of the stairwell, which said 'This is A Floor' – we freshers would point at it and say 'No it's not. It's a Wall!') These floors were packed with tiers of traditional bench-seated lecture theatres, high-ceilinged laboratories and smaller tutorial rooms, and behind the college was an eating hall (which, we were soon told, was *not* a canteen; it was a refectory). When I went there from my poky secondary modern school, the Tech shared a campus with the Royal College of Advanced Technology (RCAT), Salford Museum and Peel Park. I had accidentally entered a different world about which I knew nothing. I went with the expectation that it would be like school, only with harder sums to do, and that I would not have to study English; it turned out to be almost a university in miniature. It was the only college in that area which allowed students to study just maths and physics, and without it I would never have become a scientist.

There was a student union, housed in its own building, which had once been a private house. It had elected officers and ran social events, sports events and dances. Wednesday afternoons were always kept free of lectures for sports, and we had a sports hall and playing fields down by the River Irwell at Littleton Road. And perhaps the most important influence on my future was that we shared facilities and mixed freely with the students of the RCAT – particularly during Rag Week, when all the students built floats on the backs of wagons, dressed up in silly, inappropriate clothes and paraded through Manchester collecting money for charity. In my first year I was elected Rag Officer for the Tech and got the job of scrounging materials and borrowing a wagon and driver from a local haulage firm to build a float for the big parade. I met lots of new people and discovered that student life could be stimulating and fun. I took to wearing a blazer and long college scarf and forgot that I had been consigned to the educational scrap heap only six years earlier.

Nobody in my family had ever been to university, and so the idea of taking a degree had never been suggested at home. My father was not keen on the idea. 'You need to get a job and learn a trade,' he told me. But by now I was beginning to realise that there were really exciting jobs in the grown-up world, jobs which involved the newly blossoming discipline of electronics and offered exciting careers. I saw fascinating applications for the mathematics I could understand so much more easily than spelling.

During the long vacation (as I now called the summer holidays) I got a job with a bakery called Craig's Pantry, driving door-to-door with daily bread deliveries around the Stockport area of Manchester. Also I still had my weekend stints pumping petrol at the garage, which had funded me through my college life of A levels. So, for six weeks, from Monday to Saturday I collected my van at 6 a.m. drove it to the bakery, loaded it with bread, which I then delivered around Stockport. I did manage to swop my Friday-night shift at the petrol station for late Saturday afternoon and evening, and managed to fit in a Saturday-morning delivery for the bakery before rushing off to the petrol station to work all weekend. I ended the summer with a comfortable pile of cash, a feeling of complete exhaustion and a firm conviction that I never wanted to be a delivery driver.

By now it had been confirmed that I had got good A levels and stood a chance of going to university. But which one? My adventures as Rag Secretary had involved attending regular meetings at RCAT, UMIST and Owens (as Manchester University was known). I liked Owens, as it was the place where computing had been invented; I liked UMIST because it had a really good physics department; and I liked Salford because it had set up the first degree in electronics anywhere in the country.

It would be nice to be able to say that I had a choice of all three, but I didn't. Both Owens and UMIST rejected my application on the grounds I had not studied either French or German at O level. All was not lost, though. The ferroconcrete Royal College of Advanced Technology might consider me. I knew that they were to become a full degree-awarding university in two years' time, and if I could get onto their electronics degree I would graduate from what would then be Salford University. I applied to RCAT. They looked at my grades in Maths and Physics and invited me for interview, where Dr Alan Cowney talked to me about why I wanted to study electronics. I can't remember what I said to him, but he didn't seem to be worried whether I had a good French accent; he was interested in how good I was at sums and if I was interested in electronics. On the basis of my answers he offered me a place, and in due course I joined his department on the opposite side of the Peel Park campus from the Tech.

Now I was an undergraduate. I spent the next three years studying the behaviour of electrons in all possible circumstances. I studied circuit design, solid-state device fabrication, electron ballistics, radio propagation, signal processing and computing. But I didn't escape languages: I had to spend two hours a week learning Russian and pass an exam in it. I was given a choice, Russian or German, and I found the shapes of the Russian words far more distinctive than the German ones. I managed to achieve a reasonable standard of reading and even a little understanding by applying the same method I had used to learn English word-shapes. I even improved on my method, because I bought a Russian–English dictionary and created a home-made thumb index by sticking little cardboard tags on the pages to show which Russian letter the section covered. This meant I could look down the tabs to find the letter which started the word I was looking up. (I did the same with my English dictionary, as I found scanning down a line of tabs quicker than flipping through the book.)

The most important lesson I learned from my studies of the electron was that, given enough of the little blighters, they became completely predictable within the limits I needed to design electronic circuits. I couldn't forecast what an individual one would do, though, as it could easily change into a photon and whizz off at the speed of light, or simply disappear and pop up somewhere completely different.

Sharing a Common Darkness

I had enjoyed probing the hidden mysteries of electron behaviour whilst studying for my degree in electronics. It was a happy and zestful period of my life. So, as I approached my Third Degree in Freemasonry, I was looking forward to learning how The Craft was involved with other hidden mysteries of nature and science. I couldn't have been more shocked when I realised just what was hidden in the Third Degree.

On the evening of my Raising I was ready for the ceremony. I was now an old hand at this procedure. I answered my test questions with confidence. I recited my obligation without hesitation, and I was given the passing grip and word to allow me to enter a Master Mason's Lodge. Everything seemed normal as the deacons took me out of the lodge and gave me over to the new Tyler, Bro. Winston.

He left me to undress and put on the familiar flimsy white suit, which was covering less and less at each ceremony. Now I had many bits of arms, legs and chest exposed.

'No blindfold this time?' I asked. 'Not like the First Degree?'

'Don't worry you won't need one,' he said, grinning in what I took to be a knowing manner.

Bro. Syd, the Senior Deacon, came out with me. When he and Winston were satisfied that I was showing the correct bits of my body for the lodge to inspect, Winston knocked on the door. Syd nudged Winston. 'Hang on,' he said. 'We've still got the outside lights on.' Winston turned off the corridor lights and we stood together in darkness. When the door opened the lodge was also in darkness. From that inner gloom came the words, 'Who comes there?'

Bro. Winston replied, raising his voice so that his answer could be heard in the darkness of the lodge. 'Bro. Robert Lomas, who has been regularly Initiated into Freemasonry, since passed to the Degree of a Fellowcraft and who now comes forward, of his own free will and accord, humbly soliciting to be raised to the Third Degree for which ceremony he comes properly prepared.'

Again the voice sounded from within the lodge. I thought I recognised is as that of Bro. Graham, the Inner Guard. 'How does he hope to obtain those privileges?' it asked.

Again Winston replied. 'By the help of God, the powerful aid of the Square and Compasses, and the benefit of a Passing Grip and Word.'

The voice from the inner darkness spoke again. 'Give me that Passing Grip and Word,' it demanded. I felt a hand, reaching through the door to touch mine. I took hold of it, in the way I had recently been shown, and gave the password.

The hand was withdrawn back into the dark. 'Halt, whilst I report to the Worshipful Master,' the voice said, and the door was firmly slammed shut.

Winston the Tyler, Syd the Senior Deacon and I stood in a row in the dark, cold corridor outside the lodge. I shivered slightly (the dress of a Candidate is not intended to be warm and comforting). The darkness in the lodge surprised me. When I had left it a few minutes earlier it was a brightly lit, cosy haven on a cold winter's evening. Now it was dark and brooding. Why was this? As a Candidate I was not allowed to wear gloves and the touch of the gloved hand in the darkness had been warm against the rapidly cooling skin of my arm. I couldn't help remembering what I had been told about the purpose of a Mason's grip when I was first introduced to it.

The Worshipful Master had taken my bare hand in his gloved one, saying, 'Take me as I take you.'

The Junior Deacon had reached over and adjusted the position of my fingers until he and the Master were satisfied that I knew how to exchange the grip. Then the Master had spoken.

'This is called the Token or Grip of an Entered Apprentice Freemason,' he said, 'whereby one Entered Apprentice knows another in the dark, as well as at noonday.'

Now I had just been given a practical example of how that grip could be used. As I stood in the cold darkness of the corridor, unable to see anything clearly, from the even darker interior of the lodge a hand I was unable to see reached out to grip my hand and reassure me that one of my brethren stood ready to guide and assist me. This was reassuring, but not enough to restrain another involuntary shiver as I waited for the lodge's verdict on my 'humble solicitation' to become a Master Mason.

After an age the door opened, and Syd took a firm grip on my elbow to guide me inside.

The voice from the darkness spoke again.

'Worshipful Master. At the door of the Lodge stands Bro. Robert Lomas, who has been regularly Initiated into Freemasonry, since passed to the Degree of a Fellowcraft, and who now comes forward, of his own free will and accord, humbly soliciting to be raised to the Sublime Degree of a Master Mason, for which ceremony he comes properly prepared.'

As my eyes slowly adjusted to the darkness I could see a faint light in the Temple. It came from the East. The Master's candle had been fitted with a metal shade so that I could not see the flame, only a faint and glimmering reflected light on the wall behind the Master. As he leaned forward to knock with his gavel, his magnified shadow jumped and jostled on the wall behind. The flickering glow on to the eastern wall of the Temple reminded me of the pre-dawn sky on a moonless night.

The Master spoke. 'How does he hope to obtain those privileges, Bro. Inner Guard?' he asked.

'By the help of God, the powerful aid of the Square and Compasses, and the benefit of a Passing Grip and Word,' Bro. Graham replied, repeating the words Winston had said on my behalf.

The Master spoke again on behalf of the lodge. 'We acknowledge the powerful aid by which he seeks admission, but do you, Bro. Inner Guard, vouch that he comes properly prepared and is in possession of the Passing Grip and Word?'

Bro. Graham spoke up again: 'I do, Worshipful Master.'

The Master seemed satisfied. 'Then admit him in due form.'

In due form? I wondered for a moment what that might mean, then, while I was thinking about it, I felt two faint prickings against my naked chest, like being gently poked with two small needles. I stood perfectly still whilst the pressure of the needles remained constant.

'Enter this Master Mason's Lodge on both points of the Compasses,' I heard Graham say. In the dim gloom I could just make out the faint outline of a pair of extended compasses being held against my chest.

As in the earlier degrees, I was told to kneel and join the lodge in prayer for the success of the ceremony. Bro. Syd led me to a low stool placed in the centre of the lodge, where I was helped onto my knees. Once I was settled, as comfortably as possible under the somewhat tense circumstances, the Master knocked with his gavel. The two Wardens echoed his action round the room and then the Master called on the Lodge Chaplain to recite the following ritual prayer.

> Almighty and Eternal Architect and Ruler of the Universe, at whose creative fiat all things first were made, we the frail creatures of Thy Providence, humbly implore Thee to pour down upon this Convocation, assembled in Thy Holy Name, the continual dew of Thy Blessing. More especially we beseech Thee to impart Thy Grace to this Thy servant who seeks to partake with us the Mysteries and Secrets of a Master Mason. Endue him with such fortitude that, in the hour of trial he fail not, but passing safely under Thy protection, through the dark valley of the shadow of death he may finally rise from the Tomb of Transgression to shine as the stars, for ever and ever.

Shining as a star for ever and ever sounded fine, but what was the Tomb of Transgression? This reference to a tomb, along with the brooding and menacing darkness of the lodge, hinted that this evening was going to be a different experience from anything that had gone before. For the first time I began to wonder about the wisdom of what I was doing.

I was already a lecturer at Bradford University when I decided to join Freemasonry, and I had based my decision on my personal knowledge of the warmth and fellowship I had sensed in the Lodge of the East Gate. But I was aware that this view of Freemasonry as being benevolent was not shared by the general public.

After the First World War Freemasonry had followed a policy of not making any public statements about itself and its purpose. This left the field wide open for non-Masons to say what they liked about

The Craft without their assertions and misunderstandings being contradicted.

The Rev. Walton Hannah first realised the possibilities of this failure to defend when he wrote an article for the January 1951 issue of the magazine *Theology*, published by the pressure group the Society for Promoting Christian Knowledge. It was titled 'Should a Christian be a Freemason?' and the answer it implied was 'No'. He was pleasantly surprised at the considerable controversy this article generated and at the number of letters he had from practising Freemasons, which he described as 'full of courtesy and forbearance'. He subsequently wrote a book to assert his opinion that Freemasonry was an evil organisation that needed to be destroyed, giving as his reason what he called the necessarily evasive answers of Masons. He wrote:

> I am firmly convinced that for a Christian to pledge himself to a religious (or even, to avoid begging the question, to a quasi-religious) organisation which offers prayer and worship to God which deliberately exclude the name of Our Lord and Saviour Jesus Christ, in whose name only is salvation to be found, is apostatic. I am also quite aware that there are many Christians, and even Archbishops, who are also Masons who do not see it in that light, either because they do not take their ritual very seriously, or because they allow other considerations such as the good works, benevolence, and moral uprightness of the Craft to outweigh the clearly pagan implications of its formulae. The Englishman is a Pelagian at heart. It is my sincere hope, therefore, that this book may be of service not only in giving information to the non-Mason, but that it may also lead the Christian Mason seriously to re-consider his position. He might well ask himself at the outset, is it morally licit to bind oneself in advance, by a solemn oath on the Bible, to secrecy and fidelity in an organization which concerns faith and morals of which nothing is revealed to him previously?[50]

He had ended his polemic by appealing to the Prophet Ezekiel to support his view, saying with the utmost seriousness:

> The Prophet Ezekiel was deeply perturbed when he saw in a vision women weeping in the Temple for Tammuz. He may have been singularly lacking in humour, and he may even have got the whole thing

out of proportion, but he considered it nothing less than an abomination. It may be pointed out in passing that the Masonic writer J. S. M. Ward in one of his more fanciful moods declared that Hiram Abif was the earthly counterpart of Tammuz, so it is quite possible that these misguided females might have been able to symbolise their tears into perfectly orthodox co-Masonic channels. Nevertheless, it is open to grave doubts whether Ezekiel would have been mollified or the anger of Jehovah mitigated had they pleaded that they didn't really mean it to be taken seriously. It was all part of a play, and everybody meant well.[51]

I recognised in the Rev. Hannah the fundamentalist overtones of my childhood introduction to the jealous and angry Jehovah.

Hannah did not achieve his aim of getting the Church of England to speak out against what he perceived as the evil of Freemasonry. This was not surprising, as King George VI and Dr Fisher, then Archbishop of Canterbury, were both Freemasons when he wrote his book.[52] But Hannah planted the seeds of a widespread belief that Freemasons could not be trusted, even under oath.

When I joined English Freemasonry in the 1990s its leaders were not prepared to defend themselves against authors such as Stephen Knight, who extended Hannah's claims. He portrayed Freemasonry as a vast undesirable network with tentacles in every area of public life. The jacket blurb of Stephen Knight's book *The Brotherhood* was not encouraging reading for potential recruits to The Craft:

Recent scandals involving police, criminals and local authority corruption have brought into question certain aspects of Masonic influence; in Italy the P2 affair shattered the government and continues to reverberate. Now Stephen Knight goes behind the scenes and looks at some of the criticisms voiced by Freemasons themselves. In the United Kingdom there are some 700,000 members of this tightly-knit all-male society, many of them in very influential positions; all are bound by fierce-sounding oaths of secrecy.

What kind of influence does Freemasonry have today, and in which areas of society? How compatible is Freemasonry with the Church? To what extent has it become a self-serving organization discriminating in favour of its members when it comes to jobs, career promotion and business? A worryingly large number of instances show how and where the Masonic ideals of morality, charity and fraternity have been abused; and in describing various miscarriages of justice Stephen Knight exposes the potential dangers inherent in the secret Masonic network.

The author's acknowledgments were even more menacing. He said.

I am free to name only a small number of the many hundreds of people who have helped me with advice and information. Most of those who helped did so only on the understanding that I would say nothing that could lead to their identification. Among these were many Freemasons who feared recrimination from other members of the Brotherhood. [53]

As I stood in the darkness of Ryburn Lodge I wondered for a moment if I was giving myself over to an organisation which carried out recriminations against its own members? I remembered Knight's words as the Worshipful Master stood before me. I had taken my obligation and had agreed that I would defend and support a Master Mason's character in his absence, as though he were present. I had promised not to revile him myself, nor willingly permit others so to do, if within my power to prevent it, but to boldly repel the slanderer of his fair name; and strictly respect the chastity of those nearest and dearest to him, in the persons of his wife, his sister or his child. If those ideals were carried out by The Craft, then witch hunts against individuals seemed an unlikely consequence.

But I was about to find out much more about the true nature of The Craft; my Raising ceremony had hardly begun. I stood in front of the Worshipful Master, barely able to see him by the flickering light of the well-shaded candle flame. He spoke.

Brother Lomas, having entered into the great and sacred obligation, a Master Mason, you have a right to demand of me that last and greatest test, by which alone you can seek to be admitted to a participation in the secrets and mysteries of this sublime degree.

He paused to take a deep breath.

But it is my duty first to call your attention to a retrospect of those degrees in Freemasonry through which you have already passed, that you may be the better enabled to distinguish and appreciate the general excellence of our whole system and the relative dependence of its several branches.

I listened intently, as this was the first hint of an explanation of what Freemasonry was about. Perhaps the older brethren had been right when they said, 'Wait and see. It will all become clear.' The Master continued:

Your admission into Freemasonry, in a state of helpless indigence, was an emblematical representation of the entrance of all mankind into this, their mortal term of existence. It inculcated the striking lessons of natural equality and mutual dependence; it taught you in the active principles of universal beneficence and charity to seek the solace of your own distress, by extending relief and consolation to your suffering fellow creatures; but above all, it taught you to bend with humility and resignation to the will of the Great Architect of the Universe and to dedicate your heart, thus purified from every baneful and malignant passion and fitted only for the reception of moral truth and virtue, as well to His glory as to the welfare of your fellow creatures.

So far, so good. The mention of entering into a mortal term of existence seemed to have slight overtones of reincarnation or the per-existence of the soul, but, perhaps because it was so vague, there seemed to me to be nothing particularly alarming in this summary.

The Master's voice continued without any hesitation, as though he had delivered this speech many times before.

Proceeding onwards, still guided in your progress by the principles of moral truth and virtue, you were passed to the Second Degree, wherein you were enabled to contemplate the intellectual faculties, and to trace them, from their development, through the paths of heavenly science, even to the throne of God Himself. The secrets of nature and the principles of intellectual truth were then unveiled before you, and to the man whose mind has thus been modelled by virtue and science, nature presents one grand and useful lesson more.

The Master took another dramatic pause. I stood and wondered what that lesson might be and why it had to be delivered in a state of total darkness. Finally he continued:

The knowledge of yourself. She teaches you, by contemplation, to prepare for the closing hours of your existence; and when, by means of such contemplation, she has led you through the intricate windings of this, your mortal life, she finally teaches you how to die.

He took my hand in the grip of a Fellowcraft.

Such, my dear Brother. are the peculiar objects of this, the Third Degree in Freemasonry. They invite you to reflect upon that awful subject and teach you to feel that, to the just and upright man, death has no terror equal to that of the stain of falsehood and dishonour.

Now I knew why the room was in darkness. I was entering the valley of death. Where would the ceremony go next, what was going to happen? The Master continued.

Of this grand truth, the annals of Freemasonry afford a glorious example in the unshaken fidelity and untimely death of our Grand Master Hiram Abif, who lost his life just before the completion of King Solomon's Temple during the construction of which, as you are doubtless aware, he was the principal architect.[54]

As I stood in the dark centre of the lodge I realised I was about to play a lead role in an ancient murder, and I was to be the victim.

The two Deacons who had escorted me through the blackness quietly melted away, and their places at my side were taken by the Junior and Senior Wardens, who moved threateningly close to me. Why the changeover? And what were they holding in their hands? Whatever it was I couldn't see much, so I stopping trying to look and concentrated on what was being said.

The Master was telling a story of unbridled ambition. The work of building King Solomon's Temple was a massive undertaking. Hiram the architect shared responsibility for the work with two other Grand Masters, Solomon, King of Israel, and Hiram, King of Tyre.

Beneath the three Grand Masters there were three hundred Rulers, three thousand three hundred Overseers, and eighty thousand Craftsmen. The Rulers and Overseers were all skilled Craftsmen, or men of science. For the purpose of instructing and dividing the employment of the Craftsmen, they were arranged into lodges, made up of seven Entered Apprentices, five Fellowcrafts, and an Overseer, who was Master of the Lodge. The Masons were organised in this way because Hiram Abif calculated it was the best way to ensure promotion for those Masons who showed merit, to preserve due discipline and to prevent confusion in the work.

Only the three Grand Masters knew all the secrets of The Craft, but they promised that they would share these secrets with Fellowcrafts who proved themselves worthy. Fifteen of these Overseers were impatient to become Masters. They were worried that the Temple was almost complete and not one Overseer had yet been given the full secrets of a Master Mason. Fifteen Fellowcrafts conspired together to force the secrets out of Hiram Abif, by force if need be.

On the evening before they had agreed to carry out this treacherous plan, twelve of the fifteen backed out of the plot. But the three remaining decided to carry on.

They knew that Hiram Abif always went into the almost finished Temple at the hour of noon to pray, while the workers took their refreshment outside. They planned an ambush and placed themselves at three gates in the South, the West and the East.

At this point in the tale the Master stopped. The blacked out room was completely silent and then a bell tolled slowly. It was clearly going to strike twelve, and as the number of strokes built up towards the hour of high twelve, I could feel the hair standing up on the back of my neck. The drama of the tale, the impenetrable darkness of the room and the eerie and remorseless tolling of the bell were building up the tension in the room. The tolling completed the stroke of twelve and the room was completely silent.

Then the Master spoke.

His devotions being ended, he prepared to retire by the South Gate, where he was accosted by the first of these ruffians, who, for want of a better weapon, had armed himself with a Plumb Rule and in a threatening manner demanded of our Master Hiram the genuine secrets of a Master Mason, warning him that death would be the consequence of his refusal; but Hiram true to his Obligation replied that those secrets were known to but three in the world and that without the consent of the other two, he neither could, nor would divulge them; but intimated that he had no doubt that patience and perseverance would, in due time, entitle the Worthy Mason to a participation in them; but as for himself, he would rather suffer death than betray the Sacred Trust reposed in him.

The Master paused for effect. I heard a shuffling noise to my right and stealthy footsteps behind me. I ignored them, keeping my eyes on the Master's silhouette, backlit as it was by the flickering, half-shaded candle flame.

> This answer not proving satisfactory the ruffian aimed a violent blow at our Master's forehead but startled by the firmness of his demeanour, it only glanced down his Right Temple yet with sufficient force to cause him to reel and sink to the ground on his left knee.

As the Master finished speaking the Junior Warden, who was standing by my right hand, turned and hit me a light but totally unexpected blow on the right temple with his plumb rule. Before I could react my arms were seized from behind, and I was forced down onto my left knee. I resisted the immediate urge to swear. The blow had been hard enough to startle me but not hard enough to cause injury. The real shock had come from being forced down onto my left knee. I could hear myself breathing hard. I concentrated on recovering my composure, and stilling the urge to panic.

The men who held me lifted me upright to face the Master who continued as if nothing had happened.

> Recovering himself from this situation, he rushed to the West Gate where he was opposed by the second ruffian, to whom he replied as before, yet with undiminished firmness when the ruffian, who was armed with a Level, struck him a violent blow on the Left Temple.

Now the Senior Warden struck a light glancing blow on my left temple with his ceremonial level, while the Master continued:

> Which brought him to the ground on his right knee.

The two men behind forced me down onto my right knee in time with the Master's words. I had no control at all over what was happening to me, and in the dark and menacing situation I felt the sort of panic which Hiram himself must have felt. The brutal and inescapable mechanics of the murder became a reality for me. Once again I was roughly forced to my feet to face the Master, whose calm and unhurried voice continued.

> Finding all chances of escape in both these quarters cut off, our Master staggered, faint and bleeding, to the East Gate where the third ruffian was posted and who, on receiving a similar reply to his insolent demand, for our Master remained true to his Obligation even in this trying moment, struck him a violent blow, full in the centre of the forehead, with a heavy Setting Maul which laid him lifeless at his feet.

The men behind me held me in an immovable grip. By now I was too startled to even think about resisting. The Master stepped towards me and took from behind his back a heavy maul. I could see him only as black outline against the faintly flickering East Wall of the Temple. For what seemed an eternity he held the maul high over his head. He's going to kill me, I thought as he brought the maul down towards my unprotected skull. He gently tapped me in the centre of the forehead.

'Such was the manner of his death,' he whispered.

I felt myself being pulled backwards. One of the Wardens put his foot behind my feet, and the two men who held me now hinged me backwards until I lay flat on the ground. 'Keep as still as the grave,' one whispered as they crossed my arms across my chest and wrapped me in some sort of winding sheet. My face was covered, as if I were a corpse.

Wrapped in my shroud I could hear the brethren moving from their seats to stand in a circle around me. My eyes adjusted to the increased dark, and through the loose weave of the cloth I could make out vague shapes of slightly darker darkness.

The Master spoke again.

> Brethren, in the recent ceremony as well as in his present situation, our Brother has been made to represent one of the brightest characters in the annals of Freemasonry, namely Hiram Abif who lost his life rather than betray the sacred trust reposed in him, and I trust that this will make a lasting impression, not only on his, but on your minds, should you ever be placed in similar circumstances of trial.

I lay on the floor of the lodge, wrapped in a shroud and arranged as if in a coffin. The organist played the opening stanza of the Dead March. I was present at my own funeral.

My mind flashed back to the first time I faced the finality of death. As child about eight years old I was riding on the top deck of a Crosville bus from Chester to Mold. I clearly remember that, as I looked out over the airfield of the De Havilland factory at Broughton, the terrifying idea came to me that every time I breathed in I was one breath closer to my death. I must have spent at least ten minutes trying to slow my lung movement so as push my inevitable demise further into the future. Yet the more I thought about that inevitable oblivion, the faster my breath came, as if trying to hurry me towards that grim destination.

Why was I on that bus? Why was I thinking about the inevitability of death? I was travelling with my parents from Manchester to Mold, to attend the funeral of Great-Uncle Teddy. That was first time that someone I knew personally had died.

His death made me realise for the first time that I and everyone I knew and loved was also going to die. Now I lay on the floor of Ryburn Lodge, wrapped in a grave-cloth and laid out as a corpse, listening to the brethren of the lodge slowly and respectfully marching past my grave to the sombre notes of the Dead March. I was again reminded that I too must die.

The music stopped, the respectful progression of the brethren ceased and the Master spoke.

> Brother Junior Warden. You will now attempt to raise the representative
> of our Master Hiram with the grip of an Entered Apprentice.

The Junior Warden unwrapped my grave-cloth, giving me a brief, murky glimpse of a circle of figures standing around where I lay. He lifted my limp arm (I was now inert and silent as I lay still, contemplating my eventual fate). He took hold of my hand in the grip of an Apprentice then pulled his hand away in a slippingly loose hold.

'This proves a slip,' he said, replacing my hand under the shroud and rewrapping me into my inner darkness.

The cheerless notes of the Dead March sounded out once more, and I could sense the brethren again progressing in respectful silence around my grave. As the dead weight of my arm slumped back to lie inert across my chest I remembered a more recent experience of death. My great-aunt Annie had been married to Uncle Joe for 53 years when he died. After his death I would go to stay with her. I had already begun to study science when I stayed with her one last time.

Uncle Joe had a brother I called Uncle Bill whose wife had died many years earlier. After Joe's death Annie would go each evening to Bill's farm and cook supper for him, then they would eat together. When I stayed with her I would go to the farm with her.

Bill had a son, Clifford, who worked the farm. He was a round, ruddy-faced, jovial giant of a cousin, but I was nervous of him ever since I'd seen him kill one of the farmyard cats with a hammer.

During the hay harvest everybody helped out. The long lush grass was cut by a machine with an oscillating knife, towed behind the tractor. The first cut would be around the outside of the field and then the mechanical knife would move in towards the centre, progressively cutting down the outer boundaries of the standing hay until only a small island of standing grass remained at the centre.

Any hares or rabbits in the field would be forced towards this steadily shrinking island. The farm dogs would roam the perimeter to pen them in. When the island had shrunk to almost nothing the rabbits' fear of the tractor would become greater than their fear of the dogs and out they would dash, darting and weaving before their furiously barking pursuers.

The black and white barn cat must have been hunting mice or voles when the hay cutting started. It had a long-standing hatred of the youngest sheepdog who always chased it on sight. The cat wasn't afraid of tractors but the standing hay made good cover to hide from the boisterous sheepdog.

When the knife caught it, it screamed a piercing howl, a sound which I have never quite managed to forget. The awful howling seemed endless. Clifford who was driving the tractor stopped and jumped down to go towards that terrible sound, with me following him. The cat's face was a mask of twisted hate as it looked up at us. Its lips were drawn back in a snarl, its mouth gaping as it wailed, but it didn't try to run away, although its tail twitched madly.

'Fetch the hammer off the tractor toolbox,' Clifford ordered.

'Why?' I asked.

'Do as you're told and quick!'

I got the hammer and gave it to Clifford who went towards the cat, which had gone quiet, looking up without trying to move away. Its pupils were deep empty pools of black resignation as it watched him approach, hammer raised. He brought the hammer down, crushing its skull with a single thudding squelch.

'Stupid bloody cat! Why did you do that!' he said, wiping the hammer on the grass.

As he picked the cat up by the tail and flung its body into the ditch, I could see why it had not tried to run away. The knife, powered by the tractor the cat was not afraid of, had cut off every one of its legs, cleanly, neatly and for ever. I felt a retching sour taste welling into my mouth.

Later I sat on the stool in the farm kitchen and watched Auntie Annie stoke the range as she prepared a pan of stew. She had taken off her brown tweed coat and had tied her hair up in a turban made from a red handkerchief. The light above the table cast a large shadow behind her on the quarry-tiled floor. The over-large floral smock pinafore she was wearing made her look small and shrivelled as she stood at the whitened table cutting up meat and vegetables.

'Why do you come here to cook for Uncle Bill?' I asked.

'There's nobody else to do it since his wife died, and he's a complete cripple now. I don't see that he'll be able to keep the farm on much longer, even if Clifford wants to. Besides what else have I got to do now your uncle Joe's passed on?' she said.

'Do you miss Uncle Joe?'

'I miss him every minute of every day and twice as much at night.'

Auntie Annie stopped chopping the carrots and looked towards me. Her eyes sparkled with a dark softness.

'Joe was a really handsome young man, tall and strong just like you. He had a lovely smile. It made me go all soft inside. He was really strong, he could lift me up just like I was a feather. I was the proudest girl in Mold when he married me and brought me to Buckley to live.'

'Why didn't you have any children of your own, Auntie Annie?' I asked.

'We wanted to, we really wanted to. Joe loved children but it just wasn't God's will that we should have any.'

I realised that she was crying, I could see the tears trickling down her face and as she started to sob I went round the table and put my arm around her; she was frail and light under my touch. She turned and buried her face in my shoulder.

'Why did he have to die and leave me? Why?' she sobbed.

She looked up, and I felt a strange coldness in the pit of my stomach. In her eyes I could see the same look I had seen in the eyes of the stricken cat.

'Why won't God let me die too and go to him?'

I stood silent. Because I had no answer for her. There was no comfort I could offer. I had long since decided that death was oblivion. Both the threats and the promised rewards of the Sunday School God were equally meaningless in the world of science I was studying. Death was the place you never came back from, and, although Annie believed she would be reunited with Uncle Joe, I no longer shared her belief.

I thought life was rather like the hayfield. As it blossomed it was cut down and although, like the cat, you might try to retreat to the centre, sooner or later the reaper's blade would cut the legs from under you and leave you stranded and helpless. I was resigned to that end.

I did not rejoice in Annie's reconciliation with Joe when I watched her coffin being carried into the church they been married in. The tears welled again in my eyes as I wept for her loss and for mine.

The dreary music stopped. The Master's voice pulled me back to reality. I felt myself shiver as the emotion of my memories almost swamped me. How much longer was this going to go on?

'Brother Senior Warden. You will try the Fellowcraft grip,' the Master said.

Again my shroud was rolled back, my limp arm lifted, the Fellowcraft grip loosely applied and dropped. And as my limp arm fell back onto my chest, like a dead weight, I felt another memory of death rise up out of the darkness to confront me.

'Worshipful Master. This likewise proves a slip,' the Senior Warden said. The Dead March resumed, and the weary funeral procession once more tramped in a respectful file around my grave. But I was at another funeral.

When my grandmother Sophia died I was bereft that the woman I always called *Nain* had left me. Of all my immediate family she was the one I loved most. She had been the one who took me to, and from, primary school and Sunday School. She made my dinner and tea, while my mother worked, and I stayed with her on Friday nights while my parents went to the cinema, She had listened to my troubles when I struggled to read, she had taught me Welsh nursery rhymes, sat by the fire with me and told me stories of her childhood, and of her sisters and brother when they were young. She had impressed on me that if I worked hard enough I would succeed and had always believed in me. She was the first to tell me I should go to university and was proud I was the first member of my family to do so. She bought me the PhD robes I wear at every graduation. Then she died.

I spent the evening after her death sitting quietly at the piano playing Beethoven's 'Moonlight' Sonata, over and over and over. I carried her to her grave. It was a last service of love to thank her for all she had given me. I carried her coffin with tears in my eyes because I knew she was inside and would never come out again. I felt the slack movement of her corpse within the box, as I helped load her into the hearse. Finally I understood the absolute nature of death.

The music stopped and the voice of the Master dragged me back from that awful memory to the ceremony in the lodge.

> Brother Wardens. You having both failed in your endeavours, there remains a third and peculiar method which, with your assistance, I will now make trial.

My shroud was unfurled, and I was raised from the grave by the Master and his two Wardens acting together to lift me bodily upright. As they did so a light in the shape of five-pointed star was lit high in the East of the lodge.

As I stood before the Master he turned and pointed to where I had lain.

> Thus, my dear Brother, have all Master Masons been raised from a figurative death, to a reunion with the companions of their former toil. Let me now beg of you to observe that the Light of a Master Mason is

but as darkness visible, serving only to express that gloom which hangs over the prospect of futurity.

The rays from the star-shaped light illuminated the unfurled shroud, which had the dark black maw of an open grave woven into it. The part of the ceremony during which I had lain in the grave could not have been more than a few minutes, judging from the number of stanzas of the Dead March which had been played, but the memories it had provoked, and the deep reflections on the nature of death they brought to the surface of my mind, made it seem much longer. I was still reeling from the impact of the image as the Master continued.

It is that mysterious veil of darkness which the eye of human reason cannot penetrate, unless assisted by that Divine Light which is from above.

He gestured towards the illuminated image of the Bright Morning Star rising in the East of the lodge.

Yet, even by this glimmering ray you will perceive that you stand on the very brink of the grave into which you have just figuratively descended, and which, when this transitory life shall have passed away, will again receive you into its cold bosom.

I had certainly descended into the grave and had lain there, inert and still. I had been forced to relive my deepest buried and most disturbing encounters with death. I could only assume that this had been an intentional consequence of the ritual and that I was intended to draw some lesson from it. Then, as the Master continued, I realised the moral of the ritual was about to arrive. He pointed towards the 'open grave' now symbolised on the lodge floor.

Let those emblems of mortality which now lie before you lead you to contemplate your inevitable destiny and guide your reflections into that most interesting and useful of all human studies the knowledge of yourself.

I looked more closely. The light of the star was directed into the grave, leaving the object in shadow. I concentrated on it, then realised that at the head of the grave was a human skull and a pair of thigh bones arranged in the shape of saltire cross.[55] The Master pointed at them, saying:

> Be careful to perform your allotted task while it is yet day; listen to the voice of nature which bears witness that, even in this perishable frame, there resides a vital and immortal principle, which inspires a holy confidence, that the Lord of Life will enable us to trample the King of Terrors beneath our feet, and lift our eyes to that Bright Morning Star whose rising brings peace and tranquillity to the faithful and obedient of the human race.

The Master turned me to face the East and told me the signs and passwords of the degree. Whilst he did this the grave and bones were quietly put away, so that when the lights were restored the lodge looked as normal as ever. A Master Mason's apron was put around my waist by the Senior Warden and he then instructed me in the symbolic working tools of a Master Mason. At the end of these instructions I heard a disturbing hint of what might be a supernatural objective of The Craft. It was made in passing and not emphasised. As the Senior Warden finished explaining the tools to me he said:

> These, then, the working tools of a Master Mason, teach us to live and act, according to His divine precepts, so that when we shall be summoned from this sublunary abode, we may ascend to that Grand Lodge Above, where the world's Great Architect lives and reigns for ever.

This remnant of the Sunday School myth of Heaven, which I thought had been put in to soften the impact of the deeply disturbing forced contemplation of death I had just experienced, would turn out to be the first clue about the inner teaching of Freemasonry. But it would be many years before I realised its import.

Because I had been pushed rapidly through my degrees I had not yet seen the full closing ceremony of a Fellowcraft lodge.[56] In that ritual there is another clue which would eventually help me make sense of the Grand Lodge Above. But for now I was more concerned about the revelation I was expecting of the True Secrets of a Master Mason. After the harrowing ceremony I was well aware that our Grand Master Hiram Abif had preserved them, refusing to reveal them to the unworthy, even under pain of death. But, now I was a Master Mason, I assumed I had proved myself worthy. The secrets and mysteries I had been promised would soon be shared with me.

But I waited in vain. Instead I was told that the purpose of Freemasonry was to search for the True Secrets of a Master Mason, which had been lost with the untimely death of our Grand Master Hiram Abif, and they had been replaced with something called 'the substituted secrets' which were to be used until 'the real secrets of a Master Mason' could be found again.

Here is the ritual exchange between the Master and the Senior Warden which dashed my hopes of a startling revelation. The Master began.

Brother Senior Warden, as a Master Mason whence come you?

From the East, Worshipful Master.

Whither directing your course?

To the West, Worshipful Master.

Why did you leave the East and travel to the West?

To seek for that which was lost, which, by your instruction and our own industry, we hope to find.

What is that which was lost?

The genuine secrets of a Master Mason.

The Master persisted:

How came they lost?

By the untimely death of our Master Hiram Abif.

Was that all there was to it? Had I exposed myself to the darkest reaches of my suppressed memories simply to be told that unfortunately the secrets I had been promised had been lost? It felt that way.

This disappointment started me on a path to discover these lost secrets for myself. It would bring me into a direct conflict with the United Grand Lodge of England, which almost drove me out of Freemasonry.

The personal notes I wrote at the time, and which eventually were used to write *The Hiram Key*, show my first and immediate response to this knowledge:

My biggest criticism of Freemasonry, or 'The Craft' as it is called by insiders, is its sheer pointlessness. It does not know where it came from, no one seems to know what it is trying to achieve and increasingly it seems improbable that it can have much of a future. Not only are the origins of Freemasonry no longer known but the 'true secrets' of the order are admitted to have been lost, with 'substituted secrets' being used in their place in Masonic ceremony, 'until such time as they are rediscovered'.[57]

When I first experienced the ritual of the Third Degree I was surprised that the central story was so simple and unremarkable, having no special dramatic structure or even any obvious symbolic value. Yes, Hiram Abif did die rather than betray his beliefs, but so have countless other men and women, before and since. I was puzzled. Why was this pivotal story so lacking in meaning? As a vehicle to force me to think about the nature of death, the ritual had worked, but surely if a group had been setting up a new society it could have come up with something rather more remarkable? There seemed to be a folk-tale flavour to the ritual. And that provoked me to start digging deeper in search of the origins of the Order. After a series of books and considerable research I arrived at a view of what Freemasonry is and why it matters, little knowing that I was entering an area of great controversy.

Personal Reflections

My impression of Freemasonry as I moved through the stages of Applicant, Candidate, Entered Apprentice to Fellowcraft, was of an eccentric and rather old-fashioned society, which had once been far more influential than it was now. I hadn't found any trace of evil in it, although I was a little concerned about traces of supernatural influence in the concept of the Grand Lodge Above.

All in all, I had warmed to the benign Great Architect and His passion for Geometry. My view of The Craft had been adjusted by what my new brethren had told me of our Order's eighteenth-century beginnings. They said that the senior brethren in the British Isles had tended to come from the aristocracy, but the massed ranks of ordinary brethren had always been drawn from the top end of the middle classes. Older members of the lodge talked of how in the Victorian period it had been socially important, almost essential, for a professional man to be a Freemason. The factory-owners of the Industrial Revolution had gained status through membership of an exclusive society that was high-profile amongst aristocrats of all levels right up to the royal family itself. In theory at least, any working man could be made a Mason, but not many asked to join their bosses' club, so the lodge had long been associated with the well-to-do. When I joined Ryburn Lodge this air of faded genteel grandeur still pervaded the smoking room of the Masonic hall.

At the time I joined The Craft the leaders of English Freemasonry were not prepared to defend themselves adequately against authors such as Walton Hannah and Stephen Knight, who, I felt, unfairly and inaccurately portrayed Freemasonry as an undesirable area of public life. The only books available to the general public were anti-Masonic books. In part my decision to publish my own thoughts on Freemasonry was in response to a failure of the leadership of the United Grand Lodge of England, who were not adequately addressing false accusations that were doing enormous damage to what I believed to be a benign and charitable, even if somewhat eccentric, Order.

The Third Degree is a very beautiful degree which, once I learned how to interpret it, summed up all that had gone before. In the First Degree the lodge was in light, and I was hoodwinked and in darkness. The lodge removed my blindfold so that I could see there was light. In the Second Degree both I and the lodge were in light, and together we climbed the spiral staircase of knowledge to approach the very throne of the Grand Geometrician. The hidden mysteries of nature and science were a shared object of study. But in the Third Degree I entered a lodge which was dark and brooding. Both the lodge and I were facing the darkness of death together. The Third Degree had disturbed me, forcing me to face up to facts about mortality which I had hidden deep in a part of my memory I avoided visiting, and making it clear that the mystery of the Centre was not to be reached without confronting and overcoming my fear of mortality.

As a component in the philosophy of the rest of the system, the Third

Degree did not then seem to me to fit. And only when I worked the Royal Arch would I finally grasp what it intended to teach. But to reach this stage I would have to find out many things for myself.

6

Making My Mark

Progress in the Hidden Mysteries of Science

FREEMASONRY WAS PROVING more complex than I had ever suspected when I first asked to join it. I had been initiated as an Entered Apprentice, passed to the degree of a Fellowcraft and finally raised to the sublime degree of a Master Mason. I had been rushed through two degree ceremonies in my mother lodge. Then I watched Bro. Keith take the same degrees. And I had been taken to the formal tracing board lectures for each of the degrees in two nearby lodges.

But nothing had been explained, and little was obvious. The brethren who were carrying out the ceremonies were sincere, but were inhibited by the hierarchical nature of the system and their obligation to keep secret the contents of the degrees I had not yet been allowed to take. Looking back, I see that it wasn't that they were trying to confuse me; it was just that they didn't know what was supposed to be secret and what they could talk about.

My experience of the Third Degree had been completely different to the previous ones. It had not followed the progression I had been expecting, and it seemed to me that it assumed I had learned things on the way that I had not. The words that the Master used just before the dramatic re-enactment of the gruesome murder of a long-dead architect assumed I possessed knowledge about the architect of Solomon's Temple that the rituals of Freemasonry had not imparted to me. He had said:

> The annals of Freemasonry afford a glorious example in the unshaken fidelity and untimely death of our Grand Master Hiram Abif, who lost his life just before the completion of King Solomon's Temple during the construction of which, *as you are doubtless aware*, he was the principal architect.

As far as my Masonic education was concerned, the name Hiram Abif had never been even whispered to me. That he was principal architect of Solomon's Temple had been a well-kept secret, and the fact he was murdered a complete surprise. Yet the ritual assumed I knew all about it. So the first thing I did was ask senior members of my lodge why the ritual expected me to know something that had never been mentioned before.

In those days the senior brethren were not used to explaining themselves to newcomers, particularly newcomers who asked questions they did not consider relevant. Before I had taken my Third it might have been because they didn't want to spoil the impact of a ceremony they knew I would eventually experience, but I also suspect that often it was because they didn't know the answers. But by now I was a fully trained research scientist and well practised in setting and answering questions for myself. I was not used to having my questions brushed aside.

Three years of undergraduate study had flown by at Salford University. I had worked steadily, applied the formulas I was given and had become completely at home with the world of electronic circuit design. But I studied a wider range of subjects too.

The most dramatic challenge to my world view had come from a basic course in relativistic physics. It was a voluntary series of seminars run by a newly qualified PhD. What I heard in that series of lectures had a mind-blowing effect on my complacent Newtonian world view. The new physics, which had been such a key factor in winning World War II, was beginning to be taught on undergraduate courses in the 1960s, when I was doing my Bachelor's degree, and the real power of physics, hitherto a closely guarded secret, was beginning to be more widely understood.

When that decade began there was no anti-proliferation treaty to restrict the development of nuclear weapons, and they were regularly tested in the atmosphere, as much to send messages between the Western and Eastern power blocks as to test the yield of the various weapons packages. The simple, low-yield fission bombs of the 1940s had been superseded by fusion bombs with a thousand times more blast potential. Two of my physicist heroes, John Wheeler and Richard Feynman, working with Edward Teller, had developed a new type of bomb which used hydrogen as fuel, just like the sun. This weapon could create a miniature chunk of exploding sun-stuff down here on earth. It had been tested on Eniwetok Atoll in the Marshall Islands on 1 November 1952. It had a strength of 10.4 megatons, far more powerful than the uranium bomb exploded over Hiroshima to end the war with Japan. It started the cold-war arms race, which drove a lot of scientific research for the next twenty years. In August 1953 the Russians exploded a hydrogen bomb of their own, and the US responded in 1954 by testing a hydrogen bomb dropped from an aircraft. It devastated Bikini Atoll.[58]

All this wonderful new knowledge had begun with the ideas of Albert Einstein. It was his theory of relativity – at first sight a weird theory about the nature of time – which unlocked such enormous power. Relativity was an easy step into the more hidden mysteries of nature. It led to questions like: If you were travelling on a very fast train carrying a flashlight and shining the beam forward, if you were moving as fast as light would the torch remain dark? (The answer was twofold. The torch wouldn't go dark – however fast you were moving light still sped away from your torch at 3,000,000 metres per sec: the speed of light in a vacuum, which Einstein called c – but the wavelength of the light would change, so it would seem to change colour, looking bluer if it was moving towards you and redder if it was moving away.)

When Newton had studied the nature of the world he made certain assumptions which all scientists until Einstein had accepted. Throughout my scientific apprenticeship at A level I had never thought to question them. They were that:

- Time is a universal constant which allows me to decide if two events at different places are taking place at the same moment.
- All movements of any object take place against an absolute realm of space, within which the length of that object may be measured absolutely with whatever precision I want. In other words, space is motionless, and all rigid objects move within it in a way which I can describe precisely.
- If I know the position and speed of an object over a series of moments in time, I can predict exactly where it will go in the future and where it has been in the past.

These ideas had been firmly drummed into me throughout my A-level studies and had proved reliable wherever I had used them. I felt they made it possible to know everything about anything. When I was six years old this style of thinking had enabled James Watson and Francis Crick to discover the structure of DNA and explain the nature of life itself. It seemed to me that there was nothing the scientific method could not explain and nothing its careful application could not accomplish. But when I was introduced to relativity that confidence was shaken. The simple geometrical thinking which underpinned the Special Theory of Relativity came as a total revelation to me.

By comparing the views of two observers moving at different speeds, I could now prove that the mass of an object was also a measure of the energy needed to create that object. When Einstein first discovered this he never considered it might be possible to turn any of this mass back into energy. (In 1934 he wrote to the editor of the *Pittsburgh Post-Gazette*, 'There is not the slightest indication that nuclear energy will ever be obtainable. It would mean that the atom would have to be shattered at will.'[59]) But by the time I could prove for myself, using basic geometrical principles, that $E=mc^2$ I already knew that this fearsome energy could not only be set free, it could be directed against anybody in the world.

Perhaps the most striking insight I got from those seminars on relativistic physics was an understanding of a secret place of hidden truth, which could be reached by any scientist prepared to tap into the knowledge it holds. Being able to prove for myself the equation which had made Einstein famous had a tremendous impact on my attitude to research. I became fascinated by Einstein – who had died when I was eight years old, long before I was old enough, or educated enough, to appreciate his greatness – and read as much as I could about his life and times.

When he realised the consequences of his study of the geometry of space–time Einstein may not have believed what he found, but by 1939 he knew that the massive source of energy he had revealed *could* be accessed. He wrote a letter to warn President Roosevelt of the possibility. The president took heed of Einstein's warning and set up the Manhattan Project.

The end result was a post-war arms race, with massive production of hydrogen bombs stockpiled by the two superpowers, the US and the USSR – bombs which guided missiles could deliver anywhere in the world at the push of a button. And all the destructive technology was controlled by electronics. The discipline I had chosen to study for my BSc was entering a boom period. All the nuclear states – the US, the USSR and Great Britain – had hydrogen bombs with the capability to destroy the world if attacked. At the beginning of the 1960s France, under President de Gaulle, joined this club when it exploded a small plutonium device in the Algerian Desert. It looked as if every country in the world would soon know how to destroy our planet.

It was an exciting time to be studying to become a scientist. The pervading ethos was that we were working to harness the power of nature to make the world a better place. Our bombs made war unthinkable and unwinnable, while our nuclear reactors would soon become a unlimited source of domestic power. Another thing I learned at this time was that the only real wealth is the ability to control and apply energy. Only energy gives access to a better quality of life – provided you avoid blowing yourself up when making it. That was where electronics played a key role. Military requirements demanded smaller, more reliable and more complex electronic circuits, and, as I would eventually learn, the only way to achieve this was to use an entirely new approach to circuits that involved a completely different branch of physics.

My Need for Hiram's Key

But what of my progress in Masonic knowledge? I had been told that once I became a Master Mason the whole beautiful structure of Freemasonry would become clear to me. I had expected that all would be explained once I had completed my three degrees. But it wasn't. Nothing at all was explained.

So I decided to answer my own questions. The end result shook both me and Freemasonry.

I asked where did Freemasonry start? I was told it began in London in 1717, but when I asked who was the first known Freemason on record, I was told it was Elias Ashmole. So I pointed out he had died in 1692, which was twenty-five years before Freemasonry began.

And what about the story that lodges of Freemasons who worked for Hiram Abif built King Solomon's Temple?

'Don't mention that name outside the temple,' they said.

'Who?' I asked.

'The other Hiram.'

'But you told me in the Third Degree that it was generally known that he was the architect. How can it be generally known if his name is never mentioned?'

'You concentrate on getting your ritual right,' came the answer, in an attempt to close down my line of questioning.

Why didn't my senior brethren want to talk to me about the nature of the lost secrets? I wanted to understand Freemasonry. I had been trained in a culture of scientific education where asking questions was positively encouraged, but within Freemasonry it seemed that a questioning attitude was *dis*couraged.

I began by looking in the library of my lodge. There was a set of the revised edition of Gould's *History of Freemasonry*, edited by Dudley Wright. There was a ritual book and a set of Masonic Yearbooks going back decades. I borrowed Gould and quickly read it. The bulk of it seemed to be about operative stonemason guilds and the history of the Grand Lodge of England. There was a brief mention of an early lodge in Aberdeen, but Wright quickly dismissed it as a purely operative set-up of stoneworkers, so I didn't pay it much attention. I wanted to know more about the rituals and the secrets which the Order had so carelessly lost. As the ritual itself claimed that Freemasons had spent the best part of three hundred years searching for them, surely they had made some collective progress? It seemed not.

The only people writing popular books about Freemasonry were the anti-Masons such Stephen Knight. But what they were saying didn't make a lot of sense. For example, Steven Knight seemed to think Freemasonry was a religion which followed a Masonic God.

My experience is that Freemasonry is not a religion. It is a philosophy, which passes on its message by re-enacting myths and uses ancient symbols to illustrate these rituals. For instance, the symbol of the two pillars which stood at the porchway of King Solomon's Temple, and was echoed behind the chair of the Master of the lodge, has a long history that goes back to pagan Egypt.

Soon after I started asking serious questions about Freemasonry I came across the first academic book on the real history of Freemasonry. It was *The Origins of Freemasonry: Scotland's Century 1590–1710* by historian Dr David Stevenson of St Andrews University. About a month after I received my Third Degree, Cambridge University Press published it as an extremely expensive hardback. I found out about it from my university librarian, who borrowed a copy for me through the interlibrary loan system, and in it I found sources of knowledge that nobody in my lodge knew about. Stevenson's book introduced me to Sir Robert Moray, who was not only the first Freemason known to be initiated on English soil (in a lodge held by senior officers of the Scottish Covenanter Army in 1641, during their occupation of Newcastle), but also an early scientist and founder member of the Royal Society.

By now the research bug had bitten me. I started to accumulate facts and dates. As I was teaching data analysis at postgraduate level I naturally applied the data-patterning techniques I had developed whilst studying science and business to look for patterns in historical events. I soon started to uncover a history far more fascinating than the one I had been told.

Back then I wasn't experienced enough to distinguish between the mythical history, which looked back to the Egyptians, and real events, such as the Aberdeen Council records of a lodge in Aberdeen in the late fifteenth century. I investigated every fact I found about Freemasonry. One was this ritual assertion:

> The usages and customs among Freemasons have ever borne a near affinity to those of the ancient Egyptians. Their philosophers, unwilling to expose their mysteries to vulgar eyes, couched their systems of learning and polity under signs and hieroglyphical figures, which were communicated to their chief priests or Magi alone, who were bound by solemn oath to conceal them.

I had no preconceived view, so I saw no reason not to look at this claim. If the first Freemasons had been the Israelite builders of Solomon's Temple, then they might have drawn on the Egyptian traditions of Moses, who was brought up in the court of a Pharaoh. And by now I knew that there were Masonic degrees such as the rite of Memphis and Mizran, which were carried out in lodge rooms decorated as Egyptian Temples.

I was also developing a deep interest in the early Scottish lodges that David Stevenson had written about. I visited Scotland during my summer vacations. I looked for Masonic graves and noted their dates. I talked to Scottish brethren and looked through Masonic texts for the earliest mentions of particular lodges, where they were held, when the fact was recorded.

I told my lodge brothers of my findings, and they were as interested as I was. They encouraged me to give a lodge lecture. So I began to share my thoughts and research about Freemasonry's Scottish roots with my Masonic brethren around Halifax.

That first lecture was a success, and other lodges asked me to lecture to them. By now I was a professional lecturer at Bradford University, so I prepared my talk to be given with a series of overhead projector slides. This was a radical innovation for Masonic lecturing in Halifax. Most lecturers stood at a lectern and read their speeches out, word for word. I didn't use a lectern, didn't read my lectures out and used an overhead projector (OHP) to throw up notes and images on a screen. In the early 1980s this was cutting-edge technology, and it got me talked about.

Soon after this I teamed up with Chris Knight, whom I have already mentioned in Chapter 2. We discovered we were both Freemasons, although Chris had resigned from his lodge many years earlier (he later rejoined The Craft, becoming a member of my lodge), and we both wanted to understand Freemasonry. As we wrote at the time:

> We shared the same frustrations concerning the vague conventional explanation of the origins of the Order. Our discussions became more frequent, and our interest grew as we sparked off each other, and it was not long before we decided to undertake a structured investigation with the joint objectives of identifying the character we knew as Hiram Abif and finding the lost secrets of Freemasonry. At that time neither of us believed that we had any chance of succeeding in this strange quest, but we knew that the journey would be interesting.[60]

It was Chris who had the idea of pooling our information and seeing what we could explain about Freemasonry and where it came from. Eventually we wrote a book together, and called it *The Hiram Key*.

My train of research into early Scottish lodges had focused on a weird little chapel to the south of Edinburgh. It was involved in the early history of Freemasonry and looked worth further investigation. Many early lodges met in its surrounding area, and the family who built it provided the First Grand Master of Scottish Freemasonry. I decided to take Chris to visit Rosslyn, as *The Hiram Key* records.

> It was two days later when we set off for Edinburgh, and Robert still had not explained where or why we were going. From the beginning of our work we had split responsibility roughly around the Templar period, with Robert concentrating on events since the thirteenth century and myself everything before it. Just at the point that I was investigating the first century AD in Jerusalem, Robert was focused on fourteenth-century Scotland. His previous visits across the border had already revealed a large number of Templar and Masonic graves, which had demonstrated just how important this country was in the development of Freemasonry. So what else had Robert come across?
>
> 'Okay,' he [Robert] said with a smile. 'You know I've been looking at the history of the Sinclair family and the Chapel that William St Clair built in what is now the village of Roslin.'
>
> 'Yes,' I [Chris] replied sharply, as an indication to get to the point without a rambling intro.
>
> 'Well, it hadn't registered at the front of my mind when I first read about it, but there is something very strange about Rosslyn Chapel. . . . The whole building is decorated inside with carvings of Masonic significance.[61]

The result of my co-operation with Chris was that we developed an origin theory for Freemasonry.[62] We explored all the myths and uncovered historical evidence that supported some of these ideas. The myths which underpin Masonic ritual are ancient. We found the stories of the pillars and of a murdered Grand Master in ancient Egypt. We traced the biblical myths of Solomon's Temple down through the Old Testament and into the New. And we put together a coherent narrative to link all these old stories with historical evidence of the first recorded lodges in Scotland. We also linked Scottish Freemasonry to a revived Masonic Order of Knights Templar. We discovered that the floor plan of Rosslyn was an accurate copy of the floor plan of Solomon's Temple and found the 'Mason Word' made sense when transliterated into Egyptian hieroglyphics. It was an exciting time. What had begun as a labour of love turned into a coherent tale of the origins of the oddball ceremonies of the three Degrees of Freemasonry.

I had set out with the simple intention of answering the questions my lodge had not been able to. But what we put together made far more sense than anything the official sources of the United Grand Lodge of England could offer. Chris proposed that we turn this personal research into a book. I was doubtful. I had previously published a textbook in 1985 and knew how much work was needed to turn a draft into something that could be published. But Chris was enthusiastic and persuaded me that we should have a go.

I am really grateful that he did, as he opened up a whole new world of writing to me, which I have enjoyed ever since. Without Chris pushing me I would never have dared believe a dyslexic could become a writer of popular books. I had long been using mathematical symbols to communicate, but I had discovered that I also enjoyed the verbal story-telling inherent in delivering a good lecture. I had been a full-time lecturer at Bradford University for well over ten years, and my lecturing skill had been developing steadily as a result of watching how my students responded to what I said and listening to their feedback. I decided to have a go at sharing our version of the story of Freemasonry with the world. The result was dramatic.

Stirring the Hornet's Nest

We were lucky that the manuscript of *The Hiram Key* was accepted by Century, an imprint of Random House, and was launched, at Rosslyn Chapel, on the Thursday before Easter in 1996.

I had been encouraged by the response to my Masonic lectures in and around Halifax, where I spoke about aspects of our findings. We decided to make sure all our Masonic brethren heard about our work. Remembering the problems I had had getting hold of any information about the origins of Freemasonry, I came up with the idea that we should write to every lodge secretary and tell them of our findings. This had never been done before, but I was easily able to create a mailing list of the lodges. We thought carefully about what we wanted to say and decided to send this letter to all the lodges in England, Scotland and Wales.

22nd March 1996

Dear Worshipful Master,

It is highly unusual for two Master Masons to see fit to write to every Craft Lodge in England, Wales and Scotland, but such is the importance of our news that we could do nothing less. Next week our book – *The Hiram Key* – will be published by Century, which we believe will change for all time the way that Freemasons, and the world in general, view our Order.

Like many brethren before us, we were very curious as to the origins of the rituals that we perform, and seven years ago we set out to carefully research the origins of Freemasonry. At the outset we doubted that we would be able to find very much that was any earlier than the sixteenth century, but we have been fortunate enough to uncover a complete and magnificent history that every Freemason has a right to know about.

We are now certain that Hiram Abif was a real person, and the story in the Third-Degree ritual was created immediately following his death in 1573 BC. Amazingly, his body, and that of one of the tortured assassins, was carefully preserved, and the blows to our first Master's head are still clearly visible. Letters written at the time tell us of the tensions that led to the murder and the loss of the original secrets.

Having identified this key moment, we were able to track the passage of the Third-Degree ritual down through the royal line of David to the last king of the Jews – Jesus Christ himself. We appreciate that this sounds almost too incredible to be true but we can assure you that our research has gained the approval and support of some of the world's foremost biblical scholars.

We are now certain the original Jerusalem Church used the ritual that we now call the Third Degree, and by interpreting coded messages buried deep in Masonic ritual we have discovered the precise location of ancient scrolls that were buried in Jerusalem shortly before it was destroyed by Titus in AD 70. A team of archaeologists and Hebrew scholars are currently evaluating the site with a view to conducting one of the most important digs of this, or any other century.

Freemasonry is very special indeed, and we would like every Brother to share what we now know. We therefore respectfully request that you allow this letter to be read to the brethren of your lodge at your next meeting.

We hope that as many of you as possible will study our findings and that you will be able to take an even greater pride in Freemasonry than ever before.

Yours fraternally,

Bro. Bob Lomas and Bro. Chris Knight

The Hiram Key was duly published on Thursday 28 March 1996 and became an immediate success. We sent pre-release copies of the book to the Grand Secretaries of the Grand Lodge of Scotland and the United Grand Lodge of England. The Grand Secretary of Scotland wrote back thanking us for the book and invited us to meet him for tea in Edinburgh on 21 June. That was the beginning of my rich and rewarding relationship with Scottish Freemasonry which continues to this day.

The Grand Secretary of the United Grand Lodge of England did not acknowledge the copy of the book. He did respond to it, though. On 3 April 1996 he wrote to all the Provincial Grand Secretaries in England and Wales instructing them to pass on this message to all their lodge secretaries.

3 April 1996

Dear Provincial Grand Secretary

You may be aware that a new book on Freemasonry has been published and is being given a great deal of publicity and is appearing in quantity in the bookshops. Entitled *The Hiram Key – Pharaohs, Freemasons and the Discovery of the Secret Scrolls of Jesus* it has been written by Christopher Knight and Robert Lomas, who are both Freemasons in the Province of Yorkshire West Riding.

Because of its sensational nature the book is beginning to attract media interest, which may increase, as we understand that the *Sunday Times* is to serialise the book. As background for you and your Information Officer, should you receive enquiries from your own brethren or the local media, I have enclosed a comment on the book by the Grand Lodge Librarian and Curator.

Yours faithfully and fraternally

Grand Secretary.

The comments from the Grand Lodge Librarian and Curator were dismissive, saying among other things that 'Masonic historians will be saddened by the authors' cavalier attitude to Masonic research over the last 100 years. Their appendix on the rise of Freemasonry is riddled with factual errors.'

The accompanying letter from the Provincial Grand Secretary said:

6th April

Dear Brother Secretary,

Re Publication – 'The Hiram Key'
You will have received a letter, dated 22nd March 1996, which has been sent to all lodge secretaries in England and Wales, by the authors of the above book, requesting that it be read out at the next meeting of your lodge.

The Provincial Grand Master has not sanctioned the letter to be read, and I am now able to inform you that Grand Lodge does not approve either.

For your information, I enclose copes of the following communications:

1. Letter from the Grand Secretary dated 3rd April 1996.

2. Comment on the book by the Grand Lodge Librarian and Curator.

You are *not* required to read these communications in open lodge but the information will enable you to answer any questions you receive from your members in connection with the book.

Yours faithfully and fraternally
Provincial Grand Secretary

This response was unexpected. All the feedback I had received from my own lodge and from the other local lodges I had talked to had been positive and encouraging. From Scottish lodges I received letters of encouragement and invitations to speak, and I was entertained to afternoon tea at the Grand Lodge in Edinburgh and encouraged to use their library.

In England our letters were intercepted. I have kept letters marked 'RETURN TO SENDER' across the text, in envelopes marked 'RETURN TO SENDER AS INSTRUCTED BY PROVINICIAL GRAND LODGE' that were sent to the secretary of Ryburn Lodge and passed on to me. Invitations to lecture in Yorkshire were withdrawn, and when I asked why, I was told that the word was out that I should not be given a platform to speak. The Grand Secretary summoned a senior Past Master of Ryburn Lodge to London to explain why two of his members had written a book about Freemasonry. That Past Master, a retired Chief Constable and a Grand Lodge Officer, told me of that summons, adding that he had refused to attend and had written to the Grand Secretary to say it was none of his business what members of a private lodge did in their own time. He asked us to give a joint lecture about our findings to the lodge and sent the Grand Secretary a copy of the summons sent out to the brethren announcing the lecture. The news of this defiance spread quickly on the Masonic grapevine, and the regular flow of invitations began again.

A Provincial Grand Master took me aside after listening to me speak in a lodge.

'Who gave you permission to write a book?' he began.

I cut him short.

'Are you aware I am a member of a university which has a Royal Charter to guarantee me full academic freedom to study and publish as I choose within the law?' I said. 'And who are you to ask me, who gave me *permission* to write a book? How dare you speak to me in such a manner? Tell whoever sent you with that impertinent message that he does not control what I think, what I write or what I publish. This conversation is now closed.'

I walked out and left him looking bewildered.

Chris and I then wrote directly to UGLE challenging its right to interfere in private letters to lodges, and to suppress freedom of speech. They were unaware that we had been given copies of the letter written to the Provincial Grand Secretaries, and wrote back saying, 'It is not the custom of the United Grand Lodge of England to comment upon the published work of Brethren, or for that matter non-Brethren.'

The following week the Grand Secretary wrote a letter to my local paper, the *Halifax Courier*, attempting to discredit the book and repeating the Grand Lodge Librarian and Curator's comment, enclosed with his own circular letter, that 'Masonic historians will be saddened by the authors' cavalier attitude to Masonic research over the last 100 years'. It was quite unprecedented for UGLE to attack a Master Mason in this way. However, it was counterproductive, because it only increased my local support among Yorkshire Masons.

In the midst of this storm, Chris and I were now both wondering if Freemasonry was worth bothering with. Then my original faith in the good intent of The Craft was restored when the Grand Secretary of the Scottish Grand Lodge sent me a copy of its new Masonic Year Book. It contained this review of *The Hiram Key* by Bro. Robert Cooper, Grand Librarian:

> Any work which will stimulate debate as to the history and origins of Freemasonry is to be welcomed. The authors, Brothers Christopher Knight and Robert Lomas (both members of the English Craft), have weaved a fascinating tale spanning over 3,500 years of human experience. Rather than submit their work to a Lodge of Research or a non-Masonic history journal, the fruits of their labours were published commercially, their findings are made available therefore to the general public. Much contained within the book stands accepted wisdom 'on its head' and it is most unfortunate therefore that there is no Bibliography from which readers might consider the authors' sources; it also deprives the reader of a useful list of 'further reading'. The enduring and romantic belief that the origins of Freemasonry are linked with the demise of the Knights Templar is given a new twist. The range of material, and its ingenious interpretation, ensures that the authors have delivered a 'right good read'. Perhaps a revision, or a sequel, would go some way to answering some of the questions the authors themselves raise.[63]

I had simply never thought of *The Hiram Key* as a scholarly tome requiring such academic gravity; it had been the story of a quest to find out about Freemasonry (and the sources were referenced in the footnotes). But in every book of historical or scientific history I have written since I have always added a full bibliography, taking heed of Bro. Cooper's constructive suggestion that such a list provides readers with a useful list of further reading.

Taking heart from the good reception *The Hiram Key* had received from Scottish Masons, from Yorkshire Masons and from the general public, I decided to continue my researches. I wrote three further books with Chris and many more on my own.

I took a great interest in Bro. Sir Robert Moray and his role in the Royal Society. I visited the Scottish Lodge of Research named after him, Lodge Sir Robert Moray 1641, and was told that to understand him and his famous Mason's mark, I needed to experience another Masonic degree, that of Mark Mason.

A Confusion of English Degrees

Once I was able to discuss the early history of The Craft freely with Scottish brethren I realised that there is a piece of the jigsaw missing from the three degrees that The Craft works in England. I learned that in Scotland there are five degrees of Freemasonry which tell the basic story, and a further one which helps you understand the context.

The ritual and the symbols of The Craft have an effect on any individual who works them, and tries to understand their meaning, but they become more powerful and easier to understand when you have the whole jigsaw. The three degrees of the English Craft contain everything that is needed for a satisfying Masonic experience, but to understand Masonic philosophy and to benefit from it in training your 'soul' you need more. If my work had not been recognised and encouraged by Scottish Freemasonry I would never have pieced together the lost secrets.

In Scotland there is a further degree between the Second and the Third. This is the degree of Mark Mason. My Scottish advisers suggested that I should take the Mark Degree, which in England has to be taken separately, under the jurisdiction of a different Masonic Order, as I would never understand Freemasonry without it. I applied to a Mark Lodge in Halifax.

When I approached the lodge they were keen to have me as a member, and I had no trouble finding a proposer and seconder. But I had a little ambition I wanted to fulfil. When Sir Robert had been made a Mason in 1641 he was given a personal Mason's mark. (This is an interconnected series of straight lines which can be cut by a chisel into a Mason's work to identify who did it.) Sir Robert took the symbol of the five-pointed star as his personal Mason's mark. After the ceremonies he signed a certificate to acknowledge he had been made a Mason, along with the brothers who initiated him, and he added this star to the end of signature.

When I became a Mark Mason I wanted to take the mark which had once been used by Sir Robert Moray, as he was both a Masonic and a scientific hero (a few years later I pieced together his story and wrote it up in a book called *The Invisible College*). As long as nobody else in the lodge had previously used the same mark I could take it, as Sir Robert had never been a Halifax Mark Mason. I knew that his mark, a five-pointed star, met the ritual definition of a Mason's mark.

> The Fellowcrafts were allowed to choose any mark not previously adopted by another in their own Lodge. It consisted of points connected by straight lines so as to form any figure desired, the equilateral triangle alone excepted.

Before I put in my application to join I met with Bro. Fred, the Master of the Mark Lodge. Fred was a bluff no-nonsense Yorkshire building inspector who looked after the local school buildings for the council. I explained how I wanted a particular mark and my reason for wanting it. He got excited about the idea of awarding such an historic mark within his lodge and said he would check and make sure it had not been previously used.

'If nobody in this lodge has used it then you can take it as your own when we advance you,' he said.

Bro. Fred was a keen supporter of the Mark Degree and he was one of the first Masons outside my own lodge to go out of his way to tell me how much he enjoyed *The Hiram Key*. He also said that he had rushed out to buy it when UGLE condemned it in the *Halifax Courier*.

'What do they know about the real history of Freemasonry down there in London?' he said. 'We had The Craft here in Yorkshire long before they knew anything about it.' He winked conspiratorially.

I winked back, and felt a broad smile spreading across my face.

'I know that,' I said. 'We got it from itinerant Masons who'd worked in Scotland.'

I decided to confide something I had recently been told by one of my Scottish brethren in Montrose.

'Did you know that the Cathedral Church of Aberdeen, which was founded in 1357, has Masons' Marks from the foundation upwards?'

'Yes,' he proudly agreed. 'And did you know that the Mark Degree has been worked from time immemorial in Yorkshire, and it spread from here to the Midlands, when Masons trained at York went to work down there?'

I nodded in agreement.

He grinned back and added another little fact to my Masonic knowledge.

'And you, being so interested in Masonic history, Robert, ought to know that it's said that Thomas Dunckerley took the Mark Degree to the Phoenix Royal Arch Chapter in Portsmouth when he set it up in 1769. But he was advanced into it here in Yorkshire, just as you will be soon.'

A few weeks later Fred got back to me, said he had checked the records, and I could take the five-pointed star as my Mason's mark. That being agreed, I put in my application, produced my Grand Lodge Certificate and waited to hear when I was to be advanced.

But there was something I didn't share with Fred until after the ceremony. When my mother-in-law had died a few years earlier, my wife had inherited all her mother's Masonic regalia, and amongst it was a mark apron. When I told my wife I was planning to join the mark she gave me her mother's apron (which was identical to the male regalia) to wear that night. She knew I would be extremely proud to wear my mother-in-law's apron when I advanced to the Degree of Mark Master. (I didn't tell the lodge that I intended to wear ladies' clothing for the ceremony. But at the festive board afterwards I showed them a lipstick stain on the back of the apron.)

Everything was looking good. My wife had given me a Mark apron to represent the spiritual warmth of The Craft that I had first experienced in my teens, and I was to take as my mark one which had been used by the first Freemason known to have been initiated on English soil. I was looking forward with growing interest and excitement to being given my mark.

My warm anticipation of the personal significance of the Mark ceremony and my hopes of progress back into the good books of the English Craft grew to a peak as I stood outside the door of the Mark Lodge, waiting to be admitted.

The Tyler knocked on the closed door. It opened partially.

'Whom have you there?' came a voice from within.

'Brother Robert Lomas, who has served his time as a Fellowcraft and is now desirous of becoming a Mark Master Mason, to qualify to preside over a lodge of Operative Masons,' the Tyler answered.

'How does he hope to obtain those privileges?' came the question through the half-open door.

'By the help of the Great Overseer of the Universe, and the benefit of a passing grip and word,' the Tyler replied on my behalf.

'Is he in possession of the grip and word?' the voice asked.

What passing grip and word? I hadn't been given one.

In previous degrees I had been taken into the lodge, tested in my present degree and given a grip and password to enter the lodge in a higher degree. Momentary panic and the thought that I'd messed up the ritual overwhelmed me as the Tyler stood waiting. Only later did I realise I had just been given yet another vision of the Deity, and it was another aspect which appealed to my inner scientist. 'The Great Overseer of the Universe' is a vision of God with profound scientific overtones, but in the panic of the impending demand for a passing grip and word I had no time to explore these thoughts.

Then the Tyler spoke. 'He is not, but I will give them for him.' He stepped forward and shielding his action from me gave the Inner Guard a grip and whispered a password into his ear. Apparently I was to be allowed in.

As I entered the lodge, I was told to wait. A chisel was held to the centre of my chest by the Junior Deacon, who said to me:

Brother Lomas, on your initiation into Freemasonry you were admitted on the point of a dagger presented to your naked left breast; in the second you were admitted on the apex of a square held against your naked right breast. You are now admitted on the Mallet and Chisel.

He then struck three very gentle taps on the chisel with the mallet he held in his other hand. 'Enter on the edge of the Chisel,' he said, lowering his chisel and stepping back.

I was reminded of the ritual of the First Degree where I had been told that:

... the chisel is to further smooth and prepare the work for the hands of the more expert workman. But as we are not all operative, but free and accepted, or speculative Masons, we apply these tools to our morals. In this sense, the chisel points out the benefits of a more liberal education by which we are the better enabled to become fit members of a well and regularly organised society.

How appropriate, I thought, for an academic scientist to enter a lodge devoted to the understanding of the Great Overseer of the Universe on the point of a liberal education. My Scottish advisers had been correct; I was going to gain something from this degree.

The lodge was laid out in a similar way to my Craft lodge but there were three additional officers who sat at pedestals in floor of the Temple with their desks placed at the points of an equilateral triangle. I did not know either their office or their function.

The Junior Deacon gave me a wedge-shaped stone to hold and led me to the centre of the lodge.

Bro. Fred, the Worshipful Master, said, 'Who comes here?'

The Junior Deacon replied for me. 'Brother Robert Lomas, who has served his time as a Fellowcraft and is now desirous of becoming a Mark Master Mason, to qualify to preside over a lodge of Operative Masons.' He pointed to the stone I was carrying. 'Here is a specimen of his work,' he said.

The Master took it from me. He gave it three heavy blows with gavel.

'This is good work and square work, and such work as we are ordered to receive for the building of the Holy Temple,' he said in a loud clear voice for the whole lodge to hear.

Then he spoke directly to me.

Brother Lomas, since the building of King Solomon's Temple, and the institution of the Degree of Mark Master Mason, as now practised, a regulation has been made among The Craft that no one shall be advanced to the rank you now desire unless he has previously been raised to the sublime degree of Master. Have you obtained that rank?

I replied, 'I have.'

As a proof of what you say, you will now go to the Junior Warden in the South, and give him the sign of an Entered Apprentice, then to the

Senior Warden in the West, and give him the sign of a Fellowcraft, returning to me with the sign of a Master Mason.

I did as I was told and proved myself to be an Entered Apprentice, a Fellowcraft and a Master. That completed I stood before Master Fred.

Formerly it was the custom in a Fellowcraft Lodge that each Fellowcraft took out his mark, which was recorded in the books of the Lodge. He was also taught how to put in his hand for wages at the Senior Warden's wicket. As these parts of the Fellowcraft Degree are at present usually omitted, we shall now supply them. You will go to the Senior Warden in the West, who will assist you to choose a mark, and teach you how to put in your hand for wages.

I went to the Senior Warden. I drew my mark, a five-pointed star, on the piece of paper I was given. The Senior Warden approved it. He told me that to receive my wages I had to put my hand into a small hole called a wicket. There was a special way to do this, and if I did not do it correctly then I would be judged an impostor and my hand struck off at the wrist by an axe. He showed me how to present my hand into the wicket in order to receive my wages. Then he said, 'You will return to the Worshipful Master and show him your mark.'

I did so. Bro. Fred looked at it, looked at me and winked. 'Bro. Lomas, do you acknowledge this to be your mark?' he asked.

I replied that I did. He then said, 'Do you promise that you will neither add thereto, nor take therefrom this mark without the consent of your brethren in lodge assembled?'

I agreed that I would not change my mark in any way in the future without the consent of my Mark Lodge. I was then sent to the Registrar of Marks where I drew my new mark in the Mark Book of the Lodge.

I took my obligation before taking part in a ritual drama which involved presenting my work for inspection to each of the three officers at their pedestals, who I was now told were called Overseers. Then, after the ceremony was complete, Worshipful Master Fred summed it up in a formal ritual lecture which he delivered faultlessly from memory:

At the building of King Solomon's Temple and before the institution of the degree of Mark Master there were 80,000 operatives employed, part of whom were hewers in the quarries of Zeredathah, and part builders of the Temple; besides these there was a levy of 30,000 in the forests of Lebanon. In order that each of the 110,000 workmen might be known to his superior officers, every part of the workmanship subjected to the nicest scrutiny, and each faithful labourer receive with punctuality the reward of his industry and skill; this immense number was divided into 1,100 Lodges of Fellowcrafts and Entered Apprentices, the latter being placed under the superintendence of the former, who taught them the work. Over the whole presided 3,300 Menatzchim, Overseers, or Mark Masters, three over each Lodge. Each Fellowcraft had a mark peculiar to himself by which his work was known to his immediate Overseers, and while the Overseers had but one mark in common by which they signified their approval of the Fellowcraft's work, they had other marks by which they denoted the juxtaposition of any two stones. Thus without any difficulty was each individual's work known and recognised as perfect, and its proper place in the building indicated. The Fellowcrafts were allowed to choose any mark not previously adopted by another in their own Lodge. It consisted of points connected by straight lines so as to form any figure desired, the equilateral triangle alone excepted. The Overseers, as already said, had but one mark in common, the equilateral triangle. These 3,300 Overseers were again divided into 100 Lodges, with 33 in each, over which presided 300 Harodim or Rulers. These are now called Worshipful Master, Senior and Junior Warden respectively. They were appointed by Hiram Abif himself, and on them devolved the duty of paying the others their wages.

When the Fellowcrafts and their Overseers or Mark Masters received their wages, they put in their hands in a different manner, and at different wickets, so that if a Fellowcraft presumed to put in his hand at the Mark Master's wicket he was instantly detected as an impostor, and the Junior Harod, or Warden, stood within with an axe ready to inflict the penalty of striking off his hand.

The Mark Master's Degree was constituted by Hiram Abif before he came to Jerusalem, as he was supervising the timber for the Temple being transported on floats by sea, and, as Masonic tradition informs us, to a place so steep that it was impossible to ascend from the rafts without assistance from above. This was effected by Brethren being stationed there for that purpose, giving a strong grip which is now called the passing grip of this Degree.

It was the Master's business to prove each stone, not only as to its soundness by giving it three blows with a mallet, as to its finish by turning it over, but as to its being made exactly according to the working plan with which each Mark Master was provided. If found perfect in every way, it received the Mark Master's mark, and was sent on to the Temple; but if not, it was condemned and thrown among the rubbish. This was effected by two or more of the Brethren taking it between them and, after swinging it backwards and forwards three times, it was heaved over among the rubbish.

Every sixth working day it was the custom of the Overseers or Mark Masters to wait upon the acting Grand Master Hiram Abif in order to receive instructions, and the necessary plans for carrying on the work and keeping the men employed. Part of one of these working plans appears to have been lost, but an ingenious and intelligent Fellowcraft, whose part Brother Lomas you have just taken in the previous ceremony, having either seen the portion of the imperfect plan in the Overseer's possession before it was lost, or, forming a good idea of it from the nature of the work, perceived that a stone of a very peculiar form and construction was wanting to complete the design, and probably thinking to gain honour to himself for displaying a superior knowledge of his work, he immediately commenced blocking out such a stone. After spending much labour on it, he ultimately finished it by putting his own mark upon it. When the imperfect working plan was examined no place was found for this particular stone, and the Fellowcraft instead of honour received nothing but angry words and reproaches for idling away his time, and in the heat of passion the Overseer ordered the stone to be heaved among the rubbish, which was accordingly done by two Brethren probably well pleased at what they considered the humiliation of their companion's vanity. The sorrowful Fellowcraft who had cut the stone, on seeing this unworthy treatment of his work, placed his head in his hands in a disconsolate manner, and felt great sorrow.

The stone long lay neglected among the rubbish. At last, however, the time drew near when the keystone of the arch of King Solomon's Secret Vault was required, to which the portion of the working plan alluded to referred. Search was made at the Temple, but no such stone could be found, and, on further inquiry, it was ascertained that no stone of the requisite form had ever been brought there. The Overseers of that portion of the building immediately sent to the Overseers at the quarries, who had received the plans and orders for that portion of the work, to inquire the reason why this stone had not been forwarded with the others. The latter declared they knew nothing about it, and that there was no plan for any such stone among those entrusted to their care. The work came to a standstill, and the reason was speedily demanded by Hiram Abif, who not only recollected drawing the plan, and writing instructions about this stone, but also giving them himself to the Master Overseer of the Hewers. The latter being sent for was reprimanded for his carelessness in losing that portion of the plan, and, on learning the shape of the stone required, it came to his recollection that one of that description had been cut by one of his workmen. He informed Hiram Abif of this, and added that, owing to his not finding it noticed in his plan, he had refused to mark it, and had caused it to be rejected. Hiram Abif instantly sent for the Fellowcraft who had cut the stone, and questioned him concerning it, when, from the answers and description of it, he immediately perceived that it must be the very stone required. Instant and careful search was ordered to be made for it among the rubbish, where it was at last found uninjured.

As the Master Overseer had displayed such ignorance of his working plans as not to be able to discover the use of the stone, Hiram Abif deposed him from his office, and deprived him of the badge and insignia thereof, which he conferred on the humble Fellowcraft, whom he made a Mark Master, and raised to fill his place.

The Fellowcraft, or newly made Mark Master, was ordered to cut the Mark Master's mark on the stone around his own on the smaller end, and outside of it a series of identification letters. The stone was conveyed to the Temple with great pomp and parade, and while it was being fixed in its place, the newly made Mark Master, in an ecstasy of joy, clasped his hands together and looking up, exclaimed, 'All Glory be to the Most High.'

As this was my fourth degree in Freemasonry, I was well versed in the interpretation of symbol and ritual. The message of the degree was to study the plans of the Great Overseer of the Universe carefully so that I could use the benefits of my education to shape the raw materials of nature into building blocks and create wonderful structures. This degree reinforced the philosophy which underpinned my training as a scientist. It proclaimed that there is a Truth about the structure and order of the world which can be discovered by careful study and application. An additional message was that this Truth may not always be obvious but hard work and careful thought will always win through.

This fitted with my scientist's view of the world. I could see why I had been encouraged to take the degree. It reinforced my view that Freemasonry and Sir Robert Moray had been important influences in the development of modern science.

I went home that night clutching a copy of my Mason's mark feeling a warm affection for English Freemasonry. But that warm glow lasted only until my Mark Master's certificate arrived from London.

Personal Reflections

The Mark Degree had planted a seed in my mind. Its deeper teaching said there is an empty space waiting somewhere within me which has to be filled by a keystone of special knowledge. An important message of the degree for me was that the shape of the keystone might not be what I was expecting. All the previous ritual had emphasised that perfectly square stones were important for building stable structures. The importance of levels, perpendiculars and squares for creating cubic structures had been hammered into me, and yet at this point, when the two supporting pillars of my spiritual building needed to be joined together and their virtues combined, I needed to use a new and different shape – a shape not before mentioned in all the previous plans. The message was that, in order to make progress, you sometimes have to rethink all your previous knowledge in a new light. I was reminded of the shock I had felt when my first lessons in relativity made me realise that the infallible three-dimensional structure of Newtonian space was not enough. I had to adapt to the strange shapes of four-dimensional space–time if I wanted to make further progress. And this lesson about the need to be open to new and different ideas about the structure of the world, and by implication, the human soul, was writ large in this degree.

I went home with a lot to think about. I was not yet sure what the special knowledge about the human soul was, but it seemed to be linked with a mysterious symbol seen by the Junior Warden at the centre of the Temple, mentioned in the closing of the Fellowcraft lodge. Perhaps I had not yet learned all I could from my previous degrees. I would have to revisit them and think more deeply about their symbolic messages.

This was my first inkling of a deep spiritual teaching which underpins The Craft. It would be a while before I understood it more fully.

7

Descending into the Hidden Chamber

Surely You Can't Be Serious?

I RETURNED FROM my Mark ceremony fired with enthusiasm for the tolerant message of Mark Masonry and its endorsement of the benefit of a liberal education. I was certain that education had shaped me into a wider-minded person and a more useful engineer. The use of a chisel as a metaphor for shaping me, as a sort of living stone, from a rough-hewn chunk into a perfect shape strong enough to support the weight of the whole arch was a powerful image. Sometimes new knowledge can hit you like a hammer blow and reshape your outlook. This was exactly what had happened to my scientist's world view when I was first introduced to the shocking implications of quantum mechanics.

Before my first classes in quantum physics I had thought of electrons as little hard balls of electricity spinning in orbit around a central nucleus; I visualised them rather like planets in a miniature solar system. In my first quantum physics classes I found that everything I had been taught so far was only an approximation of the truth. My tutor, Dr Mike Hampshire, called these ways of thinking 'classical descriptions of the electron', adding they were not a reliable way to think about electrical interactions. What was really scary was to discover that any electron could choose to appear as either a wave or a particle, depending on its mood when I decided to measure it. And what was worse was that if I changed my mind whilst making the measurement, then the electron could change too. That intimate link between what was going on in my mind and how the electron behaved came as a total shock. Then it got worse. It wasn't just electrons; light was just as unreliable!

Since the age of fifteen I had believed light was an electromagnetic wave. I carried out the classic A-level physics experiments known as

Young's fringes, shining a light through a series of slits in metal plates so the beam was separated and then recombined. It formed a beautiful interference pattern of light and dark lines. Now Dr Hampshire stood in front of us final-year undergraduates and told us light was sometimes a stream of particles, and electrons were sometimes waves. And, most importantly of all, how either of them appeared depended on what we were thinking when we measured them.

These classes had three major effects on my world view. They made me realise:

1. That the world was far more complicated than I had imagined;
2. That what I thought could change the nature of reality, and anything I did or thought might affect the world around me; and finally
3. That this fascinating world could only be accessed using the symbolic thinking of mathematics.

I felt as my hero Einstein did about quantum mechanics. There is a mystery at its centre which we have yet to penetrate. This is how Einstein described the issue:

> The last and most successful creation of theoretical physics, namely quantum mechanics (QM), differs fundamentally from both Newton's mechanics, and Maxwell's electromagnetic field. For the quantities which figure in QM's laws make no claim to describe physical reality itself, but only probabilities of the occurrence of a physical reality that we have in view . . . I cannot but confess that I attach only a transitory importance to this interpretation. I still believe in the possibility of a model of reality – that is to say, of a theory which represents things themselves and not merely the probability of their occurrence.[64]

I felt that there must be some purpose to the universe which could be understood with enough effort and study. And it was to understand more that I returned to Salford to do a PhD in solid state quantum physics. So when I worked the Mark Degree ceremony the thoughts it stimulated struck a deep resonance within me.

The key message of the Mark Degree is that there is a hidden plan to reality, but it is not a plan that we are immediately aware of. The myth says that the plan has been mislaid or accidentally destroyed by the negligent oversight of its custodians – yet, if we can but find it, or rediscover its purpose for ourselves, then the vital components of reality can be assembled to create the a perfect structure. The attitude of the 'ingenious and intelligent Fellowcraft' whose role I had taken in the Mark ceremony seemed to me to reflect exactly how I had felt when I joined Dr Mike Hampshire's research group at Salford University to search for the truth about reality.

Freemasonry had suggested to me three ways to think about a deity, and all three gelled with the way my view of physics had developed. The first view had been of the Great Architect of the Universe. This coincided with the Newtonian view of predicable particles that could be manipulated and accurately predicted; it was a human-sized view which coincided with common sense. The second had been the Great Geometrician of the Universe. This encapsulated the geometrical view of space unpinning Einstein's theories of relativity; the geometry of space–time encompassed views of vast spaces and addressed the issues of eternity and infinity. It was a view of reality on a galactic scale, way above anything a human could directly experience.

Now this third view, that of the Great Overseer of the Universe, reminded me of my shock and surprise when I learned that the way I decided to observe subatomic objects changed the way they behaved. I could make a light ray turn into a stream of particles and turn a photon into an electron just by thinking about it. The myth of the Great Overseer helped make these ideas from the cutting edge of physics more understandable. The Great Overseer knew the lost contents of the Grand Plan, and as I played the role of the 'ingenious and intelligent Fellowcraft' I was inspired to think I might recover this lost plan. Was this part of the real secrets of Freemasonry, which I had felt so cheated out of in the Third Degree?

I felt honoured to be a current custodian of Sir Robert Moray's historical mark. I was finally making progress in understanding something of the true purpose of Freemasonry. My Scottish brethren had advised me to follow up the Mark Degree with the Royal Arch, and in the first flush of excitement about the insight I had gained from working the Mark, I asked Bro. Mike Astell if he would introduce me to the Brighouse Royal Arch Chapter. Then I received a letter from the Grand Secretary of the Grand Lodge of Mark Master Masons of England and Wales.

* * *

When I saw the heading on the letter my first response was pleasure at seeing the acknowledgment of Wales as a separate nation from England. The Grand Lodge of Mark Master Masons of England and Wales looked good to me. In a happy frame of mind I read the note of welcome into the Order of Mark Master Masons. The envelope included a certificate of membership, which recorded my official registered mark. I unfolded the impressive-looking document, which showed my name, the date and lodge of my advancement and my mark.

But it wasn't my mark! It was a strange arrangement of my initials, stylised by the use of a series of straight lines. It was so obviously a mistake I decided that the best way to deal with it was to write back pointing out the administrative oversight and asking for a certificate with the correct mark on it. I carefully ringed the mistake in red ink and drew my correct mark, also in red ink, alongside it, and posted it off with a polite note drawing attention to the mistake.

A week later I received a reply. It said there was no mistake. It insisted that the certificate was correct and would not be reissued. That was my official mark, and I should use it and no other.

My first thought was that perhaps the slip-up had been made on the official return. I rang Bro. Fred to ask.

He was surprised when I told him what had happened. He said he would ring his Registrar and check. When he rang back he sounded annoyed.

The decision to change the mark, he told me, had been taken because the mark I had chosen was considered 'inappropriate', and a more suitable one had been substituted.

I protested that the star-shaped Mark had been awarded in open lodge and I had formally agreed not to change that mark in any way without the consent of the Mark Lodge that awarded it.

Fred agreed that was correct but added, 'I doubt the Grand Lodge will change its mind.' He now sounded resigned.

'We'll see,' I said as I rang off.

After careful thought I sent a registered letter to the Mark Grand Lodge pointing out that its duty was to record the marks which lodges decided to award. Its only role in the matter was to accurately record the mark and to issue a certificate to the newly advanced Mark Master confirming the conferment of that mark by his lodge.

I acknowledged that to keep accurate records it had to check that the mark had:

1. not been previously used in that particular lodge, and
2. complied with the rules for creating a mark (i.e. it must consist of points connected by straight lines so as to form any figure desired, the equilateral triangle alone excepted).

But if a mark complied (and the one awarded to me certainly did), then the Mark Grand Lodge was contractually obliged to issue a certificate for that mark, for which purpose it had received a fee. Its failure to do so in this case represented a clear failure to carry out its duty as the servant of the lodges and amounted to a breach of contract with both me and my Mark Lodge.

Next I offered to overlook this breach of contract if a revised certificate was immediately forwarded with the correct mark in place. I enclosed a fresh drawing of the mark, so there could be no misunderstanding. Then, with polite thanks in advance for the Lodge's co-operation, I posted the letter off.

A few days my phone rang at home. The call was from a Mark Provincial Grand Master. After exchanging a few pleasantries I asked him why he was calling. He said he had to speak to me about my recent letter to the Grand Mark Lodge.

'You can't write to them in that way,' he said.

'When a body is incompetent and in clear breach of contract,' I said, 'I have every right to point it out and offer them a simple way to sort the matter out. And,' I added, 'I am extremely surprised you know anything about it, as I considered it a private mistake to be sorted out without public fuss.'

'I was ordered to speak to you about your behaviour,' he said.

'Oh,' I replied. 'So the Grand Mark Lodge prefers to deal through third parties, does it? If that is the case then perhaps I should also consider using a third party to send them a message about their behaviour.'

'I don't understand what you mean.'

'Let me explain,' I offered. 'If they don't sort the matter out quickly and privately I could chose a tabloid newspaper as my go-between. I could write an article about how badly Freemasonry has treated me and how the Grand Mark Lodge appears to be withholding my legally awarded mark through what could be considered to be simple spite. I'm sure that are plenty of anti-Masonic journalists who would be interested.' I paused. 'And I will probably be listened to, as I am well known as a keen supporter of Freemasonry who publicly defends Freemasonry in the media.'

The line went silent for quite a time. 'Are you serious?' he said.

'Quite,' I replied. 'I have no wish to wash dirty linen in public, but neither am I prepared to be deprived of Sir Robert's mark because I happened to once offend UGLE.'

I waited for a moment for this message to sink in.

'Do pass on the message to the Grand Mark Lodge that I look forward to receiving my corrected certificate in the very near future,' I said. It arrived within the week.

Returning to the Keystone

But simply having the mark of a Masonic hero did not absolve me from the need to challenge myself. I had a long way to go on my quest to understand The Craft and its lost secrets. And my next step in Masonic knowledge was about to happen. I was going to be exalted into a Chapter of the Holy Royal Arch in Brighouse.

I was increasingly fascinated by The Craft's philosophy. Working the Mark Degree made me realise that the symbols and myths of The Craft could be interpreted on many levels, and I was surprised at how the rituals were forming a pattern of mental development which paralleled the path I had followed to become a scientist. I was curious about what I might learn from the Royal Arch.

I had built up a picture of what I had learned from the four degrees I had taken.

The First Degree had taught me to face up to my fears, to confront and overcome my childish nightmare visions, and to trust those who wanted to teach me. The ceremony of my Initiation had discarded the jealous and intrusive God of my Sunday School days and replaced Him with Newton's inspiring vision of the Great Architect.

The Second Degree encouraged me to develop my mind and apply it to the study of nature and science to better understand the world. I had escaped the educational scrap heap of the 11-plus by harnessing the power of education, so it was a lesson I accepted easily. The view of God as the Great Geometrician reminded me of my first understanding of space and time through the symbolism of geometry.

The Third Degree, although dramatic and beautiful in its own way, had not continued this pattern of scientific insight. It taught that death is a sad but inevitable part of the human life cycle, and that it is import-ant to make the most of the opportunities that being alive offers. Why this rather obvious truism should matter was something I did not yet understand, but I was prepared to withhold judgement until I had seen the whole picture, and I had been assured the Royal Arch would provide this.

The Mark Degree had gently stroked the dream I shared with Albert Einstein of perceiving a deep and hidden plan which explained the random predictions of quantum theory.

Working the rituals is an essential part of understanding the degrees. It is not only the words which matter. The fellow feeling exuded from the lodge, the emotional impact of the symbols as they are ritually displayed, and the power of role-playing the myths creates an emotional foundation for the teaching. Only by living through the ritual is it possible to absorb the totality of its teaching.

I had been told that the Holy Royal Arch was the completion of the Third Degree, just as the Mark was the completion of the Second Degree. I was open to whatever the degree had to offer.

I was made welcome at the Chapter but taken aside to be tested in the grips and passwords of the previous three degrees. Having proved myself a Master Mason I was told a password, told to put on my Master's apron and wait to be called into the Chapter. I was introduced to the Outer Guard, known in this degree as the Janitor, who would look after me until the Chapter was open and ready to receive me.

For the fifth time I stood outside a Masonic Temple while the Outer Guard knocked on the door. I was wearing the apron of a Master Mason and I was blindfolded and draped with a rope. But this rope was wrapped around my waist, not my neck. An officer known as the Principal Sojourner stood by my side, ready to guide me.

I heard the door open and a voice ask, 'Whom have you there?'

The Principal Sojourner replied:

Brother Robert Lomas, who has duly and truly served his time as an Entered Apprentice, passed the Degree of Fellowcraft, and has been raised to the sublime Degree of a Master Mason, in which character he has exercised himself for four weeks and upwards, and, in consequence of his proficiency, has been rewarded with a password as a test of merit, and now presents himself properly prepared and approved to be exalted to the supreme Degree of a Royal Arch Mason.

The voice asked, 'How does he hope to obtain those privileges?'

The Sojourner answered, 'By the help of God and the benefit of a password.'

I felt a hand grip mine and the voice spoke directly to me.

'I will thank you for the password.'

I gave it.

'Halt, while I report to the Principal Z,' it said, and I heard the door close. After a few minutes the door opened and I was guided inside. A different voice spoke from the far end of the hall. It was a strong, confident voice and echoed slightly in the large room.

Brother Lomas, as you seek preferment in our Order, and have been honoured with a password as a test of merit, I must now demand whether you freely and voluntarily present yourself with a hope of being exalted to the supreme Degree of a Royal Arch Mason?

The Principal Sojourner, who stood by my side, nudged me and whispered, 'I do.' I repeated the answer.

The distance voice continued. 'Do you likewise declare that you are prompted to seek admission into our Order from a desire of increasing your Masonic knowledge, and of applying the same to the welfare of your fellow creatures?'

Again I was prompted, and replied, 'I do.'

'Thus assured,' the confident voice continued, 'I will thank you to kneel, whilst a blessing from Heaven is invoked in aid of our proceedings.' The Principal Sojourner, whom I recognised from the faint, but pungent smell of stale tobacco which surrounded him, helped me kneel on some sort of padded bench. I realised there was another man standing beside me, as he assisted me to kneel in the correct posture.

Once I was settled a new voice spoke from the opposite side of the hall. I recognised Mike Astell saying:

Almighty and Eternal Father of the Universe, at whose command the world burst from chaos, and all created matter had its birth, we, Thy unworthy servants, humbly implore Thee to bestow Thy spiritual blessing on this convocation, grant that the Brother who now seeks to participate in the light of our supreme mysteries may be imbued with a portion of Thy Holy Spirit; may he not enter into our Order lightly, nor recede from it hastily, but pursue it steadfastly, ever remembering that the great object of this Institution is the happiness of our fellow creatures, and, above all, the glory of Thy holy name.

The assembled brethren spoke in unison. 'So mote it be.' I could tell by the volume and disposition of the voices there was a good crowd.

The confident voice spoke again: 'In all cases of danger and difficulty, on whom do you rely for support?'

The Sojourner prompted me to reply, 'The true and living God most high.' I must admit that resonances with my Sunday School God flitted through my mind, and I wondered if I could accept the answer. I preferred the more benign Great Architect, Great Geometrician or Great Overseer, but in the interests of Masonic knowledge I repeated the prompt.

The confident voice continued:

Since your confidence is so firmly placed you may safely rise. The Companions will take notice that Brother Robert Lomas is about to pass in view before them, to show that he is a Candidate properly prepared to be exalted to the supreme degree of a Royal Arch Mason.

The Sojourner led me round the room. It all felt like my Initiation, as I was blindfolded but could hear the rustling and muttering of the brethren. What had confident voice called them? Not the brethren but the companions.

We stopped, and confident voice spoke.

As you seek to be admitted to a participation in the Secrets of this supreme degree, I call upon you to advance towards the East, to the sacred shrine on which they are deposited; you will advance by seven steps, thrice halting and bowing with reverential awe at the 3rd, 5th, and 7th, for at each step you will approach nearer to the sacred and mysterious name of The True And Living God Most High.

I felt the Sojourners leading me forward, prompting me when to stop and bow until finally I was helped to stand on a highish platform. The voice continued. 'You are now arrived at the crown of a vaulted chamber, into which it is necessary that you should descend, and in order to do so, you must remove two of the Arch or Keystones.'

What felt like a crowbar was placed in my hand and I was guided to lever at something which moved and fell with a clatter onto the floor. I was then helped to lever at a second object which joined the first in a noisy heap on the floor.

Confident voice spoke. 'Let the Candidate be duly lowered into the vault, and then attend to a portion of the writings of our Grand Master King Solomon.'

'Keep still,' the Sojourner whispered, 'we're going to lower you downwards.' I felt the rope around my waist tighten as I was bodily lowered off the platform. When I reached the ground I was instructed to kneel. I did.

Mike's voice rang out as I knelt in darkness, feeling the rope that had supported me tight around my waist. Mike was reading a passage from Proverbs, chapter 2 (my Sunday School training was not wasted after all). '"My son,"' it began, '"if thou wilt receive my words, and hide my commandments with thee; so that thou incline thine ear unto wisdom, and apply thy heart to understanding . . ."' It continued until Mike reached the line, 'The Lord by wisdom hath founded the earth; by understanding hath He established the heavens, by His knowledge the depths are broken up, and the clouds drop down the dew."'

It was a fine statement of the importance of wisdom. I listened to it with the ears of a physicist, and it made more sense than it had when I had listened to it being read by Miss Bolds during those never-ending sunny Sunday afternoons of my childhood. She would have been proud of me recognising it.

I was jerked back from my reverie by the confident voice speaking.

'You will now endeavour to discover something in the vaulted chamber,' he said. As he did so the heavy-smoking Sojourner placed something which felt like a rolled-up paper in my hand. His undertone prompted me: 'It is found.'

'It is found,' I announced, wondering exactly what I *had* found.

Apparently the confident voice shared my wonder. 'What is found?'

(Well you can *see*, I thought. And if *you* don't know, how do you expect me to?)

But Principal Sojourner came to my rescue: 'Something like a scroll of vellum or parchment,' he whispered. I repeated the words.

'What are its contents?' the confident voice asked.

(Is it in Braille? I wondered. Or has he forgotten he ordered me to be blindfolded?)

Fortunately Principal Sojourner had an excuse ready and whispered it to me.

'Deprived of light I cannot tell,' I repeated.

Let that want of light remind you that man by nature is the child of ignorance and error, and that he would ever have remained in that deplorable situation, under the darkness of the shadow of death, had it not pleased the Almighty to call him to light and immortality, by the revelation of His most holy word and will.

He paused.

'Arise therefore, and draw forth the third arch or keystone, and receive the light of the holy word.'

I felt myself being lifted by the rope about my waist, as if I was being drawn up from the vault I was visualising beneath the blackness of the blindfold.

I stood between the two Sojourners, who helped me prise out another clattering object. I deduced it must be a third keystone. I wondered if it was shaped like the one I had submitted for my mark, the one that had been rejected.

A further command came from the far end of the room. 'Let the Candidate be again lowered into the vault, and attend to a portion of the writings of the prophet Haggai.'

I was again lowered to the ground by the two Sojourners and placed on my knees. As I knelt the organ began to play 'Glory to the Supreme on High'.

Mike began to read another portion of scripture, this time from the Book of Haggai about the instruction to Zerubbabel to rebuild Solomon's Temple in Jerusalem after the Babylonian captivity.

> In the seventh month, in the one and twentieth day of the month, came the word of the Lord by the prophet Haggai, saying, Speak now to Zerubbabel, the son of Shealtiel, governor of Judah, and to Joshua, the son of Josedech, the high priest, and to the residue of the people, saying, Who is left among you that saw this house in her first glory? and how do you see it now? is it not in your eyes in comparison of it as nothing? Yet now be strong, O Zerubbabel, saith the Lord; and be strong, O Joshua, son of Josedech, the high priest; and be strong, all ye people of the land, saith the Lord, and work: for I am with you, saith the Lord of hosts.

Mike continued to read until the verse, 'The glory of this latter house shall be greater than of the former, saith the Lord of hosts: and in this place will I give peace, saith the Lord of hosts.'

The reading finished, and I was helped to my feet. The brother with the confident voice took me through my obligation and pronounced me a Companion of the Royal Arch with the words, 'Arise Brother Lomas, now a Companion of our Order.'

The organist played a grand march while the companions seemed to be shuffling about. I wondered what they were doing.

I was led back to the far end of the room and confident voice spoke. 'What is now the prevailing wish of your heart?'

Principal Sojourner prompted me: 'To be restored to light.' I repeated it in a loud voice.

'Let that blessing be restored,' came from the opposite end of the room, and as he spoke my blindfold was whipped away.

Even though the lighting was dim the effect of the tableau which the companions had formed was breathtaking. They were standing in two parallel lines like two rows of pillars. Each was dressed in a colourful apron and sash and held a long slender pole. The two rows were forming a series of arches with their wands, so that it seemed to me that I was looking down a dark, vaulted chamber. The only light was coming from six candles on large free-standing candleholders and they were forming the shape of two interlaced equilateral triangles. At the centre of the triangles was a white altar and at the far end of the hall was a stage on which stood three magnificently robed figures. The centre one spoke in the confident voice I had come to know so well.

'Being now restored to the blessings of material light, I call upon you to read the contents of the scroll you found in the vaulted chamber,' he said.

I looked down, and in my hand was a scroll. I unfolded it, and there was written:

> In the beginning God created the heaven and the earth. And the earth was without form and void; and darkness was upon the face of the deep. And the Spirit of God moved upon the face of the waters. And God said, Let there be light: and there was light.

As I read these opening words of the Book of Genesis it occurred to me for the first time how good a description they were of the mysterious Big Bang – then the fashionable theory of how the universe was formed. However, I couldn't linger over the thought, because the central figure, dressed in the robes of a king, spoke once more in his strong, confident voice.

> Such, newly exalted Companion, are the first words of the Sacred Volume, which contains the treasures of God's revealed Will. Let us praise and magnify His Holy Name for that knowledge of Himself which He has vouchsafed to us, and let us walk worthily in that light which has shone around us. You may now retire, and on your return you will be permitted to participate in the further mysteries of the Order.

Three Lectures of Explanation and an Insight

By the time I took my place in the Chapter, which is the name given to a lodge of Royal Arch Masons, I was wearing the sash and apron of a Royal Arch Mason which my wife had inherited from her mother. I had also been told that the three grandly dressed officers in the East of the Temple were known as the Sanhedrin or three Principals. One represented Zerubbabel, Prince of Israel and the builder of the Second Temple, the others Joshua, the son of Josedech the high priest, and the prophet Haggai. The confident voice directing the ceremony of my exaltation had been that of the companion taking the role of Zerubbabel, and was referred to in Chapter as Most Excellent. All three carried large wooden sceptres which they used to knock on the floor, in a similar way to the knocking gavels of a Craft lodge.

I was seated in the Chapter between the two Sojourners who had conducted me around, carrying out the duties of guides which the Deacons had done in the other degrees. The Officer known as Most Excellent delivered, from memory, a lecture of explanation to help me, the newly exalted Companion of the Royal Arch, to understand the ceremony:

> Companion Lomas, let me now congratulate you on your admission into this sublime Degree of Freemasonry, which is at once the foundation and keystone of our whole Masonic structure. You perhaps conceive that you have this day received a Fourth Degree of Freemasonry; but such, strictly speaking, is not the case; it is only the Master Mason's Degree completed. For you will recollect that when you were raised to the Third Degree, you were informed that, by the untimely death of our Master Hiram Abif, the genuine secrets of a Master Mason were lost, and that therefore certain substituted secrets were adopted to distinguish the Master Mason, until the genuine secrets might be discovered. Those secrets were lost for a period of nearly 500 years, and were recovered in the manner which has been explained to you in a peculiar and impressive form, for the purpose of fixing more strongly on the mind the providential means by which the ancient and genuine mysteries were regained.

He paused and looked around him.

> It is now time we should impart to you the historical, symbolical, and mystical knowledge of our Order, and I request your attention first to the Historical Part from the Most Excellent Companion J.

The Officer playing the role of Joshua, the son of Josedech, the high priest, stood up to address me.

> Companion Lomas, there are three epochs in Masonry which particularly merit your attention: the history of the first or Holy Lodge; the second or Sacred Lodge; and the third or Grand and Royal Lodge.
>
> The first or Holy Lodge was opened two years after the exodus of the Israelites from their Egyptian bondage by Moses, Aholiab, and Bezaleel,

on consecrated ground at the foot of Mount Horeb, in the wilderness of Sinai, where the host of Israel had assembled and pitched their tents, to offer up prayers and thanksgivings for their signal deliverance from the hands of the Egyptians. In this place the Almighty had thought fit to reveal Himself before that time to His faithful servant Moses, when He commissioned him His high ambassador of wrath against Pharaoh and his people, and of freedom and salvation to the house of Jacob. Here were delivered the forms of those mysterious prototypes, the tabernacle and the ark of the covenant; here were delivered the sacred laws, engraven by the hand of the Most High, with those sublime and comprehensive precepts of civil and religious polity, which, by separating His favoured people from all other nations, consecrated Israel a chosen vessel to His service; for these reasons this is denominated the first or Holy Lodge.

Solomon, King of Israel, Hiram, King of Tyre, and Hiram Abif presided over the second or Sacred Lodge. It was opened in the bosom of the holy Mount Moriah, under the very centre of the ground on which the Sanctum Sanctorum was afterwards erected. On this consecrated spot Abraham had proved his intuitive faith by leading his beloved son Isaac a destined victim to the altar of his God. Here, on the threshing floor of Araunah the Jebusite, David offered the mediatorial sacrifice by which the plague was stayed, here he received in a vision the form of that magnificent temple afterwards erected by his illustrious son; and here the Almighty declared His sacred name should dwell; for which reasons we distinguish this the second or Sacred Lodge.

The third or Grand and Royal Lodge was holden at Jerusalem; it was opened after the return of the Children of Israel from their Babylonish captivity, under Zerubbabel, prince of the people; Haggai, the Prophet; and Joshua, the son of Josedech, the High Priest. Now was the kingly power restored in the person of Zerubbabel to the royal line of David and princely tribe of Judah. Nor was a vestige thereof again effaced until after the destruction of Jerusalem by the Romans under Titus, in the year 70 of the Christian era; to commemorate which restoration this is called the third or Grand and Royal Lodge; and the resemblance in the Chapter before us to these great originals is, that in every regular Royal Arch Chapter we acknowledge the representatives of the Grand and Royal Chapter at Jerusalem. The three Principals represent Zerubbabel, Haggai, and Joshua, whose names they bear; the two Scribes represent

Ezra and Nehemiah, Selectors and Expounders of the sacred law, and attendants on the august Sanhedrin, by whose names they are distinguished. Your three selves represent the three faithful sojourners, by whom the secrets of the Royal Arch were found, in consequence of which discovery they were honoured with seats in the august assembly, composed of the rulers and elders of the people, represented by the rest of the Companions now present.

Companion J sat down, and Most Excellent Principal Z stood up.
'Such is the Historical account of this Degree,' he said. 'I shall now claim your attention, while our Most Excellent Companion H gives an account of the symbolical part.'

The officer role-playing Haggai stood up, and turned to address me.

Companion Lomas, the forms, symbols, and ornaments of Royal Arch Masonry, together with the rites and ceremonies at present in use among us, were adopted by our predecessors at the building of the Second Temple, as well to preserve in our minds the providential means by which the great discovery was effected, as in our hearts those lessons of exalted morality which we, as members of this sublime Degree, are bound to practise. The form in which the Companions of every Royal Arch Chapter are arranged approaches as nearly as circumstances will permit to that of the true Catenarian Arch;[65] thus we preserve the memorial of the vaulted shrine, in which the Sacred Word was deposited, while from the impenetrable nature of this strongest of all architectural forms, we learn the necessity of guarding our mysteries from profanation by the most inviolable secrecy; it also strongly typifies that inviolable adherence to order and spirit of fraternal union, which has given energy and permanency to the Constitutions of Masonry, enabling them to survive the wreck of mighty empires and resist the destroying hand of time. And as the subordinate members of the Catenarian Arch naturally gravitate towards the centre, or keystone, which compresses and cements the whole structure, so we are taught to look up with reverence, and submit with cheerfulness, to every lawfully constituted authority, whether of Masonic or civil regulation. The keystone and two contiguous arch stones are represented by the three Principals of the Chapter; for as the secrets contained under the Royal Arch could only be obtained by wrenching forth the three principal stones thereof, so the complete knowledge of this Degree can only be obtained by passing through these several offices. In this Degree we acknowledge six lights; the three lesser representing together the light of the law and the prophets, and, by their number, alluding to the patriarchal, Mosaical, and prophetical dispensations; the three greater representing the sacred word itself, and the creative, preservative, and annihilative power of the Deity. These lights are placed in the form of an equilateral triangle, each of the lesser bisecting the line formed by two of the greater, thus geometrically dividing the great triangle into three lesser triangles on the extremities, which, by their union, form a fourth triangle in the centre, and all of them equal and equilateral, emblematical of the four points or divisions of Masonry – viz., Entered Apprentice, Fellowcraft, Master Mason, and Holy Royal Arch. This symbolical arrangement corresponds to the mysterious triple tau, which forms two right angles on each of the exterior lines, and two others at their centre, by their union, for the three angles of each triangle are equal to two right angles; this serves to illustrate the jewel worn by some of the Companions of the Order, which forms by its intersections a given number of angles; these may be taken in five several combinations, and when reduced into their amount in right angles, will be found equal to the five regular Platonic bodies[66], which represent the four elements and the sphere of the universe.

The ribbon worn by the Companions of the Order is a sacred emblem, denoting light, being composed of the two principal colours with which the veil of the temple was interwoven; it is further signified by its irradiated form, and in both these respects it has ever been considered as an emblem of regal power and dignity. The ensigns which the Companions bear on their staves were the distinctive bearings of the twelve tribes of Israel, and figuratively a peculiar blessing bequeathed to each by the patriarch Jacob, who, before his death, assembled them together for that purpose, as we find in the 49th chapter of Genesis. The leading tribes are pointed out in the 2nd chapter of Numbers. The four principal banners represent the leading standards of the four divisions of the army of Israel, as described in the Book of Genesis. They unitedly bear a device of an angelic nature, under the figures of a man, a lion, an ox, and an eagle: a man, to personify intelligence and understanding; a lion, to represent strength and power; an ox, to denote the ministration of patience and assiduity; and an eagle, to display the promptness and

celerity with which the will and pleasure of the great I Am are executed. The several bearings of the sceptres denote the regal, prophetical, and sacerdotal offices, which all were, and still ought to be, conferred in a peculiar manner, accompanied with the possession of particular secrets.

The Sword and Trowel have been adopted by Masons of the Royal Arch to commemorate the valour of those worthy Masons who carried on the building of the Second Temple, with the Trowel in their hands and the Sword by their sides, that they might be ever ready to defend the holy city and sanctuary against the unprovoked attacks of their enemies; by which they left a sacred and impressive lesson to succeeding ages: that next to the obedience due to lawful authority, a manly and determined resistance to lawless violence is the first step to social duties.

The pickaxe, crow, and shovel were the instruments used by the Sojourners in clearing away for the foundation of the Second Temple: with the pickaxe they loosened the earth, with the crow they made purchases, and with the shovel they cleared away the rubbish and loose earth. These we spiritualise thus : the sound of the stroke of the pickaxe represents to us the sound of the last trump, when the graves shall be loosened and deliver up their dead; the crow, being an emblem of uprightness, displays to us the erect manner in which the body shall rise on that awful day to meet its tremendous but merciful judge; the mortal state in which the body is laid in the grave is powerfully impressed on our minds by the work of the shovel, so that when the rubbish of the body is shovelled away we may with humble but holy confidence hope that the spirit may arise to immortal and eternal life.

Having completed his lecture Haggai sat down, and Zerubbabel stood up once more. 'Such is the symbolical account,' he said. 'I shall now proceed to explain the mystical part.'

The mystical knowledge of this Degree comprehends the nature and import of the Holy Word, and the import of our traditions. On the plinth or front of the pedestal are the initials of the names of the three Grand Masters – viz. Solomon, King of Israel, Hiram, King of Tyre, and Hiram Abif, which are intended to perpetuate their names as well as to commemorate the circumstance of their presiding during the erection of the first Temple. There is also the triple tau, which is a character affixed to the summonses of Royal Arch Mason, on more than usual occasions.

The tau comes from the Hebrew, and is the sign or mark spoken of by the angel which Ezekiel saw in spirit, when it was said to the man with the writer's ink-horn, 'Go through the midst of the city, through the midst of Jerusalem, and set a mark upon the foreheads of the men that sigh and that cry for all the abominations that be done in the midst thereof,' by which mark they were preserved alive from amidst those who were slain for their idolatry by the wrathful displeasure of the Lord. It was also a mark, in ancient times, placed on the forehead of those who were acquitted by the judges, as a proof of their innocence; and military commanders put it on those who were saved unhurt from the field of battle: for which reasons it has been denominated the mark of life. The union of the three taus here represented alludes to the grand tri-unison, by which the horrific, gloomy, and unshapen chaos was changed into regular form and peaceful existence.

There is a sacred word which you have solemnly vowed never to disclose without the assistance of two Royal Arch Companions, or in the body of a Royal Arch Chapter, when acting in the capacity of First Principal. It is a compound word, shows the True and Living God Most High to be the actual, future, eternal, unchangeable, and all-sufficient God, who alone has His beginning in and of Himself, and gives to all others their being; so that He was what He is, is what He was, and shall be both what He was and what He is, from everlasting to everlasting, all creation being dependent on His mighty will.

It may be here observed, that the upper part of the tablet in the pedestal or altar should be a plate of pure gold, and the triangle and circle consequently of the same metal. The selection of these mathematical figures, the circle and triangle, deserves your attention: the latter seems to have been always considered as bearing an allusion to the Deity; for even in the remote times of antiquity names of God, or symbols of divinity, were generally enclosed in a triangular figure. It was in the days of Pythagoras considered as the most sacred of all emblems, and when any oath of more than usual import was to be administered it was given on the triangle, and when so taken none were ever known to have violated it. The ancient Egyptians called it the sacred number Three, or number of perfection; it was an object of worship amongst the ancients, as the great principle of animated existence; they therefore gave it the sacred name of God, as representing the animal, vegetable, and mineral creation; it was also called by the Hebrews, Abohut, which signifies the soul of nature. This sacred delta is usually placed in the midst of squares and circles, indicating the vivifying principle extending its ramifications throughout all created matter; it is therefore denominated the Great All, or *summum bonum*.

The Circle has always been the particular emblem of Eternal power, for as a circle has neither beginning nor ending, it is with great propriety said to be a type of Deity, which alone is without beginning or ending, and from whom all other beings are derived; it also calls to our remembrance the great and awful hereafter or futurity, when we hope to enjoy everlasting life and endless bliss.

Companions, this sublime Degree inspires its members with the most exalted ideas of God, and leads to the exercise of the most pure and sublime piety, and a reverence for the incomprehensible eternal ruler of the Universe, the elemental life, the primordial source of all its principles, the very spring and fountain of all its virtues.

That left me with a lot to think about. This degree had confronted me with more than prayer, it accepted an existence for the soul after death. And I had been given yet another name for the Deity, this one a three-syllable word (which I am obligated not to reveal, although it can be found in any library) which brought together a range of biblical names for God, some of which Christians might consider pagan, but, as I had already seen the first lodge using the symbol of the goddess Freyja, the use of a range of concepts of God did not trouble me. What I considered important about this name was not the words used but the fact it expressed the three aspects of God which I saw from my scientific studies. These are the Relativistic God of the very large, the Quantum God of the very small and the Newtonian God of human size.

The myth of the vaulted shrine, with its impenetrable nature, built to guard the mysteries from profanation and built so that it can survive the wreck of mighty empires and resist the destroying hand of time, spoke to me of something which lies at the centre of the mystery of the intelligence. It is that secret inner attribute which makes it possible for me to carry out a scientific observation and so give reality to a range of possible choices. If I could change reality by my choices, then it was valid to ask if other intelligent entities could do the same thing. I realised that the Great Architect, if real, was certainly intelligent and so could change reality just as I could. Was Masonic prayer offering a way of communicating with such an entity and sharing with it in the implementation of universe-wide plans?

I was not yet sure how I felt about this. Perhaps at last the purpose of Freemasonry had been set out to me? Was it to try to understand the incomprehensible Universe, the purpose of life, and to discover the primordial source of all principles (which to me were the Laws of Physics)? Was Freemasonry's purpose perhaps nothing less than to ask exactly the same questions that I had been taught to ask as a physicist?

Now I knew the question, although I did not yet understand the answer, which had to be the lost key to these secrets. And the question The Craft was posing made sense to my scientist self. I had avoided confronting the issue of my belief, or otherwise, in the dreadful God of the Sunday School until Freemasonry forced me to speak up about my views on the nature of the Supreme Being before it would consent to teach me. Now the system of Freemasonry was making me face up to my belief in materialism. Materialism does not need to ask, 'Why are we here?' It is enough to ask, 'How do we function?' The lecture of the Royal Arch, which I had just listened to, was forcing me to ask, 'Do I have a purpose?' and, if I do, 'What is it?'

The lectures asked if there is something of my innate self which survives death. As a scientist I was well aware that my body is simply a pattern of atoms which are continually changing. There is nothing of the substance which formed my five-year-old self left within me, yet I remain me because of the continuity of my memories and the rejuvenating patterns of my DNA. I knew I was simply a pattern of atoms which could be reconstituted with a completely different set of particles without changing the essence of me. When that pattern ceases to replicate itself I will no longer exist. That will be death for me, and for my memories, which cannot exist without a living brain to house them. Yet the atoms which made my bodily life possible will go on to become parts of other bodies, which will in turn develop their own memories and sense of being an 'I'. Did the memory of my actions, fixed when I observed reality, mean I lived on in their ongoing consequences?

I felt a momentary panic as I realised the implications of this question. I had spent the last fifteen years ignoring it. When confronted with the philosophical implications of wave-particle duality and the effect of the intelligence of the observer on the observed, I had taken refuge in Richard Feynman's advice: 'Shut up and calculate!' Freemasonry was forcing me to admit there are serious philosophical questions about purpose and was offering me fellowship in my search for answers.

When I came to study quantum physics I learned how to predict the outcome of measurements I wanted to make and accepted that, when making that decision, I was interacting with the object of my experiment and determining its outcome. That was how I learned to make solid-state integrated circuits which worked. Perhaps the most startling example of this occurs in a device called a tunnel diode. This is a junction between two different types of semiconducting silicon crystals, one side of which was rich in electrons, the other rich in protons. Where the two crystal regions meet, an energy barrier is created, and when an electron drifts into this boundary region I know its energy value exactly. This makes the electron extremely uncomfortable, because the laws of quantum physics say it is forbidden for me know its exact energy. To avoid breaking those laws the electron is forced to jump to the other side of the junction, into the midst of the protons, without passing through the space in between. In effect, this means that I insist that the electron moves against the natural direction of current flow. This makes the device appear to have a negative resistance (which should be a physical impossibility according to Ohm's law – which says that the voltage across a device should always be positively proportional to the current through it), but I could exploit that negative resistance to build a high-frequency oscillator that I could then use to power a radar set or a UHF radio transmitter. These practical applications proved that the outcomes of measuring the external mysteries of nature and science were subject to something inside me which made decisions about what to measure.

The Royal Arch ceremony, with its teachings on purpose, had given me food for thought. I later discussed its meaning with Douglas Inglesent, a brother Mason and a friend and colleague at Bradford University. He was a member of an esoteric lodge in Leeds which had been founded by a Huddersfield solicitor called Walter Leslie Wilmshurst. Douglas was interested in the deeper meaning of Freemasonry and had been encouraging me to write about The Craft. During our discussions, over lunch in the Senior Refectory, he suggested that I look more closely at the closing ritual of the Fellowcraft Degree, where he hinted there was an important clue.

'Don't forget,' he said, 'whenever Freemasonry talks about shaping a building or a stone for a building, it is talking about building your soul.'

My soul? What did he mean by my soul? Was it the part of me that was able to collapse a wave function and decide the outcome of an experiment? Was it that mysterious thing which forced an electromagnetic ray of light turn into a stream of particles?

'Look at the closing of the Second Degree,' Doug said. 'Just after you have been instructed to study the hidden mysteries of nature and science, you are told to look deep within the darker recesses of your own personal Temple.'

This is the passage he directed me to. It occurs during the closing of the lodge, and consists of a ritual exchange between the Master and his Wardens.

Bro. Junior Warden, in your situation what have you discovered?
A sacred symbol, Worshipful Master.
Bro. Senior Warden. Where is it situated?
In the centre of the building, Worshipful Master.
Bro. Junior Warden. How is it delineated?
By the letter G in the centre of a blazing star, Worshipful Master.
Bro. Senior Warden. To what does that allude?
To God, the Grand Geometrician of the Universe, to whom you, I, and all must submit, Worshipful Master.

This would prove to be a vital clue to discovering exactly where the lost key to the secrets was to be found. But that knowledge would have to wait, because soon after being exalted to the Holy Royal Arch my Masonic life suddenly became even more complicated. I met God, when He hitched a ride in my Jeep.

Personal Reflections

I was finding out the hard way that the practice of Freemasonry is different from the theory. The theory encouraged me to demonstrate brotherly love, relief and truth, but my seemingly endless tussles with UGLE seemed to embody anything but this. I was beginning to wonder if

Hannah and Knight had been right, and that Freemasonry is a worthless and unjust institution, unworthy of serious thought. Yet the warmth and encouragement I found in my Yorkshire and Scottish brethren, and the elected Grand Lodge of Scotland, suggested to me that they knew something about Freemasonry that I had still to discover. Whatever that secret was, I felt that this lost key would be found in the teaching of individual Masters of The Craft who had found it for themselves.

I realised I did want to understand the deep emotions which working the rituals evoked in me. On the advice of knowledgeable and supportive Masonic Masters I set out to work my way through more degrees and found they challenged me scientifically and philosophically. So I decided to embrace the teaching of the individuals. This proved to be a sensible course, because by taking the Degree of the Holy Royal Arch I was finally told the real purpose of Freemasonry. It was to try to understand the incomprehensible Universe and the purpose of life.

My quest was taking on a transcendental aspect I was not entirely comfortable with. But that was soon to change.

8

The Slough of Despond

The Night is Dark, and I am Far from Home

FREEMASONRY WAS NOT proving to be the haven of fellowship and goodwill I had been seeking when I joined. The journey from my first request to enter the lodge as far as the moment when I was initiated into the secret of the hidden vault had been a switchback of highs and lows. The initial excitement of my Initiation had not opened up the steady stream of knowledge I had expected but turned out to be just one of a series of emotional and intellectual trials. And the difficulties of working through the Masonic degrees had been only part of the process.

I had learned a lot about the early history and origins of Freemasonry, but lack of progress in my quest to recover The Craft's lost secrets was making it seem a waste of time. I spent many evenings exploring hypotheses with Bro. Mike Astell, who had been my proposer into Freemasonry and was a continuing sounding board for my developing ideas.

'Has Freemasonry passed its sell-by date? Is it dying?' I asked him, as we sat in the bar at Ryburn Lodge late one Wednesday evening.

'I don't think so,' he said. 'But you must decide for yourself.'

From my first introduction to male Freemasonry Mike encouraged, mentored and assisted me. He had been a bastion of good sense and moderation at times when I felt like denouncing the Grand Lodge as the spawn of the devil. He always tried to help me see issues from their viewpoint, with varying degrees of success. I had spent many late nights at various local lodges talking with him about the finer points of Craft ritual and the historical perspective I was assembling. And when I had invited Chris Knight to rejoin Masonry in Ryburn Lodge, Mike had seconded him.

Mike enabled me to experience the warmth of being a valued member of a supportive lodge and showed me that not everyone agreed with UGLE.

'The Craft is far bigger than any individual brother, no matter what his rank,' he said, when I complained that it should be possible for me to be able to look up to the Grand Lodge for moral guidance.

'I'm encouraged to search for Truth and then punished for sharing what I find,' I complained. 'When I try to emulate Bro. Robert Moray by adopting his mark, I'm slapped down.'

'But you argued your case and they backed down,' he pointed out with a grin.

'True,' I said, 'but only when I threatened them. That shouldn't be necessary.'

He just laughed and suggested we toast The Craft, and for a while I thought that there might still be a way forward. I would always lift my glass to his toast, despite my internal misgivings.

Then the bombshell struck. It began when Mike decided to take early retirement from his teaching job, saying he was finding it too exhausting. For a month or so he thrived on his release from responsibility and the copious free time he could now devote to his Masonry. But one evening he phoned me with bad news.

'I went to see the doctor today,' he began. There was a sadness in his voice which I had never heard before.

'And?' I said.

'I have cancer,' he said.

All the usual platitudes rushed through my head. I thought to speak of treatments, of encouragement, to make positive statements . . . but nothing seemed adequate.

'What's to be done?' I asked.

'Nothing, I suspect,' he said. 'But they're going to operate anyway.'

Within a week he was in Leeds Infirmary, and after his operation I went to visit him. He was sitting up in bed looking drawn.

'Have they fixed you?' I asked, smiling, even though I could see in his eyes that the news was not good.

'It's too advanced,' he said.

'I'm so sorry,' I said, for all that this was a totally inadequate response.

'Let me give you some advice,' he said. 'If you ever think you might be dying and get the chance to ask your doctor to be honest with you about your chances – don't ask.'

'Why?'

'Because it's better to have hope than be certain of despair.'

I would have liked to have been able to offer him a religious hope of a better life after death, but I couldn't, and he wouldn't have believed me if I'd pretended. Instead I pointed out that as a headmaster he had shaped hundreds of children and equipped them for a better life. He had carried out his tasks while it had still been day, and a generation of children would thank him for that.

'They will remember you as long as they live, and as long as you are remembered by those you taught and helped,' I said, 'you are never really gone. Everyone remembers a good teacher.'

He tried to smile, and almost succeeded.

He died soon afterwards. An honour guard from the lodge escorted his coffin into church. At its foot were the square and compasses of a Master Mason. Later, in lodge, we stood together in silence to honour his departed merit, and I felt a great sadness at my loss. I was nurturing a real fear that the Freemasonry I had seen as a youth no longer existed in a form I could access.

I had devoted considerable time and effort to the study of Freemasonry, but Mike's death seemed to emphasise the finality of the dead end I had reached. I felt alone and bereft. I had wanted to understand The Craft and become a part of the warm fellowship I had once glimpsed. But after a decade spent studying ritual, history and vague rumours, trying to make sense of what seemed to be an inchoate muddle, I could no longer see a way forward. Freemasonry had become an important influence in my life, but perhaps its secrets truly were lost.

To make matters worse, the lodge discovered that its rooms at Eaglescliffe needed major repairs which we could not afford. We would have to sell up and move, or increase the lodge fees to such an extent we would drive away our membership. The lodge became a war zone. It split into two camps: those who wanted to move as soon as possible, and those who did not want to move at any price and would rather bankrupt the lodge by trying to patch the leaking roof. Although I wasn't really bothered about where the lodge met, I found I could not escape the arguments. I stopped attending, and, with Mike dead, no one tried to talk me into giving it another try.

Even my intellectual study of The Craft lost its savour. The first two degrees, and the Mark, were full of positivist philosophical attitudes which appealed to my inner scientist, but the Third Degree, the Royal Arch and the Knights Templar degrees were mystical and transcendental, verging on the weird. I couldn't see how to reconcile their conflicting teachings, and I had lost my other trusted confidant when Chris had resigned. The Craft looked like nothing more than a confused hangover from a previous age. Should I cut my losses and get out? I daydreamed about resigning and stopped attending lodge. I was travelling through a valley of Masonic despair.

Moving Forwards

I have often heard it said within my current lodge that when a Candidate is ready a teacher will find him. A teacher was about to find me, but I needed to be struck by a thunderbolt before I was ready to listen.

Douglas, my colleague at Bradford University, belonged to what he described as 'a very special lodge' in Leeds. I discussed my frustrating research into the 'lost secrets' with him over a morning coffee in the Senior Common Room, and he suggested some philosophical reading to help clarify my ideas.

'If you like this approach,' he said, 'then perhaps you might enjoy a visit to Living Stones. We're a lodge who take a deep interest in the transcendental side of The Craft.'

Douglas lent me a book by Dr Giuliano di Bernardo (of the Italian Society of Logic and Philosophy of Sciences). I found two ideas which offered a way forward. The first confirmed the deep emotional appeal of Masonic symbols and how they hint at something deeper than words can convey. Di Bernardo wrote:

> In Freemasonry the symbols express one secret, the initiation secret. There is only one initiation, which consists of seeing oneself as a link in the ideal chain of brotherhood. Anyone incapable of understanding this will always be in the position of the profane who happens to walk into a

Masonic Temple and observes objects familiar to him such as the square, compass, mallet and book, but cannot understand their symbolic meaning. In order to 'read' what he sees, he needs Masonic light, which can only be granted to him through initiation. Only then will he understand the Masonic secret and become part of a new moral dimension, entering into a symbolic union with others to whom the same secret has been revealed. It is this very symbolism that represents the foundation common to all Masonic circles throughout the world. By learning the symbols and allegories which they express, the mason is in a position to understand the supreme principles of Universal Freemasonry, whatever the language and in the simplest way possible. When a mason enters a Temple anywhere in the world he can take part in the initiatic works whatever the language or culture.[67]

The purpose of the ritual, then, is to enable a Mason to understand and learn about symbols to develop more powerful ways of thinking. This idea was reinforced by di Bernardo's statement that:

Through its use of symbols Freemasonry manages to speak, regardless of historical contingencies, a unique and universal language, reflecting the characteristic of immutability. Indeed, once the basic thought has been formulated in symbols, it is transmitted without any substantial modification. In this way a continuity of tradition is guaranteed.[68]

A great puzzle of the mundane history of Freemasonry was that all the symbols, even those used in the most recently introduced degrees, dated right back to the earliest speculative Freemasonry in the Lodge of Aberdeen. This implied that the symbols predated all but the simplest of verbal rituals, and that Freemasonry was tapping into some pre-existing mystical stream of thought. Di Bernardo said that the use and manipulation of the symbols was a key to the deep purpose of The Craft. This gelled with me. I knew that if I couldn't write down an equation for a process, then I did not understand it; the symbols of mathematics explain far more than mere words ever can.

Di Bernardo made a further point about the sense of communal purpose that I was not always able to find in male Freemasonry.

Initiatic work, which is both everlasting and historical, is not carried out by each individual mason, but rather by the community of men who share the same principles and ideals of Freemasonry. In the Temple each mason smoothes his rough stone in collaboration with other masons. Thus each mason is a link in the chain of the Brotherhood: just as a chain cannot exist without its individual links, so the links, taken one by one, cannot form a chain. Both the chain and the single links are therefore essential to each other . . . One cannot be initiated into this secret without the use of symbolism, since to be initiated means embarking upon a practical process of betterment that the candidate can take up only if he understands the symbolic and ritual significance of its stages . . . Thus symbolism as an instrument of expression of the initiatic secret, and the oath as a commitment not to transgress it, represent the line of demarcation between Freemasonry and any other non-initiatic society. If the secret is destructured from its symbolism, the foundations of Freemasonry immediately come to nothing. A Masonic circle without any initiatic foundation is nothing but an ordinary society with philanthropic aims.[69]

He put into words what I had felt at the Lodge of the East Gate so long ago. The benefit of Freemasonry comes from the way a lodge works together and transmits its feelings and insights. Later I came to appreciate that to understand a degree you must experience it. By collaborating with your lodge you grow in understanding. I suddenly understood that this was why I had stalled in my quest. My aims, to understand and practise Freemasonry, no longer coincided with the aims of Ryburn Lodge, which was to progress all its members, in order of date of Initiation, through the various ranks in order to provide a continuous supply of new Worshipful Masters. By falling out with UGLE I had scuppered this process. As di Bernardo had said: 'In the Temple each mason smoothes his rough stone in collaboration with other masons.' Without that necessary collaboration within the lodge my stone was staying stubbornly rough. My progress had stopped.

To move forward, perhaps I ought to visit Douglas's Lodge of Living Stones. If it was as special as he claimed, then I could learn from it. To decide if I wanted to get involved with another lodge, I asked him to tell me about it.

Douglas said his lodge had been founded by a Huddersfield solicitor by the name of Walter Leslie Wilmshurst, who on Saturday 16

December 1927 was installed as its first Master. WLW (as Douglas called him) had been born in 1867 in Sussex. His mother died when he was six years old, and the following year his father remarried. He was sent to Cranleigh School, where he was a star pupil. At the age of 13 he won prizes for his achievements in Acoustics and Inorganic Chemistry, and became president of the school Debating Society; two years later he won more prizes for Inorganic Chemistry and Modern Languages. At the age of 15, after a row with his father, he left school and took a job as an articled clerk in the offices of Moseley and Co. in the mill town of Huddersfield, in the West Riding of Yorkshire.

He became as accomplished a legal student as he had been a scholar of science and language. He passed his law exams by the age of 22 and set up his own practice. His next move was to join the Huddersfield Masonic Lodge, and he was initiated in 1889. He quickly progressed to the rank of Master Mason and in 1891 joined the Royal Arch Chapter of Prosperity in Huddersfield. He married Miss Emma Hanson, the daughter of the family that ran a successful local transport company. Now a settled family man he joined first the Huddersfield Operatic Society and the Huddersfield Choral Society and became President of the Huddersfield Discussion and Debating Society in 1897.

By 1898 he was secretary of the Huddersfield Lodge, and wrote his first Masonic booklet, *The History of the Royal Arch Chapter of Prosperity No. 290.* Then he resigned from both lodge and chapter to join the Lodge of Harmony. This lodge suited him better, and he became Worshipful Master in 1909. He showed an interest in Eastern mysticism and published a pamphlet discussing the conflict between scientific and religious modes of thought for the Huddersfield Discussion Society. Fortunately Douglas had a copy of this and lent it to me. Reading it I began to warm to WLW.

> To understand how Science and Religion express opposite sides of the same fact, the one its near or visible side, the other its remote or invisible side, is our problem. How to find this harmony, how to reconcile the two, is the question to be answered. We have to seek out that ultimate truth which both will avow with absolute sincerity. But, if the two are to be reconciled, the basis of reconciliation must be this deepest, widest, and most certain of all facts – that the Power which the Universe

manifests to us is utterly inscrutable . . . as we scan the scientific horizon and watch the accumulating portents of the times, as we piece together fragments of new knowledge that are coming out of the laboratories, and study the deductions that speculative thought is drawing from that new knowledge, it is possible to venture upon, at all events, some provisional forecast. And what will be the effect of the new disclosure upon religious thought and belief? Will it tend, as the increase of scientific knowledge has hitherto done, to the further rout and destruction of ideals of faith? Or will it tend to restore and strengthen them?[70]

Wilmshurst wrote this just four years after Max Planck discovered that all energy is split into discrete packets, and one year before Albert Einstein discovered light was also packed in granules, and so triggered the quantum revolution.

He continued:

The theories of Science, like the dogmas of Theology, are mere working hypotheses; conclusions drawn from certain premises, and capable of adjustment to the demands of increased knowledge as knowledge itself increases. Gravitation cannot be proved any more than the Incarnation; evolution is an inference as much as the doctrine of the Trinity; the ether a postulate as necessary a basis for scientific thought as the existence of a Deity is a basis essential to the practice of religious thought. In each case certain assumptions are necessary, and these assumptions may differ at different times, but in any case Science is as dogmatic as Theology, and Theology as theoretical as Science; and no finality is practicable for either . . . Hence, there must always be a place for Religion, which under all its forms is distinguished from everything else in that its subject matter is something that passes the sphere of ordinary experience. Science, on the other hand, is simply the higher development of common knowledge. But if both Religion and Science have bases in the reality of things, then between them there must be a fundamental harmony. There cannot be two orders of truth in absolute and everlasting opposition.[71]

As Douglas said, when he gave me this crash course on his lodge's founding Master, 'He was an outstanding scholar of the sciences, but, once he'd been exposed to the influence of Freemasonry, he came to realise there is more to life than materialistic determinism. And that is what the lodge he created still teaches.'

Wilmshurst had said 'There cannot be two orders of truth in absolute and everlasting opposition.' Now I was struggling to match the transcendental messages of parts of Freemasonry with the pragmatic science of other degrees.

'Is Masonic truth different from religious or scientific truth?' I asked.

'You need to experience the aura of Living Stones,' Douglas replied, adding to my puzzlement rather than clarifying it.

On another occasion Douglas told me about a lecture Wilmshurst gave in 1905 entitled 'The Scientific Apprehension of the Superphysical World'.

'You don't accept there is a superphysical world to apprehend,' Douglas said. 'Do you?'

'No I don't,' I replied. 'If I can't solve the equation for the process then it's probably not real.'

Douglas is an academic mechanical engineer and had worked with me for many years at Bradford University. He knew my scientific background and also the issues I had had with UGLE since writing *The Hiram Key* and the other books which followed it. He was teasing me with the possibility that there is a layer of Masonic thinking that I had yet to experience.

'I think you'll enjoy Living Stones,' he said. 'Come along as my guest on the fourth Friday in March, and you'll see something that will rekindle your enthusiasm. And who knows? It might even broaden your view.'

How right he was. After one meeting I was hooked. The more I visited Living Stones the more the mists of despair dispersed, and I was able to break free of the boggy valley of dark confusion and climb towards the distant high hills of secret Masonic knowledge.

Attending a Perfect Lodge

Living Stones meet in Leeds at Castle Grove Masonic Hall. Quite a few other lodges meet there too, and I had given lectures there, so I knew my way. The lodge meets in a side temple. Douglas greeted me in the entrance hall and introduced me to his lodge brethren. We went up to the little temple which held about 40 people. The room was full but there was none of the bustle, mild horseplay and banter which had characterised the pre-meeting chaos of my mother lodge. Everyone sat quietly, as if composing their thoughts, while we waited for the meeting to start. It was more peaceful and calming than I had ever experienced before, and I could sense the unity of purpose which had so impressed me at the Lodge of the East Gate.

This feeling continued throughout the meeting. The Worshipful Master was quietly spoken with a calm, commanding presence. The opening ceremony of the lodge was more complex than anything I had seen before. They performed a ritual of lighting the officers' candles which involved lighting a taper from an eternal flame at the centre of the lodge and carrying the light to its periphery. The Master announced that the lodge was going to work a ritual lecture, known as 'The Book of the Perfect Lodge', which had been devised by their founding Master Bro. W. L. Wilmshurst to explain the purpose of a lodge and how it should work together to fulfil its purpose. Then, to my surprise, the Master announced that we would spend a few minutes in silence whilst we prepared ourselves for the task. I was even more surprised when the lights were lowered, and everyone fell quiet. For two or three minutes we sat in a dark, rich silence. I felt myself getting calmer and more focused. The faint, flickering light of the four candles, one by each of the officers' pedestals and one high in the centre of the lodge, reminded me of the darkness of my Third Degree. As I listened to the deep breathing of the otherwise silent men surrounding me I could hear the rhythm of their respiration moving towards a harmonious concord.

The Master knocked with his gavel, and the light was gently restored. The temple was calm and alert. The Master began by explaining the purpose of the ritual.

'A Lodge is much more than an assembly of persons,' he began.

When duly formed and opened it represents the inner working of each individual Mason who is a part of it. It is purposely designed as to be an object lesson in that most interesting of human studies, the knowledge of yourself. For the true work of The Craft, that of disciplining and perfecting yourself, cannot be undertaken until you know what your self is.

As I listened to the calm and soothing voice of the Master I wondered how this teaching related to what I had understood from the Royal Arch. From that degree I had taken the idea that the objective of Freemasonry was to understand the incomprehensible Universe, the purpose of life, and search for the primordial source of all truth. This lodge was telling me that the object of The Craft was to look inside yourself for answers. I decided to suspend judgment until I understood its teaching better. The atmosphere and feeling which filled the lodge suggested a deep confidence in its own purposes. Freemasonry does not give up its secrets easily, and while I was musing the Master moved on to discuss the soul and its nature.

'Man is a threefold being. He has an outside personality through which he confronts the world. This persona has mysteries of its own that are the subject of worldly science but not part of our Masonic Craft.' He paused, with dramatic emphasis and looked directly at me. 'The science and concern of The Craft is of a higher purpose.'

Douglas had already told me that my reputation had preceded me. Many brethren of Living Stones had read my work and were curious to meet me. At that moment I felt that the Master was speaking directly to me and was about to tell me something important for my quest. I looked back into his eyes and waited.

Man also has an inside personality. A psychological field usually called the Soul, which animates his outside self. It bears the same relation to the outside self as the interior of the Lodge does to its exterior. And it is to the mysteries of this human soul that the science of The Craft is entirely directed.

This was the most direct statement of purpose I had ever heard about Freemasonry: far clearer than the words of the Royal Arch. I listened carefully as I felt on the verge of a breakthrough in understanding. 'The Lodge is formed as a visible model of the Soul to show how, by the discipline of The Craft, this inner part may be developed from a state of chaos to one of order and beauty,' the Master continued.

This reflected the state of my inner part. I felt I was in a state of chaos, on the verge of abandoning English Freemasonry. I had not long since written *The Invisible College*, which involved undertaking a detailed study of Sir Robert Moray and the impact his knowledge of Freemasonry had on the formation of the Royal Society. When I compared the novel and innovative thinking of the Masonic founders of the Royal Society with that of the United Grand Lodge of England, I despaired at what had been lost. But, listening to the Master of Living Stones, I felt hope stirring in the soul I didn't have. Giving myself a quick mental shake, I paid full attention as he continued.

> But beyond man's outward person and inward soul, there abides a third and supreme factor in him, one which affiliates him to the root and source of all being. This is the divine immortal Spirit at his Centre. This Spirit, like the outer body, is also outside the scope of the science of The Craft. But it has its Mysteries. They are known as the Greater Mysteries, and you will never be able to comprehend them until you have assimilated the Lesser Mysteries of the Craftsmen in both theory and personal experience.

He claimed that the path to Masonic Truth was found by journeying into the soul. I remained unsure if I had a soul, but I set my doubts aside as I listened to his explanation of the 'science' of The Craft.

> The Spirit indwells the Soul, just as the Soul suffuses the Body; but only in the Soul which is rectified, purified and worked from the rough ashlar to the perfect cube can the 'Centre' be brought to life and consciousness in the mind.

I visualised my consciousness as this triple-layered onion. It made sense. If there is such a thing as the soul it must be that inner core that makes a measurement possible. It must be the essential part of the observer which forces the haze of probability to collapse into a particular outcome. The nature of the human soul, then, is connected with the puzzle of what scientific measurement means, and what an intelligent observer does when it interacts with the result of its measurement.

The Master of Living Stones continued discoursing on the relationship between the human mind, soul and spirit in the Masonic lecture, and he had my full attention.

> The Lodge is a model of that intermediate psychological field of Soul which lies between the Spirit above and the Material below. The Soul can direct its energies to either of these poles, becoming illumined or

darkened, spiritualised or sensualised, according to its dominant tendencies. The open Lodge exhibits the mind, in its various aspects of intuition, reason, and will, the emotions, and the sense tendencies, as all forming a community of so many Brethren who must not only learn to dwell together in unity, but also to work together for their common good, namely, the regeneration of the whole organism. These different components are shown in the Lodge as separate entities, occupying various appropriate places, according to their corresponding functions in the Soul. Some rule as Officers, others obey and learn. Some are active, others passive; some are fixed in their places, others mobile; for in the constitution of the Soul there are permanent elements and transitory features.

This was a revelation. I was hearing Masonic ideas which, although mystical, complemented my understanding of science. I thought of Richard Feynman, who pointed out that Nature, and hence God, has to be impossible to understand in any rational manner. And when asked why things were as they were, he answered:

The more you see how strangely Nature behaves, the harder it is to make a model that explains how even the simplest phenomena actually work. So theoretical physics has given up on that.[72]

I thought of Frank Tipler, Professor of Mathematical Physics at Tulane University, New Orleans. Tipler studies quantum measurement and the physics of cosmology. He has come to the conclusion that intelligent observation has a key role to play in the development of the cosmos.[73] He is an expert on relativity and points out that it is a theory that covers all space and time, the mathematics making no distinction between the past and the future (and sometimes casting doubt on the sequence in which events happen). He also notes that intelligence can affect the state of the universe by deciding what to measure. He concludes:

The possible presence and actions of intelligent life cannot be ignored in any calculation of the evolution of the far future . . . Its very survival [the future] requires life to impose order on the universe. Taking biology into account allows us to do the physics of the far future.[74]

In Masonic terms Tipler has quantified the Cosmic Plan of the Great Architect which Living Stones was telling me I could access this Plan by allowing my soul to become aware of the mystical Masonic Centre. I realised that Tipler had also written about the effect of the ego.

> We physicists are by and large an extremely arrogant group of scholars. Our arrogance stems from the reductionist perception that ours is the ultimate science, and from our undoubted achievements over the past few centuries. What we promise, we generally deliver. Whatever one thinks of the social significance of the nuclear bomb, there is no doubt that it works. Solar eclipses occur exactly when we predict they will. As one who has spent his entire life as a physicist I not surprisingly share this arrogance.[75]

As I sat in the body of the lodge of Living Stones and looked into my own, freshly admitted soul I saw the arrogance Tipler speaks of. The Master of Living Stones had explained this as allowing my ego to control my spirit. He was trying to convince me that I must subdue or kill my ego if I was to make Masonic progress.

Most physicists are atheists and think spirituality a relic of a pre-scientific world view. They are convinced there in no need for God, and any hypothesis involving interaction with a Cosmic Plan and a Great Architect is by definition nonsense. But, as Einstein showed when he disproved Newton's concept of absolute space and universal time, on occasion we physicists are forced to reconsider long-rejected theories, because our existing understanding no longer matches our improved observations of reality. I knew that I was going to have to revisit the God hypothesis, not from the viewpoint of theology but from that of physics. I felt a momentary panic, until I thought of Enrico Fermi. He helped build the first atomic bomb and won the Nobel Prize for Physics in 1938 for building the first atomic reactor. I had spent years using a mathematical tool called Fermi-Dirac statistics (which he and Paul Dirac jointly discovered) to manipulate electrons. It is not often mentioned that Bro. Fermi was made a Mason at the age of 22, in the Lodge Adriano Lemmi in Rome, long before he made his world-shattering discoveries in physics. If Fermi felt comfortable announcing in open lodge that he put his trust in the Great Architect, why should I not follow his lead in this, just I had done in mathematical reasoning? Now comfortable that I was not alone in exploring this view, I returned my attention to the ceremony.

I became enthralled as each officer in turn explained his role and the function his office played in the corporate enterprise of the lodge. The recitation complete, the Master summed up.

> Brethren, even as we are separate individuals who combine into unity to form a Lodge, each of us is also an entire Lodge in himself. Each a composite assembly of many, not always harmonious, elements, needing to be shaped into due form, and made perfect for the Great Architect's use. By the help of our united work in this Lodge, may it fall to each of us to achieve this task and rule as Masters over ourselves.

He paused and once more looked me in the eye, seeming to see deep into the confusion of my thoughts.

> May each Brother learn how to tyle the door of his Soul, so that none but Masonic elements are present in it, and then to open the Perfect Lodge of his own being to welcome the Great Architect at his Centre and so qualify himself for those Greater Mysteries for which the lesser ones of our Craft are a necessary preparative.

The ritual complete, the Master called again for darkness and silence. In that deep-breathing, dark contemplation I felt the urges of my scientific training preparing to counter the emotionally charged vision of purpose which I had just seen. I needed to think these ideas through in my own time.

Later at the meal, the Master mentioned that no visitor was ever invited twice. 'If you feel you wish to attend you may come. If you feel we have nothing to interest you then you will not wish to come again. The choice is yours.'

I was going to come to this lodge again. I was still unsure if I had a soul but I was prepared to consider that I might, and see if I could learn more about it.

Over lunch in the Senior Refectory at Bradford University a few days later I asked Douglas about 'The Book of the Perfect Lodge'.

'It was written by Wilmshurst in 1928,' he said. 'It was the culmination of his ideas that the spirit is a divine spark which can communicate directly with the Great Architect, and the job of a Mason is to train his soul to communicate with his divine spark.'

I asked if Douglas had any other writings by Wilmshurst showing how he had come to the view expressed in the Perfect Lodge. He pointed me to a paper by Wilmshurst called 'The Scientific Apprehension of the Superphysical World'. In it WLW had written:

> At the fiat of some mighty energy working in the invisible, the process of creation of the earth and stellar worlds have become manifest; at the withdrawal of that fiat they would cease to be; a momentary relaxation of the will which holds the objective universe together would cause it instantly to dematerialise.
>
> The mechanical laws of the ether are not yet known; something of its potentialities is obvious from the phenomena of light and of the waves of electro-magnetic force artificially generated for the purposes of wireless telegraphy, which travel at the same rate as light, but differ from light-waves in length and their ability to produce vision. But what of its potentialities of which we are ignorant? When its laws come to be understood and it becomes possible to link up the further knowledge thence derived with that of psycho-physics, there will doubtless be at our disposal an intelligible and demonstrable explanation of those complex interactions of mind and matter.[76]

When I read this I was a little disturbed that WLW seemed to suggest that the Great Architect was some sort of Cosmic Mind which sustained creation by continuously willing it into existence. I wasn't sure I could accept that idea. But I decided to read more of his writing to see what else he had to say. Douglas showed me other Masonic papers written by WLW, one of which said:

> Both Freemasonry and religion deal with the same subject and lead to the same goal, but in the approach to it there is a marked difference. If we translate our philosophical reasoning into familiar religious terms we recognise that a transcendental condition of consciousness is within you. The Mason learns this as a science, and so has an exact scientific understanding of truths about which the non-initiate has but shadowy notions; he knows what others must only conjecture . . . The text of our rituals and lectures discloses a strange combination of two different and

easily distinguishable levels of teaching; a lower and common-place level which is simple and intelligible to everyone; and a higher and esoteric level relating to matters of advanced philosophic wisdom.[77]

WLW had spelt out the conflict between the two messages I had found in the rituals of The Craft. The ritual had two strands: a practical teaching and a transcendental message. But I still could not see how they might be reconciled.

When I asked, Douglas told me that WLW had taught that the gap was bridged using ritual meditation to induce a state of mind called 'cosmic consciousness'. In a paper published in the *Occult Review* in March 1924 WLW described this as:

> An inner vision which transcends sight as far as sight transcends touch, and a consciousness in which the contrast between the ego and the external world and the distinction between subject and object fall away.[78]

In a way it was fortunate that I had a vague awareness of this state before I experienced it. When it strikes the unprepared it can induce visions to turn its subjects into religious fanatics.

Lightning Strikes the Prepared Mind

Walter Wilmshurst taught that the purpose of the Third Degree was to bring alive a divine spark which can only be accessed when you force your chattering ego to become quiet. He called this event 'the death of the ego'.

The philosopher William James also described this state, calling it *Samadhi*,[79] but gave a warning to anyone who casually toys with this emotional state:

> One may stumble into superconsciousness sporadically, without previous discipline, but it is then impure. The test of its purity, like our test of religion's value, is empirical: its fruits must be good for life. When a man comes out of *Samadhi* . . . he remains 'enlightened', a sage, a prophet, a saint, his whole character changed, his life changed, illumined.[80]

I never expected to experience it. I had read that 'awareness of the Centre' was a form of Masonic superconsciousness, but whether this amounted to 'previous discipline' I am not sure. The experience did not make me religious, but it did make me aware that the sensations religious mystics report are real.

The Masonic mystery of the Centre became real for me during a moment of ecstatic insight during a thunderstorm.

It all began as I was driving over a high hill in West Yorkshire towards a threatening storm cloud. It was late afternoon in early autumn as my Jeep Cherokee climbed out of Bradford on the winding rural road towards the high peak of Queensbury. I was listening to the Steve Wright Show on Radio 2. The skies to the west were dark and threatening. Black clouds shrouded the hilltop, and the reflected warm light from the surrounding lowlands created a scene that reminded me of a Van Gogh painting, done on a day when the flocks of crows blocked the cornfield skies and obscured the sun.

I remember thinking, There's going to be one hell of storm coming as my Jeep twisted and turned up the narrow road, between the darkening fields.

The air felt heavy and oppressive, and I shivered as I felt the deepening chill. I reached down and turned the heating up, but it made little difference because the cold was seeping into my mind not my body. The dark clouds above were swooping down to meet me like a great black maw as the road climbed the hillside. I was beginning to feel an unfocused uneasiness – nothing in particular, just a general nervousness, as though I were in the pervading presence of an unseen and diffuse threat. I felt the hairs on my body standing up, starting with the hairs on the backs of my hands, and a slight tingling spreading up my arms. Then the hairs on the back of my neck quivered and shook with a life of their own. I felt as if some fearsome, all-powerful presence was staring at me, measuring my position, ready to jump onto me and tear at my flesh – and I wanted to run away before it caught hold of me. Whatever it was had somehow got into the back of my Jeep; my rational mind knew this was not possible, but my emotions told me it was real. The sky was now so dark that I needed to put the headlights on, but I was afraid to move my hand in that awesome presence. I was torn between the need to look back and reassure myself that I was alone in the Jeep and a deep fear that, if I did so, I would see a manifestation so dreadful I would be driven mad. I knew I could not continue to drive in this state, so pulled the car to the side of the road. The voice on the radio was still chattering away – a cheery lifeline from a different, safer world I had left far behind and might never get back to.

Once I had stopped the Jeep I knew I must force myself to turn and face the source of the fear and dread which was still making the hairs on my neck quiver. Visions of the God of Job whirling out of a desert storm to confront my scientific blasphemy swirled around my mind and threatened to swamp my reason. It took an enormous effort of will to turn around and face whatever it was – I was quite sure I was about to see something dreadful.

But the back of the Jeep was empty. The threatening, vengeful God-presence disappeared as I turned to confront it. It was replaced by a new feeling, a very different one. I was at the centre of a rose-coloured cloud of celestial fire which was spreading outwards. As it swept outwards it took my mind with it. It filled the Jeep and spilled out over onto the hillside. It filled the land and spread up into the sky. It filled the solar system and continued to grow until I could see and feel the whole of the cosmos swirling in beauty and splendour about me. I lost all sense of time and experienced the awe of an astronomer given access to the whole beauty of creation. My mind felt too small to hold the splendour of what I was seeing, and I could feel my reason exploding outwards as it tried to take in all the wonders on display. I felt a deep joy in the glory of creation.

How long that moment lasted I can never be sure. Subjectively it seemed endless; it felt outside of time. But I was torn away from that joyous state, back into my parked Jeep by a terrifying experience. A flash of unbearably bright light washed through the cab, and I realised it was a flash of lightning, but what made it so frightening was that I heard the light 'zizzing' as it ripped through the air.

I know light is silent: it never makes a 'zizzing' sound. So to hear light moving was scary. But my scientific training quickly kicked in, and I made careful notes about my perceptions immediately after the experience, while it was fresh in my memory. I reconstructed this sequence from those notes and recorded this analysis of what had happened.

First I felt a period of ecstatic insight, in which I sensed my mind expand to become at one with all creation; next I heard the 'zizzing', and this coincided with the pulse of light from the electrical discharge of the lightning; then I heard the electromagnetic impulse of the strike, via the radio speakers; and finally I heard the sound of the thunder, caused by the wave-front of displaced air reaching my ears. The interval between the 'zizzing' and the light pulse had been almost impossible to separate: it had felt as if I had heard electrons being dragged upwards from the Earth to neutralise the positively charged thunderclouds as the insulation of the air broke down. The perceived volume of the 'zizz' had increased in time with the intensity of the light, while I had not 'heard' the noise from the radio until the 'zizz' had finished.

There was ample time for me to react, and start to count, before the sound wave hit me, so what ever caused the 'zizz' travelled as fast as light. It had to be an electric field which directly stimulated my audio nerve so that I interpreted it as a sound. The fact I heard the zizzing before I saw the light tells me it was caused by the collapse of the electric charge build-up on the hilltop (I must have been close to the centre of the charge build-up that caused the strike). As the atmosphere ionised during the lightning spark this electric field rapidly drained away, which caused the voltage fall that I heard as a zizz. The fact that the sound seemed to come from about five degrees left of straight ahead implied that my left audio nerve had processed the signal marginally faster than my right, or the electric field had been delayed or attenuated as it passed through my head. I don't think there is much in my head to absorb and attenuate an electric wave front, but the sheathing of the axon of the audio nerve would offer a capacitive load to the fast-changing electric pulse. This could have caused a differential rise time between the two nerves, so creating the very slight time delay which my brain had interpreted as a slightly off-centre positioning.[81] It would also account for the way the volume of the 'sound' seemed to rise and fall.[82]

I now understand that an electrical overload of my brain caused my mystical episode. It was fortunate that I was listening to the radio when it happened, as the noises from the radio gave me the additional data to analyse the event rationally. Without that supporting data I could easily have been convinced that the God of my childhood had risen up, confronted me and then given me a vision of His creation. The timing of the light, radio pulses and sound waves, however, allowed me to reconstruct what had really happened, but, from my Masonic reading, I recognised it as the target state of Masonic awareness that Wilmshurst had studied. I later found that brain scan studies have shown that the all-consuming synchrony of neurons I had experienced is the state William James calls *Samadhi*. [83] He used the term to describe a mystical state which he had observed in occult or religious situations. I now knew it could also be a mental reaction to a physical stimulus.

I was lucky to fall accidentally into the mental state that is the focus of the Lodge of Living Stones without spending years in hopeless striving. It was wonderful but it was a real phenomenon, caused by the exposure of my brain to an intense electrical field and the triggering of countless numbers of neurons in synchrony. Yet it felt subjectively real. I experienced the presence of the Great Architect. I might have dismissed it as a purely physical phenomenon had I not been alerted to the fact that the brethren of Living Stones thought it a valuable thing to strive for. They later told me that this state of mind can take many years to achieve through focused meditation.

I was lucky in two ways. Firstly I felt the full nature of the experience and was able to record and appreciate it, and secondly it happened in circumstances which made it possible for me to analyse and understand what had caused it, and to appreciate that it was a consequence of physical processes not magical miracles. But it still felt as though I had communicated with something far bigger than me.

Could The Craft teach me to access that sense of connection with something so much greater than myself without the stimulus of a strong electric field? That remained to be seen, but I now realised that to learn more I needed to join the Lodge of Living Stones and train my soul so I could return to that mysterious Centre I had encountered in a Jeep in Yorkshire.

Personal Reflections

At my lowest ebb during my quest to understand the lost purpose of Freemasonry I had been ready to abandon The Craft and concentrate on science. I had decided that science was the only way to approach the big questions of life, like 'What is reality?' and 'Why am I part of it?' My extensive researches into the history of Freemasonry had not given me any insight into its purposes. And my attempts to understand it and explain it to my brethren had met with responses ranging from support and offers of assistance and research material (from the officials of the Grand Lodge of Scotland and their members) to downright hostility from the United Grand Lodge of England.

The insights and consolations of science had replaced the simple and brutal religion of my childhood as a basis for understanding the world, and I hoped that Freemasonry's principles of Brotherly Love, Relief and Truth might provide a more logical and supportive alternative to that religion. Wilmshurst had written a ritual lecture which summed up the purpose of a lodge and the meaning of Masonry. Known as 'The Book of the Perfect Lodge', it was read aloud in lodge at the vernal equinox. Symbolically this is the beginning of the new astronomical year and symbolises the rebirth of the lodge after the death of Installation, when all the officers are replaced. The ritual spoke of a great mystery known as the Centre, which could not described in words, but had to be experienced.

Wilmshurst described the lodge as a composite mind formed by each brother contributing an element of understanding to the whole, so that the group mind of the perfect lodge was greater than any individual member. He taught that the Perfect Lodge, spaced around the circumference of the mysterious Centre, should be able to share its inspirational vision of the Centre with all its members.

I was at first sceptical of this approach, suspecting that Wilmshurst's deeply held Christian beliefs had made him think that way. He wrote of a state of 'cosmic consciousness' that was the objective of every Mason. I suspected this state of mind was simply a delusion brought on by desire. Then I experienced it for myself, alongside a bolt of lightning, and I understood what inspired him. Awareness of the Centre is a physical state of mind and offers subjective experience of something transcendental at that mysterious Centre.

But what was it? I felt as if I had met *something* during that frightening moment just before the lightning strike, but my brain had not been functioning normally. The intense electrical field had swamped the normal perception systems of my brain. I would need to open my mind to the esoteric teaching of Wilmshurst's lodge if I wanted to rediscover what The Craft had lost. And I would have to revisit what my Sunday School teachers had called 'my immortal soul'. As immortal means 'not subject to death' I saw difficulties in absorbing the concept into my scientific world view, but with the dictionary definition of the soul being 'the actuating cause of an individual life' I thought there might be room for some accommodation.

I was puzzling over these questions when I met my Guide.

9

Questioning My Soul

A Whiff of the Promised Secret

At last I found a Master of The Craft who was aware of the lost secrets and prepared to teach me. I remain in regular touch with this brother but he would prefer me not to name him, so I shall refer to him only as my Guide.

I met my Guide soon after Douglas had invited me to the Lodge of Living Stones to see the ceremony of reading 'The Book of the Perfect Lodge', and he impressed me with his calm presence and the effortless way he worked the ritual. He later explained to me that the reason for learning the ritual so carefully is to concentrate on the emotional impact of its delivery to the lodge. He likened it to playing a piano piece: first you learn the notes, then you practise the fingering and rhythm, but only when playing the notes has become automatic can you perform the piece and draw out its beauty. The words of the ritual are the notes, but only when you know them so well that they seem to be your own words can you deliver them in a way which helps the lodge focus on their import. I did not realise why his ritual spoke so clearly to me when I first heard him, but I did know that I was held spellbound as the meaning of the words became clear for the first time. In fact the words seemed to disappear, so that only the beautiful meaning remained. I knew I could learn from this brother, and I sought him out after the meetings in order to question him. I wanted to know more about the mystery of the soul.

Mysteries are different from secrets. Secrets are known information which can be revealed if the holder chooses. Mysteries are things that are difficult to comprehend but can be understood with effort and guidance. To uncover and understand these mysteries my Guide warned me that I would have to work and study. He explained that 'the Soul suffuses the Body; but only in the Soul which is rectified, purified and worked from the rough ashlar to the perfect cube can the Centre be brought to life and consciousness in the mind'. That was my challenge.

We have seen how Freemasonry grew out of the insight of Bros Menzies and Stuart that certain symbols, when displayed in public, bring about changes in people's minds and attitudes. They were probably making use of a pre-existing tradition but, by developing a sensitivity to symbols and an explanatory mythical tradition based in ritual re-enactment, they discovered how to pass on this knowledge to their Apprentices, their successors and perhaps to me.

The Craft's mythical history taps into a source of practical knowledge. My Guide told me that the real purpose of The Craft is to provide spiritual training for the soul. But where was I to find the mental artefact that this source of spiritual knowledge is intended to improve? He suggested that I begin my search by looking at others' characterisations of a soul.

I soon found there is no shortage of definitions but they seem to conflict. Here are three typical ones.

The Catholic Encyclopedia defines the soul as:

> the ultimate internal principle by which we think, feel, and will, and by which our bodies are animated. The term 'mind' usually denotes this principle as the subject of our conscious states, while 'soul' denotes the source of our vegetative activities as well. That our vital activities proceed from a principle capable of subsisting in itself is the thesis of the substantiality of the soul: that this principle is not itself composite, extended, corporeal, or essentially and intrinsically dependent on the body, is the doctrine of spirituality.[84]

Philosopher Bertrand Russell defines the soul differently:

> The most essential characteristic of mind is memory, and there is no reason whatever to suppose that the memory associated with a given person survives that person's death. Indeed there is every reason to think the opposite, for memory is clearly connected with a certain kind of brain structure, and since this structure decays at death, there is every reason to suppose that memory also must cease.[85]

Biologist Richard Dawkins sides with Russell, saying:

> Human thoughts and emotions emerge from exceedingly complex interconnections of physical entities within the brain. An atheist in this sense of a philosophical naturalist is somebody who believes there is nothing beyond the natural, physical world, no supernatural creative intelligence lurking behind the observable universe, no soul that outlasts the body and no miracles − except in the sense of natural phenomena that we don't yet understand.[86]

This introduces the idea that the soul might be a means of accessing some natural phenomena that we don't yet understand. Sir Fred Hoyle, the cosmologist who discovered how carbon is created within stars, suggested how to approach this issue.

> An examination of the origins of the major religions will show that in spite of contradictions their tenets spring from a common aim: the identification of Man with the Universe. To be sure this aim is a little difficult to discover in contemporary religions. There is a reason for this. Contemporary religion is based on the religious teachings of bygone eras, often teachings that are very much older than the adherents of the modern religions realise, so old indeed that they belong to days when men understood comparatively little either about themselves or about the Universe . . . serious mistakes were made, mistakes that cannot survive a modern scrutiny by the rationally minded. But instead of recognising this, contemporary religion has preferred to stick to the letter, rather than to the spirit, of the old beliefs. Faced then with outrageous contradictions it has become necessary to be increasingly vague about the meanings of the labels that describe the religious concepts . . . it seems far more profitable to attempt to rebuild our ideas of Man's relation to the Universe from a new start, putting aside the older beliefs until some rational basis for discussing them has been achieved.[87]

I was not surprised to see the Catholic definition of the soul at odds with the philosophical and scientific ideas of Russell and Dawkins. But all three are only statements of faith. (I categorise both Russell and Dawkins as religious believers, as they are proselytising atheists.) They stem from different faiths and represent different expectations, but none is supported by any appeal to observation. Perhaps Richard Dawkins will argue that there is no need to base his beliefs in observation, logic is enough, but as a physicist I know that the logic of Aristotle had to be replaced by the observations of Newton before real progress could be made.

All three of these definitions of the soul are unprovable assertions. Only Hoyle offers an open-minded scientific way forward when he suggests we rebuild our ideas of humanity's relation to the Universe from a new start. Hoyle is a benign agnostic who rules nothing out, but pushes for a rational basis for any spiritual belief. Freemasonry may have stumbled upon just such a rational basis, and I was now ready to explore the possibilities it had opened up.

Like the major religions Freemasonry makes unprovable assertions that are based on concepts which are over five hundred years old and predate the birth of modern science. My first clue came from a brother of Living Stones, Tony Baker, who, whilst giving a toast to our visitors, adapted an old story to explain the purpose of the lodge.

> When the ancient gods met in council to decide where to hide the secret of the meaning and purpose of the cosmos they were concerned that mankind would discover it and misuse it. They thought long and hard about where to conceal it. The first suggestion was to hide it on a high mountain. But the objection was made that humans were attracted to high places, and, no matter how high the hill on which it was hidden, humans would climb it and discover the secret. Another of the council members suggested that the great secret should be hidden in the depths of the ocean. But the objection was made that humans were inquisitive and ingenious creatures and would in time explore the depths of the sea and discover the secret. Then the oldest and wisest of the gods spoke. 'Hide it within the human soul. That is the last place mankind will think to look. So it will remain hidden except from those who are worthy of being trusted to know it.'

In 'The Book of the Perfect Lodge' Walter Wilmshurst took these thoughts much further. This is what I learned from taking part in his ceremony.

- At the centre of my soul there is a divine spark that links me to the Great Architect of the Universe.

- I am a multi-layered being. I have an emotional and physical body, a mind with intellectual abilities, a soul which is that essential part of myself which I call 'I', and a spirit to contain that divine spark.
- I can train my soul to commune with the Great Architect, to contact the centre which spawned my individual divine spark and from it learn to understand the Great Plan of the Universe and my role in it, and so give my life purpose and direction.

I became so uncomfortable with the concept of a soul that I wrote a little book called *The Secret Science of Masonic Initiation*, in which I tried to understand how to train it to be aware of the Centre. But I had to include a reservation that I have italicised below.

> Freemasonry offers a system of training the soul. Whether or not you believe in the concept of a soul, the Masonic system works and improves your life. To benefit from Masonic Initiation you must be prepared to accept that you can train your soul (*whatever that might be*) and that if you do so you will benefit. *But questions about the nature of the soul must wait for another time and another place.*[88]

Since becoming a member of Living Stones, I accept that I can train my soul – but to show my soul is real I must go further, as Wilmshurst did.

Now is the time, and this is the place, to tell the story of the search for my soul and the nature of the Great Architect with which it is intimately entangled. I now had a Guide, who was as scientifically qualified as I was, encouraging me to think the scientifically unthinkable. But where was I to start? Fred Hoyle's advice to seek a rational basis for discussing humanity's relation to the Universe seemed the most logical place to begin.

The Random Discipline of Physics

Freemasonry says it is based on three Grand Principles – Brotherly Love, Relief, and Truth. But the search for Truth is often neglected. Masonic Truth tells of a Great Architect at the Centre of Creation, a Divine Spark which resides in the soul of each Freemason, and a Divine Plan for creation which every Freemason can become a part of. After my mystical experience I was prepared to consider that this Great Architect might be a natural phenomenon that we don't yet understand.

Fred Hoyle recognised the human need to search for a Divine Plan.

> Religion if it has any sensible meaning does not consist in holding beliefs by 'faith' that are denied by rational thought . . . if it is not to be pernicious nonsense, it must be based on rational thinking . . . let us approach the subject from an unexpected direction . . . Imagine that you have all the things that you would like, and that you have achieved all your ambitions. What then? A very dull life indeed . . . It is clear then that an 'end' in life, or better still many such 'ends,' are important to the individual . . . The sense of purpose in the life of an individual seems incomplete unless the whole community in which he lives possesses a common sense of purpose.[89]

Freemasonry meets this criterion, providing a common sense of purpose as a basis for a rational set of spiritual beliefs, but this does not prove any Masonic Truth. The possibility of it being by itself nothing more than an irrational comfort blanket remains.

Whilst wrestling with this idea I revisited the work of another of my scientific heroes, Paul Dirac. Dirac, along with Bro. Enrico Fermi, discovered mathematical processes which underpin the solid-state physics that I studied as a young postgraduate scientist. He also predicted the existence of anti-matter many years before it was discovered, let alone before it was regularly used in everyday medical technology.[90] I knew his work because when I returned to Salford University to study for a PhD under Mike Hampshire, Dirac's 'band theory' of semiconductors became the focus of my working hours for three full years.

As a PhD student I learned many different skills. I built all my own vacuum systems and remote handling equipment. I learned how to shape and fabricate metals into working machines. I learned how to build high-powered electronic switching units.[91] In order to process large amounts of data I learned how to program mainframe computers and produce both text and graphs. But most of all I learned the theory of how an electron behaves within semiconducting crystals. And that is how I came to know the theories of Paul Dirac.

The quantum world he described was magical *yet useful*. And he forced me to consider the mystery of the human mind. I have touched on his view that all the Newtonian and Relavatistic physics I had studied previously made a basic assumption that my material body, and the mind it gave life to, obeyed the same laws of physics as every other object in the universe. But now I entered a different quantum world where external reality was a complicated wave function of possible outcomes and it only changed into a real event when a conscious observer made an observation. And the intent of that conscious observer could change the outcome.

This was a useful thing to be able to do when I wanted to bombard a thin film of semiconductor with photons of light and turn photons into moving electrons or create a tunnel diode. But the implications of the power of the mind over matter was staggering. Simple organisms cannot reduce wave functions. Only conscious observers (i.e. scientists) above some ill-defined level of complexity are able to do this trick.[92]

As I carried out more measurements I knew the effect was real. But I still had a sense of how outrageous its reality was. The big question that presented itself to me was this. How had reality ever come to be established at all under such weird conditions?

There is a basic idea about the creation of matter which underpins all theories of the origin of the universe. It is immaterial whether the universe is in an eternally expanding steady state or started with a big bang. The quantum theory which I had been trained to apply to semiconductor devices insisted that matter existed because of the random emergence of entangled groups of particles which popped out of the vacuum because of a mechanism known as the Uncertainty Principle. This law decrees that it is not possible to know both the exact energy and the exact position of anything, not even a point of nothingness. There is always a finite probability that such a point of nothingness will be forced to break down into particles of matter which fly off somewhere else to avoid the observer knowing too much about them. This is a recipe for complete chaos. And yet I knew from observation that something had structured this primeval chaotic matter into organised systems which gave rise to conscious observers, at least once in the history of the cosmos. Bro. Enrico Fermi had summed up this mystery clearly when he asked, 'Why is there something rather than nothing?' Quantum theory told me that the existence of Fermi's 'something' was the result of an observation creating a distinct history for that 'something' out of the vast range of calculable probabilities which existed side by side before the observation was made.

There was no escaping the implication of quantum mechanics that, throughout much of the universe, and through all the time before life began, there had to be conscious observers. How else could the wave function of an early lifeless universe become reduced to one containing life?

Did it mean that all the possibilities inherent in the development of the universe's wave function since the beginning of time had persisted, unresolved, until the first conscious observers appeared by accident? I couldn't help wondering who, or what, did the necessary observations to create the first observers?

Choosing a Steady Option

When I was a student in the late 1960s there were two conflicting views about the origin of the universe, and both were scientifically respectable. One said that the universe had always existed, and that new matter was continually being created within strange stellar objects called quasars. The alternative view was that the cosmos had been created at a fixed moment in time, some 10 billion years earlier. George Gamow put forward the fixed moment of creation, whilst Fred Hoyle supported the steady state view.

Gamow's moment of creation idea (which Hoyle scathingly referred to as 'The Big Bang theory') did not address what carried out the necessary quantum observations to bring about the emergence of intelligent observers. The Steady State model sidestepped the problem, because, if the cosmos had always existed, then there would always have been observers somewhere to collapse wave functions.

Gamow's theory, taken in combination with quantum theory, implied a definite moment of unique creation. However, it seemed to me that such a theory could not avoid the implication of a possible creator. The quantum aspect implies that an observer had to collapse the wave function into its present form. If God was that primeval observer responsible for the reduction of the original wave function which caused things, then the intent of the observation required it to cause other conscious observers to exist. This implied that God must have intended these other observers and what they would later measure. As a postgraduate student I was disturbed because it seemed to me that a direct consequence of Gamow's fixed moment of creation idea was that it implied a God who willed the moment of creation and then observed its early wave function, causing it to collapse into a form to ensure the evolution of human consciousness.

Since leaving Heys Road School I had almost forgotten about my Sunday School God who roared out of the desert to challenge Job for daring to question him. But, just as I was approaching my ambition of becoming a scientist, His shade had come back to haunt me. Gamow was offering a bizarre scenario by which I could explain the quantum coupling coefficient which had the arbitrary value of 137.05587.[93]

There was no theory to explain why it should be this number, and I only know its value because it has been measured many times. If Gamow was right, then the explanation for it being this number value was that it was a quite arbitrary decision taken by God one morning when Mrs God was nagging Him at breakfast. When He collapsed the initial wave function of the universe He set the quantum coupling coefficient to a very peculiar numerical quantity. My problem was that I could measure it over and over again, and I could use it to predict outcomes of things like microchip manufacture, but I had absolutely no idea why it couldn't be 138, or even a nice, round 140. If God intended to observe that value when He triggered the big bang, then there He was again roaring out of the desert to tell me not to question His decisions.

I put aside my philosophical misgivings and concentrated on making devices which forced electrons to do what I wanted them to. (After first graduating I had worked at Ferranti Semiconductors in Wythenshawe, South Manchester, before returning to Salford to work for a PhD. After getting my PhD I returned to Ferranti to apply my knowledge of quantum mechanics first to power transistors and later to integrated circuits and early microcomputers.)

Now, though, with the three principles of Wilmshurst's 'Book of the Perfect Lodge' bubbling around my mind I remembered something that might help. Paul Dirac, the father of modern solid-state physics and the inspiration for string theory, had also developed a methodology for studying the existence of God.

He had followed in the footsteps of Newton to become Lucasian Professor of Mathematics at Cambridge and shared the Nobel Prize in Physics with Erwin Schrödinger in 1933. This entitled him to attend the annual Lindau Nobel Laureate meetings, a forum for Nobel Prize winners and young researchers to exchange ideas.

When I was in the second year of my PhD, Dirac posed the controversial question, 'Is there a God?' Then, he had laid down a methodology to answer the question:

> To test the God hypothesis a physicist should build two models of the universe, one of which contains God and one which does not. He should then seek to find clear distinctions between the two models before comparing the results to the actual universe to see to which class it belongs to.[94]

Dirac thought the case for the God was unproven. But if future scientists showed the creation of life was overwhelmingly unlikely, then he would accept that as evidence for the existence of a God.[95] In the light of the current orthodoxy of the Big Bang hypothesis and the ideas of the Perfect Lodge, my Guide suggested I revisit Dirac's suggestion.

Sir Fred Hoyle was Paul Dirac's research student. Hoyle's most prestigious scientific achievement, apart from the Steady State theory, was to predict how the carbon atom, a vital building block of life, is created in the normal nuclear processes of any average-sized star. This unexpected result, later tested by experiment, revealed the cosmic process which made life possible.[96]

Inspired by Dirac's thoughts on testing for God, Hoyle investigated the role of chance in evolution. A year before Dirac's death in 1984 Hoyle published an analysis of the statistical probability of life originating by chance in the real universe.[97] Five years later his mathematical study of the neo-Darwinian theory of evolution led him to propose there might be a purpose and plan behind the spread of carbon-based life. The antagonism of the neo-atheists stopped him publishing this work until two years before his death.[98] He continues to draw posthumous criticism from the neo-Darwinians, in the form of Richard Dawkins, who damns him with faint praise in the *Oxford Book of Modern Science Writing*:

Fred Hoyle was a distinguished astrophysicist and cosmologist whose uncompromisingly blunt Yorkshire character – or so I felt – found expression in the heroes of all his science fiction novels . . . The passage I have chosen is from *Man in the Universe* and is an example of the insight that a physical scientist can bring to biology. *It was written before Hoyle began the perverse campaign of his old age, against all aspects of Darwinism.*[99] [Italics mine]

Hoyle's crime was to demonstrate that Dawkins's biology lacks mathematical rigour and can lead to uncritical acceptance of improbable events.

Biological knowledge . . . has no proper foundation . . . Just as our physical knowledge is expressible in mathematical form, so must biological knowledge if it is ever to have a real impact on society. Here I can only give a few hints of what might be possible.[100]

To the gentle amusement of my Guide I reported Hoyle's conclusion that the emergence of intelligent life in a 14-billion-year-old universe is overwhelmingly unlikely without the intervention of intelligent action. But, I argued, a plan might not be needed if the universe is much older than the Big Bang theory implies. My Guide simply smiled and encouraged me to meditate about the issue.

Hoyle's analysis threw me back to my philosophical problems with Gamow's fixed-moment-of-creation hypothesis. Not only did it require a God to be the Great Primeval Observer, it also needed Him to be the Master Genetic Engineer who drew up the blueprint for DNA. Was this evidence for the existence of the Great Architect of the Universe? Did it vindicate Wilmshurst's claims? I wasn't yet prepared to admit that, but I had to review the evidence.

'You think it through and then come back to discuss it,' my Guide said. 'You won't believe me because I speak from personal awareness, not mathematical proof.'

How could I resist such a challenge?

The Litmus Test for God

Because biologists know little about cosmology or the evolution of solar systems, they fail to take physics into consideration. Hoyle said:

> As early as 3600 million years BP, possibly as early as 3800 million years BP, many of the biological problems of crucial consequences to all life had been solved. If life originated earlier than this in the Universe at large, there is of course no difficulty in seeing how the biochemical complexities of life could have been imported onto the Earth from the moment the Earth could first sustain life. But if one attempts to follow orthodox biology, according to which life originated here on Earth, the severe problem arises of how to explain the origin in a narrow window situated near 3800 million years BP.[101]

For DNA-based life to evolve in a geologically short time poses great difficulty for Charles Darwin's 'little warm pond' theory, which Richard Dawkins states as an accepted fact in *The God Delusion*.

It *is* an accepted fact that all the necessary elements were available. It is also an accepted fact that if those elements are brought together in the correct sequence they can make a living creature, as Craig Venter has shown by making an artificial life form.[102] But Dr Venter is an intelligent genetic engineer working to a plan to create his artificial microbe. How likely are these basic elements to come together in the wild to form DNA by happy accident?

The basic elements need to combine into proteins and enzymes. Proteins are chains of amino acids, but only a few combinations cause life. Many naturally occurring amino acids are found, but only twenty of them figure in the process of life.

The amino acids that underpin life are tangled chains of hydrogen, carbon, oxygen, sulphur and nitrogen atoms. There are at least four hundred ways in which these atoms can link together. The individual amino acid molecules are coiled and knotted together so that additional chemical bonds form to hold them together. A protein consists of strings of particular amino acids linked together in a linear chain which folds into a globular shape. Enzymes are proteins that increase the rates of chemical reactions at low temperatures and make life function.[103]

The issue for neo-Darwinists is, How did this complex process of highly efficient duplication of organic molecules start? The process needs enzymes, RNA and DNA to exist all together. If any of the components are missing the system cannot work. Fred Hoyle worked with his ex-student, Chandra Wickramasinghe, Professor of Astronomy at Cardiff University, to consider this issue.[104]

How many possible different enzymes could be assembled at random from the 20 biologically useful amino acids to form the typical chain of 300 amino acid strings needed for a protein? It works out to be 10^{390}. Now divide this number by the number of outcomes which will make a living protein and call that number f.

Hoyle and Wickramasinghe calculated ranges for f.[105] Taking their estimate of the value of f, I calculated the number of one-shot trials needed to create a working DNA system to underpin the reproduction of various organisms. To make a simple bacterium needs about 2000 individual enzymes to be assembled in the correct order. The number of trials needed to do this would be:

$$((10^{390}/f) = 10^{270})^{2000} = 10^{340,000}$$

That is 10 with 340,000 zeros after it.

For a complex organism such as a human you need about 75,000 different enzymes. So the number of trials needed to guarantee you have the correct formula for all 75,000 is $10^{25,000,000}$, that is, 10 with 25 million zeros after it.

This is an extraordinarily large number. Just to write it out, writing at a speed of 3 zeros per second for 12 hours a day, seven days a week, would take you almost a month!

An immediate implication of this calculation is that intelligent life is so unlikely that it can only be created either deliberately *or*, if randomly, then over a much longer time than the Universe is supposed to have existed. If the Big Bang theory is correct, it implies that any intelligent observer arising from this process must be linked to the intelligence of the Primeval Observer.

Let me explain why. There has simply not been time for enough independent random trials to have taken place after the Earth formed before the first simple life forms appeared for it to be accidental. The oldest rocks on the Earth are about 4.5 billion years old. The oldest life forms are 3.5 billion years old. That leaves, at best, a window of 1 billion years for life to evolve by accident. But the earliest form of bacteriological life needed water to develop. Earth was not a watery place until after the late massive bombardment during which Earth was repeatedly struck by watery comets, which deposited the water which formed the seas and any 'little warm ponds'.[106] This happened about 3.85 billion years ago, so the window of opportunity for the accidental beginning of DNA-based life shrinks to about 350 million years.

To ensure enough separate trials of bringing together the raw chemicals can be carried out (and, remember, each attempt has to be completely separate, because, once the basic building blocks have stuck together, they can not be unstuck to allow another attempt at making a living molecule) requires $10^{339,987}$ trials to be carried out every minute of that period. That number is 10 with 339,987 zeros after it! The implications of this simple calculation are threefold:

1. Either we are extremely lucky, and life formed within the first few million attempts of the basic elements coming together randomly, purely as the result of an accident which can never be repeated (i.e. a miracle).
2. Or the comets which brought in the water which formed our oceans also carried in bacteriological life forms which formed elsewhere (this implies a very old universe, to allow time for life to arise by accident).
3. Or life was created by intelligent intervention, in the same way the human scientists can create an artificial bacterium (this fulfils Paul Dirac's test for the existence of a Great Architect).

Wilmshurst deduces from his study of The Craft that there *is* such a Great Architect, and it is possible to link to this Primeval Observer by becoming 'aware of the Centre'. He called the phenomenon 'cosmic consciousness'.

Before experiencing the spiritual bonding of Living Stones and the expansion of consciousness which accompanied being almost struck by lightning I would have dismissed his propositions in 'The Book of the Perfect Lodge' as nonsense. But now I was properly prepared to make a further step in Masonic knowledge.

'Do you think Wilmshurst was right about the role of cosmic consciousness in Freemasonry?' I asked my Guide.

'If you have experienced it yourself then you don't need me to tell you what you became aware of,' he replied. 'Either you experienced something larger, more purposeful and more benign than anything you had met before, or you didn't.' He smiled. 'Only you know what happened inside your brain.'

The Universe Inside My Head

My Guide was right. I *had* experienced a oneness with the cosmos. But I still had a nagging worry that it was simply a feature of an electrically induced neurological overload.

Nobody can hope to understand the phenomenon of super-consciousness without experiencing it. I first experienced it as an introverted fear of a physical darkness which was watching me. When I turned to face the fear my sense of self was suppressed and became dead to earthly concerns. I became 'aware of the Centre'. It was like touching the source and root of all being. My mind experienced union with the bright cosmic centre, and it inspired my spirit. I became a small part of a vast interconnection of what I can only call spiritual force. (It is tremendously difficult to put into words.) I felt a union between my human spirit and a Cosmic Mind which understood the whole nature of reality and wanted to share its knowledge.

My studies of early Christianity showed that when a religiously inclined person is abruptly thrust into this mental state (e.g., St Paul on the road to Damascus) it makes them intensely religious. It feels like meeting God and seeing the world from His omnipotent viewpoint. My childhood Sunday School experience had burned out any religious empathy I might once have had, so my training as a scientist kicked in when it happened to me; I identified the electrical cause, which I realised was a non-mystical explanation. As a scientist I expect to understand reality, and when something apparently supernatural happens I look for simple reasons. And even if the reasons turn out not to be simple, I always expect them to be natural.

Around that time I was approached by a new marketing manager at Lewis Masonic, the oldest Masonic publisher in the world. Before I knew it, I'd put together a synopsis for a book exploring the deep feelings that my experience of the Masonic Centre evoked in me, first by lightning strike and later by deliberate, focused meditation under the guidance of my Guide. It was a totally new genre for me.

I knew Colin Wilson had written about this super-conscious state of mind, and I had had interesting discussions with him about the mental state that he called 'peak experience'. Colin was convinced that it gives a vision of the real nature of underlying reality and is the creative force that drives poets and artists. His first book, *The Outsider*, dealt with those who experienced moments of super-consciousness and how they had to learn to overcome the sense of fear and alienation so that they could change from within. Colin encouraged me to write about my experience, and the result was *Turning the Hiram Key*, the first book Lewis ever published for the general public.

Whilst I was investigating this state of consciousness I was thrust into a realm populated by religious mystics and experimental psychologists. Then, whilst researching the inspirational role that Masonic symbols played in the moon landings of Project *Apollo*, I came across a book by a brother Mason-scientist.

I was researching Freemasons who had been to the moon (there were seven among the *Apollo* astronauts) and seeking to discover how the experience had affected them. I read *The Way of the Explorer* by Bro. Dr Ed Mitchell, who flew on *Apollo 14* and walked on the moon. Imagine my surprise when I found he had experienced super-consciousness during his flight back from the moon on *Apollo 14*. Our experiences were remarkably similar. We had both been subjected to a religious upbringing as a child, both had the rigorous scientific training of a PhD physicist, and both experienced the ritual teachings of Masonic philosophy. And perhaps the most significant similarity was that neither of us was made a religious convert by the experience.

This is how Bro. Mitchell describes his first moment of super-consciousness:

> There was a vast tranquillity, a growing sense of wonder as I looked out the window, but not a hint of what was about to happen. Perhaps it was the disorienting, or reorienting, effect of a rotating environment, while the heavens and Earth tumbled alternately in and out of view in the small capsule window. Perhaps it was the air of safety and sanctuary after

a two-day foray into an unforgiving environment. But I don't think so. The sensation was altogether foreign. Somehow I felt tuned into something much larger than myself, something much larger than the planet in the window. Something incomprehensibly big. Even today, the perceptions still baffle me . . . looking beyond the Earth itself to the magnificence of the larger scene, there was a startling recognition that the nature of the universe was not as I had been taught. My understanding of the separate distinctness and the relative independence of movement of those cosmic bodies was shattered. There was an upwelling of fresh insight coupled with a feeling of ubiquitous harmony – a sense of interconnectedness with the celestial bodies surrounding our spacecraft . . . I was part of a larger natural process than I'd previously understood, one that was all around me in this command module as it sped toward Earth through 240,000 miles of empty black space . . . its silent authority shook me to the very core. Here was something potent, something that could alter the course of a life.[107]

I could identify with the experience, the emotions and the difficulty of expressing what had happened. I had written, 'I felt my mind expanding to fill the cosmos. Time froze, and I felt a great peace and clarity. I could feel the stars moving in their courses as the spiral arm of the galaxy twirled slowly above me.' Mitchell described it thus:

What I felt was an extraordinary personal connectedness with the cosmos. I experienced what has been described as an ecstasy of unity. I not only saw the connectedness, I felt it and experienced it sentiently. I was overwhelmed with the sensation of physically and mentally extending out into the cosmos. The restraints and boundaries of flesh and bone fell away. I realized that this was a biological response of my brain attempting to reorganize and give meaning to information about the wonderful and awesome processes I was privileged to view from this vantage point . . . I am convinced that it always has been and always will be a largely ineffable experience. What was clear, however, is that traditional answers to the questions, 'Who are we?' and 'How did we get here?' as derived both by science and religious cosmologies, are incomplete, archaic, and flawed. There is more to the process than we have yet dreamed.

Super-consciousness creates a subjective impression that there is a greater intelligence behind the universe, and those who experience it think that it is possible to make contact with this intelligence. A comparison with the literature on this state agrees with my experience, but that does not make it fact.

Ed Mitchell is puzzled by the issue of quantum observation and puts forward an interesting view on scientists' increasingly desperate attempts to remain passive observers.

> The physical universe was conceived by Newton as a deterministic machine grinding inexorably toward whatever destination God had in mind. The universe was simply there. It was absolute, and man was only the passive observer who needed to discover its physical laws in order to understand it completely, and thereby better follow God's commandments.[108]

The Newtonian world is where all scientists begin their apprenticeship. Until we master Newton's laws of motion and gravity we cannot progress further in knowledge of the universe. But when we do, nowadays we discover that we are forced to play an interactive role in the outcomes of our experiments.

Ed Mitchell and I were lucky to have been prepared by training as physicists and Freemasons to accept and investigate our 'mystical' experiences. Mitchell confirms this.

> Where mystics have believed the more startling insights to be a supernatural phenomenon, I was reasonably sure it was entirely natural, even normal; perhaps an emergent characteristic of ongoing evolution . . . I believe, while on that fateful journey from the moon . . . an evolutionary product (the brain) spontaneously reorganized its information to produce a new insight at the level of conscious awareness . . . I wanted to know why and how it happens. I wanted a more secular, scientific answer.

So he rejected a supernatural explanation of his first moment of mind-expanding ecstasy, just as I did.

> I was convinced that these were natural events, not supernatural or magical, though certainly beautiful and profound. The ecstasy I experienced was somehow a natural response of my body to the

overwhelming sense of unity I received. I saw how my very existence was irrevocably connected with the movement and formation of planets, stars, and galaxies – the ineluctable result of the explosion of an immensely hot and dense dot at the center of the universe billions of years ago. Or, if quasi-steady state theorists are correct, as it now appears they may be – the ineluctable result of continuous matter creation in super clusters of galaxies.[109]

Feeling part of the vast quantum entanglement between all particles of matter throughout the cosmos seems to be a natural development from the idea of an interactive quantum observer.

An important consequence of a quantum view of the world is that no reality exists – past, present or future – until it is observed. Physicist Roger Penrose wrote about this strange feature, explaining how it is possible for an object to be in two places at once.[110] This strange mathematical consequence is called *quantum linear superposition*, and, although it may seem an abstract idea, it has a real effect. Experiments show that a quantum object really *is* in two places at the same time. But that is not the end of the story, as Penrose explains.

Quantum linear superposition is quite puzzling enough . . . [but] any physical object, itself made out of individual particles, ought to be able . . . to 'be in two places at once'. The formalism of quantum mechanics makes no distinction between single particles and complicated systems of many particles. Why, then, do we not experience . . . say, cricket balls, or even people, having two completely different locations at once? This is a profound question, and present-day quantum theory does not really provide us with a satisfying answer.[111]

He goes on to say that the apparent unchallengeable reality in the existence and position of large objects, which makes them appear in only one place at a time, is because they have been observed many times, by many observers, and so all the uncertainty about where they are has collapsed into a known position. But he adds that this might not be true of objects which have never been observed at all. This raises the intriguing question, 'Did the moons of Jupiter exist before Galileo first observed them?' Quantum mechanics allows the shocking possibility that, by observing them, Galileo called them into existence and created their orbital history.

This proven ability of the human consciousness to collapse a range of possibilities into one fixed state is a natural mechanism for managing the possibilities open to an unresolved wave function. Dr Mitchell thinks this property of consciousness can be trained.

> Psychoactive people,[112] either naturally or through training, have a greater range of actions they can intentionally and directly initiate with their mind. I was coming around to see that there is actually nothing more complicated conceptually about these unusual processes than that psychoactivity is merely a means of managing energy and the patterns of energy that we term information. However, there are many subtleties involved in training oneself to better employ the process, particularly outside the body, and considerable complication in explaining how it fits within the theories of physics. There is also still considerable mystery as to how the brain actually accomplishes these feats. The processes are not simply the mechanical processes of gears and levers, nor the electrical processes of moving charges, as classical theories would have it.[113]

After I had succeeded in reproducing the 'lightning strike' experience of cosmic consciousness in lodge, and during sessions of private meditation, I came to accept that mystic awareness of the Centre is a real and reproducible mental state that leads to feeling part of something larger then me. In this state of mind I can believe I interact with a great Divine Plan of the Universe, and that the spark in my soul is linking to the Plan of the Centre. But am I really linking to anything outside myself? If so, what? Is the universe itself intelligent? Or am I just deluding myself?

The father of the hydrogen bomb, Dr John Wheeler, after listening to a lecture by Hoyle, said:

> If the universe is necessary to the creation of life, could it be that life is necessary to the creation of the universe? Do acts of observership, in the quantum sense, have anything to do with bringing about that which appears before us. Nothing is more mysterious in the subject of quantum mechanics than the role of the observer in the scheme of things.[114]

Wheeler went on to suggest that a Divine Plan might exist, and humans could be a part of it, as intelligent observers. This is the view Wilmshurst expresses in 'The Book of the Perfect Lodge'. I was fast becoming convinced this is an important insight into Freemasonry. In The Craft the clockwork God of Newtonian determinism has been replaced by the quantum-aware Great Architect who is ready and willing to allow us to contribute to His malleable Plan for the cosmos.

Personal Reflections

'The Book of the Perfect Lodge' says that I have within me a Divine Spark which is a part of the Great Architect, referred to as 'the Centre'. And when I work with my lodge brethren together we can pool our individual sparks to become a fire to illuminate the darkness of ignorance with the light of Truth.

Wilmshurst tells me that if I pool my small spark with those of my lodge brethren and work with them I can link my soul's spark to the light of knowledge at the Centre. In this way I can become part of the Divine Plan of the Universe. Wilmshurst summarises this idea in a poetic metaphor towards the end of 'The Book of the Perfect Lodge':

> I have sat in gross darkness in the North. I have wandered in the moonlight of the West. I have stood in the noontide sunshine of the South, and from the hill-tops of the exalted mind beheld the glory of the Great Architect from afar. And thence I have been led down to the valley of the shadow of death, where no light was, save the glimmering star of my own deathless spirit.
>
> But, because of points of fellowship between my soul and the Grand Geometrician, the right arm of the Most High was stretched forth to me and drew me into union with Himself. I have been raised from the dead and have passed for ever from darkness to light. I have been throned in the chair of Wisdom and ruled in the Craft as Master of a Lodge and as governor of my own soul.[115]

This seemed a weird and mystical claim, which I would have dismissed out of hand, had I not experienced the expansion of consciousness which Wilmshurst said was the key to accessing this knowledge.

My Guide suggested that I should investigate this for myself, as all he could offer me was anecdotal insight from his own inner knowledge. He recognised that this would not be enough for a doubting physicist.

He encouraged me to revisit Nobel Physics Laureate Paul Dirac's ideas on how to test for the existence of God as a natural phenomenon. This forced me back to a worry about the origins of the universe I first had as a postgraduate student. If the universe is as young as the Big Bang theory implied, then the emergence of intelligent life is so improbable as to constitute sufficient evidence to satisfy Dirac's criteria that God exists.

Other physicist Freemasons, such as Bro. Sir Edward Appleton, the discoverer of the ionosphere, Bro. Enrico Fermi, the discoverer of the atomic reactor, and Bro. Ed Mitchell, the astronaut, had concluded that the state of Masonic super-consciousness that Wilmshurst had advised as a way of understanding the nature of the Great Architect's Divine Plan is a natural phenomenon.

And Paul Dirac, John Wheeler, Fred Hoyle and Chandra Wickramasinghe had all speculated that some form of Cosmic Intelligence might exist.

That was my next area to investigate.

IO

Isn't The Cosmos Older Than That?

The Despiritualisation of Science

Before 1940 the practice of physics involved much thought about the basic questions of time, matter and space. The heroes of the new physics, Einstein, Born, Dirac and Planck, were all comfortable working within the broad philosophical tradition that Newton, Laplace and Gauss had occupied. They were not afraid to mention the possibility of God's purpose, even when they doubted the conclusions of religion.

Wheeler, Fermi, Feynman and Dyson, the last productively creative generation of physicists, developed a new hard-nosed and focused approach that was pragmatic and favoured mathematical skill over considered reflection, although all quietly considered possible roles for a Great Architect. Only Hoyle publicly flirted with questions of purpose, and so missed out on a Nobel Prize for raising difficult questions with the intellectual establishment. The generation of physicists working during and immediately after the Second World War achieved tremendous success with a wide range of practical problems. They produced fusion and fission bombs and calculated the implications of quantum effects on the movement and transmutation of basic particles with solid materials (solid state physics). However, whilst developing clever engineering solutions, they avoided confronting the fundamental questions of the role of the observer in cosmology, in quantum measurement and in space–time.

My generation, the scientists who came after them, learned their pragmatic techniques as postgraduates and were actively encouraged to ignore the spiritual misgivings of the founding fathers. The ironic outcome of this pragmatic teaching is that science has moved towards a theoretical view of itself which is little different from the musings of medieval theology. Our most profound theoretical studies are far away from any contact with experiment or observation. We speak of multiple universes, hidden dimensions, god-particles and dark matter, but we don't know if any of them really exist outside our calculations.

As I look back to the founders and early followers of the quantum revolution I can't help noticing that most of them were looking for an underlying order which they assumed to pervade the universe, and which they sometimes called by the name of God.

> I believe in Spinoza's God who reveals himself in the orderly harmony of what exists, not in a God who concerns himself with the fates and actions of human beings.
>
> Albert Einstein [116]

> God does not care about our mathematical difficulties; He integrates empirically.
>
> Albert Einstein [117]

> Everything we call real is made of things that cannot be regarded as real.
>
> Neils Bohr [118]

> If God has made the world a perfect mechanism, He has at least conceded so much to our imperfect intellect that in order to predict little parts of it, we need not solve innumerable differential equations, but can use dice with fair success.
>
> Max Born [119]

> If there is a God, he's a great mathematician
>
> Paul Dirac [120]

> All matter originates and exists only by virtue of a force . . . We must assume behind this force the existence of a conscious and intelligent Mind. This Mind is the matrix of all matter.
>
> Max Planck [121]

> The issue of whether the universe is purposive is an ultimate question that is at the back of everyone's mind . . . the greatest mysteries one has in quantum mechanics is with the role of the observer . . . There are very many aspects of the universe where you have either to say there

might have been monstrous coincidences, which there might have been, or alternatively there is a purposive scenario to which the universe conforms.

Fred Hoyle[122]

These ground-breakers of modern quantum science looked for the hand of a Great Architect and practised what my Masonic training calls studying 'the hidden mysteries of nature and science in order to better understand the ways' of that Great Architect. They didn't assume that considering a role for some sort of God was a dangerous and outdated concept that had to be suppressed with fundamentalist zeal.

Why are so many modern scientists afraid of thinking in terms of the intervention of intelligence in the formation of the cosmos? Is it because they do not think such an intelligence could be a natural phenomenon? Do they assume that to even postulate such an intelligence must involve superstition, magic and unscientific nonsense?

The late 1960s and early 1970s, when I was a science student, was a time when opportunities were counterbalanced by devastating threats. On the one hand I was living in the midst of the Cold War and was very aware of the threat from nuclear strikes – I had been drilled in exactly what to do in the event of a four-minute warning in order to maximise my chance of surviving an atomic blast. But it was also a time filled with hope at the technological possibilities that the new physics of relativity and quantum mechanics were opening up.

Dirac and Fermi put forward theories (hole theory and band theory) which made it possible to build semi-conductors from cheap sand (silicon). Solid-state devices (the newly invented transistor) could be used to fabricate wonderful computing machines. The digital revolution got under way on computers the size of a small community hall and with less than a thousandth of the processing power of a modern mobile phone, but it soon moved on to machines a million times more powerful that could fit on a sliver of silicon glass less than a tenth of an inch square. When I began as a research student a calculating job involved booking time on a shared computer days in advance, and then waiting hours for the results to be printed out; if I wanted to run the graph-printing software that formed Appendix 1 of my PhD I had to book a slot days ahead and collect my output the following morning. It was a far cry from the powerful computers I now have on my desk for my own exclusive use. By the time I graduated with a PhD I could carry in my jacket pocket a programmable calculator with a hundred times the computing power of the building-sized KDF9 computer I had first learned to program. I thought it a wonderful breakthrough, after my slide rule.

My generation of physicists were heirs to a world where science made anything possible, and knowledge knew no limits. We were the heroes of the whole population, and everybody assumed that science would solve all the problems of society and make everyone rich; it only needed a sufficient concentration of trained minds to be brought together, and it would happen. As a group we studied the success of the Manhattan Project, which had created the atomic weapons. We watched how our elders (the generation of John Wheeler and Dick Feynman) brought down to earth the fiery furnace of the sun and commanded it to burn in the form of the hydrogen bomb. Control and manipulation of the forces of Nature was an open book to us. We were taught all the skills needed to predict the outcome of bringing certain materials together in a particular way, and our predictions were always right. We knew all anybody needed to know about manipulating reality. We could bend it to our will. The spaceships we designed flew to the moon, our X-ray probes unravelled the coiled mystery of DNA-based life, and our miniature, affordable computing machines revolutionised the availability and accessibility of information. All this progress, the fruit of focused and unquestioning intensity, was the product of a battle between Einstein and Bohr, which culminated in the truce that goes by the name of the Copenhagen Interpretation.[123]

Yet Einstein and many other fathers of the quantum revolution retained a sense of awe about the nature of reality. They were all convinced there was an intelligent force which underpinned reality and made it understandable. They saw no limits to what they could discover about that force.

The Copenhagen Interpretation does impose limits on what a physicist can know, though. It says that when objects are treated as if they are waves of probability, it is impossible to know anything about their nature. All that can be done is predict their behaviour.

My generation of physicists was taught that there is no rhyme or reason in the behaviour of populations of small wave-like objects, but we were shown how to became skilled manipulators of these tiny bits of matter and packets of energy, able to create a whole new range of technologies from our predictive equations. But the price we paid was not just the loss of our sense of awe and wonder but a complete interdict on dabbling in spiritual metaphor. We were treated as stupid heretics if we even considered that there might be interactions between reality and the intelligence of a conscious observer at the quantum level. And to suggest that we might even be able to understand such interactions was way beyond the pale.

In summary, a sense of awe and wonder inspired Einstein and his colleagues to look for reason and purpose in the construction of the cosmos. The nihilistic Copenhagen viewpoint has advanced the technological application of science enormously, but it has robbed it of any inspiration to inquire into why the quantum world is as it is.

In my opinion the lack of progress which characterises modern physics, and the vehement hostility with which the neo-atheists attack any knowledge drawn from spiritual insights, arise from the obstacles that the Copenhagen Interpretation puts in the way of any role for intelligence in the evolution of the cosmos.

Wilmshurst claims there is a small spark in my soul that is able to interact with the Great Architect and help carry out the Divine Plan. As a physicist I have to agree with him. There is an unexplained, and widely unacknowledged, implication of quantum theory. For an observation to take place, so that a fixed past is assigned to an object, an intelligent mind has to interact with the measurement. Fred Hoyle explains it from the scientist's viewpoint:

> Certainty comes in an individual experiment only after it has actually been done, and certainty comes only by observing the outcome of a particular experiment, with our consciousness telling us the result . . . It comes as something of a shock to find one's consciousness being involved in this way, and many scientists, while accepting the basic ideas of quantum physics, try to avoid the involvement of consciousness by what seems to me to be a deception.[124]

The words may be different but the implication is identical. Wilmshurst called that consciousness the Divine Spark. The deception referred to by Hoyle, by which scientists avoid thinking about this Divine Spark, is the Copenhagen Interpretation. Throughout his life Hoyle struggled with its implications for quantum physics, as Einstein did before him. Both of them concluded that consciousness and intention, that is to say intelligence (or, speaking Masonically, the Divine Spark which implements the Divine Plan), have a role in determining the outcomes of observations. Hoyle was deeply troubled by this.

> Einstein . . . sought to give expression to his worries by arguing that quantum mechanics was wrong, a point of view which brought him into collision with most physicists, a point of view which over the years has not been substantiated. Experiment persistently shows quantum mechanics to be without the internal contradictions which Einstein thought it had . . . Instead of picturing ourselves as external observers, quantum mechanics seems to imply that we cannot separate ourselves from the events we are observing, sometimes to the extent of actually determining what takes place.[125]

Quantum mechanics is *not* wrong. It gives highly accurate predictions of what will happen in a wide range of circumstances, but it *is* incomplete. It does not try to explain the interaction of intelligence with the creation of reality. The idea that we might be helping bring about some intentional purpose by our choice of observations is dismissed by many current scientists as mystical claptrap. But I believe the reason modern science is failing to make progress in understanding the basic problems of reality is because it is fighting a rearguard action to maintain the fiction of a detached observer. It needs to understand the role of the mind as it interacts with a quantum observation to register an event. Freemasonry has taught me that my consciousness has an important role in defining my function within the Divine Plan of the Cosmos.

By now you may well be asking, How do you physicists know all this is true? Is it simply an artefact of mathematics? The answer is that it has been demonstrated by experiment in the so-called 'delayed-choice experiment', first proposed by John Wheeler in 1980 and actually carried out by Alley, Jakubowicz and Wickes (AJW) at Maryland University in 1984. (The detail of this experiment is described in Appendix II.)

The implication of this experiment is profound. Its findings worried me, and I believe they should worry you as well. John Wheeler expressed this worry:

> If delayed choice is real in a laboratory, then it is real in the universe at large . . . we must conclude that our very act of measurement not only revealed the nature of a particle's history on its way to us but in some sense determined that history. The past history of the universe has no more validity than is assigned by the measurements we make now.[126]

As we look further and further back into the past with better and better telescopes, we may perhaps be bringing that past into being. The universe is potentially a system that creates its present form by shaping its past, and this is possible because the existence of a fixed past history comes about when intelligent observers, in either the present or the future, make a first-time observation of previously unmeasured quantum uncertainties in the distant past.

The idea that the Divine Spark within each of us can take part in building the Perfected Temple of the Cosmos by playing a part in enacting the Divine Plan of the Great Architect is looking less crazy. But the implication is that the Great Architect could be the composite mind of a multitude of intelligent observers, or souls containing Divine Sparks.

The critical matter seems to be the choice of what to measure, and the intent of the measurement, as these choices turn an uncertain past into a measured reality. Wheeler summed it up:

> Not all potentiality is converted to actuality in any finite time. There are innumerable clouds of probability running around the universe that have yet to trigger some registered event in the macroscopic world [i.e. to be observed by an intelligent observer]. We have every right to assume that the universe is filled with more uncertainty than certainty.[127]

He went further in another paper:

> How can the machinery of the universe ever be imagined to get set up at the very beginning so as to produce man now? Impossible! Or impossible unless somehow — preposterous idea — meaning itself powers creation. But how?[128]

He warns 'you should be careful what you wish for, or choose to observe', because by doing so you could well bring it about. An intelligent observer can create a particular past by the choice of observation s/he makes in the present. This ability is not restricted to humanity. The theory which leads to this result says any intelligent observer can perform the trick. It also implies that if humanity is the only group of intelligent observers in the cosmos, then we are responsible for forming our own past and are the architects of our own Divine Plan. But if there are other intelligences elsewhere in the universe they can also shape our past as well as their own, and we can potentially shape theirs.

In my next discussion with my Guide I accepted that nothing in 'The Book of the Perfect Lodge', including its description of a Great Architect and the possibility of an interactive Divine Plan, clashed with my understanding of quantum physics. As I let the ancient ritual work its magic on me, I was inspired to look with fresh eyes at issues I had entertained about the philosophy of physics but had ignored for years.

Soon after joining Living Stones, Bro. Bert, the senior Past Master of the Lodge, had spoken to me about the practice of meditation. It was clear from what he said that he regularly practised a form of Masonic meditation and sometimes achieved awareness of the Centre. He pointed out that there is no easy method for achieving the state of insight, but regular practice of systematic meditation, using Masonic passwords as mantras to chant, or focusing on tracing boards to cut out distractions, helps the process. I followed his advice, set aside time for meditation and followed his suggestions. In this way I found that I also was able to occasionally achieve a state of awareness of the Centre. It was remarkably similar to the experience of the lightning strike, as the opening of my mind to the totality of the cosmos seemed to be inevitably preceded by an overwhelming feeling of dread that I had to confront before my awareness expanded.

My visits to Living Stones, the advice of my Guide and the ongoing experience of cosmic consciousness were encouraging me to listen to the inner voice of my spirit and to link with the mystery of the Centre, so that I might learn more of the Divine Plan of the Cosmos.

'Are you ready to attempt to define your soul yet, Robert?' my Guide asked.

'I am,' I replied. And here is my definition.

> My soul is that continuing awareness of the nature of self that carries my spirit through the dark unconsciousness of sleep to awake to a fresh knowledge of itself in the cold light of dawn. It is also the seat of the mechanism by which I experience the nature of larger reality in the form of creative insights, the way I acquire knowledge of unprovable truths and the means by which I am able to collapse wave functions by deliberate acts of observation.

This allows for the communication of knowledge and intent of observation to take place once a certain complexity of awareness has been attained. But what does my 'soul' communicate with when it feels it is having an audience with the Great Architect, and what is the mechanism of communication it uses? These are parts of the lost secrets I have still to recover.

Many scientists prefer to dissect the mysteries of the world in a manner that leaves no place for the soul. But the mystery of quantum observation involves the interaction of a conscious entity with the wave function to collapse its range of probabilities into a single reality. A living entity, such as a bacterium, is not enough; without self-conscious awareness it is unable to take part in the measurement. But life is not a divine gift. It is something we can make in a test tube.

The intervention of intelligence can create life. Completely artificial life was created in 2010 by Dr Craig Venter who 'constructed a bacterium's genetic software' and transplanted it into a host cell. The resulting microbe looked and behaved like the species 'dictated' by the synthetic DNA.[129] This shows there is nothing supernaturally unique about the creation of DNA-based life. It may be statistically unlikely, but it is not miraculous. From the bits and pieces lying around in the jars on their lab shelves scientists can take the basic chemical constituents of a cell, assemble them in the correct sequence and produce a living bacterium. Of course, such life is not the 'intelligent observer' which effects a quantum measurement – but, given time, it might evolve into that.

Is it possible for my soul to link to a collective intelligence? I have collected together some ideas about the nature of the sort of intelligence which might have intervened to create life, but I still do not know how my soul communicates with this Great Architect.

Perhaps the answer lies in the nature of knowledge. How is it that I know a measurement has happened? Is it when the pointer on the dial moves, when the particle creates a path in the bubble chamber at CERN, when a charged particle hits the phosphor of a display screen, when my optic nerve pulses and quivers from the impact of a photon, or is it when my soul registers the outcome of the observation and confirms it by informing the Great Architect that the next step in the Divine Plan has been completed?

The statistics of life have forced me to consider it possible that some form of intelligence was involved in its creation. Quantum physics tells me that the choices made by intelligent observers in the present (or the future) can shape and fix the past or our present. This opens a different possibility for the nature of any intelligence involved in the creation of life. The Great Architect of the Universe may be a natural observer, or even an amalgamation of natural observers: a sort of collective Cosmic Mind of widely separated individuals, not a supernatural supreme being. But if there has not been sufficient time for such a Cosmic Mind to evolve, then the issue becomes a different one. Then the question is, Is the Great Architect supernatural, and Freemasonry a religion rather than a spiritual and philosophical training system?

From the Beginning of Time

At Bradford University I have a colleague who is a committed Christian; I will call him Peter. He is highly intelligent, numerate, educated to PhD level and beyond, and a firm believer in Intelligent Design. He is in no way a biblical creationist and totally accepts the popular view that the universe is about fifteen billion years old. He fully understands that the process of selection can change and modify living forms: as he says, you only have to look at the variety of dog breeds to see that. He also accepts the Big Bang theory's claim that the universe was created from nothing by a single unique event. He differs from Richard Dawkins, however, in that he believes it was a deliberate act by a supernatural intelligence which he calls God, and that the God he believes in set up the conditions so that life would appear. He even enlists Hoyle's discovery of the mechanism for fabricating carbon as evidence of deliberate intelligent intervention in the development of life.

When I questioned him about the possibility of life beginning by accident in Darwin's 'little warm pond' he said he found it a highly unlikely scenario, as he was fully aware of the interlocking nature of DNA, enzymes and proteins and the fact all the parts have to come together at once for life to begin. However, when I asked him to estimate the probability of life beginning spontaneously he put forward an estimate which was a billion orders of magnitude less than the real probability. When I told him the true value he was highly amused, and pointed out that I was supporting his position.

When I asked him why he thought there was a benign intelligence behind the beginnings of life, he told me he had experienced a moment of super-consciousness in the midst of a religious service. (He did not call the experience super-consciousness, however; he spoke of experiencing God's all-enveloping love.) That, in conjunction with his own reasoning, convinced him that the Big Bang was evidence of a Creator God.

In part, Peter is right. The Big Bang describes a universe which was created by a miracle, in that it is not a fully explained scientific process. It does not explain how widely separated photons from opposite ends of the observable universe, which is known to be at least 28 billion light years wide, are in a state of thermal equilibrium. This is a state usually found only in particles close enough to interact and balance out energy differences.

The fact that these widely separated photons are all so extremely close to the same temperature became an issue in 1929, when astronomer Edwin Hubble (the man honoured by the naming of the Hubble Space Telescope) published details of observations that showed that the further away a galaxy was from the Earth the faster it was moving away from us.

He did this by recording the colour of the light which these distant objects gave off. Objects coming towards us are blue-shifted, as the wavelength of the light gets shortened (blue light has a higher frequency than red), and those moving away from us are red-shifted, as the wavelength is stretched out). Hubble measured the colour-shift of hundreds of different galaxies, expecting to find as many moving towards us as he found moving away. Every distant light-emitting object he measured was moving away from us, and the smaller, fainter ones were moving faster than the larger and brighter ones. If all the objects in the universe were speeding away from us, why was the background temperature so uniform?

An obvious conclusion to draw was that the universe is expanding and, because the fainter objects were assumed to be farther away, and because they were moving faster, this expansion must be speeding up. If fainter objects are more distant than brighter ones, then the light from them must have taken longer to reach us than the closer ones, and so they must be older.

This was a startling result. One interpretation was that all the star clusters which were speeding away from each other came from a single, central point. The media posed the question, Does this mean the Solar System was at the centre of the universe? But it was quickly pointed out that the whole of space–time was expanding, so there is no centre. This can best be imagined by thinking of a two-dimensional analogue such as the surface of a balloon. It the galaxies are thought to be spots on the surface of the balloon, then as it is blown up all the spots will be moving away from each other, no matter which one you choose. There is no centre spot, and the more distant ones move more quickly than those close by for any spot you choose. This is what seemed to be happening to the universe. Space–time was continually expanding.

One implication of this is that the universe had a distinct beginning, the moment when the expansion began. The attraction of a 'genesis' moment was irresistible and resulted in a fixed-time-of-creation theory, 'the Big Bang theory'. This claimed that the early universe was a very hot and chaotic place, but as it expanded the gas within it cooled, and the first stars formed.

But if the Big Bang began in the extreme chaos of the greatest explosion ever known, why did it then spontaneously organise itself into stars and galaxies? And why did it then drift back towards chaos?[130]

One claim of the Big Bang theorists was that as a consequence of this original chaos, the universe should be filled with radiation that is literally the remnant heat left over from the Big Bang. This was called 'cosmic microwave background radiation', or CMB for short. When such background radiation was found, that seemed to be conclusive proof of the Big Bang and its implications for the relatively brief lifespan of the universe.

Belief in the Big Bang is an Act of Faith

To be respectable as a scientist I am expected to accept that time began around 14 billion years ago. And what came before time? Well, that is a question I am not allowed to ask, because the beginning of time was a singularity, and so had no 'before'.[131]

Hubble's measurements of the light from distant cosmic objects suggested the speed of any object was related to its distance from Earth. This relationship became known as Hubble's Law, and from that time forward the amount of red shift observed in any new object was used to estimate its distance. The idea that the universe has expanded from a single point (the Big Bang) is based entirely on these measurements and their shortcomings. Then, in 1990, it was discovered that the expansion of nebulae can cause red shift.[132]

Early estimates of the date of the Big Bang suggested an age for the universe of 1.7 billion years, but this conflicted with calculations about the age of stars, worked out using their mass and the rate at which they radiated energy. More embarrassing, the atomic age of many stars was older than the estimated age of the universe. To add to the fun, Rutherford, the man who discovered the atom, estimated that the age of key elements in the solar system to be ten times older than the Hubble-predicted age of the universe.

Hubble's Law assumed that all distant galaxies are speeding away from us at known speeds and used them to calculate when they all started from a single point. Hubble's Law, however, asserted that all observed red shift was caused by the relative movement of the observer and light sources. This is not true. That form of red shift, which is caused by relative motion, is known as Doppler red shift, but there are two other things which cause red shift. One is cosmological red shift, which is caused by the expansion of space–time, and the other is gravitational red shift, caused by strong gravitational fields pulling at photons and reducing their energy (gravity cannot slow down the photon, so this reduction in energy appears as a stretching out of the photon's wavelength, moving its colour towards the red end of the spectrum).

After the Second World War many things changed, and there was an expansion in scientific research which was still in full swing when I was studying for my PhD. Larger optical telescopes were built, radio astronomy became possible, and the vast expansion in knowledge of nuclear processes gained from building atomic bombs towards the end of the war led to a deeper understanding of the process of creating chemical elements within stars.

In the late 1950s radio telescopes found a new type of object in the skies. It was called a quasar (meaning quasi-stellar object). Quasars are enormously energetic objects which have large black holes at their centres and often give off massive plumes of matter, which can then condense into stars. All quasars have a very high red shift. Hubble's Law predicted that they were so far away that they must have appeared in the very early stages of the formation of the universe. But they could be nearer and manifesting gravitational red shift.

If they were formed soon after the Big Bang, then they are hard to explain, because the Big Bang theory's account of cosmic background radiation assumed that the initial state of the universe was highly uniform. The problems thrown up by the discovery of quasars led to the invention of a miraculous inflation as a means of getting around the issue.

Hoyle pointed out this weakness underlying the Big Bang theory. He drew attention to the fact that quasars have a peculiarity in the structure of the gravity-distorted space surrounding them, which causes higher red shift.[133] The implication of this is that quasars may be not as far away as they are assumed to be. Moreover, as distance is used to estimate the age of an object, quasars may not be as old as we assume they are. We may yet have to reconsider what they really are. Measurements of the red shift of radio galaxies also show wide divergences from Hubble's simple rule of steady expansion.[134]

The Steady State cosmological theory put forward by Hoyle, Bondi and Gold proposed that the creation of matter was an ongoing process in an eternal universe, not a once-and-for-all act of creation. Hoyle described how this theory was received.

In the steady-state universe, matter is created at a uniform rate determined by the expansion . . . The concepts underlying the theory were thought to be of doubtful validity when the model was under intense discussion in the 1950s and 1960s, but by the 1980s with the introduction of inflation they had become more respectable. This early view of the theory is one of the reasons why it was received with considerable hostility, but there were clearly other strong emotions. For some the idea of creation was acceptable if it took place at an early time and only once, i.e. a big bang, but for it to go on steadily at a rate which made it undetectable locally was unacceptable. For some it is clear that western religion is important when origins are being considered; parallels between the big bang and the creation described in the Old Testament are inescapable, and it is clear that in part at least some of our colleagues were driven by religious motives.[135]

This, then, is the crux of the issue: early public interest in the Big Bang model owed more to its biblical acceptability than its physics.

In his early development of the Steady State theory Hoyle, normally a very quick thinker, missed a trick. Today the main argument advanced as 'proof' of the Big Bang theory is the so-called 'fossil' cosmic background radiation left by the explosion. Hoyle's Steady State theory predicted that there should be a background microwave radiation observable uniformly throughout the sky. His colleague Tom Gold calculated it should be around $2.78°$ K. This figure was not published at the time, as Gold was overruled by Hoyle and Bondi. Hoyle explains why:

[In] 1955 . . . Bondi, Gold and Hoyle admitted [their theory] . . . required a universal radiation background in the far infrared. There was some difference between the three authors as to how the argument should be presented. Gold argued in favour of a thermalized background, because nature always turns out to be more efficient at degrading the quality of energy than we expect it to be. Whereas Bondi and Hoyle argued that because no adequate thermalizing agent seemed available, the more cautious position should be taken of simply placing the background generally in the far infrared. And on a vote of two-to-one, this was how the matter was published.

In subsequent years a great deal turned on this decision, which it should not have done. But when it comes to how the world decides broad issues in science, far too much depends on chance. Had Gold's picture of nature being an arch-degrader of energy been followed, a calculation of the resulting thermodynamic temperatures would have followed immediately . . . [yielding] T = 2.78 K. Had this elementary step been taken in 1955, it is easy to contemplate that when the cosmic microwave background was detected in 1965 to have a temperature somewhat below 3 K, this estimate made in 1955 would have seemed stronger than the estimates 'above 5 K' of . . . [the Big Bang theorists] made in 1948. And as subsequent determinations of T lowered its observed values bit-by-bit towards the modern value of 2.73 K, big-bang supporters would not have been able to hold centre-stage to the extent they actually have . . . it is likely that the big-bang theory would not have been on-stage at all.[136]

The Steady State theory has since been developed and revised. Instead of the spontaneous eruption of hydrogen atoms out of the zero-point energy field, the new quasi-Steady-State theory proposes that quasars are where matter is continuously created.

In 1995 a mechanism which transforms starlight into microwave radiation was discovered. Tiny crystallised iron granules, thrown into interstellar space by exploding stars, absorb starlight and emit microwaves. It fully explains the cosmic background radiation without any need for a Big Bang. As Hoyle wryly commented:

By 1995 . . . the means to thermalize the background inferred by Bondi, Gold and Hoyle in 1955 was at last available. But, of course, it was 30 years too late to influence the big-bang advocates who remain unimpressed, either by the data or by the result T = 2.78 K to which the argument of 1955 leads. However, in our view such properties as iron whiskers are now seen to possess would, if they were of no relevance to the cosmic microwave background, be freakishly accidental.[137]

The strongest public argument for the reality of the Big Bang, and hence the short time for life to evolve, is based on the measurement of cosmic background radiation (CBR).[138] Once that is called into question, it is possible to question the whole thing.

How Long is Time?

The Steady State theory made a prediction for the value of the CBR which was four times more accurate than the Big Bang theory, yet, because of the 'Creation' connotations, which physicist George Smoot likened to 'seeing the face of God' in his press conference announcing the results of the NASA COBE satellite measurements,[139] the Big Bang has become an article of unquestionable scientific faith.

The 'miraculous' instantaneous expansion of space that had to be postulated to explain the present distribution of galaxies by Big Bang believers only adds to the popular religious impact of the theory. It purports to explain how the universe was conjured from nothing 14 billion years ago by inferring an unexplained act which is outside both time and space. This hidden miracle has captured the popular imagination and most of the scientific establishment. It is a religious viewpoint which is comfortable for many people to hold, as it gels with St Augustine's idea of a God outside of space and time, who created the universe from nothing at the beginning of time.

But if the universe is much older, or even eternal, it makes many of the unanswered questions about the origins and role of intelligence much more compatible with the philosophical ideas that are taught by Freemasonry. There is time for life to develop, evolve intelligence and coalesce into a Cosmic Mind. The remaining unknown is the mechanism by which such a Cosmic Mind communicates with its constituent parts. A scenario such as a Steady-State universe, where matter and possibly quanta of space–time are being continually created in quasars, allows scope for a Great Architect to emerge from a self-reflecting feedback loop of quantum observation of the far past. As geologist Professor Norman Newell said in 1993:

> The Big Bang theory has brought wide attention to the origins of the universe and creation. But let us ask, how did the chemical elements, energy, and the natural laws and forces of physics originate? The old problem of first cause has now become a major concern for scientists, as it always has been for the theologians.[140]

There is scope within the theories of modern physics to put aside the Big Bangers' claims for the relatively brief age of the universe, along with the even shorter claim made by the Creationists, and assume that there has been sufficient time for a Great Architect to evolve.

The most recent observations from the Herschel Far-Infra-Red Telescope show that about 12 billion years ago luminous infrared galaxies were already 'creating stars at such phenomenal rates that they defy conventional theories [i.e. Big Bang theories] of galaxy formation'.[141] This seems to confirm that the steady formation of galaxies was well under way at a far earlier stage than the popular Big Bang theory predicts.

What I have learned from Freemasonry makes me question both the Big Bang and the Copenhagen Interpretation. And I am not alone in questioning these articles of faith of the neo-atheists. I found support for my position in something John Wheeler wrote in 1986:

> We know that the way the quantum theory works is no mystery. It is expounded in a hundred texts. But from what deeper principle does its authority and its way of action derive? What central concept undergirds it all? Surely the magic central idea is so compelling that when we see it, we will all say to each other, 'Oh how simple, how beautiful! How could it have been otherwise? How could we have been so stupid so long?' But what is the decisive clue to it all that we of today are missing? [142]

Physicist Frank Tipler makes a mathematical case that once intelligent life arises in the universe it changes the nature of cosmic evolution, and that quantum mechanics and general relativity require what he calls a Cosmological Singularity – an uncaused first cause that he claims must emerge from this scenario.[143]

Abner Shimony of Massachusetts Institute of Technology agrees that the ability to collapse wave functions by observation may not be limited to just human observers.

> More decisive is the vast evidence of the evolutionary link of higher animals with the simplest organisms and even with inorganic matter. It is difficult to see how irreducibly stochastic behavior [the ability to collapse a wave function by observation] could be a structural characteristic, which could occur in a complex organism even though it is absent from all the components of the organism. Consequently, if

there is an irreducibly stochastic element in the behavior or experience of higher animals, then one should expect a stochastic element in the primitive entities at the base of evolution. And if this is correct, then the Schrödinger equation, which is usually supposed to govern deterministically the state of a physical system except when it is being observed, can only be approximately valid. This possibility should, in my opinion, be taken very seriously.[144]

Shimony says that once an organism develops the will to observe, then it will be able to force a fixed state onto the uncertainty of any as yet unobserved reality. But that organism does not have to be human, and it does not have to be on Earth. It is not an unreasonable assumption to consider that life in the cosmos might have co-evolved into a Great Architect, by observing and creating its own past. But if this has happened, how would we know? When we observe the distant past through our telescopes we are not trying to communicate our ideas to alien intelligences, we are simply trying to discover what we can about reality. Why should any other distant intelligence be different from us? The answer to my question, 'Why has the Great Architect not communicated with us?' might be that that we haven't found any message because there is no intention to communicate. But that does not mean that we can never see the *consequences* of non-human observations.

Personal Reflections

My search for Freemasonry's lost secrets has led me to believe that:

1. The assumption of an extremely ancient Steady-State universe, where matter is being continually created, makes it much more likely that there are a vast number of carbon-based intelligent observers scattered throughout the universe, all forcing order on to newly created matter by their observations.

2. This sea of souls, all capable of collapsing wave functions, are likely to be way beyond the range of any hope of making electromagnetic communication with them. And, as Paul Dirac said, if something is beyond your ability to observe it then, as far as you are concerned, it doesn't exist. This implies that we may never be able to make contact

with other intelligent life forms elsewhere in the universe, because the more successful ones are all isolated by the speed of light, which limits how far into time and space we can see.

3. The surprisingly consistent order we see in the laws of physics might have been brought about by the observations of countless intelligent observers, all collapsing wave functions at the very limit of their observational ranges. And, because there is no speed or distance limit on the instantaneous collapse of a wave function following a deliberate observation, we see outcomes even when the sharing of information carried by light waves is not possible because of the vast distances involved.

This leads me to make the assumption that it is possible that there might be intelligent life elsewhere in the universe. To satisfy the Fermi criteria (which asked, 'If there are aliens out there, where are they?' and went on to show that if intelligent life existed in our galaxy it would have contacted us by now) this intelligent life must be so thinly spread that it can never make contact using radio or light rays. But I can also be confident that any such intelligent life will be able to collapse the clouds of uncertainty at the limits of its observational range into patterns of reality, which we might also observe in our far distance. This would mean there is no deliberate attempt to create and communicate a Divine Plan by a single Supreme Being. But the Divine Plan could be the combined output of the community of observers widely scattered through the space–time of an infinitely old and infinitely large universe.

When I put this thought to my Guide he reminded me that Freemasonry suggests a way to test this idea. It teaches that the Great Architect communicates Truth by the contemplation of mathematics.

The importance of mathematical Truth in Freemasonry and science must be my next step towards reassembling the lost secrets.

11

The Instantaneous Sharing of Truth

The Mysterious G

Freemasonry teaches about a Temple which is not made by human hands: this is the Masonic metaphor for the soul. There is a mysterious symbol at the centre of this Temple. It is the letter G, which stands for Geometry and God the Grand Geometrician of the Universe. I first learned of it when I became a Fellowcraft, but until Bro. Douglas Inglesent specifically drew my attention to it I did not grasp its import.

As I mentioned in Chapter 7, Douglas reminded me that during the closing ceremony of the Second Degree this ritual exchange takes place between the Master and his Wardens:

> Bro. Junior Warden, in your situation what have you discovered?
> A sacred symbol, Worshipful Master.
> Bro. Senior Warden. Where is it situated?
> In the centre of the building, Worshipful Master.
> Bro. Junior Warden. How is it delineated?
> By the letter G in the centre of a blazing star, Worshipful Master.
> Bro. Senior Warden. To what does it allude?
> To God, the Grand Geometrician of the Universe, to whom you, I, and all must submit, Worshipful Master.

The Master then sums up this exchange for the benefit of the brethren of the lodge in a form which I must admit I did not fully appreciate until my Guide later explained it. The Master says:

> Then Brethren, let us remember, wherever we are, whatever we do, He is with us. His all-seeing eye ever beholds us, and whilst we continue to

act as faithful Fellowcrafts, may we never forget to serve him with fervency and zeal.

At a simple level this reminded me of the all-knowing, meddling God of my childhood Sundays. However, it can also be interpreted as acknowledging that at the centre of every human soul there is a Divine Spark that knows and shares in the Truth of the Grand Geometrician: 'wherever we are, whatever we do, He [in the form of the Divine Spark] is with us.'

'There are certain self-evident Truths which are given to the soul to know by the Grand Geometrician, allowing any faithful Fellowcraft to access them and know and prove them for himself,' my Guide said. 'I think that during your scientific education you might have come across this sort of Truth under the name Platonic Truth.'

As a man of science my Guide would be well aware of the unprovable yet self-evident Truths, such as $1 + 1 = 2$, which underpin mathematics.

This set me off on a whole new direction. Throughout my scientific career, and my later lecturing career, I searched for scientific Truth that can only be found using symbols. Without the symbolic language of mathematics I could never have become a scientist. Did this simple ritual exchange hold the final key to the lost secrets of Freemasonry? Is the path to Truth found by understanding and manipulating symbols?

The ritual definition of Freemasonry echoed in my mind and I blurted it out. 'A peculiar system of morality, veiled in allegory, and illustrated by symbols.'

My Guide smiled. 'Exactly,' he said. 'You have passed the challenge of the Warden and are now entitled to climb the winding stairway to the hidden mysteries of the middle chamber.'

My Guide had earlier gently nudged me to think about a Masonic teaching given in open lodge: a ritual myth concerning Euclid, who had developed Plato's ideas concerning Truth to create geometry. The ritual says that Euclid taught The Craft that the study of the relationships between the symbols of geometry makes it possible to access eternal Truths. It is worth recalling that traditional history which I mentioned in Chapter 4.

The River Nile, annually overflowing its banks, caused the inhabitants to retire to the high and mountainous parts of the country. When the waters subsided they returned to their former habitations; but the floods frequently washing away their landmarks, caused grievous disputes among them, which often terminated in a civil war. They hearing of a Fellowcraft's Lodge being held at Alexandria, the capital of their country, where Euclid presided, a deputation of the inhabitants repaired thither, and laid their grievances before him. He with the assistance of his Wardens and the rest of the Brethren, gathered together the scattered elements of Geometry, digested, arranged, and brought them into a regular system, such as was practised by most nations in those days, but is bettered in the present by the use of fluxions, conic sections, and other improvements. By the science of Geometry he taught the Egyptians to measure and ascertain the different districts of land; by that means put an end to their quarrels: and amicably terminated their differences.

The reference to the 'fluxions' of Newtonian calculus dates this passage to after the eighteenth century. In this piece of ritual the mythical history has been intertwined with the mundane history to make a philosophical point. Euclid was said to have recorded the symbols of geometry, and as a result a Masonic catalogue of basic symbols is taught to all Candidates.

The symbols of geometry were celebrated during the flowering of ancient Greece. They were nothing less than symbols of visual reasoning. Using only a pencil, ruler and a pair of compasses they make it possible to prove relationships that cannot otherwise be known. I had used the basic rules of Euclid to analyse vector force interactions whilst an A-level student. The symbols are simple to understand, apply and teach.[145]

Nobody is sure whether the historical Euclid was a real person or a group of scholars writing under a shared pen-name. But the book which carries the name Euclid's *Elements* makes three important claims.

1. All humans know truths about geometry which they have not learned through education or experience.
2. This knowledge is held in the changeless, universal dominion of Platonic truths which all souls can perceive and recognise.
3. There exists a realm of absolute, unchanging truth which is the source and the basis for our knowledge of what is True.

Masonic myth tells how Euclid built on Plato's teaching that the symbols of geometry are a key to understanding the world and searched for symbols to reveal them. In the training of a Mason's soul the symbols lead him to discover Truths which are even more hidden.

Plato said that to question the validity of Truths which are self-evident to the soul is a sign of either ignorance or insanity. Freemasonic ritual explains why, in this exposition from the First Degree lecture:

> Geometry, the first and noblest of sciences, is the basis on which the superstructure of Masonry is erected. By Geometry we may curiously trace nature through her various windings to her most concealed recesses. By it we may discover the power, wisdom, and goodness of the Grand Geometrician of the Universe, and view with amazing delight the beautiful proportions which connect and grace His vast machine. By it we may discover how the planets move in their different orbits, and mathematically demonstrate their various revolutions. By it we may rationally account for the return of seasons, and the mixed variety of scenes which each season produces to the discerning eye. Numberless worlds are around us, all formed by the same Divine artist, which roll through the vast expanse, and are conducted by the same unerring law of nature. While such objects engage our attention, how must we improve, and with what grand ideas must such knowledge fill our minds. It was a survey of nature, and an observation of her beautiful proportions, which first induced men to imitate the Divine Plan, and study symmetry and order. This gave rise to society, and birth to every useful art. The architect began to design, and the plans which he laid down having been improved by time and experience, have produced some of those excellent works which have been the admiration of every age.

Freemasonry teaches that geometric reasoning enabled the art of building to advance, and for hundreds of years great public temples were designed using the infallible guidance of the symbols of geometry. Knowledge of the nature of the symbols of geometry was needed by every builder in stone, and over time bigger and more magnificent temples were built, as awareness of geometry was accumulated to develop the processes. Access to knowledge of symbols opens up this realm of previously unknown information. As the ritual says, 'the hidden mysteries of science and nature are illuminated by symbols'.

My Guide explained: 'Freemasonry developed symbology[146] to communicate its ideas in a universal cosmic language. Once an idea is formulated in symbols it is transmitted without corruption. This guarantees continuity of tradition. A modern Mason carries out symbol work in exactly the same way a Mason of five hundred years ago did. The Mason of today faces the same spiritual problems and basic questions about Truth that a Mason of 1490 had to face, and the symbols provide the same answers.'

I waited to see if he would say more. 'But . . . ?' I said, smiling.

'But,' he echoed, 'there are greater depths to this subject which only the more esoteric Masonic lodges teach. Go and meditate about equations.'

He was right. There is an incredible mystery attached to simple equations.

We have already touched upon the way the idea of the equation was developed by John Wallis, the father of modern algebra, a founder of the Royal Society and a Freemason.[147] Wallis used the idea of the equality of powers, expressed by the two pillars of The Craft, to express Truths about the world. The 'equals sign' of mathematics, '=', is the symbol of the two pillars rotated by an angle of 90°, or the fourth part of a circle. As my Guide pointed out, this is mentioned by the Junior Warden during the ritual of opening the lodge in the Second Degree, when the Worshipful Master asks the Junior Warden if he is a Fellowcraft.

> I am Worshipful Master. Try me and prove me.
> By what instrument in architecture will you be proved?
> The Square.
> What is a Square?
> An angle of ninety degrees or the fourth part of a circle.

To put it another way, if you rotate the symbol '=' through an angle of ninety degrees or the fourth part of a circle, you see the main Masonic symbol of perfect equality. Thus inspired, Wallis developed the equation, the most important tool of all physics, which enables access to core ideas that make a universe work and keep it working.[148]

The development of the symbolic language of mathematics has led to a remarkable spiral of consistency. The actions of the mathematical laws of physics produce complex systems, and these complex systems lead to brains and consciousness that then produce symbolical reasoning, which leads to mathematics, which can encode the underlying laws of physics that gave rise to the beings who observe them.

Cosmologist Paul Davies had an interesting reaction.

We wonder why the power of simple mathematical symbols allows the emergence of precisely the sort of complexity that leads to minds and mathematics which can then encode those laws in universally understood symbols in a simple and elegant way. It's almost uncanny, it seems like a conspiracy.[149]

I thought to myself, 'Is it a conspiracy perhaps . . . with the Cosmic Mind of the Great Architect at the Centre of it?'

Plato's Perfect Symbols and Equations

Could there really be a conspiracy between a collective cosmic intelligence and the creation of reality? One Greek philosopher thought there was, and his ideas influence physicists today. Plato (427–347 BCE) said that for a theorem to be discovered it must already exist before anyone thinks about it.

He said that a transcendental world of absolute forms exists, and our souls can access the knowledge this world contains. We have knowledge of these supra-sensible realities that we cannot possibly have obtained through bodily experience, and this knowledge must be a recollection of what our souls were acquainted with before our births. He believed that the world was essentially intelligible, and it is our intellect, not our senses, that has the ultimate 'vision' of reality.

Freemasonry, with its powerful idea that the symbols of geometry are hidden in the Centre of the Mason's soul, takes this idea forward by teaching that if we need to know Truth we discover it by looking inwards towards that Divine Spark which connects us to the Great Architect.

A vision of Platonic perfection drives scientists and is at the heart of all the systems of scientific research which have been developed in the twentieth century.[150] Physicist Roger Penrose, a committed scientific Platonist, explains why.

A Platonic viewpoint is an immensely valuable one. It tells us to be careful to distinguish the precise mathematical entities from the approximations that we see around us in the world of physical things. Moreover, it provides us with the blueprint according to which modern science has proceeded. Scientists will put forward models of the world – or, rather, of certain aspects of the world – and these models may be tested against previous observation and against the results of carefully designed experiment. The models are deemed to be appropriate if they survive rigorous examination and if, in addition, they are internally consistent structures. The important point about these models is that they are basically purely abstract mathematical models. The very question of the internal consistency of a scientific model, in particular, is one that requires that the model be precisely specified. The required precision demands that the model be a mathematical one, for otherwise one cannot be sure that these questions have well-defined answers.

If the model itself is to be assigned any kind of 'existence', then this existence is located within the Platonic world of mathematical forms. Of course, one might take a contrary viewpoint: namely that the model is itself to have existence only within our various minds, rather than to take Plato's world to be in any sense absolute and 'real'. Yet, there is something important to be gained in regarding mathematical structures as having a reality of their own. For our individual minds are notoriously imprecise, unreliable, and inconsistent in their judgments. The precision, reliability, and consistency that are required by our scientific theories demand something beyond any one of our individual (untrustworthy) minds. In mathematics, we find a far greater robustness than can be located in any particular mind. Does this not point to something outside ourselves, with a reality that lies beyond what each individual can achieve?[151]

The complex malleable sub-world of quantum reality was only discovered using mathematical symbols, as we have seen. The key steps in developing these mathematical methods of thinking were discovered by men steeped in the symbolism of Freemasonry.

Where do the mathematical laws that allowed scientists to predict the outcome of delayed-choice experiments come from? Freemasonry teaches me that these symbols come from a mystical Platonic heaven of perfect symbolic forms which grows from my awareness of the Centre. Physics teaches me they come from 'the Platonic world of mathematical forms, from 'a reality that lies beyond what each individual can achieve'.

Is this a common symbolic repository that both Freemasons and physicists are taught to access, but in different ways: physicists by mathematical training and creative inspiration and Freemasons by transcendental awareness and quiet group meditation? But the original inspiration came from Freemasonry and its influence on Isaac Newton.[152] Since Newton, mathematical reasoning and the manipulation of symbols has helped scientists to understand the universe; Nobel Prize winner in physics Richard Feynman elaborates:

> If you are interested in the ultimate character of the physical world . . . our only way to understand that is through a mathematical type of reasoning . . . I don't think a person can fully appreciate . . . these particular aspects of the world . . . without an understanding of mathematics . . . there are many, many aspects of the world that mathematics is unnecessary for, such as love . . . [but to] not know mathematics is a severe limitation in understanding the world.[153]

He also observed:

> Mathematics is not just another language. Mathematics is a language plus reasoning; it is like a language plus logic. Mathematics is a tool for reasoning . . . By mathematics it is possible to connect one statement to another.[154]

The scientific system of mathematics is founded on the Masonic idea that symbols convey deep meaning. Freemasonry teaches, further, that symbols influence parts of our brain that conscious thought does not affect. Much of Masonic ritual is about sensitising Candidates to the meaning and import of symbols. Special care is taken to promote an interest in the mathematics of geometry, as the introductory lecture to the First Degree shows:

> Brethren, Masonry, according to the general acceptation of the term, is an Art founded on the principles of Geometry, and directed to the service and convenience of mankind. But Freemasonry embracing a wider range, and having a more noble object in view, namely, the cultivation and

improvement of the human mind, may, with more propriety, be called a Science, although its lessons for the most part are veiled in Allegory and illustrated by Symbols.

This shared belief in a Platonic heaven of perfect mathematical forms is explained by Penrose.

> Science and mathematics have themselves revealed a world full of mystery. The deeper that our scientific understanding becomes, the more profound the mystery that is revealed . . . Physicists, who are the more directly familiar with the puzzling and mysterious ways in which matter actually behaves, tend to take a less classically mechanistic view of the world than do the biologists . . . According to Plato, mathematical concepts and mathematical truths inhabit an actual world of their own that is timeless and without physical location. Plato's world is an ideal world of perfect forms, distinct from the physical world, but in terms of which the physical world must be understood. It also lies beyond our imperfect mental constructions; yet, our minds do have some direct access to this Platonic realm through an 'awareness' of mathematical forms, and our ability to reason about them . . . Whilst our Platonic perceptions can be aided on occasion by computation, they are not limited by computation.[155]

I returned to discuss these ideas with my Guide.

'Where did these mathematical truths and their accompanying insights come from?' I asked. 'How do human minds gain access to them? Can any intelligent life form, anywhere in the universe, access the same bank of Platonic Truths? Is the transfer of the knowledge in these Truths restricted by the speed of light or not?'

'You need to meditate on what you just said,' replied my Guide. 'If the Great Architect's Divine Plan is written in mathematics, then perhaps it was intended that any intelligent observer could access it. Have you read Richard Feynman's thoughts about maths and the Great Architect?'

I found the quote he was referring to in *The Character of Physical Law*:

> The Great Architect seems to be a mathematician. To those who do not know mathematics it is difficult to get across a real feeling as to the beauty, the deepest beauty, of nature. I really think that two cultures

separate people who have and people who have not had this experience of understanding mathematics well enough to appreciate nature. It is too bad that it has to be mathematics, and that mathematics is hard for some people. It is reputed – I do not know if it is true – that when one of the kings was trying to learn geometry from Euclid he complained that it was difficult. And Euclid said, 'There is no royal road to geometry.' And there *is* no royal road. Physicists cannot make a conversion to any other language. If you want to learn about nature, to appreciate nature, it is necessary to understand the language that she speaks in. She offers her information only in one form; we must not be so unhumble as to demand that she change before we pay any attention.[156]

But where does this mathematical insight come from? Does the Platonic heaven arise from the interaction of a cosmos-wide corps of intelligent observers collapsing reality into forms that allow mathematical truths to emerge? Richard Feynman says:

Nature uses only the longest threads to weave her patterns, so each small piece of her fabric reveals the organisation of the entire tapestry.[157]

So are the minds of our physicists and Freemasons tuning into the thoughts of a natural Cosmic Intelligence, or are they tapping into the Mind of a Supernatural God? If there are other intelligent observers somewhere in the universe, then Bro. Fermi's argument demonstrates that they must be beyond the range of any communication mode which is limited to the speed of light.[158]

How might it be possible to communicate physical laws instantaneously across vast distances?

The Problem of Distance

The question of how quantum action takes place over intergalactic distances with apparent instantaneous communication is called the paradox of non-locality. Einstein first explored this mechanism in an attempt to disprove quantum theory. He hoped to show that a more complete 'hidden-variable' quantum theory could exist and might one day be discovered. He showed that under certain, clearly defined circumstance it is possible to create a pair of entangled particles which instantaneously know exactly what is happening to the other particle, no matter how far apart they are. This result defied the rule that nothing can travel faster than the speed of light. It is now known as the EPR paradox (after Einstein and his co-authors Podolsky and Rosen). They also proposed a simple thought experiment and analysed its implications through the predictions of quantum theory. This experiment emphasised the non-local nature of quantum events.[159]

The EPR paradox result showed that events that are widely separated in space–time can be instantaneously linked, even though the two particles involved in the linked events are light-years apart. As physicist David Bohm explained, quantum theory allows for particles separated by vast intergalactic distances to communicate the outcome of an observation of either particle to their entangled partner instantaneously.[160] Euan Squires, of Durham University, explains this.

> Quantum mechanics creates the puzzling situation in which the first measurement of one system should 'poison' the first measurement of the other system, no matter what the distance between them. One could imagine the two measurements were so far apart in space that special relativity would prohibit any influence of one measurement over the other.[161]

In 1966 John Bell carried this analysis further and proved these predictions are real.[162] It is a fact that quantum communication mechanisms work over cosmic distances and are not limited by the speed of light. Roger Penrose says Einstein hoped there was a deeper theory to be found which would reconcile this with relativity, but he never found it.[163] Einstein himself later wrote:

> Quantum mechanics is very impressive. But an inner voice tells me that it is not yet the real thing. The theory produces a good deal but hardly brings us closer to the secret of the Old One. I am at all events convinced that He does not play dice.[164]

Unlike Einstein, though, I am comfortable with the idea that the Great Architect has a gambling problem. Such a weakness makes Him far more attractive than the know-it-all control freak I met at Sunday School.

Freemasonry, however, has convinced me that the Great Architect does not load the dice, and He will allow us to work out the odds for any outcome which is possible using the mathematics of quantum theory. Roger Penrose agrees with this position, saying that the description of the world, as provided by quantum theory, is really quite an objective one, though often strange and counter-intuitive.[165]

Einstein's followers, particularly David Bohm, developed a viewpoint that there must be some 'hidden variables', which would enable us to define reality. Roger Penrose accepts that such a hidden-variable theory can be consistent with all the observational facts of quantum physics, but only if the theory allows for instantaneous communication over intergalactic distances.[166] It is this strange 'non-locality' effect, where two particles, light-years apart, instantly 'know' what is happening to the other, that offers a physical method for any Cosmic Intelligence to communicate.

When I next discussed this problem with my Guide he said, 'I suggest you read the work of the mystic who inspired the physicist David Bohm.'

'Who is that?' I asked.

'Krishnamurti,' he replied.

'I've never heard of Krishnamurti,' I said. 'But if he managed to inspire David Bohm, the guy whose textbook helped me learn my trade, then that's good enough reason to read him with an open mind.'

'He held a long series of discussions with Bohm about the nature of the Cosmic Intelligence that we call the Centre,' my Guide replied. 'I'll send you a selection of his writings.'

He was as good as his word. I started to read the thoughts of spiritual philosopher Jiddu Krishnamurti (1895–1986), and this comment stood out as soon as I did:

> Belief is one thing, reality is another . . . One leads to bondage and the other is possible only in freedom . . . Belief can never lead to reality. Belief is the result of conditioning, or the outcome of fear, or the result of an outer or inner authority which gives comfort. Reality is none of these . . . The credulous are always willing to believe, accept, obey, whether what is offered is good or bad, mischievous or beneficial. The

believing mind is not an enquiring mind, so it remains within the limits of the formula or principle.[167]

I was struck by the similarity of this statement to one made by physicist Richard Feynman, who said:

> The worst times, it always seems that they were times in which there were people who believed with absolute faith and absolute dogmatism in something. And they were so serious in this matter that they insisted that the rest of the world agree with them. And then they would do things that were directly inconsistent with their own beliefs in order to maintain that what they said was true.[168]

'Is there is any evidence that single subatomic particles can produce measurable effects on human senses which can be detected within human consciousness?' I asked my Guide.

He had read the thirteen discussions that took place between David Bohm and Krishnamurti in 1980[169] and told me they had come to a conclusion that insight is an energy which illuminates the activity of the brain. When this illumination is perceived by consciousness the brain itself begins to act differently.

'As you study The Craft it changes and develops your soul,' my Guide said. 'Bohm and Krishnamurti talk of "the ground" and "the Universal Mind", which seems similar to the energy of the vacuum and the Cosmic Mind you have been talking about.'

I agreed.

'Krishnamurti said that the ground becomes manifest when attention is paid to it by a receptive mind,' my Guide said. 'When we sit together in the dark silence of contemplation we make our corporate mind receptive to what Krishnamurti called the ground and what we call the Centre.'

'But what are we making our mind receptive to?' I asked.

'The mystery of the Centre,' he replied. 'And the nature of that is something that you must discover for yourself.'

I got a further clue a few days later. I gave a talk at the Bradford Astronomical Society. In the general chat afterwards I was told that astronaut Charlie Duke was due to visit West Yorkshire and give a lecture. While talking about Project *Apollo* I was reminded of the special mission which Astronaut Duke had carried out during his NASA moon flight. His observations, conducted during the later *Apollo* missions, showed that human senses are quite capable of registering the reception of a single subatomic particle.

Astronauts on the first Moon landing, *Apollo 11*, had reported seeing strange flashes, even with their eyes closed. NASA decided to investigate this effect, which only happened outside the Earth's natural electromagnetic shield. It was found that the flashes were caused by a single high-energy particle stimulating the astronauts' optic nerves or retinas. Here is the official report.

> Crew members of the *Apollo 11* mission were the first astronauts to describe an unusual visual phenomenon associated with space flight. During trans-earth coast, both the Commander and the Lunar Module Pilot reported seeing faint spots or flashes of light when the cabin was dark and they had become dark-adapted . . . these light flashes result from high-energy, heavy cosmic rays penetrating the Command Module structure and the crew members' eyes. [170]

This proves that human senses can detect a change in a single subatomic particle.

Combining the proven quantum communication effect with the knowledge that human senses are sensitive enough to register single wave packet interactions means that there is no technical reason why distant interactive measurements should not be possible.[171] The implication of this is that if an intelligent observer in some distant part of the universe forces a particular state onto an entangled particle which has a partner within the sense apparatus of a human, then those human senses could detect and react to it.

This means distant observations on the entangled twins could have noticeable effects on human minds. This would not require any intention on the part of the human, or the distant observer, for shared effects to be experienced.

Here, then, was a mechanism for communication. Human brain conditions trigger state changes in the particles which make up the synapses of the brain. If those particles are entangled with similar particles in other non-human brains, then there will be perfect correlation between the state changes which occur. If one mind forces a state change in the particles which make up its synapses, then any other mind which had entangled particles in its synapses could resonate with it. (Indeed, recent research into quantum computing has found that strands of DNA are capable of detecting spin changes in a single electron.[172])

This idea that the minds of intelligent observers could resonate through the mechanisms of quantum entanglement had occurred to Ed Mitchell. Indeed he had experienced such interactions for himself. He understood that if such an effect happened, then it would occur instantaneously over vast distances. He had one of the first opportunities in human history to make such an experiment with minds so far apart that even light was taking many seconds to make the journey. It is often argued that the quantum communication effect cannot be used to carry information, and it only transfers correlations of particle states. But, provided there are a few entangled particles in each of the sharing minds, then their correlated states may provide a mapping of thought patterns between the two minds.

Mitchell carried out a thought-transfer experiment to test for such effects over extraterrestrial distances, from the far side of the moon when out of radio contact. He describes the experiment, carried out during the *Apollo 14* mission.

> Every evening as the crew settled in for an attempt at sleep in zero-gravity, and the cabin grew quiet, I would take a moment and pull out my kneeboard, on which I had copied a table of random numbers, along with the five 'Zener symbols' used in ESP experiments and made popular by Dr J.B. Rhine: a square, a circle, a star, a cross, and a wavy line. Then I promptly and discreetly began the simple experiment that Ed Boyle, Ed Maxey, and I had devised. Not even Al or Stu knew what I was up to. On four evenings, twice on our way to and from the moon, I matched one of the symbols with a random number between one and five, and then organized the numbers with a random number table copied from a math textbook. In this setting I would concentrate on a symbol for 15 seconds. Meanwhile, through tens of thousands of miles of empty space, my collaborators in Florida would attempt to jot down the symbols in the same sequence that I had arranged on my kneeboard.[173]

The result of the experiment produced statistically significant evidence of correlation between events in co-operating minds. It may require sensitivity training to be able to reproduce it almost at will, but that is exactly the type of training which certain lodges in Freemasonry offer.

Ed Mitchell was carrying out a practice which my lodge of Living Stones does every day at noon. We all repeat the same ritual and visualise ourselves meeting in the Temple. When talking about this practice among ourselves we often seem to be able to tell who is present, and who is not. Later, when comparing notes, I have asked brethren who I felt were missing if they had carried out the ritual, and more often than seems likely by chance (although I have not kept detailed records) they had been unable to spare the time to work the ritual.

For a moment, consider that intelligent observers who share entangled particles in their thinking systems can become aware of each other. The Great Architect can be defined as the combined intelligence of many sentient observers scattered widely throughout the universe, so far apart they can never communicate with any signals limited by the speed of light, but able to resonate with each other's thoughts, able to calculate the laws which their observations bring into being and able to access each other's mathematical concepts.

Does this explain the mind-expanding awareness of the Centre I have experienced within Freemasonry? That feels as if I am becoming aware of a vast intelligence. Perhaps Freemasonry is right when it tells me I must feel the knowledge of the Centre to understand it.

Is the lost key to Freemasonry and the mystery of the Centre within my soul?

Personal Reflections

Freemasonry's teaching about the Platonic world of mathematical techniques is the strongest evidence for the existence of a Cosmic Mind or Great Architect I have found so far. The Platonic realm of eternal truths, which both Freemasonry and physics have developed methods of accessing, must arise from somewhere. I suspect it is not mystical but a supranatural phenomenon which we are only just beginning to understand.

The existence of other natural intelligences which might have played some role in the creation of the 'Laws of Physics' is not an unreasonable idea. It causes no clashes with the laws of physics and seems to be leading me to answers to the questions Freemasonry has posed me.

Was my study of the basic tenets of Freemasonry pushing me to consider that the emergence of life and intelligence is an inevitable consequence of the laws of physics, despite the highly improbable possibility that it happened on Earth in the last 4 billion years simply by chance?

When intelligent life happens once, by chance, then it starts to observe its environment, and by its choice of observations changes that environment to make the emergence of life elsewhere in the universe more likely. No intent by this Cosmic corps of distant intelligent observers to communicate is required for us to become aware of them through access to the Platonic realm of Truth. Did this mean that the first Freemasons of the Lodge of Aberdeen realised the inherent power in symbols, and The Craft has since developed their use over generations as a means to communicate with the composite Cosmic Mind of the Great Architect?

I knew that I must apply myself to the Masonic system of focused meditation and see where it could lead me. I had the guidance of Wilmshurst's writings and the support of my Guide and mentors, who were able to advise me on techniques. I was about to venture into the dark Centre of my soul to search for the lost secrets, and I had the goodwill of an aware lodge to help me.

12

Entering the Lodge Within

Braving the Hidden Mysteries of My Mind

THIS FINAL STAGE of my quest was the most demanding task I had yet approached. Having spent years systematically erasing from my mind the superstitious religious attitudes that had been forced upon me in childhood, I was now preparing to regress towards something which looked suspiciously like a more sophisticated version of the same thing. Wilmshurst's teaching was forcing me to consider that those magical and fantastic processes of religion I had discarded for the hard-nosed mathematical reality of scientific investigation might actually embody an element of truth.

As a way of creating changes in the human environment, science has long outstripped religion. Yet religion has not faded away; it continues to address areas of truth which modern science denies exist at all. Some of the more extreme forms of religion take the intellectual weapons science has developed and use them as tools to try to force oppressive change based on mystical experiences. My experience with the lightning storm convinced me of the subjective reality of mystical experiences, and I cannot deny its experimental reality. But mystical experiences that happen to charismatic individuals can lead them to use the insights of their 'audience with God' to become powerful forces in the world. Then, when their followers seek similar mystical experiences, their expectations can result in apparent supernatural confirmation of their predisposed views. I suspect that many of the miraculous answers to prayers that have confirmed the belief of religious leaders from Ezekiel or St Paul to modern times have arisen from this phenomenon.

I was now planning to investigate this process within a group which was not looking for confirmation of a religious attitude when seeking this mystical experience. As my Guide pointed out, Wilmshurst's lodge had been influenced by the mystical philosopher Krishnamurti.

'And,' he added, 'you will find his views have a close affiliation to the views of Einstein, Dirac, Wheeler and Hoyle.' He drew my attention to this:

> One has to investigate without any motive, without any purpose, the facts of time and if there is a timeless state. To enquire into that means to have no belief whatsoever, not to be committed to any religion, to any so-called spiritual organisation, not to follow any guru, and therefore to have no authority whatsoever.[174]

I agreed that the mysteries of reality should be approached with no preconceptions. And Krishnamurti is right that time is one of the great mysteries of reality. When I have experienced moments of super-consciousness my sense of time has been suspended, and all the accounts of this experience I have read suggest this is a defining feature of such a state of mind. One reason for practising meditation is to experience this timelessness, which is a feature of awareness of the Centre.

Two of the great theories of reality are rooted in time. Relativity explains how events which took place in the past can be observed in the present (when the light rays from the event finally reach the observer), and quantum mechanics explains how events in the future can be accurately predicted by knowledge of the present. The third great theory of reality, Newtonian mechanics, avoids the issue by accepting time as a God-given property.

I was being offered a method of initiatory training which was designed simply to let me develop knowledge and awareness of the mystery at the centre of creation and of myself. This mystery of the Centre was the creative force that was creating reality; it was expressed in metaphors of a Great Architect of the Universe and a Divine Plan for the Cosmos. But was that creative force real? I was being encouraged to sense it, so that its plan could be understood and I could play a part in it.

After experiencing super-consciousness I understood that it is subjectively powerful and susceptible to taking on the expectations of the individual experiencing it. Had I been prepared for it by religious indoctrination, rather than scientific discipline, it could easily have turned me religious. However it did not; rather, it convinced me that there must be a scientific explanation for it.

If I wanted to explore this idea further I must suspend my disbelief in the reality of the immortal soul and allow the traditional Masonic method of teaching to work its mental magic on me. The lost secrets of The Craft are claimed to be in the inner lodge of my soul, and to reach them I would have to knock on the mental door of that lodge and prepare to face the terrors of my inner psychic landscape.

Must a Scientist be an Atheist?

I had to move from conventional atheism, as preached by Richard Dawkins, and embrace the uncertainty of agnosticism. To prepare myself, my Guide advised me to look at what my scientific heroes had written about this matter. 'Don't forget one of your main heroes of science, Enrico Fermi, was a brother mason before he became a great scientist,' he reminded me. He was right. From Newton down to Hawking a majority of the physicists whose work I admire have expressed views about the existence or otherwise of some sort of God.

Albert Einstein accepted the existence of a superior intelligence that he felt revealed itself in the harmony and beauty of nature. But he didn't extend this view to include a 'God who rewards and punishes the objects of his creation and whose purposes are modelled after our own'.[175] When he was asked directly to define God he wrote:

> I'm not an atheist and I don't call myself a pantheist. We are in the position of a little child entering a huge library filled with books in many languages. The child knows someone must have written those books. It does not know how. It does not understand the language in which they are written. The child dimly suspects a mysterious order in the arrangement of the books but it doesn't know what it is. That, it seems to me, is the attitude of even the most intelligent human being toward God. We see the universe marvellously arranged and obeying certain laws but only dimly understand these laws.[176]

Werner Heisenberg made this forthright statement:

> It may be argued that certain trends in Christian philosophy led to a very abstract concept of God, that they put God so far above the world that one began to consider the world without at the same time also seeing God in the world . . . then a new authority appeared which was completely independent of Christian religion or philosophy or of the Church, the authority of experience, of empirical fact . . . it spoke of two kinds of revelation of God. One was written in the Bible and the other was to be found in the book of nature. The holy scriptures had been written by man and were therefore subject to error, while nature was the immediate expression of God's intentions.[177]

When I became a Fellowcraft Freemason I was told it was my duty to study the hidden mysteries of nature and science so that I might better understand the Great Architect. This view has never been more clearly expressed than in these words of Heisenberg.

Erwin Schrödinger, the man who discovered the quantum wave function and invented the famous experiment with the cat in the box, was more explicit about the nature of God. He rejected the idea of a personal, interfering and vengeful God, but he also rejected the idea that scientists had to be atheists. His words suggest that he had experienced a mind-expanding contact with the Great Architect:

> Let me briefly mention the notorious atheism of science . . . Science has to suffer this reproach again and again, but unjustly so. No personal god can form part of a world model that has only become accessible at the cost of removing everything personal from it. We know, when God is experienced, this is an event as real as an immediate sense perception or as one's own personality. Like them He must be missing in the space–time picture. I do not find God anywhere in space and time . . . for . . . God is spirit.[178]

The super-consciousness which I suspected might link a human mind to some cosmic intelligence is a deliberately cultivated state of being which Freemasonry calls 'awareness of the Centre'. The rituals of The Craft, and the support of a lodge, are intended to help individual Masons to achieve this state of insight. When they do, they know what Schrödinger called 'experiencing God as an immediate sense perception'.

Richard Feynman, the discoverer of quantum electro-dynamics, explained how a sense of spiritual inspiration lay at the heart of his physics.

> The same thrill, the same awe and mystery, comes again and again when we look at any question deeply enough. With more knowledge comes a deeper, more wonderful mystery, luring one on to penetrate deeper still. Never concerned that the answer may prove disappointing, with pleasure and confidence we turn over each new stone to find unimagined strangeness leading on to more wonderful questions and mysteries – certainly a grand adventure! . . . Few unscientific people have this particular type of religious experience . . . This is not yet a scientific age.[179]

Fred Hoyle, too, came to the view that there is a cosmic intelligence that plays a part in the workings of the universe.

> We learn in physics that non-living processes tend to destroy order, whereas intelligent control is particularly effective at producing order out of chaos. You might even say that intelligence shows itself most effectively in arranging things exactly as the origin of life requires. This point is so important that it is worth pausing to consider the very great difference that intelligence can make, not by thunder and lightning methods like Thor and his hammer, but by the subtlest of touches . . . Where is this intelligence situated? Exactly what does it do? What is its physical form? A generation or more of scientific consolidation is needed before risking a shot at such ambitious questions . . . Is intelligence outside the Earth inaccessibly remote or is it close enough to be contacted if only we knew how?[180]

I believe that Freemasonry may well have found a way of communicating with this cosmic intelligence using that mystical experience that many religions encourage. But, of course, here is the crucial difference between Freemasonry and religion. The Craft imposes no supernatural theology upon how this experience is to be understood.

Even Stephen Hawking, not noted for his spiritual sensitivity, when challenged in the letters page of *American Scientist* about being afraid to admit the existence of a Supreme Being, defended the physicist's sense of awe and freedom to interpret it, saying:

I thought I had left the question of the existence of a Supreme Being completely open. It would be perfectly consistent with all we know to say that there was a Being who was responsible for the laws of physics. However, I think it could be misleading to call such a Being 'God' because this term is normally understood to have personal connotations which are not present in the laws of physics.[181]

It is interesting to compare the words of Karen Armstrong, an academic writer who trained as a nun and felt damaged by the religious process, with those of Fred Hoyle, who trained as a scientist, and was inspired to study creation throughout his life.

First Karen Armstrong:

What if God is also a mental aberration? The ecstatic celestial vision of the saints could be just as fantastic as my own infernal sensations. What we called God could also be a disease, the invention of a mind that had momentarily lost its bearings. I was slightly dismayed to find that this idea did not trouble me over-much. If there were no God, then much of my life had been nonsense, and I should surely have felt more upset. But then, God had never been a real presence to me. He had been so consistently absent that he might just as well not exist.[182]

Compare her disappointment when the Great Architect failed to appear or speak out of a burning bush to Fred Hoyle's grudging acceptance of a cosmic intelligence as real:

'God' is a forbidden word in science, but if we define an intelligence superior to ourselves as a deity, then we have arrived at two kinds – the intelligence . . . [of other evolved intelligent observers elsewhere in the cosmos] and the 'God' of the infinite future . . . In contemporary Western religions it is said that 'God' created the Universe and that 'God' can interfere with the Universe to suit himself. However, the Universe cannot interfere with 'God', so that, unlike the situation in science, action and reaction are not equal and opposite. This lopsidedness leads inevitably into a logical morass. One is impelled by such concepts to ask a question which turns out to be unanswerable; the question why the Universe should exist at all. As a distinguished modern theologian said, 'What we cannot understand is that God who has no need of the world should have reason to create it,' but this morass is avoided when it is seen that 'God' exists only by virtue of the support received from the Universe.[183]

The modern science of physics, which grew out of the work of John Wallis and Isaac Newton, who were in turn inspired by the injunction now given in the Second Degree of Freemasonry 'to study the hidden mysteries of nature and science to better know the Great Architect', provides a route to spiritual understanding which is sometimes denied to devout religious believers. Fortified by the knowledge that scientists I respected had not been afraid to think about God and of cosmic Intelligence, I was ready to open my mind to the teachings of Freemasonry in general and the Lodge of Living Stones in particular.

Learning to Communicate with the Great Architect

I became a regular visitor to the Lodge of Living Stones, and the more I learned, the more convinced I became that its founding master under-stood the mystical experience of interacting with the Great Architect and had developed ways of passing on his knowledge. Finally I took the decision to apply for membership. After submitting some samples of my Masonic writing – all its members have to be prepared to write research papers – I was admitted. As a member I was given access to the library and the bank of research papers which the lodge had accumu-lated. I was also given guidance and advice from Douglas, from the Past Masters of the lodge and from my Guide, who had taken me under his wing after my first experience of 'The Book of the Perfect Lodge'.

Once I was a member, my Guide encouraged me to practise Masonic meditation on a regular basis and also set me a course of directed reading of the lodge papers, so that I could understand the purpose of the lodge.

During the consecration of Living Stones, its founding master Bro. Walter Wilmshurst said:

> The direction of inquiry towards matters to which the Craft was specially designed to lead us are 'the hidden mysteries of nature and science,' involving that 'knowledge of yourself' which is the most important of all human studies. These matters go far beyond the mere 'system of morality'

which the Order also provides. In our system, it is not until the neophyte Mason has been disciplined to a high state of morality and virtue, has been trained in physical and mental self-control, been educated in detachment from ordinary worldly possessions and ideals, and habituated to the practice of self-giving instead of self-getting, that, as we say, he is 'permitted to extend his researches' into more deeply hidden things. And it is at this point that the 'system of morality' opens out . . . into a system of Initiation-science.[184]

In Lodge Paper No. 6 he added to this message:

The first lesson imparted to Candidates for Initiation in all ages was Know Thyself, since truly to know oneself involves a knowledge of all else even of The Great Architect, in whom everything lives, moves, and has its being.[185]

In preparing me for the 'more deeply hidden things' of our Craft, the lodge first helped me through a series of trials and tests of merit. The disciplines of morality, virtue, self-control and self-giving are not easy to acquire, and even though I felt I should have mastered them, when put to the test by a brother's 'unreasonable' behaviour I sometimes found I did not live up to my professed intentions. Indeed, looking back at the difficulties I encountered with the English Grand Lodge, I realised that despite the official antagonism, many more sympathetic and perceptive brethren had helped me use the experiences to develop my own attitudes.

Freemasonry tells me I should 'judge with candour, admonish with friendship and reprehend with mercy'. Judging with candour comes easily, as I have no trouble noticing when people are talking nonsense (particularly if they talk about science without actually knowing anything about it) and can often do quick calculations to highlight the gross stupidity of any spurious claim they might make. So it's easy to be candid in pointing out just how wrong they are. Admonishing with friendship comes harder: the fun thing to do is to publicly point out just how daft they are and get a laugh at the expense of their ignorance – but that is not friendly. It would be more friendly to explain the issue privately and help them understand, but that is never my first instinct. I have to work at controlling my sarcastic tongue and containing my urge to poke fun, and I don't find that easy. Finally, reprehending with mercy. My instinct, which showed itself in my spat with the Grand Mark Lodge, was to bite back and threaten. But now I understand that I would not have been showing mercy; that would have been vindictive, and vindictiveness would not make me a better person. Once the poor behaviour had been corrected, the merciful course was to leave them in peace, which I did.

I have sometimes discovered things inside myself I was unaware of. Every time I reach the point during my meditations when I feel as if my mind is about to expand, I have to face the irrational fear that wells up out of my subconscious and threatens to overwhelm me. Much as I would like to believe I am in total control of myself and my emotions, I have often found I am not. What I say and how I behave is not always in harmony. Often I regret a hasty put-down or a careless brush-off. My Guide tells me it is because my soul is not always in balance, and I should work on developing calmness.

The teaching of 'The Book of the Perfect Lodge' says that the fullness of the human mind is like a lodge, which I can learn to open and enter. But it also warns that within that lodge there can be darkness as well as light. Certain lines in the closing prayer of the lodge warn of the joys and perils I might encounter in the personal lodge of my mind. This is part of that warning:

> Be unto us the Lesser Warden, and in the meridian sunlight of our understanding speak to us in sacraments that shall declare the splendours of Thy unmanifested light;
>
> Be Thou also unto us the Greater Warden, and in the awful hour of disappearing light, when vision fails and thought has no more strength, be with us still, revealing to us, as we may bear them, the hidden mysteries of Thy shadow;
>
> And so through light and darkness, raise us, Great Master, till we are made one with Thee, in the unspeakable glory of Thy presence in the East.

In these few ritual words the paradox of the secret knowledge is summed up. When the ritual sacraments spoke to me I felt I was standing amid the splendours of unmanifested light, but when my thought and reason failed to give answers I had to face the terrors of the night.

Such were the perils that beset me when I turned from that which is without (my scientific view of the world) to that which is within (contact between my soul and an intelligence greater than my own).

Scientific reasoning had carried me a long way along my journey from rational scientific West of the lodge towards its mystical East.[186] But to re-experience the vastness of creation, my rational science had to be set aside. Until I learned to quieten my mind and still my thoughts there was no space for the faint spark of the Centre to glow into brilliance.

A key part of this mental discipline occurred when the lodge prepared itself for the ritual task of the meeting. We sat in silence with the lights lowered while we stilled our thoughts. My Guide told me that the lodge lowered the lights and let darkness flood the minds of the brethren so that the splendour of light would not distract us from the silence of unspoken sacraments. Only when we could still our worldly thoughts could we experience the great mystery of the Centre.

The paradox of this search for light is that I had to learn how to embrace my natural dread of darkness to prepare myself to work with the love and harmony that is needed to form a Perfect Lodge. I had to learn to withdraw from the intimate fellowship of shared understanding which discussion in open lodge provides, and sojourn in individual darkness, to allow each new fragment of shared Truth to veil itself in shadow, so that its brilliance would not dazzle me into incomprehension. By the experience of light and darkness, of thought and fear, I was shown how to approach the gate of the Temple and pass out beneath its portal towards the mystery of the Centre.

In this strange fashion I was shown how the lodge builds up spiritual capital. A lodge meeting is far more than a ceremonial spectacle, it is a means of leading each individual towards participation in the corporate spirit that is a Perfect Lodge. Each successive meeting, when we formed a Perfect Lodge, increased the atmosphere that Masonic practice should engender. This was a return to something I had first felt at the Lodge of the East Gate. For the first time in male Freemasonry it always felt good to enter the lodge, and after every meeting I felt refreshed, no matter how weary I was before the ceremony.

But there were aspects of Wilmshurst's teaching I struggled with. He said that the purpose of a Perfect Lodge was to forge a connecting link between a lodge of brethren in this world and invisible hierarchies in what he called the Grand Lodge Above. The corporate mind of a Perfect Lodge, he said, was able to form a channel to conduct an unobstructed current of spiritual energy between the Great Architect, who exists in the light of the Eternal East, and the Perfect Lodge, in which perforce must dwell the Earth's lengthening shadow of the West. This had disturbing overtones of the angelic hosts of my childhood, continually singing the praises of the vengeful Lord of Hosts.[187]

This message is not one which my scientific mind had been trained to accept. It is not a testable material message, rather it is an esoteric enigma. But if I was not prepared to be open to things I did not know then I could never hope to find out the unexpected. The unknown, by definition, is trackless and unexplored. The nature of Truth is contradictory, and whenever I tried to capture it in language I was inevitably drawn into paradox, yet to avoid all paradox led to distortions.

This is why the lodge works in two ways, in darkness and in light, by individual reflection and by corporate reiteration. Truth, I was taught, lies in the deep structure of the world and is experienced by thought and by awe, by reason and by intuition. What I was beginning to experience, both in lodge and in private meditation, was more certain than anything I could learn from listening to other people trying to describe what they had experienced. Most people did not understand what they had experienced and would filter it through their religious expectations. So the retelling of their experiences was not enough to reveal truth unless I could also experience the emotion and inner vision for myself.

The lodge was training me in experiencing and thinking about truth, it was providing a forum to share truth, and it was offering opportunities to demonstrate truth and chances to work together to provide group experiences of truth. In this way I was helped to internalise truth, so that I could make a daily advancement in Masonic knowledge.

Wilmshurst had said that the strength and worth of a lodge does not depend upon numbers and popular attractions, but upon the quality and intensity of the corporate life of its members, upon their united and consistent co-operation towards a common ideal, and upon their ability to form a 'group-mind' or 'group-consciousness'. I experienced this group-mind not as we opened the corporate lodge together, but between the dark silences which enclose our inner workings, whilst the Perfect Lodge was formed.[188]

Until I had experienced this sensation of a group mind seeking Truth together I would not have considered it possible. But as I allowed myself to be open to the spiritual teaching, so I became aware that it was changing the way I thought. I was now making a conscious effort to become part of the corporate mind of the lodge, and I did seem to be experiencing a greater clarity of thought. But I could not be sure if this was a placebo effect, brought on my wanting to become accepted, or a real physical change. It did not, however, stop me thinking about the physics of the different levels of consciousness I was experiencing. Although the ritual practices were presented in a mystical Masonic format, it was clear that I was being shown how to focus my mind on observing detailed parts of reality.

I decided to write a series of lodge lectures to test my knowledge of each of the stages I had been guided through. I kept a journal of each step and noted what I had learned and the ways of practising the spiritual exercises I had found successful in approaching the rituals. Over many months I delivered each of the lectures to the lodge and listened carefully to the informed feedback and comments of my lodge brethren. In this way I refined my understanding of the process and learned how to open my mind to 'knowledge of the Divine Plan'.

I began to practise what can only be described as a system of remote viewing that had been developed by Walter Wilmshurst. He had written that because our corporate lodge does not meet daily, if we were to work each day on the smoothing and squaring of ourselves as living stones to offer to the fabric of the Great Architect's Temple of humanity, then we needed to do more than just attend once a month.

As I have explained, he invited all lodge members to co-operate actively and systematically with the rest of the brethren to form a regular organic unity of minds, not merely a temporary association of persons. He said that we should follow the guidance of Grand Master Hiram Abif and at the hour of high twelve banish every other thought from our heads and visualise our Perfect Lodge together, in peace, concord and unity. Each brother was to separately visualise himself in his normal place in the lodge during a dark silence.

At high twelve I seek out a quiet place, close my eyes to feel the comradely warmth of the dark silence before mentally tyling and opening my personal inner lodge. Then in that silent inner temple of my soul I invite the Eternal Spirit of Wisdom to address the brethren of my body, mind and spirit by repeating these ritual words, knowing my lodge brothers are all doing exactly the same thing. This is what I say:

> Here, in the presence of the Great Architect and in fellowship with my lodge of brother Masons, I offer myself as a living stone of a building raised to the service of the Great Architect and his Craft.
>
> May the power of the Grand Geometrician overshadow and descend upon us! May Light illumine and Love unite us, that we may know ourselves one in the presence of the Great Master of the Universe, so that from our unity may go forth to all beings Light, Love, Peace!

Eventually I wrote a little guidebook describing my progress towards awareness of the Centre, calling it *The Secret Science of Masonic Initiation*, and in it I wrote about this practice.[189]

I find the ritual helps me relax for a few moments even on the most hectic of days. When I have slightly more time I use one of the Masonic tracing boards as a symbolic focus for meditation. I have obtained some small reproductions of the tracing boards, and I set aside fifteen minutes or so (using a small electronic timer so I don't have to clock-watch). I find that for me it works best in the late evening, when the household is quiet. I turn off the main lighting and use a single lamp to shine on the tracing board of the degree I wish to think about.[190] Each of the tracing boards has an associated posture and sign, which I adopt whilst reflecting on the board. My aim is to maintain my body in perfect stillness, whilst holding the correct posture. I do not try to suppress all my thoughts, I simply focus on the images on the tracing board, maintain the posture of the degree and let my thoughts about those images go where they will. Occasionally I feel the terror which, for me, always precedes full awareness of the Centre, but I now know that if I turn and face the fear my mind will expand to encompass the whole cosmos. But usually when the timer summons me back to reality I simply find I feel relaxed and alert, and have a deeper understanding of the material of the degree.

I also make the lodge room a psychological meeting-place. Every day, I make an opportunity to project my will in an effort to realise corporate unity with the lodge. In a mental, but real, sense I feel the spiritual refreshment of a lodge meeting every day, not just at monthly intervals.

At the hour of high twelve, I try to banish every other concern from my thoughts and visualise myself and my lodge brethren gathered together in lodge, in peace, concord and harmony. This creates a subjective impression that the lodge meets every day, not just at infrequent intervals, and it contributes to harmony of thought, unity and concentration of purpose on occasions when we meet physically.

I find this practice helps induce harmony of thought, unity and concentration of purpose on those less frequent occasions when the lodge meets physically. Thereby the lodge room becomes a focus for collective thoughts and aspirations.

As I got into the habit of contributing my daily quota to this concerted work at the lodge room, I realised that I had committed myself to what the ritual called 'daily Masonic labour'. At first the exercise felt futile or even fanciful. I didn't think I was experiencing any benefit from it. But as I persisted I began to experience results. I mentioned this to my Guide.

'Remember no one can enter the lodge without first meeting opposition and giving the proper knocks,' he said. 'In this higher sense of seeking to enter the lodge you may meet with barriers of inertia, diffidence or unbelief in yourself. These will only give way when you apply knocks of resolute effort to them.'

Relating this advice to physics, I realised that I was being advised to plan my experiments carefully.

I was still struggling to calm my thoughts and to allow my mind to be still enough to lose its sense of confinement. I knew from my occasional successes that if I could still the constant chattering of my thoughts I would feel that sense of up-welling mind-expansion which was the first stage of the super-conscious state.

The process of mastering Masonic meditation was teaching me how to recognise my feelings so that I could direct my attention to parts of my brain which were susceptible to awareness.

I think communication with the Cosmic Mind utilises entangled quantum fields. A quantum field has a wavelength. By activating neurons of some critical length in my brain I was setting up a system that might be sensing instantaneous quantum changes in the consciousness of intelligent observers elsewhere in the universe.

A pattern emerged from my regular attempts at Masonic meditation. First I would feel the fear of a brooding entity just out of my field of view. If I persisted, kept calm and focused, this fear would give way to a mind-expanding moment when time stopped, and I felt great peace and clarity. Then I would feel the stars moving in their courses and the galaxy twirling slowly above me. The practice of Masonic meditation was able to reproduce subjective effects similar to those I had felt during the thunderstorm – but I knew I was creating the state myself, it was not being imposed by an intense electric field. Yet during these transient moments I felt certain there was an intelligence, and its purpose was to impose order onto the chaos of matter.

The ritual of the group mind was training me to use those parts of my brain which produced this effect. I had no way of knowing if the effect was real or if it was an illusion brought on by forcing myself into what has to be by any standards a strange state of mind. The more I tried to contribute to the group mind of the lodge the easier it became to enter this transcendental state of mind. Wilmshurst said that by drawing from the common pool of thought-energy the weaker and less efficient contributor becomes enriched by the contributions of the more capable ones, and so is gradually raised to equality with them. That seemed to be what was happening to me. Was I being taught to observe the Divine Plan of the Great Architect, or was I just enjoying a euphoric state of mental intoxication?

If the effect was as real as it seemed to be, I needed to be careful. The choices I was making in my observations and practices were encouraging certain outcomes and precluding others. I was playing with a powerful tool, as I knew that quantum choices were theoretically capable of either inflicting what we fear or fulfilling our dreams.

Certain lodges within Freemasonry do seem to have stumbled upon a method of accessing the Platonic realms of Truth. The ritual says that Freemasonry is based on three grand principles. 'Brotherly Love, Relief[191] and Truth'. Some of the main principles of Freemasonry now seemed to make more sense:

- In this context Brotherly Love could be understood as creating a group mind to support my sanity as I ventured into the mysteries of the dark Centre.
- Truth could translate as the ability to visit the Platonic realms of the truth about reality.
- Relief could be seen as making sure I would use this power to contribute to the wave function of the cosmos in such a way as to bring about the greater good.

But one thing was quite clear: I needed to learn to be careful what I wished for.

Personal Reflections

To see if there was any substance in the claims of esoteric Freemasonry I knew that I would have to submit to training a soul I was not sure I possessed. To prepare me intellectually for the challenge my Guide recommended that I read the mystical philosopher Krishnamurti, who had been an influence on some Past Masters of Living Stones. He also suggested that it was not absolutely necessary for scientists to be atheists.

'Many of your scientific heroes have been prepared to think about the idea of a God,' he had told me. 'Check it out for yourself.'

I did, and he was right. My will strengthened by this information, I allowed the lodge to help me train my soul, and, with practice and the support of the lodge, I was occasionally able to revisit that timeless realm of cosmic-consciousness. But I remained uncertain about the nature of my experience. I could not be sure whether the effect was real or whether it was an illusion I induced in myself by deliberately seeking out a strange state of mind.

13

The Lost Key is Found

Back to the Beginning

IBEGAN THIS book by describing an intense discussion about the nature of Masonic Truth held by three widely different individuals in a dark and cold car park late on a wet, foggy September evening. The participants were the most recent recruits to the Lodge of Living Stones – Bro. Hew, Bro. Tony and me. We were all working on the same project, to train our souls in the discipline that Wilmshurst bequeathed in order to learn the Truth about reality. I also posed a question: 'What is the nature of the force which can bring together such a disparate collection of individuals to share their innermost feelings?'

The force which brought us together is the ability of Freemasonry to open a portal to the nature of reality and show us that we have a purpose in the great scheme of the cosmos. We are all interested in investigating the nature of the Cosmic Mind that we sense at the mysterious Centre.

With the Lodge of Living Stones I have rediscovered the spiritual warmth which attracted me as a youth during the social evenings at the Lodge of the East Gate. And I have also found the deep purpose of The Craft. Its most important and inspirational teachings are:

1. The Great Architect has a Divine Plan for the creation of the Temple of Perfected Humanity.

2. Deep within my soul there is a Divine Spark which can make contact with the Great Architect, at the Divine Centre, and so learn about the purpose of the Creation.

3. The rituals tell of a Grand Lodge Above, with a Grand Master and Grand Officers. I believe this myth expresses an idea which is part of the stream of esoteric tradition throughout the ages. It says that

a supernal Assembly not only exists, but that it existed before the world did and played a part in creating the world.

4. If I make daily steps in Masonic Knowledge I can understand the Great Architect's Divine Plan and play a part in its completion.

5. The symbolic working tools, superficially appearing to be the tools of a worker in stone, teach me how to shape my soul to become a Living Stone and take my place in the perfected Temple of Intelligent Observers.

6. The Glory of the Centre is within myself, and my mind and consciousness are an image of the Great Architect.

7. A lodge can work together to create a group mind, and it is capable of greater mental feats than any individual brother.

8. I have learned how to access a state of mind which feels as if I can link to the souls of my lodge brethren and to the Cosmic Mind of the Great Architect.

9. The Cosmic Mind of the Great Architect is too vast for its thoughts to be comprehended by any individual. Seven Masons are required to make a Perfect Lodge, and together they reproduce the seven-fold mind of the Great Architect and so learn the purpose of the Great Plan.

10. I have learned how to hold a virtual lodge by means of remote viewing. Daily, at the hour of high twelve, I pause for a moment to quieten my mind and think about the corporate purpose of the lodge.

None of these things are scientific activities but I am convinced that Freemasonry shares a basis with observational science. It is not superstitious and does not call upon its members to embrace supernatural belief.

Freemasonry teaches using myths, metaphors and symbols. The myths of Freemasonry do not have to be scientifically framed for the method of training to create tremendous insight. And it has inspired enormous steps in scientific and social knowledge over the last five hundred years.

There is a little tale I tell my students to demonstrate how mistaken beliefs can still produce scientific results. The military success of the Roman Empire was partly based on the ability to manufacture a short, strong sword known as a *gladius*. There is a mythical story about how the Romans came to discover how to temper and anneal[192] these steel swords.

Their blacksmiths thought they were making iron swords, but the incorporation of carbon into iron creates steel. The Roman blacksmiths heated their iron swords in carbon-fired furnaces, and so accidentally created steel edges to their swords. They also discovered the process known as quenching, where the blade is heated until it glows cherry-red (a temperature of 750–800° C). It is then plunged into a bath of oil which is held at a temperature of about 40° C and allowed to cool to the bath temperature. This results in a much stronger blade, as the steel crystallises into a stronger internal structure during the sudden rapid cooling.

The Romans had a slave society, and the story goes that one day a Roman blacksmith was working with a particularly annoying slave. The blacksmith had heated the sword blade to red heat and had just finished shaping the blade edge when the slave so annoyed him that he plunged the red-hot sword into the slave's body, killing him in the process. As it was late in the day the blacksmith left the dead slave with the hot sword inside him until the following morning, when he removed the sword before the body was taken away to be disposed of. He discovered that that sword was far stronger than any he had made before and assumed that the soul of the slave had passed into the blade of the sword and strengthened it. As a theory of metallurgy, based on the available evidence, it works. The sword was much stronger because it had been annealed at body temperature, and the slave functioned like a bath of oil does by quenching the blade. Every time the blacksmith plunged a cherry-red sword into a slave and left the body overnight before removing it, a stronger sword resulted. As the Romans knew nothing about the structure of steel, the assumption that it was the slave's soul which strengthened the blade appeared reasonable. It did, however, make the position of blacksmith's slave a high-risk one with a short life expectancy. As I tell my students, a bath of oil at about body temperature and with a thermal mass about a thousand times higher than that of the sword will work just as well, and the oil bath has no soul to transfer to the sword.

Just as the Roman blacksmith thought the sword's strength was caused by migration of the slave's soul into the sword, so The Craft thinks it accesses the mystery of the Centre by training the soul. And its system works. But Freemasonry has discovered a way of tapping into the strange world of quantum observation and entangled subatomic particles. That is the lost key to Freemasonry.

The Craft has realised that it can provide three things:

1. Access to the Platonic world of symbolic Truths, which is created by the build-up of all intelligent observations over all space–time, not just by human intelligence.
2. Linkage to the accumulated mind of all the observers of reality throughout space–time.
3. A ritual and method to focus the observer's intentions to create a past which leads to an intelligent mind's ability to collapse quantum wave functions.

But this is not how Freemasonry describes its teaching. It teaches that the Platonic world of geometric truth can be accessed by the study and use of symbols. Its rituals tap into the accumulated wisdom of all the observers through space–time and call it the Mind of the Great Architect. It teaches that individuals can bring about beneficial changes in reality by focusing on the needs and wants of others, and this deliberate fine tuning of key features of the world makes life better. It calls this becoming a part of the Divine Plan of the Great Architect. What it teaches is real. Its explanations, though, are myth. Freemasonry is indeed 'veiled in allegory and illuminated by symbols'.

The lost key to the secrets was broken into two with the formation of the Royal Society – which took over the study of the hidden mysteries of nature and science – and the parallel creation of a structured Grand Lodge system in London, which took over the standardisation of ritual. The bow or head of the lost key, the part which enables the user to rotate the blade within the lock, was used to drive forward the symbolic language of mathematics. It powered the drive to relate the symbolic equations of Truth to the practical applications of physics. But the blade, or ward, of the key, the part which actually fits into the centre of the lock and releases the bolts, remained within the increasingly formalised rituals which the new Grand Lodge structure forced onto all subservient lodges. The lost key is hard to find because it is broken and scattered, not just within the degrees of The Craft but also in its wayward and wilful child, experimental science.

The Craft had shown me how to control and initiate the state of mind known as super-consciousness, which I had first experienced during that lightning storm on a Yorkshire hilltop. It has taught me how to face up to the dread and terror which manifests itself in me just before the mind-expanding moment of cosmic consciousness is reached. It has given me a mythical structure of symbols to help me override any fear that life is purposeless.

The eternal, infinite space that we call the heavens frightens everyone. The Craft knows that this fear is reduced if the universe has a purpose. It reveals this by teaching awareness of the mystery of the Centre and the oneness of creation. Its metaphor of the circumference, which at every point is equidistant from the Centre, helps individual Masons work through the fear of visible darkness to reach the glory of purposeful light.

A human is a conscious being, born into a world where people die. We know we must die, but we cannot imagine the reality of being dead. So we experience anxiety about the inevitable future of our inner self. The Craft teaches Masons how to face up to this darkness without despair or fear. It teaches that our contribution to the growing pattern of reality will continue to play its role in the Grand Lodge Above and in the ongoing plan of the Great Architect.

As human beings we are born to the question of God, and, although we are free to turn our back on it, we cannot pretend it is not asked. We can choose to say 'I will God to exist, and I have faith' and create an agnostic sense of order we can live with, or we can choose to say 'I will God not to exist, and I have faith in his non-existence', as the atheist does. The God within our mind can range from the oppressive tyrant, who ruled my Sunday School education with an iron fist and overbearing presence, to the depressing, nihilistic none-ness of the neo-atheists.

The Craft offers the alternative symbol of a Great Architect, a co-operative intelligence which is working on a purposeful plan and is pleased to involve us in the ongoing task of constructing and maintaining reality. It has shown me that to be a scientist I don't have to be a neo-atheist. I don't have to subscribe to the view that life is a meaningless consequence of a heedless accident of curdled molecules festering in a stagnant 'little warm pond'. The idea of the Great Architect as a Cosmic Mind which controls the evolution of the universe is not necessarily meaningless just because it cannot be proved or disproved by scientific method. The Craft has realised that experiencing that Cosmic Mind belongs to another order of consciousness, and that is its contribution to the lost key. The awareness it offers is of a portal into that transcendental part of reality where the equations which command the hidden mysteries of nature and science are waiting to be discovered.

Here is the first part of the lost key, the blade of the key which fits into the transcendental knowledge of the Centre and engages with the Cosmic Mind of the Great Architect. But without a bow the blade of the key can not be turned, and the bow of the lost key is hidden in the deeper teachings of physics. What links the two, the shaft which connects the bow to the blade of the key, is the transcendental knowledge of symbols which Freemasons and physicists share.

Both The Craft and physics agree that symbols are eternal things sitting in a Platonic heaven waiting for us to discover them and their power. Science and Freemasonry both set out to sensitise and imprint symbols in the minds of their followers by ritual exposure. Over time the imprinted symbols become a focus for meditative power and a means of increasing depth of understanding. The intense schooling of mathematical training is as demanding and severe as the Initiatory ritual discipline imposed by The Craft on its Candidates. Both paths increase the Initiate's power to reason and understand reality.

Modern Freemasonry began in Aberdeen in the 1480s, and the symbolism it uses today was fully known from this early time. For well over five hundred years Freemasonry has passed on a message about Truth and reality, largely unchanged. This incredible longevity has led many people to assume that there must be a secret hereditary conspiracy of manipulators who gain some personal advantage from such an Order and so perpetuate it for personal gain. But this is not so.

There *is* a secret hidden within Freemasonry, but that secret is not selfish. For at least five hundred years The Craft has been striving to understand the incomprehensible universe, the purpose of life and the primordial source of the laws of physics.

The lost secrets are three key ideas:

1. Symbols can convey messages which transcend and exceed the limitations of words.
2. There is a commonly accessible transcendental region where all the symbolic knowledge about reality lies waiting to be discovered.
3. Individuals can work together to understand and access this symbolic repository and use the knowledge they gain to understand, manipulate and contribute to reality, so giving their lives purpose. By working together the sum is greater than the parts.

Freemasonry has not been sustained by a secret order of cultist priests, but by training thinkers, who in their turn have created societies to illuminate the hidden mysteries of nature and science by the power of symbolic reasoning.

The ritual training of Freemasonry continually makes new Masons who are sensitised to the same timeless symbols of Truth, exposed to the same myths and inspired by the same ideals as the first speculative Masons who created the Kirkwall Scroll. The ritual progression of degrees creates new Masons who are trained and prepared identically to the Masons they are replacing. They are left free to draw inspiration from the process and apply it to their lives outside Freemasonry. They are encouraged to contribute to the Divine Plan of the Great Architect. It is a form of self-organisation inspired by transcendental symbols.

As physicist Paul Davies said, self-organisation which creates intelligent systems has a widespread effect. Once intelligent life arises it has the ability to collapse quantum wave functions and cause a past which ensures it exists in the present.

> Self-organization abounds in physics and chemistry: in super-conductors, lasers, electronic networks, turbulent fluid eddies, non-equilibrium chemical reactions, the formation of snowflakes. We even see it occurring in economic systems. It would be astonishing if self-organization did not occur in biology too. Yet any suggestion that biological order might arise spontaneously – i.e., that complex biological systems may already possess an inherent ordering capability – is considered a dangerous heresy.

Systems that self-organize in some circumstances often become chaotic in others. Researchers have identified a new regime dubbed 'the edge of chaos', where systems are highly sensitized to chance without becoming completely unstable. At the edge of chaos unpredictability coexists with creative and coherent adaptation. This seems to capture the elusive quality of life, which combines freedom and flexibility with holistic integrity. The key property of self-organization at the edge of chaos is that systems can suddenly and spontaneously create organized complexity with surprising efficiency.[193]

It only needs one species of intelligent observer to arise by chance anywhere in the universe for a cosmic plan to begin to appear, as this group makes observations and fixes the past. Every time a new theory with specific experimental consequences is proposed, then its relevant community of sciences sets out to make observations to confirm or deny the result. These observations collapse the existing uncertainty until they create certainties with a timeline stretching back as far as the consequences of the measurement allow.

By its choice of observations and the use of powerful instruments which extend the range of observation into the far reaches of space–time, our science is creating present, past and future by observing areas of the cosmos which might have already been observed by others and so collapsed into a reality which seems to have a purpose.

As John Wheeler pointed out:

> If delayed choice is real in a laboratory then it is real in the universe at large . . . we must conclude that our very act of measurement not only revealed the nature of a particle's history on its way to us but in some sense determined that history. The past history of the universe has no more validity than is assigned by the measurements we make now.[194]

This is the explanation for the transcendental realm of Platonic Truths. It is the accumulation of all observations throughout space–time, by any species of intelligent observers creating a past which has a purpose out of what was once pure confusion.

New observations made by any newly emerging species of observers link to the 'laws of physics' which have accumulated from all past observations. The laws collude to give a sense of purpose to the past and a sense of discovery to previously random information.

One of the functions of Masonic training and Initiation is to make individuals aware of their place within the framework of the cosmos and draw attention to their ability to form and shape reality by their own heightened perception of it. Hence the importance of being properly prepared, as the seeds of self-destruction lie in making the wrong choices for shaping our past. Such dangers are real, and John Wheeler has attempted to explain them.

> The great lesson of quantum mechanics is that if we choose to measure one thing, we thereby prevent the measurement of something else. We can decide what we want to measure, but we can't decide to measure all properties of a system at once . . . we make the whole idea of following a single path meaningless.[195]

This implication of quantum theory is profound and terrifying. When deciding what to observe we change the nature of the reality we are observing. By observing we interact with reality and modify it for ever and throughout all space–time. But, most importantly, there are choices in this process which are affected by the intentions of the observer.

By deciding to make an observation today we might make quite drastic changes to the very distant past of the cosmos, our very distant past and the distant past of all other species of intelligent observers which might exist out of range of our light-speed-limited perceptions. And if we can do this so can we be affected by other species involved in the same instantaneous process.

Our species evolved because of the conditions which influenced us over the eons. By observing and changing those conditions we might be changing ourselves in ways we have no way of detecting.

Since matter, in the form of intelligent observers, developed the ability to become curious about itself it has had an impact on the history and development of the universe. Curiosity has driven humans to make observations of the earliest phases of the universe and in doing so has forced a particular form of reality on the past. Jonathan Black summed up this idea.

> In the mind-before-matter view, mind created the physical universe precisely with the aim of nurturing human consciousness and helping it to evolve.[196]

Quantum physics says that the past of the physical universe was not resolved and fixed until it was observed by minds which desired to nurture consciousness. But that consciousness does not necessarily have to be human.

Science tells me that it is quite possible that the universe is a self-creating system which has evolved an interest in itself and, by means of that interest, has created a particular history to confirm the evolution of life. John Wheeler drew this idea in the form a large letter U. At one end there is the chaos of unresolved wave functions, while at the other is the eye of a conscious observer looking back at the clouds of uncertainty collapsing into a reality to cause consciousness to evolve.

My Masonic training has taught me not to take seriously the strident atheistic certainties of biologists and nihilistic philosophers. Freemasonry and physics represent the Old and New Testaments of science respectively. Freemasonry has evolved a spiritual system of studying the human mind that does not have the superstitious baggage of religions. The cosmic observations of the Great Architect have made a kind of intellectual sieve, to create brains and intelligences which can deal with the laws of nature. Freemasonry offers a route to study this inner mystery of human consciousness in a way totally compatible with quantum physics.

In the nineteenth century many scientists rejected Freemasonry's science of the human spirit, and many Freemasons turned away from physics, as it denied the need to know yourself that lies at the centre of the Masonic system. But relativity and wave mechanics changed everything. They gave the observer a key role in defining the nature of a system. In the early twentieth century the scene was set for revisiting the secret science of Masonic Initiation, as an alternative means of approaching the problem of a self-conscious observer with an independent spirit. The concepts put in motion then are now beginning to flower. So what of the future?

It could be bright! Freemasonry offers an inspirational spiritual path to scientists that is free of the superstitious-metaphysical certainty that characterises religious thinking. It offers training in the use of symbolic language to discuss the real questions of existence. It offers a portal into the transcendental realm of Platonic Truths where the accumulated observations of the distributed Cosmic Mind of the Great Architect dwell. Scientists need spiritual inspiration as much as the next person, but they don't need to be told to abandon their questioning uncertainty and accept a blind faith in impossible things to gain it. The time has come for Freemasonry to welcome its prodigal scientist children back into its lodges. For with its blanket ban on the discussion of religion and politics The Craft encourages its brethren to concentrate on what they hold in common, not those things which split them. And it does not exclude from its ranks those with different views about the nature of the world or different theological beliefs. It is truly inclusive of all who can express a belief that there might be order and rationale within the universe.

Freemasonry sums up the mystery of its purpose in Wilmshurst's Closing Prayer for a lodge.

> Oh Sovereign and Most Worshipful of all Masters, who, in Thy infinite love and wisdom, hast devised our Order as a means to draw Thy children nearer Thee, and hast so ordained its Officers that they are emblems of Thy seven-fold power,
>
> Be Thou unto us an Outer Guard, and defend us from the perils that beset us when we turn from that which is without to that which is within;
>
> Be Thou unto us an Inner Guard, and preserve in our souls that desire to pass within the portal of Thy holy mysteries;
>
> Be unto us the Younger Deacon, and teach our wayward feet the true and certain steps upon the path that leads to Thee;
>
> Be Thou also the Elder Deacon, and guide us up the steep and winding stairway to Thy throne;
>
> Be unto us the Lesser Warden, and in the meridian sunlight of our understanding speak to us in sacraments that shall declare the splendours of Thy unmanifested light;
>
> Be Thou also unto us the Greater Warden, and in the awful hour of disappearing light, when vision fails and thought has no more strength, be with us still, revealing to us, as we may bear them, the hidden mysteries of Thy shadow;

And so through light and darkness, raise us, Great Master, till we are made one with Thee, in the unspeakable glory of Thy presence in the East.

So mote it be.

POSTSCRIPT

A Further Step in Understanding

A S MY THOUGHTS about The Craft and its relationship to the knowledge contained in quantum physics developed I regularly discussed my ideas with my Guide. As I was finishing this book he asked me which aspects of the lost secrets of a Master Mason made me most uncomfortable.

'As a scientist you always seek a materialist explanation for things of the spirit,' he commented. 'There must be some areas of Masonic practice where this causes you problems. Which are the most disturbing?'

I didn't need to think long; my areas of discomfort were easy to identify.

'Angels, chakras and the power of prayer and rituals to influence events,' I said immediately.

'And why have you missed astrology off your list?' he asked, his face creasing into a knowing smile.

'You well know that when I investigated Masonic astrology I found a scientific explanation,' I said, smiling back.

I thought back to how I had come to study Masonic astrology. After the success of *Turning the Hiram Key*, which had looked at the science underlying the practice of Masonic ritual, my American publishers were keen to do a follow-up. I mentioned to my editor Ellie Phillips that I had a whole bundle of mathematical calculations which seemed to offer an explanation of the Masonic myth of the effect of the Bright Morning Star. When I added that I had become interested in studying the reality of Masonic astrology after reading the diaries of George Washington and noticed how he had taken its principles into account whilst establishing the federal city which bears his name, she encouraged me to write up the material. The book began by looking at the influence of Masonic astrology on George Washington, moved on to a study of what Masonic astrology implied, which was that great leaders were born when the Bright Morning Star appeared just before sunrise (an issue previously touched on in *The Book of Hiram*), and ended with a detailed scientific study of mechanisms which might explain how the appearance of bright planets close to the sun could enhance the brains of growing children.

What had surprised me was that I had been able to find a possible scientific explanation for the claims of Masonic astrology.

Interest in the idea of the Bright Morning Star having a beneficial effect on the welfare of the human race had been a consistent theme in my early investigations of The Craft. Whilst writing *Uriel's Machine* I had looked closely at the way the rising of the planet Venus (the planet which is known Masonically as the Bright Morning Star) had played a key part in megalithic culture,[197] and I spent many cold, damp nights sitting in stone chambers watching how the light of Venus cast shadows inside tunnel mounds at certain seasons of the year. Using this knowledge I had been able to put forward a rationale for the purpose and alignments of certain mounds in the Boyne Valley in Ireland (Knowth, Dowth and Newgrange). Knowth was aligned with an eight-yearly appearance of Venus as both an evening and a morning star. At the evening of the vernal equinox the light of Venus shone down its western tunnel, and in the morning shone down the eastern one. And at the winter solstice of such a year Venus would rise half an hour before the sun and shine its pale, ghostly light into the central chamber of Newgrange. Most importantly, though, I also discovered that this event was heralded by the light of the setting Venus shining onto a spiral symbol within the western side of Dowth in the seventh year of the Venus cycle, so indicating to anybody with the knowledge that the spectacular events at Knowth and Newgrange would inevitably follow in the coming year. I was later able to show that the three stone rings on the mainland of Orkney (the Ring of Brodgar, the Stones of Stenness and the Ring of Bookan) served a similar purpose, with Bookan acting as the warning that the celestial event of the double appearance of Venus was coming, and Stenness playing the role of marker of a double appearance at morning and evening, whilst Brodgar highlighted the winter rising of Venus before the sun, when its light also shone into the chamber of Maes Howe. This work was mainly published as a series of lectures given at the Orkney Science Festival, some shared with Prof Archie Roy, which have since become popular talks I give to various astronomical societies.

But perhaps the most frightening moment of this research came just before dawn at Bryn Celli Ddu in Anglesey. The June sun was just tinting the eastern horizon as I crossed the rough grass towards the mound. But I was startled to hear a strange rhythmical grunting sound coming out of the dark entrance. It sounded like the steady breathing of a great beast.

Now I'm not the sort of person who is easily spooked by legends of ghoulies and ghosties, but listening to this regular rumbling brought to my mind the legend of *Brenin Llwyd,* the Grey King or Monarch of the Mists. *Y Brenin Llwyd* – always attended by the *Bwbach Llwyd*, ugly little hobgoblins – was big and fearsome, with an appetite for human flesh and a mouthful of sharp teeth to match his size. I knew that he usually sits on top of mountains – hiding in the grey clouds and mists, where he can make a meal of any hapless hikers who get lost on the peaks – but there was nothing to stop him waiting to trap me in the dark depths of Bryn Celli Ddu.

My *Nain* had warned me as a child that I could spot *Brenin Llwyd* by the sound of his deep breathing, and when I did I should get ready to run. I looked towards the gloom of the north-east, trying to make out if the sky was lightening, but all I could see was the mist rolling over the fields. Where there's mist the *Brenin Llwyd* is sure to be, I thought, my heart beating faster.

Stop being silly! I told myself. It's a sheep that's got itself stuck. But my inner child kept urging me to turn and run. The speed of the grunts increased and got louder. I inched carefully down the passage, shining my torch down at my feet to see where I was stepping. I entered the chamber with my gaze fixed on the ground. Then, as I swung the torch beam around I saw something writhing on the floor. It looked like a tangle of old clothes. It rolled towards me, trying to get up. I shone the torch to get a better look then quickly turned it off.

'Oh,' I said. 'Happy solstice,' and quickly withdrew (as also, I suspect, did the gentleman). I waited outside. The grunting did not resume, but was replaced by snorting and giggling. When the young couple came out the dishevelled girl smiled at me.

'And you have a good solstice too,' she said, walking off hand in hand with her swain. 'The chamber's free now if you want to use it.'

I stood for a moment on the top of the mound, looking east. A faint glow was spreading slowly westwards, and as the sky lightened I heard the first straggling snatches of birdsong. Off to the north sounded the faint roar of an intercity train rushing across the island on the first leg of its long trip from Holyhead to London. The occasional bleating of distant sheep sounded almost like a fretting child. The stars faded into the steadily lightening blue of the sky. Far off, towards the village, a car engine churned into life, then rumbled for a while before whining away into the distance. I could see more and more detail of the surrounding countryside as the sky grew brighter, its greys and blacks turning almost imperceptibly into greens, golds and blues. Then the first ray of the sun's disc glinted off the windows of a house standing right on top of the hill. Any moment now the sun would shine on the forecourt of the mound. I rushed down and hurried back along the blackness of the tunnel to its now empty chamber.

Bryn Celli Ddu consists of a long narrow tunnel leading into a five-sided chamber, formed by setting up enormous stones in the shape of a pentagon. On the opposite side of the chamber from the entrance is a pillar, and across from the pillar there is a slot between the stone and the roof slab which allows light to shine on the pillar at certain times. I had seen a precision line of sunlight shine on the pillar many times, but this morning I saw something completely unexpected.

As the sun lifted above the horizon its first rays shone down the tunnel, hitting the bottom of the south-westerly wall slab which contained the light-slot. This sunbeam was reflected from the lower part of this slab, which I could now see was concave. As the sun climbed slowly skyward the passage flooded with light, and there was a broad golden path along the floor of the tunnel penetrating into the chamber.

The base of the slab now acted like a crude concave mirror. The sunlight was reflected back towards the entrance aperture, where it illuminated a small, roughly carved spiral, carved into the stone surface in a place I had never expected to be illuminated by sunlight. Within minutes the sun moved to the south, its light no longer hit the reflector, and the spiral was once again in darkness. Before I saw this I would never have believed that sunlight could ever fall on that crudely carved spiral, but it does – for just a few moments of the summer solstice sunrise, once a year.

This basic observational research, carried out over many years, convinced me that certain Neolithic builders had been acute observers of the movements of the heavens. Later, when I came to research *The Book of Hiram* I traced the myth of the Bright Morning Star and its role in creating great leaders back to the real Hiram King of Tyre.[198] This was a significant advance for my understanding of the founding myths of The Craft, because Hiram King of Tyre plays an important role in the Masonic story of the building of the Temple. At this time I used statistical analysis to test if there was any substance to the idea that when the Bright Morning Star appeared before dawn at the vernal equinox it had a beneficial effect on society. This Masonic myth is re-enacted during the climax of the Third Degree in which the ritual had encouraged me to 'lift my eyes to that Bright Morning Star whose rising brings peace and tranquillity to the faithful and obedient of the human race'.

I was surprised to discover that there was a statistically significant association between the birth of greater numbers of highly achievement-motivated people and the appearance of the Bright Morning Star. At first I thought it might simply be a motivational placebo effect, but, by comparing the findings of statistician Michel Gauquelin (who compared thousands of horoscopes to their owners' professional records)[199] with those of Harvard University anthropologist David McClelland (who studied levels of achievement in human societies over the last 2000 years),[200] I soon discovered that that there was a real effect going on. Masonic astrology was more than a romantic myth, it seemed to be a real physical effect. What was not clear was how the rising of bright planets just before the sun could possibly be influencing the brain structure of newly born infants.

Once convinced there was something more than a placebo to explain, I now set out to search for a possible mechanism. I began with a detailed literature search to find out how babies' brains grow and what makes some children more motivated than others. I found that there was a link between intelligence, motivation and exposure to situations which helped the children stimulate extensive neuronal interconnections. I also found that changes to the patterns and density of neurone connections in growing brains could be caused by exposure to pulses of electromagnetic energy. This left me with a puzzle about how bright planets, appearing in the dawn sky close to the sun, could possibility be causing chains of energy pulses.

My next step was to investigate patterns of radio and radar propagation in the Earth's ionosphere, and I soon found that patterns of radio pulses, of a wavelength which could stimulate neurone connections in growing brains, had been observed. At that stage I revisited the work of Nobel laureate Bro. Sir Edward Appleton on the nature of the ionosphere and how it changed throughout the day under the influence of sunlight. I noticed a radiation pattern within one of the ionospheric layers which showed that the degree of exposure to these pulses of brain-shaping radio energy changed with latitude. This suggested to me that if the pulses were affecting the proportion of achievement-motivated individuals in a society, there should be a correlation between the latitude of that society and its degree of economic success. I tested out this hypothesis and found it to be statistically significant. By now I was convinced I was onto something interesting, but I did not have a mechanism to link this effect to the rising of the Bright Morning Star.

At this point I realised that these brain-forming pulses were generated by rapid movements of free electrons in the ionosphere. I thought about what could cause such movements and realised that the clouds of free electrons would be subjected to intense tidal forces from the sun, the moon and the heavier planets (which also happened to be the bright ones).

It took me almost three months to complete and check my equation that described the tidal forces on a free electron and derive a function to predict its radio output. I plugged this equation[201] into a piece of software to simulate the change in pulse-chains with, and without, Bright Morning Stars rising, and I found that the gravitational attraction of the rising planets did indeed cause an electromagnetic environment which could encourage greater interconnections within the developing brains of children born at that period.

I then realised that this work offered a potential solution to the puzzle of why our species suddenly developed new skills about 50,000 years ago. I plotted the latitude of the major advances in skill development against the predicted intensity of brain-shaping pulse exposure: the correlation was statistically significant.[202] We developed as a successful species when we moved to latitudes which exposed the brains of our children to these beneficial pulse chains.

What was fascinating to me, as a student of The Craft, was how one of its founding myths, based on thousands of years of observation of the heavens, could give me an insight into a previously unknown evolutionary influence and put forward what could be described in scientific terms as a potentially falsifiable theory. This is how I summed up what I had found:

> [My] theory of Masonic astrology says that the earth's electromagnetic environment causes changes in the brain structure of some individuals, and this enabled *Homo sapiens* to exploit an inherent evolutionary advantage. Once this process of high-speed copying of useful survival tricks, such as language, was established, then Darwinian processes took over and the rapid rise in the human population became inevitable. What a strange conclusion to arrive at from a consideration of the 'superstition' of Masonic astrology! But, as a Freemason, perhaps I shouldn't be surprised: The Craft has always claimed to hold secrets of great worth.[203]

I had found what I believed to be a complete and self-consistent theory of how bright stars in the sky near the sun could cause changes in the developing brains of children. I wait with interest to see if anybody follows up my deductions and equations with further experimental investigation. (So far I have not found anything to disprove the theory, only theoretical and statistical support to indicate that it might be correct. Time will tell.) But I do know of two famous Freemasons who used the idea that the rising of the Bright Morning Star could encourage positive mental influences on the most able people in a society. They set out to create giant city-sized sundials to draw the attention of the rulers to the arrival of these auspicious periods for the rest of Eternity, and one carried out a successful experiment.

After the 1666 Great Fire of London the architect and Freemason Sir Christopher Wren put forward to the Stuart king Charles II a plan that would have created a special Masonic alignment in the rebuilt London. Wren drew on his Masonic background to create two focal points for his new plan for London. He wanted to build an avenue linking them that pointed to Eternity, and he wanted it to point to a key sunrise in the Masonic calendar. If Wren had ever built his brave new city, you would have been able to stand in front of St Paul's Cathedral at dawn on 2 April, look up the great avenue, and see the sun rise over the Royal Exchange. (And, once every eight years, you would see the Bright Morning Star of Venus rise there just before the sun.) The alignment of the main avenue of Wren's new London would thus have been a giant sundial marking the date that Masonic tradition assigns to the first day of work on King Solomon's Temple.

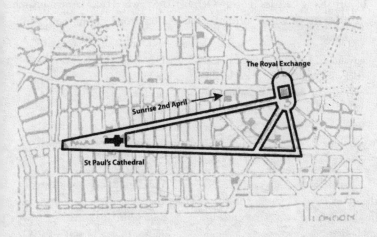

Figure 1: Bro. Sir Christopher Wren's proposed layout for a new city of London.

Inspired by Wren, Bro. George Washington, the first US President, used ideas from Masonic astrology to design his federal city in 1790, and from his diaries I found that he studied the appearances of the Bright Morning Star and seemed to accept that its appearance just before the rising sun had some sort of beneficial effect. He had drawn on two tenets of belief that seem to be firmly rooted in Masonic astrology. He had arranged the line between the President's House and the Capitol to point towards the sunrise on 6 February, a day of high Masonic significance. Secondly, this same alignment also pointed to a periodic rising of the Bright Morning Star on the same day. That sunrise marks the position of the stars of the zodiac on the day the Temple of Solomon was consecrated and when, Masonic myth says, the Bright Morning Star shone into the newly built Temple. Washington chose a single alignment to coincide with both the yearly rising of the sun and the eight-yearly rising of the Bright Morning Star of Venus above the Capitol when viewed from the President's House. Having, like Wren, aligned the main avenue of his federal city to a significant Masonic sunrise, he then carried the similarity through to the laying of the cornerstone of the Capitol on the autumnal equinox in 1793. I suspect he had in mind to repeat the ceremony carried out by Bro. King Charles II on 23 October 1667, when the Mason monarch 'levelled in Masonic form the foundation stone of the new Royal Exchange'.[204]

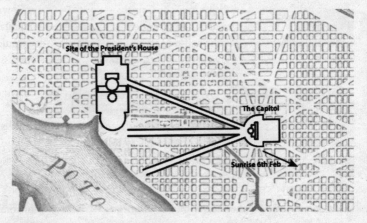

Figure 2: The layout of Bro. George Washington's federal city.

I began to study Masonic astrology when I realised that there was a strong statistical correlation between the proportion of high-achieving individuals in a society and how often Bright Morning Stars had appeared close to the sun around the time those individuals were born. When I investigated the physics I was able to put forward a possible theory of Masonic astrology. However, this is quite different from popular astrology and much more limited in its prophecies. It can only predict when a greater proportion of the children born will grow up to be high-achievers. The objective of The Craft has always been to improve society and each individual's contribution to it, so Masonic astrology is not an astrology of individuals, it is an astrology of societies. Its predictions are statistical, and I have found it to have a solid observational basis, although I suspect there are only two types of question it can answer:

1. What proportion of a group of people will be stimulated to act in a certain way by chains of ionospheric radio pulses?
2. In which times and places will these pulses have their greatest effect?

But a study of Masonic astrology inspired Bro. Washington to align the Capitol and the President's House, so that once every eight years the Bright Morning Star will rise over the Capitol and shine its rays down Pennsylvania Avenue towards the President's House on a particular morning in February. And he believed that, if he did this, society would benefit. He might well have been correct, as he founded a very successful superpower.

My Guide interrupted my reverie. 'And perhaps there are scientific explanations for the other things that still disturb you,' he said.

'My most uncomfortable thought is the underlying assumption that the lodge creates supernatural presences within its walls when it's opened,' I said. 'I feel that the lodge becomes a sort of corporate mind but I see it as something generated by the shared thought processes of the brethren not by the presence of angels.'

'And why should the idea of higher intelligences make you uncomfortable?' he asked. 'I thought you admired Uriel, the patron archangel of the North of the lodge.'

'Because I don't know what these higher intelligences might be,' I said. 'To me Uriel is a metaphor for the majesty of the heavens. He's the archangel of the North and responsible for leading us into the light and away from the paths of darkness.'

'And don't forget his element is earth,' my Guide added. 'And he controls the strength of the wind of knowledge and understanding. The wind you feel within your mind.'

'Is that what it is, when I think I'm feeling the corporate mind of the lodge strengthening my insight?' I asked.

'You have suggested that other intelligent observers, in the far distant reaches of the cosmos, may be observing reality and calling into being the laws of physics you so admire,' he said. 'Why should The Craft not draw on the symbol of an archangel to represent the lodge's contact with those groups of observers?'

'But do you believe in these whirling wheels of light forming around the officers that Leadbeater writes about?' I asked. 'The things he calls Chakras?'

I had in mind a graphic passage in C.W. Leadbeater's *The Hidden Life of Freemasonry*.

The gestures and words taught in Freemasonry are not chosen at random; each has a definite meaning and a definite power in the world of the unseen, quite apart from its signification on the physical plane . . . [These signs focus on] force-centres [which] exist as points of connection at which energy flows from one vehicle or body of a man to another. Anyone who possesses a slight degree of clairvoyance may easily see them in the etheric double, where they show themselves as saucer-like depressions or vortices in its surface. When quite undeveloped they appear as small circles about two inches in diameter, glowing dully in the ordinary man; but when awakened and vivified they appear as blazing, coruscating saucers, much increased in size. We sometimes speak of them as roughly corresponding to certain physical organs; in reality they show themselves at the surface of the etheric double, which projects slightly beyond the outline of the dense body. If we imagine ourselves to be looking straight down into the bell of a flower of the convolvulus type, we shall get some idea of the general appearance of a *chakra*. The stalk of the flower in each case springs from a point in the spine, so another view might show the spine as a central stem, from which flowers shoot forth at intervals, showing the opening of their bells at the surface of the etheric body . . . When at all in action, these centres show signs of rapid rotation, and into each of their open mouths, at right angles to the surface of the body, there rushes a force from the higher world – one of those which T.G.A.O.T.U. is constantly pouring out through His system.[205]

'I've never seen anything like that in lodge,' I said. 'And I use the signs and postures to help focus my mind on the objects of the degree when I practise my meditation.'[206]

'Neither have I,' my Guide smiled. 'Perhaps we're not clairvoyant. But I have met a Brother who was, and whom I trusted. He said he could see these things'.

'Who's that?' I asked.

'His name was Bro. Geoffrey Hodson, and, although he died some thirty years ago, he did write about the way he perceived these manifestations of spiritual forces within the open lodge. I met him and trust his judgement.'

My Guide directed me to a book called *At the Sign of the Square and Compasses,* suggesting that I begin by reading the section entitled 'Modern Scientific Evidence', which said:

> Certain modern scientists have affirmed their belief, formed from their investigations, in the existence of what they refer to as 'a directive Intelligence in nature'. Sir James Jeans, for example, states that for him the universe looks 'less like a great machine than a great thought. We discover that the universe shows evidence of a designing or controlling power that has something in common with our own individual minds . . . The universe can be best pictured . . . as consisting of pure thought, the thought of what, for want of a wider word, we must describe as a mathematical thinker.'

> Sir Arthur S. Eddington writes, 'Modern physics has eliminated the notion of substance. Mind is the first and most direct thing in our experience . . . I regard consciousness as fundamental. I regard matter as derivative from consciousness . . . The old atheism is gone . . . Religion belongs to the realm of Spirit and mind, and cannot be shaken.'

> Sir James Arthur Thomson: 'Throughout the world of animal life there are expressions of something akin to the mind in ourselves. There is, from the amoeba upwards, the stream of inner, of subjective, life; it may be only a slender rill, but sometimes it is a strong current. It includes feeling, imagining, purposing as well as occasionally thinking.'

> The occult scientist thus agrees with the physicists but takes one step further and only one, I suggest, finding as we have seen, that the life-giving and the form-producing processes of Nature are aided, directed indeed, by the actions of hierarchies of Creative Intelligences. As embodiments of universal Intelligences, they know in varying degrees, according to evolutionary stature, the design or archetype or computer

programme in the Universal Mind, and by allying themselves with the emitted Word-Force, enhance or amplify its formative capacity.[207]

This gelled with my own ideas about the Cosmic Mind – which is probably not surprising, as the people writing the comments are all physicists.

Hodson also defined what he understood by the term chakra:

A spinning, vortical, funnel-shaped force-centre with its opening on the surfaces of the etheric and subtler bodies of man and its stem leading to the superphysical counterparts of the spinal cord and of nerve centres or glands. There are seven main Chakras associated severally with the sacrum, the spleen, the solar plexus, the heart, the throat and the pituitary and pineal glands. Chakras are both organs of superphysical consciousness and conveyors of the Life-Force between the superphysical and physical, bodies.[208]

Hodson saw the chakra as an organ of communication between the Great Architect and accepted that it was something he could see, glowing, within the open lodge. He took its purpose as a focus for what he called Hierarchies of Creative Intelligences.

The ritual of opening was designed long ago by the great Adepts in collaboration with certain lofty Angels belonging to the ceremonial order. The questions and answers concerning orientation, solar positions and functions of the principal officers, establish the thought that the two temples, that of the universe and the Lodge, are associated with currents of will-thought and sound-force flowing between the master and the principal officers. Thus, by the voice of man and by arrangement with the Angelic Hosts, the Masonic temple is 'formed' from the dynamic point of view and is put in circuit with corresponding currents of universal power . . . when the master in the name of the G.A.O.T.U. declares the temple 'open,' universal power begins to flow along the established circuit into and through the four quarters of the temple.

Thus the temple, having been put in circuit with the four quarters of the compass, the four types of energy associated with them, and the Angelic presences having taken up their stations, is dynamically 'alive'. Later, the labours of the day being ended, the temple is 'closed' and then the current is cut off as it were. The ceremonial Angels withdraw . . . Thus in an opened temple great forces are flowing through the four quarters of the compass and particularly through the officers and pedestals at the East, South, and West. Those who have officiated as officers on occasions, feel these forces flowing about and through them.[209]

Had I read this account when I first entered Freemasonry I would have dismissed it as mystical nonsense, but since my own 'mystical' experiences with the lightning strike and focused meditation I was more open to consider that it might be a poetic attempt to put into words experiences which are extremely difficult to make sense of.

But Leadbeater, in particular, seemed to be able to see what I could only feel. He said:

> The generation of the proper atmosphere is one of the most important features of Freemasonry, indispensable to efficient working. Any one who is at all sensitive to such influences may feel the change which takes place when we pass from one degree to another, but only those who have opened the sight of the soul can see the variations of colour, or watch the busy workers who are so energetic in producing them.[210]

I had learned that at the centre of The Craft there is a belief that it is possible to develop and improve your soul. But I have never been quite sure how to deal with the issue of the soul. My natural tendency is to think as a physicist, not as a mystic. But, despite his poetic allusions to angels and chakras, Hodson evidently thought that some real form of communication with a Cosmic Mind takes place. As he explained:

> Not only the reigning Master but every duly initiated brother both personifies and is potentially a channel for extra-planetary powers . . . each duly initiated member being consciously aware of his or her active relationship with Planetary, Solar and Cosmic Beings. Indeed, the revelation received and the illumination attained in those Mysteries includes deepening comprehension of spiritual, occult and physical laws of Nature and progressively conscious collaboration with the Archangelic and Angelic Hosts who may be thought of as the occult 'Engineers' in the space-free 'Power House' of the universe.[211]

Hodson had felt the need to consider the view of physicists in arriving at his position. I decided that I also needed to look at the physics of what these strange manifestations might be.

A Scientific Basis for Angels, Chakras and the Cosmic Mind?

During my search for the lost secrets of Freemasonry I have looked closely at attitudes of the leading physicists who have developed knowledge of the laws which help me predict the behaviour of reality. Since the time of Galileo physics has developed as a challenge to theological orthodoxy. There seems to be a repeating pattern in the way new areas of physics develop. They begin as esoteric subjects of intellectual curiosity, move into the area of providing military advantage, so becoming the focus of military aspirations for national security, before becoming a threat to existence which needs to be controlled internationally.

John Wheeler wrote of an emergent property of simple items of information forming something that could be as complex as the Cosmic Mind of the Great Architect.

> The rich complexity of the universe as a whole does not in any way preclude an extremely simple element such a bit of information from being what the universe is made of. When enough simple elements are stirred together, there is no limit to what can result.[212]

Here, I felt, was a recipe for the emergence of a Great Architect by natural processes. If the universe is as old as I suspect it might be, then there has been plenty of time for many observers, scattered so widely through out space–time as never to come into contact, to conduct separate experiments which helped fine-tune the laws of the universe to make them hospitable to all intelligence. This might be the source of that sense of intelligent purpose that creates awe in all physicists.

In Chapter 11 I discussed possible mechanisms of quantum entanglement by which human minds could link to the minds of non-human conscious observers beyond the range of normal communication channels.[213] There is general agreement that matter is a condensation of vacuum energy which causes a spontaneous eruption of quarks and electrons from the zero-point energy field that pervades the whole of space–time. (This is sometimes rather poetically referred to as the Dirac Sea.) The quarks quickly form groups together to make protons and neutrons, sometime creating many other strange unstable particles as they do. But this method of formation ensures that such particles are created in entangled pairs, so the implication is that all matter in the universe is made of particles which are entangled with other particles, and the pairs are widely dispersed. No matter whether all the matter in the universe was created during the Big Bang or, as I have come to suspect, over a longer period by the ongoing action of quasars, this remains true. With every particle being one side of an entangled pair, and a human brain having about 10^{51} – that is, about 10, 000,000,000,000,000,000,000,000,000,000,000,000,000,000,000,000,0 00,000particles[214] – involved in its neuron structure, the chances of an opposite of the pair being used to build an intelligent system elsewhere is a finite possibility. If the Big Bang theory proves to be true, then this strengthens the argument, as all the particles, even those in the furthest reaches of outer space, were once close enough have been entangled. And if the quasi-Steady State theory is true, then new pairs of entangled particles are being continuously created throughout eternity and have had plenty of time to spread throughout space–time. This means there is nothing scientifically unreasonable in suggesting that non-human intelligent observers in vastly distant parts of the universe may share entangled particles within their thinking organs. (For humans these organs are brains, but for extraterrestrial life forms . . . who knows what they use to think with?)

There is no generally accepted mechanism to explain how entangled particles communicate faster than light, but I have put together some ideas about how it might work, and I have already mentioned current research which shows that DNA can detect the sign of a single electron's spin.[215] When Einstein was thinking about how the photo-electric effect worked he realised that he couldn't explain all the results of the experiments unless he threw away the idea that light was a continuous stream. Instead he worked out what would happen if it was made of tiny particles, which he called photons. He found that by changing his assumptions he was able to understand what was happening. I think a similar approach is needed to try and understand how it is possible for pairs of particles to communicate instantly across vast distances, when all other means of communication seem to be limited by the speed of light.

The possibility occurred to me that space–time might not be what it appears to be. For thousands of years nobody noticed that almost everything in the world came in tiny, tiny portions called quanta. Since Einstein's work we know that light, energy and even matter are all made up of separate standard-sized portions, and those portions can look like either small, hard marbles or fuzzy little packets of waves, depending on how we decide to measure them. We humans only see lumbering great conglomerations of these indecisive quanta, so we think that matter is solid, that light is made of rays, and that we can be quite certain of where something is and where it has been. But if we look more closely we find this just isn't true. Look too closely at a quantum, and you change it, whether you mean to or not, and you change not just how it is now, you also change how it was in the past. It may be counterintuitive, but this theory underpins all our modern technology and explains how it works.

Likewise, we think that space and time are a continuous whole, like the rubber skin of a balloon. We also expect space to be continuous, so we can rove all over the surface of the balloon without falling down any cracks. Likewise we think that time flows from the past through the present to the future without any holes or lumps to upset our cosy view. We expect that if we travel from A to B we will always stay within space. But it might not be true.

Einstein disturbed this view first, when he showed that space and time are parts of the same thing, and that both space and time can bend. We never expect space–time to break and fragment, though. But what if it does?

Just imagine for a moment that space–time might be made up of tiny, tiny granules[216] – think of them as very small grains of rice filling up a very big jar, about the size of the cosmos. If space–time was like these grains of rice, then it would be possible to fall into the gaps between them – and out of space and time. Then what would happen?

If these granules of space–time were small enough, then most standard subatomic particles, like protons, neutrons and electrons, would be so big that they would sprawl across many of these tiny, spherical grains, which I will call textoids, and not notice the cracks. Most large objects would fit within a clump of textoids with nothing sticking out. Big objects like a pencil, a sock, a human or a galaxy, would never see the tiny, tiny gaps in space and time. But some odd particles – those with funny-shaped waveforms – might find that their boundaries slipped down the gaps between the grains of space–time.

And there will be gaps. For at last the last four hundred years humans have studied the mathematics of how to pack as many spheres as possible into a given space without leaving niggling gaps. The close packing of cannonballs was an issue for the navy of Charles II – one that the Freemasons of the Royal Society looked at. (They wanted to pack as many cannonballs as possible into the smallest space, so a man-of-war could carry lots of ammunition whilst still leaving room for the gunners to load the gun.) Newton studied the problem of closely packing spherical balls,[217] and found that for spheres on a flat plane there are seven other spheres touching any individual one; when the analysis is extended to three dimensions, there will be thirteen. (How odd that these are mystical numbers in Freemasonry!) His analysis also showed that there is always free space between these spheres, even when they are packed extremely tightly. Likewise, spherical textoids of space–time cannot pack perfectly into any given volume, and there will be gaps between them which are not part of space–time. But what could fill that interstitial space, which by definition has to be outside of space–time?

Paul Dirac put forward a possible answer. He suggested that this space was filled with the background energy of the vacuum, what he called an interstitial aether. He had revisited and brought up to date the old theory of the aether, which at one time scientists thought was an elastic substance that carried the vibrations of light waves. A famous experiment known the Michelson–Morley experiment[218] showed that such an elastic substance could not exist and inspired Einstein to produce his alternative explanation of how light moves, known as the theory of relativity.[219]

But Dirac's take on interstitial aether was different. His mathematics suggested it must be an inelastic and non-relativistic substance. It was a place which was separate from, and yet connected to, every single textoid of space–time in the universe.[220] This meant that if the edge of a particle slipped into this interstitial aether it could pop out anywhere else in the whole universe. And it also provided a mechanism to explain the non-localised communication effects between entangled particles that are such a troubling aspect of quantum measurement. If entangled particles maintain a thread of connection through interacting with this aether, then their linkage is not restricted by the speed of light, and the information about an observation is transmitted instantly to the paired textoid where a particle's twin resides.

As Dirac's interstitial aether is non-relativistic, if the waveform of a particle collapses into that interstitial place, rather than into the space–time of a textoid, the speed of the particle will not be limited to that of light. This would mean it could slip through the interstitial aether to appear instantaneously at another point in space–time. This type of behaviour has already been investigated in the theory of 'wormholes'.[221] Are entangled particles therefore linked by a sort of golden thread which tangles its way through Dirac's non-relativistic interstitial aether?

Recently there has been experimental evidence that this non-relativistic aether exists. It comes from the MAGIC telescope array.[222] MAGIC – the Major Atmospheric Gamma-ray Imaging Cherenkov telescope – scans the sky for high-energy photons from distant objects. Most nights nothing much happens, but once in a while brief flashes of energetic light bear witness to violent explosions in distant galaxies. On the night of 30 June 2005, though, something amazing happened. It was reported in the *New Scientist*:

> What MAGIC saw on that balmy June night came like a bolt from the blue. That is because something truly astounding may have been encoded in that fleeting Atlantic glow: evidence that the fabric of space–time is not silky smooth as Einstein and many others have presumed, but rough, turbulent and fundamentally grainy stuff.
>
> It is an audacious claim that, if verified, would put us squarely on the road to a quantum theory of gravity and on towards the long-elusive 'theory of everything'. If it were based on a single chunk of MAGIC data, it might easily be dismissed as a midsummer night's dream. But it is not. Since that first sighting, other telescopes have started to see similar patterns. Is this a physics revolution through the barrel of a telescope?[223]

The source of the data blip – a 20-minute burst of hugely energetic gamma rays from a galaxy some 500 million light years away known as Markarian 501 – was different. The lower-energy photons from Markarian 501 outpaced their higher-energy counterparts, arriving up to four minutes earlier.[224] This should not happen. If an object is 500 million light years away, light from it should always take 500 million years to get to us: no more, no less. Whatever their energy, photons are supposed to travel at the same speed, the implacable cosmic speed limit of light. But do their different wavelengths cause them to occasionally take short cuts, through a medium where they travel faster than the speed of light? Such a medium is Dirac's non-relativistic aether. It is possible that this aether could be acting like some sort of interstellar rat-run, or short cut, for critical wavelengths of photons.

Of course, this is only a first clue, and the idea needs more study, but it does show that it is possible that quantum particles may not be completely limited to the speed of light. Summed over billions of light years, such interactions could account for the MAGIC light speed anomaly.

Perhaps the Great Architect has provided us with particle accelerators – distant galaxies – whose eruptions might allow us to test predictions of quantum gravity, and non-relativistic interstitial, against hard experimental evidence.

But does this imply that the contact I feel I have with Cosmic Mind of the Great Architect, in open lodge, has a basis in reality? I cannot yet present a full mathematical justification of this idea, but I can describe what I experience, using the metaphors and symbols of The Craft.

A Personal View of a Living Lodge

In the Lodge of Living Stones the most inspiring ceremony of the Masonic year, at least in my opinion, is the reading of 'The Book of the Perfect Lodge'. On this occasion the lodge not only comes together to form a corporate mind, but each of the contributing brethren explains the role they have to play to bring about this.

The brethren of Living Stones meet in Castle Grove and greet each other as they arrive. We will sit and chat and catch up with events in the way friends do who have not met since last month. The formal evening will then begin with a few moments of quiet contemplation within the Temple where the lodge will later be formed. The eternal flame of the Centre (a candle suspended within a circle circumscribing a letter G and hung above the central altar) will be lit. The officers' chairs remain empty, with their collars draped over the chair-backs. Each individual brother sits quietly immersed in his own contemplations. When I take the role of organist I will check that the organ is properly prepared, the correct stops are drawn out, the swell pedal is moving freely, that power is there when the switch is flicked and that the score for the opening ode is in clear view on the music desk. Unlike the custom in many other lodges I do not play incidental music during this period of pre-meeting contemplation. Having made sure the organ is ready I take a spare seat in the temple and sit quietly. Usually I have come to this meeting directly from the university, and my mind will be full of the activities of my academic day, so I sit and try to still my mind. I deliberately set about slowing my thoughts and listen to my rate of breathing, trying to take steady, deep and deliberate breaths.

At the appointed time for the ceremony the Director of Ceremonies (DC) will ask the officers to gather outside the Temple. As they get up and move away I take my place at the keyboard of the organ and turn it on.

When the officers of the lodge are assembled into a procession the DC gives me a nod to start the opening ode. He will call the brethren to order (meaning to stand to attention), and I will play the introduction. As I play the verses all the brethren sing the words as the officers process around the Temple, carefully following a square route around the lodge as they gradually drop off officers to stand in their correct positions. By the time I complete the third and final verse all the officers are standing by their appointed seats and have placed their collars of office around their necks. The DC invites us all to sit down and passes control of the ceremony over to the Master. I remain seated at the organ stool, but turn off the power.

The Master welcomes us all and carries out the ceremony of opening the lodge. During this ceremony the Immediate Past Master lights a taper from the Eternal Flame, and the deacons carry this flame first to the Master, then to the two Wardens who each light their candles in turn. The two Guards are entrusted with their weapons (a sword and a dagger) and reminded that the power they exercise comes not from themselves but that all power comes from the Centre.

When the lodge is properly formed (by getting each officer to briefly outline his duties) the Master declares it open. He will then announce the business of the evening, to read 'The Book of the Perfect Lodge', before calling for a period of reflection to allow the brethren to prepare themselves for the ceremony we are about to work. The brethren fall silent and the lights are dimmed. The only illumination comes from the Eternal Flame and the candles of the Master and his Wardens.

During this period I concentrate first on relaxing the muscles of my body; next I work on slowing down and increasing the depth of my breathing until my body is calm. Then I focus on stilling my mind. I do this by half-closing my eyes and looking across the black and white squares which form the floor of the temple. I allow my mind to wander over the patterns and shapes of light and dark which shimmer in the gloom before me. I allow my eye to pick out lines and lozenges, diagonals and horizontals, and become peaceful and still. Sometime I can feel the beginning of the mind-expanding process that sometimes occurs during my private mediation skirting the edge of my consciousness.

The sharp sound of the Master's gavel knocking and the gentle restoration of the Temple lights pulls me back to the lodge. As the brethren become quietly alert I feel what I can only describe as the corporate mind of the lodge manifesting as a living presence.

The Master introduces the ceremony by reading Bro. Wilmshurst's description of a Mason as a threefold being:

> The Spirit indwells the Soul, just as the Soul suffuses the Body; but only in the Soul which is rectified, purified and worked from the rough ashlar to the perfect cube condition can it, as the 'Centre', be brought to life and consciousness in the mind. To achieve this is the work of The Craft Mason, and its achievement means Mastership.

He will later explain that:

> The Lodge is a model of that intermediate psychological field of Soul which lies between the Spirit above and the Material below us. The Soul can direct its energies to either of these poles, becoming illumined or darkened, spiritualised or sensualised, according to its dominant tendencies. The open Lodge exhibits the mind (in its various aspects of intuition, reason, and will), the emotions, and the sense tendencies, as all forming a community of so many Brethren who must not only learn to dwell together in unity, but also to work together for their common

good, namely, the regeneration of the whole organism . . . The Lodge, to be perfect, has seven primary Officers. These personify, broadly, the sevenfold structure of the Soul.

Each of the seven Officers explains in turn his role in the corporate mind of the lodge. The Officers, who together meld into a harmonious Master of The Craft, are:

Worshipful Master, who represents the Spirit.
Senior Warden, who represents the Mind.
Junior Warden, who represents the Outer Personality.
Senior Deacon, who represents the link between Spirit and Mind.
Junior Deacon, who represents the link between Mind and Outer Personality.
Inner Guard, who represents the inner sense-nature (astral).
Outer Guard, who represents the outer sense-nature (physical).

There are also seven secondary Officers, whose function is to represent the activities of a soul that has become well organised by working upon itself. These are:

The Chaplain, who reminds the Brethren that the power of prayer or meditation can focus the soul on the paths of Wisdom.
The Treasurer, whose function is to attend to the material needs of the Lodge to receive material wealth in order to conserve and distribute it for the well-being of the whole body.
The Secretary, whose role is to send forth the Master's summonses to the Brethren to attend the duties of the Lodge, just as the Great Architect sends forth a call to labour on the construction of the Cosmic Temple.
The Director of Ceremonies, who presides over the rites and ceremonies of The Craft and ensures they are performed according to ancient usage.
The Almoner, who goes freely among the Brethren to collect alms and to secretly distribute them. He prides himself on not letting his left hand know what his right doeth, so that he can imitate the Divine impartiality which scatters upon the just and unjust alike.
The Organist, whose role is to provide music for the Brethren's ceremonies and remind them of the eternal melodies of the heavens.

The Steward, who serves sustenance and refreshment to the Brethren and Visitors of the Lodge and sees that they are amply provided for and lack nothing.

At the point in the ceremony where the Organist explains his role within the corporate structure of the lodge I rise and deliver my description (and in doing so I am reminded how important it is for each Officer to play a distinct role in the formation and sustaining of the lodge mind). I point out that 'As worlds were made by the music of the Divine Creative Word, so, as a fellow-worker with the Great Architect, I aspire to build the temple of my humanity with harmony and concord.'

Finally the Immediate Past Master of the lodge explains his role. He sits in silence in the East of the lodge to assist in the opening and closing and to give charges and counsel to the brethren when needed. But he also explains that the progressive nature of The Craft is revealed as the Mason moves systematically through the offices.

I sit in the perpetual Light of the East and gaze back into the West, whence, long ago I was moved in my heart to set forth and seek for that which was lost to me. And now, by God's help and my own industry, I have found it! For me all hoodwinks have been lifted, all veils removed, and today the sight of my soul is keen. With enlarged vision I behold the world as a vast Lodge wherein Divine Mysteries are celebrated perpetually, whereof those of our Craft are an image. I perceive all life as a procession entering at the West and journeying to the East, ascending from the dust of the earth to the heights of heaven and I know the Mysteries of Our Brotherhood to be a means of grace divinely appointed to help men on their way.

Brethren, this is the conclusion of the Mysteries of The Craft, and after this manner shall they be fulfilled in every one who turns from darkness to light. Ponder them in silence, for in silence the Mysteries fulfilled.

The Master knocks his gavel, the lights are lowered, and we sit in silence to ponder the lost mysteries of The Craft which have just been so poetically expounded.

I used the first dark silence to still my body and mind. In this second dark silence I allow myself to focus on the purpose of the Cosmic Plan which underpins the reality I study as a scientist, and I muse on how I might better understand and apply it.

I have been taught that the fullness of the human mind is like a lodge, which I can learn to open and enter. But I have also been cautioned that within that lodge there is darkness as well as light, and I think of the moment of dread which for me always precedes awareness of the Centre.

Words, thoughts and symbols are the natural tools I use as I search for my inner Truth. And words have carried me a long way on my journey from West to East, but when they finally fail, as they must, I eventually I have to trust my feelings.

Much of The Craft is founded on words. Its ritual is built from words, and Masons jealously guard each and every one as, reverently spoken, it flows across the silent Temple pavement to be absorbed by the attentive brethren sitting around the circumference. When a brother speaks, his lodge brethren suck in his words and echo them in the silent spaces of their own souls, copying his example within the personal lodge of their mind. I vehemently shun the substituted secrets of synonyms and disdain the false vision of extended verbal explanation. For only when our inner and outer lodges unite as a single voice do we feel at one with each other. And this only happens when we all reach internal tranquillity, so that the harmony of our inner and outer lodges is not disturbed.

Before we engage in silent and intimate union with the ritual words, we prepare ourselves by stilling our thoughts in moments of dark silence. We lower the lights and let darkness flood our temple, so that the splendour of the light will not distract us from the silence of unspoken insights.

The paradox of my search for light is that I must learn to embrace my dread of darkness in order to prepare myself to work with that love and harmony which should at all times characterise a Perfect Lodge. And then, when we withdraw from the intimate fellowship of shared understanding which the group mind of the open lodge provides, we first sojourn awhile in individual darkness to allow the new fragment of shared Truth to veil itself in shadow, so that its brilliance will not dazzle us into incomprehension. Our experience of light and darkness, of thought and fear, are made one as we prepare to leave the Temple and pass out beneath the portal of holy mysteries.

This is how we build the spiritual capital of the lodge. A lodge meeting is more than a ceremonial spectacle, it is a means of leading each individual brother towards the shared knowledge of that corporate spirit which is the Perfect Lodge. Each successive meeting of a Perfect Lodge will increase the palpable atmosphere which Masonic practice should engender, so that it will always feel good to enter the lodge – for members, for Candidates and for visitors.

The nature of Truth is contradictory, and whenever I try to capture it in language I am inevitably drawn into paradox – yet all my attempts to avoid paradox lead to distortions of Truth. This is why the lodge works in darkness and in light, by individual reflection and by corporate reiteration. Truth lies in the deep structure of the world and is experienced by thought, by awe, by reason and by intuition. What we experience ourselves is more certain than what other people tell us about what they have experienced. But most people do not understand what they experience, so experience on its own is never enough. The Craft offers training in experiencing and thinking about Truth, it offers a forum to share Truth; it offers opportunities to demonstrate Truth and times to work together to share group experiences of Truth. In this way brethren are helped to internalise Truth, so that each can make a daily advancement in Masonic knowledge.

The strength and worth of a lodge does not depend upon the number of its members and the size of attendance at its popular attractions, but upon the quality and intensity of the corporate life of its members, upon their united and consistent co-operation towards a common ideal, and upon their ability to form a 'group mind' or 'group consciousness'. We experience this group mind not when we open the corporate lodge together, but between the dark silences which delineate our inner workings. Before we work our ceremony we lower the veil of darkness to encourage us to open the inner lodge of our own consciousness ready to allow to it resonate with the inner lodges of our brethren, so that the open corporate lodge becomes a grand lodge of inner lodges. It is this grand lodge of personal inner lodges that creates the group mind of the corporate lodge. Then, after the work of the ceremony is done, we lower the lights to afford us the privacy of darkness while we close our inner lodges before sharing in the closing of the material lodge.

During the noonday prayer, when I feel the fellowship of the Perfect

Lodge grow within me, I experience and understand Truth. When I carry out this ritual, metaphorically I feel the breath of my chosen guardian angel, Uriel the archangel of the North, blow the wind of knowledge and understanding onto the Divine Spark at the Centre of my soul.

If I visualise the lodge as a roaring fire of understanding, and myself as a single coal within that blaze, then I know that whilst I am in the body of the conflagration I aid my brethren to radiate the light and warmth that is knowledge of the Truth. But if I am plucked from the hearth and placed alone on the hob, then my inner ember will quickly cool to a dark cinder. The ritual of the high twelve meeting of minds gives me access to a quickening force of oxygen feeding my Divine Spark to encourage it to flare into brightness.

This spiritual metaphor does not interfere with my scientific understanding or make me less of a scientist. I still investigate and test evidence using the tools of mathematics, scientific observation and conscious measurement. But the ritual helps me feel that I am not purposeless and alone. Freemasonry offers me the possibility that my efforts are contributing to the work of the Cosmic Mind of the Grand Geometrician and helping to spread Brotherly Love, Relief and Truth throughout the cosmos. For Freemasonry looks to share that which I have in common with all people of good faith, especially my brother Masons, whilst forbidding discussion of the religious and political views that would otherwise drive us apart.

APPENDIXES

APPENDIX I

Challenging my Physicist's Faith

Probing the Great Silence

Dirac's ideas on how to approach the existence of God forced me to consider the basic assumptions of science. If I accepted the Fixed Moment of Creation theory espoused by many current scientists, then I was forced to conclude that intelligent intervention in the act of creation is likely.

This intervention could be from a miraculous supernatural being, as most religions assert. Or it could be from a natural but unknown physical entity. Either way, the statistics say that life is too unlikely to have appeared by chance within the widely accepted constraints of space–time.

But if God is out there, then why won't He/She/It communicate with me? I was not the first person to ask this question, and there was scientific approach to it that I could use to move my quest forward. It had first been asked by Bro. Enrico Fermi, one of the discoverers of the atomic bomb, not about God but about flying saucers.

Fermi was born in Rome on 29 September 1901. In 1922 he got a doctor's degree in physics from the University of Pisa, and the following year, at the age of 22, he was initiated into The Craft by Lodge Adriano Lemmi in Rome. In 1927 he became Professor of Theoretical Physics at the University of Rome. In 1938 he was awarded the Nobel Prize for Physics for his work on the artificial radioactivity produced by neutrons, and for nuclear reactions brought about by slow neutrons.[225] Fermi took his family to the award ceremony in Sweden and then fled to America. He never returned to Mussolini's fascist dictatorship in Italy.

In 1950, while he was working at Los Alamos National Laboratory, Fermi, Edward Teller, Herbert York and Emil Konopinski were discussing a spate of UFO stories in the newspapers of the time. Fermi – who was well known for his ability to do rapid calculations based on simple observations (he is famous amongst scientists for accurately calculating the energy output of the first atom bomb by timing the speed of the blast wave between two scraps of paper he placed on the ground) – worked out an estimate of the number of civilisations there should be in our galaxy if life was common. He then asked the question, 'Where is everybody?' He concluded that if life was widespread, then Earth should have been visited long ago and many times over. This question and calculation has become known as the Fermi Paradox.[226]

What inspired Fermi to ask the question was the formulation by radio astronomer Frank Drake of an equation predicting the probability (N) of finding alien life by searching for radio transmissions. The Drake equation says:[227]

$$N = R * p(P) * NL * p(L) * p(I) * p(C) * L$$

where

R = the average rate of star formation per year;

p(P) = the probability that these stars have planets;

NL = the average number of planets that can support life per star with planets;

$p(L)$ = the probability that life will develop on such a planet;

$p(I)$ = the probability that that life will be intelligent;

$p(C)$ = the probability that intelligent life will develop civilisations capable of space communication;

L = the length of time such civilisations continue to emit signals.

Drake estimated that there must be at least ten alien civilisations within our galaxy, provided life arose spontaneously on Earth-like planets as quickly as it did on Earth.

Fermi's reasoning is as follows. A civilisation will inevitably end up seeking to spread itself beyond its planet of origin for one of three reasons: exploration, colonisation or survival.

Exploration involves sending a mission towards other stars once the necessary technological level is reached. There is little doubt that this must happen one day, for reasons either of curiosity or prestige.

Colonisation has been a goal of most terrestrial civilisations since the earliest times, for religious as well as for economic or political reasons.

Unless we assume that other intelligent beings would be more reasonable than us – simply accepting their lot and never wanting to find out what's over the next hill or the next solar system – the temptation of colonisation will be widespread, and hence it will happen.

As for survival, the lifespan of a star is limited, and in about 5 billion years the Sun will cease to be stable: it will become a red giant and absorb the Earth. Sooner or later, therefore, space flights and interstellar travel will be essential to humanity's survival. All extraterrestrial civilisations will also face the same problem with their sun.[228]

Fermi assumed the existence of just one extraterrestrial civilisation capable of interstellar travel (at a speed lower than the speed of light) within our galaxy. Using the previous assumptions, he calculated that this civilisation would conquer the Galaxy in a series of jumps, colonising a planet over a few hundreds or thousands of years, and then using that planet as a platform and manufacturing base for sending more vessels towards new conquests. This calculation showed that after only 10 million years the whole Galaxy would come under the influence of this extraterrestrial civilisation (the low rate of travel being compensated by the exponential increase in the number of vessels involved).

If just one extraterrestrial civilisation would spread in a relatively short time, why don't we see extraterrestrial visitors, and why don't our radio telescopes hear intelligent signals? It's a good question. Life may be widespread, but intelligence may be less common.

In 1974 Chandra Wickramasinghe discovered that most interstellar dust is freeze-dried bacteria. This is evidence of widespread life, but not of other intelligent observers. As he explains:

> I decided to take a closer look at the visual extinction curve of starlight, the way that starlight is extinguished by dust at visual wave lengths . . . There were many unresolved problems . . . there was no homogeneous solid material that had the desired property . . . [however,] a particle made of organic material with bulk refractive index n = 1.5 could have an average refractive index of 1.2 or less if it contained minute vacuum cavities . . . When I pointed this out to Fred [Hoyle] his interest in the possibility of bacterial grains in space was immediately aroused. We got to work on discussing ways in which bacteria would freeze-dry in space leading to the production of vacuum

cavities within them . . . Freeze-drying in a vacuum, such as in outer space, would maintain the cell wall intact and also retain the interior organic content and bound water, while free water will escape and lead to the production of vacuum cavities . . . The result was staggering: we had discovered a perfect fit to the average interstellar extinction over the visual waveband with just the one assumption that interstellar grains were freeze-dried bacteria.[229]

These results were published in 1977 and put Chandra into a self-imposed scientific exile, simply for presenting strong observational evidence that the space between the stars is full of microbial life.[230] The implication of this for my quest to discover the lost secrets of Freemasonry is far-reaching. Firstly, it implies that life is not limited to, or centred on, the Earth, but is a widespread cosmic phenomenon; this makes the existence of other intelligences apart from humanity more likely. It also shows it is possible that a Great Architect, a guiding intelligence which interacts with life, exists somewhere. Human scientists have made artificial bacteria. Until scientists did it, the creation of life was considered a supernatural skill of God alone. Who knows what a more highly evolved intelligence is capable of creating from the raw materials of stellar furnaces?

Life is unlikely to have arisen by chance. What is the implication for Dirac's test for the existence of God that life, in its simplest form, is widespread throughout the cosmos?

The number of possible ways to bring basic elements together in combinations that do not result in intelligent life is $10^{25,000,000}$. Remembering that each of those attempts results in the elemental atoms sticking together so tightly that they are not available for a second attempt at structuring them into the correct sequence, this means each of the trials have to be carried out in a fresh 'little warm pond' of free atoms.

The cosmos is a big place, so it's possible lots of attempts can happen at once. But did other successful attempts happen close enough to the Earth for them to affect us? There is a cosmic speed limit which stops anything exceeding the speed of light, and it takes four years for light to get here from the nearest star (it takes 2 million years to arrive from the nearest galaxy). Life, even tiny particles of bacterial life, travel much slower than the speed of light.

As a physicist I am expected to believe that the universe is just over 14 billion years old. Knowing the age of the universe I can make the assumption, from the Drake equation, that no DNA-based life began until after stars had formed and begun to manufacture carbon. Results from NASA's Wilkinson Microwave Anisotropy Probe (WMAP) released in February 2003 suggest this happened about 200 million years after the Creation.[231] For the sake of argument I will assume that the universe is around 15 billion years old or 1.5×10^{15} years.

These numbers allow an estimate of the number of combination trials which would have had to be carried out each year to be certain that life would have developed by the time it was found to have begun on Earth. To comply with the Big Bang theory this would have to be when the universe was 1.1×10^{15} years old.

This gives the number of random trials per year needed to ensure the emergence of life by accident as $(10^{25,000,000})/(10^{15})$. This works out at as $10^{24,999,985}$ trials per year, or $(10^{24,999,985})/(10^{10}) = 10^{24,999,975}$ trials per second.

Now just remember how big this number is. It is a 1 with 24,999,975 zeros after it. Using an estimate of 3 seconds to write out each zero, and writing for 24 hours a day, it will take you 97 days to write it out; if you only write for eight hours a day it will take just under 11 months. And that is just to write down the number of trials needed each *second* after the Big Bang, in order to be sure that intelligent life will arise by accident on a 'little warm pond' on an early- Earth-type planet.

Wickramasinghe's discovery that bacteriological life is widespread in intergalactic space makes the problem worse. Bacteria thrown into space by comet or meteor collisions with hospitable planets spread extremely slowly. They are pushed outward from their parent suns by being bombarded by photons, but move much slower than the speed of light. How did they become so widespread unless they were formed everywhere almost as soon as the universe was created?

The numbers force me to accept that random emergence of life is extremely unlikely, because of the time restrictions imposed by the Big Bang theory. If I cannot assume the age of the universe is greater than 15 billion years, there has not been enough time for sufficient random one-off trials to have occurred by chance. Accepting the Big Bang theory makes Dirac's test for the intervention of some sort of God in the creation of life mathematically so highly probable that to all intents and purposes it is certain.

This made my physicist's cold, analytical heart scream in protest. Since I escaped the clutches of my Sunday School God I had always had faith that physics can explain everything. So have I been misled? I seemed to have argued myself into having to take seriously Wilmshurst's suggestion that there is a meddling Great Architect of the Universe who created life deliberately to some Divine Plan. This conclusion did not make me happy. A scientific spirit of curiosity drives me to study the hidden mysteries of nature and science and reinforces my attitude that anything and everything may be questioned within the enforced humility of scientific uncertainty. All assertions must be tested. But my calculations were forcing me to entertain the existence of a supernatural, interfering God, even though I had no experimental evidence of His actual interference.

One certain truth I had learned from my lifelong study of physics was that the real miracle is that there are no miracles. At the heart of every mystery the laws of physics continue to hold fast, if we understand them properly. I wouldn't change this view (which has never yet failed me) without a fight. Scientific thinking led Fermi to ask, 'If aliens are so probable, where are they?' In like manner I asked, 'If God is such an obvious meddler, why did He stop fiddling with life forms about four billion years ago and leave all future development to the random lottery of evolution?'

What My Scientist Self Thinks It Should Believe

Investigating the teaching of Freemasonry had forced me to question scientific assumptions. How much of my scientific knowledge is tested fact, and how much blind faith?

I decided to summarise what it means to be a scientist and what baggage the role carries with it.

- Being a scientist makes me an acolyte of an elite cult which owns knowledge of the power which rules our world.
- We can call up forces of destruction which are capable of destroying the planet.

- We intercede in the mechanisms of life and death, of health and disease.
- We manage and facilitate the only real source of wealth, the production of energy.
- By our efforts over the last four hundred years we have made the world what it is today.
- To join this elite group requires decades of dedicated study, years of detailed examination and a desire to think about the great mysteries of life.

In the Middle Ages this definition would have described a god-like being, because, as Arthur C. Clark pointed out, any sufficiently advanced technology seems to be magic to those who don't understand the science.

Different groups of people hold different ideas about scientists, and it is sometimes surprising to discover what people believe and why. Dr Ed Mitchell repeats a delightful story told to him about Yuri Gagarin, the first Russian to fly in outer space. When Khrushchev, the Russian President, spoke to Gagarin after the flight, he said that although he was quite sure that Yuri had seen God during the flight it might be better if he didn't say so in public. Later, when Gagarin had a private audience with the Pope, the Pontiff said that although he was quite sure that Yuri hadn't seen God during the flight it might be better if he said in public that he had.[232]

I am proud to be a scientist, but scientists are not gods. Over the last thirty years or so my generation of physicists has failed to make any major advances in extending human knowledge about reality. We have made tremendous strides in technology and engineering. The Large Hadron Collider at CERN is a stupendous feat of engineering. But it is also the last hope of vindication for the string theorists. If it finds the Higgs boson, often nicknamed the 'God Particle', then string theory will have made a prediction which has at last been shown to be correct.[233] If the Higgs boson does not appear in the cloud chambers of the Large Hadron Collider's particle collectors, then string theory remains as unproven as the existence of God.

The Higgs boson shares with proof of the existence of God the same elusive quality as the end of the rainbow – just when you think you have followed it far enough to examine it, it jumps into the far distance. When the Dirac criterion might demonstrate the existence of a God, the Fermi Paradox calls the result into question. Like the Higgs boson, the closer I get to analysing the nature of the Great Architect the quicker the answer retreats.

On the CERN website I found this statement of unsubstantiated faith in a creation myth followed by an unlikely event (the disappearance of antimatter). Had I read this on a theological website I would call it a miracle.

> Fourteen billion years ago, the Universe began with a bang. Crammed within an infinitely small space, energy coalesced to form equal quantities of matter and antimatter. But as the Universe cooled and expanded, *its composition changed*. Just one second after the Big Bang, antimatter had all but disappeared, leaving matter to form everything that we see around us – from the stars and galaxies, to the Earth and all life that it supports.[234]

How convenient! But what made all that antimatter disappear, and where did it go? This is another mystery, just as great as how, with only one chance in $10^{25,000,000}$ of success, the right sequence of elemental atoms came together in a 'little warm pond' amid the chaos of the newly formed planet Earth to create DNA-based intelligent life. Both beliefs are unprovable acts of faith, and their immensely small probability of happening puts them firmly in the class of events that theologians call miracles.

I don't believe in miracles. Whenever I apply the laws of physics to a problem I get predictions which fit reality, provided I understand the laws. The last great work on understanding the world in this way was done by Richard Feynman's generation of physicists when discovering quantum electrodynamics, and even that was a tidying-up exercise, not a major breakthrough. Since then we physicists have not come up with any new theories offering unique theoretical predictions that have been tested by experiment or observation.

We have applied the ideas of an earlier generation, such as Paul Dirac and Enrico Fermi, to the problems of technology and become immensely successful in electronics, information manipulation, biology and engineering. But these concern *how* to do things. We have made no progress in understanding *why* things happen. The unanswered questions of the twentieth century remain unanswered. We scientists have failed to come up with a basic description of reality. The best we can offer is a statement of probability (a guess) which can only be tested by carrying out a measurement. All the successes of our technology depend on our ability to guess what will happen, not on our ability to explain why it happens. My generation of scientists has lost its way. As Lee Smolin, from the Perimeter Institute for Theoretical Physics in Ontario, says:

> Physics should be more than a set of formulas that predict what we will observe in an experiment; it should give a picture of what reality really is.[235]

Confronting the Great Architect's Gambling Problem

In 1905 Albert Einstein discovered that light is made of little particles (photons). This was the first inkling that physicists had that all the basic quantities of everything – light, energy, subatomic particles, gravity and possibly space–time itself – are tiny fixed-size portions. It seemed that God employed an obsessive weights and measures angel to make sure that everything in the cosmos conforms to a set of divine packaging specifications. This is a counter-intuitive idea, but it explained many of the problems of optics and founded the discipline of electronics.

As quantum physics was developed, a philosophical problem emerged at its root. It was possible to write down equations and accurately predict the outcomes of experiments involving any quantum object, but it was not possible to explain *why* the object did what it did. A traditional scientific belief dating from Aristotle says for every effect there is a cause. But quantum mechanics says things happen by chance. The history of a quantum particle can be changed by the choices made by experimenters. The fact that no outcome is ever certain, and every outcome can only be estimated, seemed to abolish any possibility of finding absolute scientific truth.

Physicists split into two camps over these discoveries. In 1920 two groups, headed by Albert Einstein and Niels Bohr respectively, fought a battle for 'the soul of physics'. This phrase was used by Schrödinger in his 1933 Nobel lecture, when he claimed his work on the wave function was an attempt to save 'the *soul* of the old system' of mechanics.[236]

The soul Schrödinger wanted to save was the concept of causality. He proclaimed that there is a reason for everything, and you can deduce this reason. A different interpretation put forward by Niels Bohr was, known as the Copenhagen Interpretation. It embraced indeterminism, a principle which says there is no purpose to physical events, only statistical probabilities of outcomes, which can be calculated from the rules of quantum wave mechanics.

All previous scientific truth, from Euclid, Plato and Aristotle down to Newton, accepted that nothing happened without a reason. Science assumed that all that was needed to understand the cosmos was enough detail about the laws of interaction between objects. Now Bohr put forward an interpretation of the atomic world that said quantum mechanics could not explain causes: something classical physics prided itself on being able to do.

Bohr said that whenever an intelligent observer decided to measure a subatomic particle the apparatus and the particle interacted in an uncontrollable way. It became impossible to measure everything about the particle. He believed that the measurement apparatus disturbed the particle. Then in the mid-1930s Einstein, Podolsky and Rosen (EPR) published a paper[237] which demonstrated that if two particles are entangled, they remain linked throughout the rest of space and time, and when one is measured it can communicate the results of the measurement to the other, instantaneously. The message is not limited by the speed of light. This finding defies all conventions of classical physics and relativity.

Einstein said this showed that wave-mechanical calculations were incomplete, as they did not give a 'reasonable definition of reality'. His paper had a major impact on Bohr, who realised that speaking of observers disturbing atomic objects by measuring them assumed the particle to be the sort of billiard-ball-type objects which Newtonian mechanics could interpret. He made a series of statements which have become known as the Copenhagen Interpretation saying 'the whole situation in atomic physics deprives of all meaning such inherent attributes that classical physics would ascribe to such objects.' He said there is no meaning to be found in the actions of objects at the quantum level, all that is possible is to predict the outcome of measurements. This statement set Bohr firmly in the anti-realist camp. He believed quantum mechanics can only be used symbolically to predict observations made under well-defined conditions. The theory says nothing about any reality that *causes* those outcomes. The Copenhagen Interpretation asserts that science cannot study the cause of reality, because reality does not exist.

The Copenhagen Interpretation was the basis of how I was taught to do quantum physics. I have mentioned how my early questions about the need for a Primeval Observer got lost in my urge to calculate outcomes and make semiconducting devices. This way of working has enabled physicists, chemists and engineers to calculate and predict a vast number of situations. It has built new and advanced technologies. But Bohr's theory challenges our imagination because it violates a fundamental principle of human knowledge: that every action has a cause – part of Western common sense since the Renaissance. But Bohr's Copenhagen Interpretation insists that the price we pay for technological progress is to accept that there is no reality behind our calculations. Nothing has a cause, and all outcomes are down to chance. This is a high price to pay. In this scenario the Great Architect is a hopeless gambling junkie.

Einstein did not accept this. The philosopher Immanuel Kant had argued there is an absolute truth for science to find. Einstein agreed with this and believed that every event must have a cause, but some of the things that cause reality are not yet understood. He believed in the existence of absolute transcendental truth and could not accept that God might be a gambling addict.

The Copenhagen Interpretation allows scientists to avoid thinking about reality and confronting the Great Architect's addiction to gambling. It assumes reality is a purely mechanical process created by the act of making an observation; in Bohr's jargon this is called bringing about 'a wave function collapse'. The probability of a particle's future position and energy is described by an equation called the 'Schrödinger Wave Function', and this has no definite values or physical meaning until the particle's state is measured by an intelligent observer. Once it is measured, the wave function 'collapses' into a reality, and a past history for the wave instantly springs into existence. Before the measurement was made the object had no definite past, and a vast range of different histories were all possible.

Physicist John Wheeler regularly worshipped in the Unitarian faith (a faith that requires a belief in *causality*).[238] *He was disturbed by the implications of the* Copenhagen Interpretation for, like Einstein, he believed all causes can be discovered.[239]

> I see no bedrock of logic on which quantum mechanics is founded. What is the underlying reason for quantum mechanics? I keep asking myself. It has to flow from something else, and that something else remains to be found.[240]

As he explained:

> Different ways of examining the system under observation are 'complementary.' Think of the blind men who reached different conclusions about the nature of an elephant depending on what part of the beast they touched. Quantum physicists examining a system not only reach different conclusions depending on how they 'touch' the system; they find that the very act of making one measurement rules out making a different kind of measurement at the same time. It is as if when one blind man touches the elephant's trunk, the elephant's leg disappears into a kind of fog, escaping the touch of another blind man. Yet if the blind men return to the 'quantum elephant' later, they can touch the leg – provided they don't try to grasp the trunk at the same time.[241]

Wheeler says that the problem of making observations in physics is dependent on the circumstances of when and where an event happens. Three factors make this so, none of which was known before Einstein's discoveries. The first is that there is a maximum speed at which the knowledge of an action can be carried from the event to the observer. The second is that there is a minimum amount of energy that has to be transferred between the event and the observer in order to make the observation happen. If the event measured involves very small objects, the energy of the messenger particles carrying the results to the observer can be as large as the energy being measured.[242] The third factor is that there is no absolute frame of reference for the time when an event occurred. Past, present and future depend on the speed and position of the observer and the event. My past can be another observer's future.

Two of these factors impose limitations on what a physicist can hope to know. Because of the universal speed limit it is impossible (within the theory of relativity) to separate measurements of time and space without knowing where the observer and the object are, and how they are moving. And when dealing with quantum objects it is impossible to separate the behaviour of the object and the means by which it interacts with the method of observation. However, this is not the end of the story.

The motive of the observer when making a measurement creates a history for an observed particle which did not exist before that observation happened. By choosing a course of action in the present a physicist can bring about changes in the remote past. This scary idea pushed John Wheeler to try and come up with a more comfortable explanation.

Working with his student Hugh Everett in 1957, he attempted to solve this problem of the observer's intentions affecting the outcome, by thinking of circumstances which avoided the need for a wave function to collapse into a specific reality. The main issue is that quantum mechanics treats observers as *external* to the system it is describing. A major consequence of this is that it cannot be used to describe the whole cosmos, since the cosmos also contains the observer. Wheeler and Everett suggested instead that when an observation is made, reality splits into a range of different worlds, in each of which one of all the possible outcomes is real. The observer's consciousness can only perceive one of these many worlds, as all the others have separated and contain different versions of that observer. The implication of this is that part of me, the essential self-conscious observing me, dies to a whole range of possibilities and lifelines every time I observe something. My personal history can only follow a single world line. This is an extravagant solution (creating billions of parallel worlds every second) but, within the Copenhagen Interpretation's rules, there is nothing illogical about it,.

The act of measurement is the deepest mystery in quantum cosmology. It may be true that a part of the observer has to die each time s/he measures the outcome of a prediction or decides to make an observation. This would mean that most of the possible 'mes' have to die every time I make a decision.

This idea that a part of the individual's consciousness needs to die every time a decision is made is central to the Third Degree of Freemasonry. The ritual tells me:

> The Secrets of nature and the principles of intellectual truth were unveiled before you, and to the man whose mind has thus been modelled by virtue and science, nature presents one grand and useful lesson more: the knowledge of yourself. She finally teaches you how to die.

When I heard this Masonic idea, that my ego must die in order to free my spirit to a full awareness of reality, I thought of the Everett–Wheeler theory that a range of possible 'mes' dies every time I take a decision to follow the reality of a particular world line. The fact that the ritual of Freemasonry contained ideas about what for me is one of the greatest mysteries of physics was a key factor in forcing me to try to find a way of melding my viewpoints, of the scientist and the Freemason.

Reconciling My Science and My Freemasonry

Being a Freemason as well as a scientist has forced me to adopt a world-view that is neither scientific nor religious. But it is spiritual and draws me towards insights into the nature of consciousness and its impact on reality.

There are seven basic tenets, broadly accepted by scientists, that clash with the philosophical system of Freemasonry. I will compare and contrast my scientific and Masonic views.

1. As a scientist I am encouraged to accept that the universe is an absurd and meaningless accident.[243] As a Mason I am taught that the Great Architect has a Divine Plan for the creation of a Temple of Perfected Humanity which leads to my soul acquiring knowledge of the Divine Centre. I have also been taught that if I make daily steps in Masonic knowledge I can both understand the Great Architect's Divine Plan and play a part in its completion.

    Is the universe planned or is it accidental? Classical physics told me the cosmos was planned, but the Copenhagen Interpretation tells me it is a random accident.

2. My scientist self is encouraged to believe that this accidental universe and all its constituent contents were created from nothing at a precise moment, about 13.7 billion years ago.[244] Before this unusual moment there was no time and no space – which conveniently sidesteps the question what was there before the universe? Answer: there was no 'before', because time began at the Big Bang.

   As a Freemason I work rituals which say that a Grand Lodge Above, having a Grand Master and Officers, existed before the universe was created. They testify to an idea which forms part of the long stream of esoteric tradition throughout the ages, that a supernal Assembly not only exists, but that it preceded, in time and constitution, the Masonic Order on earth. The rituals says that earthly Freemasonry is but a shadow and projection upon the physical world of a corresponding hierarchical Order in some superphysical place. (These supernal Grand Officers are sometimes given the names of angels.) In other words, I am taught that the Masonic Order on earth is simply a reflection of the Grand Lodge Above. This Grand Lodge Above seems to have seeped into modern physics in the form of the discovery of Platonic perfection, as I have discussed elsewhere.

   My study of Dirac's criteria for the existence of God has already caused me to question the Big Bang theory. Perhaps I should revisit alternative interpretations of the facts.

3. As a scientist I believe the laws of physics are derived from a transcendental and eternal world of Platonic truths which has always existed and always will.[245]

   As a Mason I am taught that geometry is the basis on which the superstructure of Masonry is erected. By geometry Masons trace nature through her various windings to her most concealed recesses. By it we discover the power, wisdom and goodness of the Grand Geometrician of the universe and view with amazed delight the beautiful proportions which connect and grace His vast machine. By it we discover how the planets move in their orbits and mathematically demonstrate their various revolutions. By it we rationally account for the return of seasons and the mixed variety of scenes which each season produces to the discerning eye. Numberless worlds are around us, all formed by the same Divine artist, which roll through the vast expanse and are conducted by the same unerring laws of nature. It was a survey of nature and an observation of her beautiful proportions that first induced men to imitate the Divine Plan and study symmetry and order.

Is there a non-physical world of ideas which contains unprovable truths? The work of mathematician Kurt Gödel suggests there is. He showed that for any system of mathematics, there is always a statement about numbers which is true, but which cannot be proved by that system. In other words, mathematics will always be a little fuzzy around its edges.[246] It can never be the rigorous, unshakable, logical tool that physicists would like it to be. But Freemasonry has always assured me that certain truths can be accessed only by my soul. The assertion that $1 = 1$ is just such a truth.

4. The idea of God is a dangerous and outdated concept. 'There is no God, no designer, no teleological principle, no destiny.'[247] As a Freemason I have been taught that by setting the Divine Spark within me free from the slavery of the human ego I link my soul to those of my brethren and also to the purposes of the Great Architect.

    Is the idea of a Great Architect irrational and unnecessary?

5. Human life is just a chemical scum floating on the surface of an uninteresting, moderate-sized planet.[248] As a Mason, I have been taught that deep within my soul there is a divine spark which can make contact with the Divine Centre.

    Does the human soul really have a role in the cosmos?

6. Life on Earth started spontaneously in 'a little warm pond' of primordial soup.[249]

    I have been taught that the Glory of the Centre is to be found within myself, as all humans are deliberately made in the image of the Great Architect.

    Is there more to the origin of carbon-based life than biologists realise?

7. When I decide to take a measurement I cause a change in reality to occur which destroys all alternative possibilities and fixes the outcome of the experiment for ever.

    My experimental results in quantum mechanics imply that nothing exists until it is observed by a conscious entity (which might be by definition a soul). In a lodge I try to work together with my brethren to form a group mind, which is capable of greater mental feats than any individual brother. The Seven Masons who make a Perfect Lodge, are intended to reproduce on Earth the heavenly nature of the sevenfold mind of the Great Architect. I have been taught that the rising of the Bright Morning Star has a beneficial influence on mankind, and its rays kindle the divine spark in my soul. A Mason's working tools, although superficially the tools of a worker in stone, I have been taught are a means of shaping my soul into a Living Stone to fit into a perfected Temple of Humanity. I believe from practical experience that a lodge can work together to create a composite mind. I carry out a daily ceremony of holding a virtual lodge by means of remote viewing at the hour of high twelve. I try 'to stand in the meridian sunlight of our understanding so that the Great Architect can speak to me in sacraments that reveal the splendours of unmanifested light'.

Is this unity of souls having an effect on the cosmos?

All these concepts have played an important part in making me a scientist.

But my position as a Freemason is quite different. I have acquired conflicting viewpoints of the world from science and Freemasonry. Wilmshurst's teaching about Freemasonry has revealed a spiritual view that gives me, and the universe, a purpose. This clashes with my scientific training and the beliefs of my generation of scientists, who think the universe is an absurd and meaningless accident that we can easily manipulate if we apply the laws of physics to the mechanical task of predicting outcomes – and never ask why.

'How can I reconcile these positions?' I asked my Guide.

'Look at the neglected spiritual views of the founders of your scientific knowledge,' he said. 'It's a recent development that scientists have become proselytising atheists. In the past things were different, and perhaps in the future they might change again.'

And, as I explained in Chapter 10, this is exactly what I did.

APPENDIX II

The Delayed-choice Experiment

The Implementation of Wheeler's Thought Experiment

THE 'DELAYED-CHOICE EXPERIMENT' was proposed by John Wheeler in 1980 and carried out by Alley, Jakubowicz and Wickes (AJW) at Maryland University in 1984.

The reason this experiment was necessary stems from certain odd results which were observed in what has been an A-level Physics experiment carried out by every aspiring science student. Known as the 'two slits' experiment, it was first done by Thomas Young in 1801 and was intended to prove the wave nature of light.

Young pointed a source of light at a slit in a light-proof barrier. The light beam fanned out from that slit to act as a focused light source. This beam of light was then pointed at a pair of slits in another light-proof barrier. Both slits fanned out the light, so that they too acted as individual sources of light. Then the light from these two slits was allowed to shine on an observation screen. Either of the two slits could be closed off.

When either slit was open and the other closed, the light falling on the observation screen was bright at its centre and faded away towards the edges, but when both slits were open an interference pattern of alternating light and dark fringes, known as 'Young's fringes', appeared on the observation screen. This seemed to show that light travelled in waves just as Huygens's wave theory of light had predicted. This proof of the wave nature of light was accepted for the next hundred years and not even questioned until Einstein suggested that light was really made up of little particles called photons.

In 1961 Claus Jönsson performed the same experiment using a stream of electrons. Before the discovery of the Schrödinger wave equation, electrons were thought to be little particles, rather like tiny billiard balls. Schrödinger had predicted they should also behave like waves, and this is what Jönsson tested. He found that the stream of electrons created interference patterns on the observation screen, so behaving like waves.[250]

The obvious next question to ask was, what would happen if a single electron at a time was fired through this system of slits? By 1974 the technology to fire single electrons had been developed, and the experiment was repeated for a single electron by Pier Merli et al.[251] This was when the weird solutions of the Schrödinger equation showed themselves to be real. If the electrons were really little particles, then if a series of single electrons was fired through the slits each electron should only pass through one path at a time; it should not be possible for an interference pattern to be seen. But Merli found an interference pattern, thus showing that the wave function which described each electron spread out, with the result that the electron passed through both slits at once and hence interfered with itself to build up a set of Young's fringes. But that wasn't all he saw.

When the experiment was repeated with a detector that could tell whether or not the electron passed through a given slit, then the interference bands disappeared. When they know they are being watched the electrons behave like particles and stay in one place at once. The moment we stop watching them then they spread out and appear in different places at the same time. The intelligent act of measuring which slit the electron uses removes its wave aspect completely. The electron acts exactly like a particle. The observer's uncertainty about the electron's position causes the wave effects.[252]

Paul Dirac had looked at this problem and made a prediction that 'each photon then interferes only with itself'.[253] It wasn't until 1984 that this prediction could be tested, and another issue could be looked at in the process. We knew that if an observer decided to measure which path an electron followed, the electron could not pass through both slits at once. However, John Wheeler asked 'but what if the decision whether or not to observe which path the photon had followed had been delayed until after the photon had already passed the slits, but before it reached the observation screen?' This is the delayed-choice experiment, which was first carried out by Alley, Jakubowicz and Wickes in 1984[254] and confirmed by Hellmuth, Walther and Zajon the following year.[255]

This experiment has a profound implication for the history of the cosmos.

The experiment consists of a low-power laser which squirts out a single photon at a time. This source is situated at Point 1 in Figure 3. Beyond Point 5 we have two detectors, A and B, which tell us how many photons are hitting them.

At Point 2 is a half-silvered mirror (which randomly reflects half the photons which hit it and allows the other half to pass through). At Points 3 and 4 are two fully silvered mirrors which reflect every photon which reaches them.

Now consider what happens if the source at Point 1 is set to emit a continuous stream of photons.

Before I reveal the results of the experiment, let's reason out what *should* happen, if we assume that the classical view of reality is correct, and a particle can only be in one place at a time. This means that it would have a fixed history which might be unknown but could theoretically be determined.

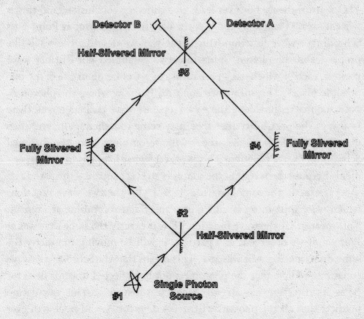

Figure 3: The Delayed-choice Experiment

When a photon is emitted from Point 1 it strikes the half-silvered mirror at 2, and there is an equal probability that it will pass through the mirror and head towards Point 4 or be reflected towards 3.

If Point 1 is set to emit a long string of photons, then half of them will be reflected and half allowed to pass through (as this is the definition of a half-silvered mirror). At Points 3 and 4 we have fully silvered mirrors, and every photon which reaches these mirrors will be reflected. Those from 3 are reflected towards Point 5 from the left side, and those from 4 are also reflected towards 5 but approach it from the right side.

Now, if reality is fixed, and all we are doing is observing it, then each photon will have passed along only one of these possible paths, but we did not know which. If this is true, then when the photons reach the second half-silvered mirror at Point 5, half will be reflected and half transmitted. The implication of this is that we would expect both detectors on average to register the arrival of half the number of photons emitted from Point 1.

Quantum theory however leads to a different conclusion, and this is what it says. When a photon hits the half-silvered mirror at Point 2 its Schrödinger wave function (this is the way we describe the wave-like properties of the photon) splits into two entangled but distinct wave packets, each of which has a probability of 0.5 of being in one of the two possible places. This means we don't really know where the photon is. Now, no matter how long these two separate wave packets travel, there is always the possibility that they may come together again, and then quantum mechanics says they will recombine into the original Schrödinger wave function. This is exactly what happens in this experiment. Because the layout of the routes is an exact square – the path [1 2 3 5] is exactly the same length as [1 2 4 5] – the two wave functions which were split into two at Point 2 meet and recombine at Point 5. This means that the wave function PE is it exactly the same as it was at Point 1. If we observe it as a particle, it will be moving in exactly the same direction at 5 as it was at 1. This means that the Schrödinger wave equation predicts that the photon cannot be deflected towards detector B, as its direction has already been measured at 1. This calculation predicts that all the photons will strike detector A, and none will ever strike detector B. This conclusion is counterintuitive from the classical viewpoint, which assumes that there is a reality to the particle's history (meaning it must have gone via either Point 3 or Point 4, not both at once) and that half the photons should strike Detector A and half Detector B.

The experimental results (since repeated many times) show that every photon emitted from Point 1 ends up striking Detector A, and none reach Detector B. This result shows that the photon had to be in two places at once, at Points 3 and 4, for it to be able to recombine at 5 and still be travelling towards Detector A in the same direction we observed it to be travelling when it passed Point 1.

But all this changes if we decide to observe the photon's route, rather than its direction of travel. We can do this by placing light-proof shutters between paths {3 5} (Shutter C) and [4 5] (Shutter D).

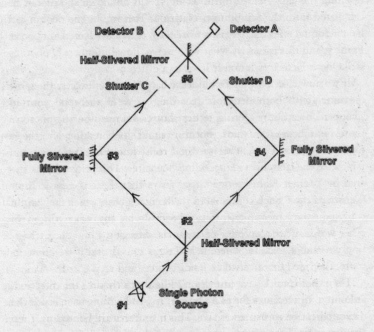

Figure 4: The Delayed-choice Experiment with the addition of shutters

If we close both shutters then no photons reach either detector. But if we only close Shutter C, leaving Shutter D open, then send a string of photons from 1, we record half of them hitting Detector B and half hitting Detector A. What the calculation tells us is that, even though the original wave packet which left 1 split into two separate wave packets, the one which went via Point 3 was stopped when it hit Shutter C. The only path left open to the photon is via Point 4. This means the wave packet which split at Point 2 has no chance of recombining with the part which we know travelled via Point 4. The probability of it completing the path via Point 3 falls to zero because of the closed Shutter C, and the remaining part of the wave packet which we observe to follow the path {1 2 4 5} immediately becomes 100% likely (i.e. it becomes reality), as we have now fixed by observation the path which the photon travelled. Hence the photon's the direction of travel after reaching the half-silvered mirror at Point 5 is unknown and cannot be calculated from the Schrödinger equation. This means the photon can be randomly reflected or transmitted by the half-silvered mirror at Point 5, and this is exactly what we observe. Equal numbers of photons strike both Detectors A and B.

If we now close Shutter D and leave C open we get exactly the same outcome (with both detectors recording 50% of the total emitted photons), because by closing either shutter we measure the photon's route, and hence can know nothing about its direction after it is randomly reflected by 5. This is a direct consequence of a basic quantum law called the Heisenberg Uncertainty Principle. This principle, discovered by Werner Heisenberg in 1927, says that there is a basic limit (known as the Planck constant) to the accuracy with which any pair of complementary measurements can be made on any wave packet. In other words, if we accurately measure the direction a photon is travelling we cannot measure where it is (i.e. its route), and if we know its route, then we cannot calculate its direction.

The experiment I have just described either measures the direction, at Point 1, or measures the route by opening and closing shutters. If the direction is not measured (that is, both shutters are left open), then the direction of the photon after it strikes the half-silvered mirror at 5 can be predicted, and the experiment confirms the prediction. If, however, we decide to measure the route taken, by choosing which shutters to open and close, then we can predict nothing about the direction in which the photon will move after striking the mirror at Point 5.

This experiment gets even more interesting when we delay the decision about what to measure until the very last moment. We can make one of three measurement choices. We can leave both shutters open, so measuring the momentum of the photon at Point 2, or we can choose to close one or other shutter, thus measuring which path the photon follows around the perimeter of the square. As we are using a single photon source, we can, if our shutters are fast-acting (this is possible using a piece of technology called a polarising filter), fire off a photon and then randomly choose what to measure just before the photon reaches the shutters.

This experiment has been done, and the results confirm that a single photon travels along both possible paths at once. Not until we decide which measurement to perform does it have a fixed history. Before the measurement it wasn't just that we didn't know what it was doing: it was that it was doing everything possible all at the same time, and only when we made our measurement did it have a real past.

Roger Penrose has said that 'quantum mechanics makes no distinction between single particles and complicated systems of many particles'. At one time all the present-day particles existed in the great, hot, tangled mess of their own eruption from the zero-point field energy of space–time (either in the Big Bang or in far-flung quasars). John Wheeler summed up the question of how intelligent matter arose from this hot tangled mass to create its own past:

> Some who investigate the anthropic principle put forward the notion of an ensemble of universes . . . In the overwhelming majority of cases, they argue, intelligent life is and always will be impossible. We belong, on this view, to one of the rare exceptions, a universe where awareness can and does develop.
>
> We can reject some of these ideas without rejecting everything. We can forgo the notion of an ensemble of universes as outside the legitimate bounds of logical discourse . . . But how can the machinery of the universe ever be imagined to get set up at the very beginning so as to produce man now? Impossible! Or impossible unless somehow – preposterous idea – meaning itself powers creation. But how?[256]

The implication of this thought is that, once early humans started to observe and measure the movements of the lights in the sky (i.e.

Marshack's evidence for lunar observation 30,000 years ago, which I mentioned in *Uriel's Machine*,[257] and the earlier evidence of sun movement lozenges recorded 70,000 years ago at Blombos Cave[258]) then by observing the motions of the heavenly bodies we gave them a history.

SOURCES

Printed Sources

Aberdeen Minute Book (1483), vol. 1, no. 39, Aberdeen Burgh Council.

Aberdeen Burgh Minute Book (1483), vol. 1, no. 39, Aberdeen Burgh Council.

Aberdeen Burgh Minute Book (1493), vol. 1, no. 52, Aberdeen Burgh Council.

Aberdeen Burgh Minute Book (1498), vol. 2. no. 14, Aberdeen Burgh Council.

(The four items above are also in the University of Dundee Digitised Archives.)

Alley, C.O., O Jakubowicz, C.A. Steggerda and W.C. Wickes (1984), 'New Type of Einstein-Podolsky-Rosen-Bohm Experiment Using Pairs of Light Quanta Produced by Optical Parametric Down Conversion', *Proceedings of the Second International Symposium on Foundations of Quantum Mechanics in the Light of New Technology*, Physical Society of Japan, Tokyo, p. 158.

Alleyne, R. (2010), 'Scientist Craig Venter creates life for first time in laboratory sparking debate about 'playing god', *Daily Telegraph*, 20 May.

Anderson, J. (1723), *The Constitutions of the Free-Masons*, William Hunter, London.

Armstrong, K. (2004), *The Spiral Staircase*, Harper Perennial, London.

Arthur, G. (1909), *The Story of the Household Cavalry*, Constable, London.

Aspect, A., P. Grangier and G. Roger (1981), 'Experimental Tests of Realistic Local Theories via Bell's Theorem', *Physical Review Letters*, 47, 460.

Barker-Cryer, N. (2006), *York Mysteries Revealed*, Barker-Cryer, York.

Barrow, J., F. Tipler and J. Wheeler (1988), *The Anthropic Cosmological Principle*, Oxford University Press, London.

Bell, J. S. (1966), 'On the Problem of Hidden Variables in Quantum Mechanics', *Reviews of Modern Physics*, 38, 447.

Black, J. (2007), *The Secret History of the World*, Quercus, London.

Bohm, D. (1980), *Wholeness and the Implicate Order*, Routledge, Oxford.

Brian, D. (2000), *The Voice of Genius: Conversations with Nobel Scientists and Other Luminaries*, Perseus, New York.

Burbidge, E.M., G.R. Burbidge, W.A. Fowler and F. Hoyle (1957), 'Synthesis of the Elements in Stars', *Reviews of Modern Physics*, vol. 29, pp. 547–650.

Chown, M. (1993), *Afterglow of Creation*, Arrow, London.

Darwin, C.R., ed. F. Darwin (2001), *The Life and Letters of Charles Darwin*, vol. 2, Adamant Media, Boston MA.

Davies, P. (1995), *Are We Alone?* Penguin, London.

—— (2007), *The Goldilocks Enigma*, Penguin, London.

Davis, P.J., and Hersh, R, (1981), *The Mathematical Experience*, Penguin, London.

Dawkins, R. (2006), *The God Delusion*, Bantam, London.

Dawkins, R., ed. (2008) *The Oxford Book of Modern Science Writing*, Oxford University Press, Oxford.

Deutsch, D. (1997), *The Fabric of Reality*, Allen Lane, London.

Di Bernardo, G., trans Gillian Mansfield (1989), *Freemasonry and Its Image of Man: A Philosophical Investigation*, Freestone, Tunbridge Wells.

Dirac P. (1930), *The Principles of Quantum Mechanics*, Clarendon Press, London (4th edition 1981).

Eales, S.A., and S. Rawlings (1996), 'A Panoramic View of Radio Galaxy Evolution from a Red shift of 0 to a Red shift of 4.3', *The Astrophysical Journal*, 460, 68.

Edwards, G.P. (1985), 'William Elphinstone, His College Chapel and the Second of April', *Aberdeen University Review*, 1, i, pp. 1–17.

Einstein, A., trans. A. Harris (1949), *The World As I See It*, Philosophical Library, New York.

Einstein, A., B. Podosky and N. Rosen (1935), 'Can Quantum Mechanical Descriptions of Physical Reality Be Considered Complete?', *Physical Review*, May 13, vol. 17, pp. 777–80.

Farmelo, G. (2010), *The Strangest Man*, Faber, London.

Farmelo, G., ed. (2003), *It Must Be Beautiful: Great Equations of Modern Science*, Granta, London.

Feynman, R.P. (1965), *The Character of Physical Law*, BBC Publications, London.

—— (1985), *QED: The Strange Theory of Light and Matter*, Princeton University Press, Princeton NJ.

—— (1988), *What Do You Care What Other People Think?* Unwin, London.

—— (1998), *The Meaning of It All*, Penguin, London.

—— ed. Jeffrey Robbins (1999), *The Pleasure of Finding Things Out*, Penguin, London.

Flett, J. (1976), *Lodge Kirkwall Kilwinning No 382*: Shetland Times, Lerwick.

French, A.P. (1979), *Albert Einstein*, Harvard University Press, Cambridge MA.

Gauquelin, M. (1994), *Cosmic Influences on Human Behavior*, Aurora Press, Santa Fe NM.

Gordin, M.A. (2007), 'Bohr's Grand Battle', *American Scientist*, Oct, pp. 572–3.

Gould, R.F. (1886), *The History of Freemasonry*, 3 vols, Caxton, London.

Gourlay, K. (2000), 'Orkney Scroll may be Priceless Relic', *The Times*, 21 July.

Grand Lodge of Antient Free and Accepted Masons, *Year Book of the Grand Lodge of Antient Free and Accepted Masons of Scotland* (1997), Grand Lodge of Antient Free and Accepted Masons, Edinburgh.

Gribbin, John R. (1984), *In Search of Schrödinger's Cat: Quantum Physics and Reality*, Bantam Books, London.

Hannah, W. (1952), *Darkness Visible: A Revelation and Interpretation of Freemasonry*, Augustine Press, London.

Hawking, S.W. (1985), Letter to the Editors, *American Scientist*, vol. 73, no. 12.

Hay, G., ed. J.A. Glenn (1993), *The Prose Works of Sir Gilbert Hay*, vol. II, Scottish Text Society, Edinburgh.

Heisenberg, W. (1958), *Physics and Philosophy*, Penguin, London.

Hellmuth, T., H. Walther and A.G. Zajon (1985), 'Realization of a Mach-Zehnder "Delayed-choice" Interferometer', report presented at the June 1985 Finnish symposium, Foundations of Modem Physics.

Hodson, G. (1976), *At the Sign of the Square and Compasses*, Vasanta Press, Madras.

Holroyd, S. (1991), *Krishnamurti, The Man, The Mystery and The Message*, Element, Rockport MA.

Hoyle, F. (1957), *Man and Materialism*, Allen & Unwin, London.

—— (1983), *The Intelligent Universe*, Michael Joseph, London.

—— (1993), *The Origin of Universe and the Origin of Religion*, Moyer Bell, Wakefield RI.

—— (1999), *Mathematics of Evolution*, Acorn Enterprises, Memphis TN.

Hoyle, F., G. Burbidge and J.V. Narlikar (2000), *A Different Approach to Cosmology*, Cambridge University Press, Cambridge.

Hoyle, F., and N.C. Wickramasinghe (1979), 'On the Nature of Interstellar Grains', *Astrophysics and Space Science*, 66, 77–90.

—— (1993) *Our Place in the Cosmos*, Phoenix, London, p. 167.

—— (1997), *Life on Mars?* Clinical Press, Bristol.

Infeld, L. (2007), *Quest: An Autobiography*, American Mathematical Society, Providence RI.

James, W. (1983), *Varieties of Religious Experience*, Penguin, London.

Jammer, M. (1999), *Einstein and Religion*, Princeton University Press, Princeton NJ.

Jönsson, C. (1961), 'Electron Diffraction at Multiple Slits', *Zeitschrift für Physik*, 161, pp. 454–74.

Knight, S. (1984), *The Brotherhood: The Secret World of the Freemasons*, Granada, London.

Krishnamurti, J., and D. Bohm (1985), *The Ending of Time*, Harper & Row, San Francisco.

Leadbeater, C.W. (1925), *The Hidden Life in Freemasonry*, Theosophical Publishing, Adyar.

Lomas, R. (2005), *Turning the Hiram Key*, Lewis Masonic, Hersham.

—— (2006), *The Secrets of Freemasonry*, Constable & Robinson, London.

—— (2007), *Turning the Templar Key*, Lewis Masonic, Hersham.

—— (2009A), *The Invisible College*, Transworld, London.

—— (2009B), *The Secret Science of Masonic Initiation*, Lewis Masonic, Hersham.

—— (2009C), *Turning the Solomon Key*, Transworld, London.

—— (2010), *Mastering Your Business Dissertation*, Routledge, Oxford.

—— (2011), *The Secret Power of Masonic Symbols*, Fair Winds, Rockport MA.

Lomas, R.A., M.J. Hampshire and R.D. Tomlinson (1972), 'A Sensitive Method of Hall Measurement', *Journal of Physics* (E), vol. 5, no.8, p. 819.

Lomas, R. and C. Knight (1996), *The Hiram Key*, Century, London.

—— (2000), *Uriel's Machine*, Century, London.

—— (2003), *The Book of Hiram*, Century, London.

McClelland, D.C. (1961), *The Achieving Society*, Free Press, New York.

MAGIC Collaboration (J. Albert, E. Aliu, H. Anderhub et al.) (2008), 'Probing quantum gravity using photons from a flare of the active galactic nucleus Markarian 501 observed by the MAGIC telescope', *Physics Letters B*, vol. 668, pp. 253–7.

Merli, P.G., G.F. Missiroli and G. Pozzi (1976), 'On the Statistical Aspect of Electron Interference Phenomena', *American Journal of Physics*, 44, pp. 306–7.

Mitchell, E., and D. Williams (2008), *The Way of the Explorer*, New Page, Pompton Plains NJ.

Newton, I. ([1725] 1934), *Mathematical Principles of Natural Philosophy*, University of California Press, Berkeley CA.

Osborne W.Z., L.S. Pinsky and J.V. Bailey, 'Apollo Light Flash Investigations' in *Biomedical Results of Apollo,* NASA, http://lsda.jsc.nasa.gov/books/apollo/S4CH2.htm.

Pagels, H. (1982), *The Cosmic Code: Quantum Physics As the Language of Nature*, Simon & Schuster, London.

Pais, A. (1982), *The Science and Life of Albert Einstein*, Oxford University Press, Oxford.

Penrose, R. (1989), *The Emperor's New Mind*, Vintage, London.

—— (1994), *Shadows of the Mind*, Oxford University Press, Oxford.

—— (2004), *The Road to Reality*, BCA, London.

—— (2010), *Cycles of Time*, Bodley Head, London.

Pickover, Clifford (2008), *From Archimedes to Hawking: Laws of Science and the Great Minds Behind Them*, Oxford University Press, Oxford.

Preston, W. (1795), *Illustrations of Masonry*, G. & T. Wilkie, London.

Russell, B. (1947), *What is the Soul?*, Heyes Barton Press, Raleigh NC.

Sandage, A., and J.M. Perelmuter (1990), 'Properties of Galaxies in Groups and Clusters', *The Astrophysical Journal*, 350, 481.

Schrödinger, E. (1967), *What is Life?* Cambridge University Press, Cambridge.

Shimony, A. (1963), 'Role of the Observer in Quantum Theory', *American Journal of Physics*, vol. 31, no. 10, p. 761.

Short, M. (1989), *Inside the Brotherhood: Further Secrets of the Freemasons*, Grafton, London.

Smolin, L. (2008), *The Trouble with Physics*, Penguin, London.

Squires, E. (1986), *The Mystery of the Quantum World*, Adam Hilger, Bristol.

Stevenson, D. (1988), *The Origins of Freemasonry: Scotland's Century 1590–1710*, Cambridge University Press, Cambridge.

Thomson, W.P.L. (1987), *History of Orkney*, Mercat Press, Edinburgh.

Tipler, F. (1995), *The Physics of Immortality*, Macmillan, London.

Tonomura, A., J. Endo, T. Matsuda, T. Kawasaki and H. Ezawa (1989), 'Demonstration of Single-Electron Build-up of an Interference Pattern', *American Journal of Physics*, 57, pp. 117–20.

Vibert, L. (1924), Foreword to *Anderson's Constitutions of 1723*, Masonic Service Association of North America.

Weinberg, S. (1977), *The First Three Minutes*, Flamingo, London.

Wheeler, J.A. (1986), 'Hermann Weyl and the Unity of Knowledge', *American Scientist*, vol. 74, July–August 1986, pp. 366–375.

—— with K. Ford (1998), *Geons, Black Holes and Quantum Foam: A Life in Physics*, Norton, New York.

Wickramasinghe, C. (2005), *A Journey with Fred Hoyle*, World Scientific, London.

Wilmshurst, W.L. (1904), *The Present Aspect of the Conflict between Scientific and Religious Thought*, printed by E.W. Coates, Huddersfield.

—— (1924), 'Concerning Cosmic Consciousness', *Occult Review*, March 1924.

—— (1925), 'The Fundamental Philosophic Secrets within Masonry', paper read to London Masonic Study Circle.

—— (1927) 'The Purpose and Aims of the Lodge', Lodge Paper No. 1, The Lodge of Living Stones, Leeds.

—— (1928), 'The Book of the Perfect Lodge', Lodge Paper No. 4, The Lodge of Living Stones, Leeds.

—— (1929), 'The 1st Degree tracing board', Lodge Paper No. 6, The Lodge of Living Stones, Leeds.

—— (2010), *The Scientific Apprehension of the Superphysical World*, Kessinger, Kila MT.

Internet Sources

http://202.38.126.65/navigate/math/history/Mathematicians/Wallis.html.

http://lunarscience.arc.nasa.gov/articles/the-solar-systems-big-bang.

http://magic.mppmu.mpg.de/.

http://map.gsfc.nasa.gov/.

http://nobelprize.org/nobel_prizes/physics/laureates/1938/fermi-bio.html#.

http://ota.ahds.ac.uk/headers/0220.xml.

http://physics.about.com/od/glossary/g/wormhole.htm.

http://plus.maths.org/issue23/features/kissing/.

http://rmp.aps.org/abstract/RMP/v29/i4/p547_1.

http://scienceworld.wolfram.com/physics/Michelson-MorleyExperiment.html/.

http://www.brad.ac.uk/webofhiram/?section=walter_leslie_wilmshurst&page=Secrets.html.

SOURCES

http://www.brad.ac.uk/webofhiram/?section=walter_leslie_wilmshurst
&page=Cosmic.html.

http://www.cscs.umich.edu/~crshalizi/Russell/what_is_the_soul.html.

http://www.fermisparadox.com/.

http://www.fermisparadox.com/Fermi-paradox.htm.

http://www.jcvi.org/cms/press/press-releases/full-text/article/first-self
-replicating-synthetic-bacterial-cell-constructed-by-j-craig-venter-
institute-researcher/.

http://www.lhc.ac.uk/About+us/What+is+the+LHC/Detector+experiments
/14438.aspx.

http://www.newadvent.org/cathen/14153a.htm.

http://www.newscientist.com/article/mg20327210.900-late-light-reveals-what-
space-is-made-of.html.

http://www.newton.ac.uk/newtlife.html.

http://www.phys.unsw.edu.au/einsteinlight/.

http://www.robertlomas.com/preston/padlock/index.html.

http://www.telegraph.co.uk/science/7745868/Scientist-Craig-Venter-creates-
life-for-first-time-in-laboratory-sparking-debate-about-playing-god.html.

http://www.universetoday.com/2010/05/26/galaxies-like-grains
-of-sand-in-new-herschel-image/.

http://www.maths.qmul.ac.uk/~pjc/preprints/goedel.pdf.

http://www.archive.org/stream/storyofhousehold01arthuoft/storyofhouse-
hold01arthuoft_djvu.txt.

http://www.freemasons-freemasonry.com/beresiner11.html.

ENDNOTES

1   Hannah (1952).

2   Knight (1984).

3   Short (1989).

4   In a paper I presented to my lodge I calculated the number of males over 21, using UK and US census data, and compared this with the number of Freemasons in the same populations. This gave me a measure of the popularity of Freemasonry as a 'market share' of the male population that Freemasonry has normally achieved over the generations. The UK data goes back the further, as lodge records go back to 1598 in Scotland and 1717 in England.

5   After Elizabeth's death William married 20-year-old Lady Marjory Sutherland. She bore him four more children, two daughters and two sons, dying whilst giving birth to the second son. At the age of 73 he married Janet Yeman, a woman almost fifty years younger than himself, but fathered no children with her.

6   Hay (1993), p. ii.

7   http://ota.ahds.ac.uk/headers/0220.xml (accessed Feb 2011).

8   Aberdeen Burgh Minute Book (1399), vol. 1, no. 6.

9   Aberdeen Burgh Minute Book (1483), vol. 1, no. 39.

10 Gould (1886), vol. I, pp. 422–3.

11 Aberdeen Burgh Minute Book (1493), vol. 1, no. 52.

12 Aberdeen Burgh Minute Book (1498), vol. 2. no. 14.

13 Stevenson (1988), p. 24.

14 Edwards (1985).

15 Stevenson (1988), pp. 24–5.

16 Lomas (2006), pp. 130–47.

17 If you want to see more of the mundane history of Freemasonry, I tell the full story in Lomas (2007).

18 Gourlay (2000).

19 *Ibid*.

20 Wilmshurst (1929).

21 I explain why the side pieces were added in Lomas (2005), Chapter 12.

22 Wilmshurst (1929).

23 Stevenson (1988), p. 14.

24 Thomson (1987), pp. 207–9.

25 Flett (1976), p. 155.

26 See Lomas (2009A).

27 See Lomas (2007).

28 Anderson (1723), p. 31.

29 Anderson (1723), p. 33.

30 Feynman (1985), p. 10.

31 *Ibid.*, p. 129.

32 Einstein (1949), p. 28.

33 See Lomas (2011).

34 Newton ([1725] 1934), p. 370.

35 Giuliano di Bernardo, Professor of Philosophy at the University of Trento, has analysed these statements and come to the view that if all four statements are to hold fast, as UGLE asserts they do, then the Great Architect must be understood as 'a regulative ideal in a non-exclusive sense'. A regulative role as the Guardian of the Laws of Physics could not be a better description of my view of what a Supreme Being should be.

36 How does The Craft's demand for the acceptance of the Great Architect as a non-exclusive regulative ideal fit in with the fact that a wide range of holy books are opened in various lodges?

    A pamphlet published by UGLE, *Freemasonry and Religion*, says 'The Bible, referred to by Freemasons as the Volume of the Sacred Law, is always open at every Masonic meeting.' When I consulted di Bernardo's philosophical interpretation of this remark (di Bernardo (1989), p. 83), he says. 'This statement tends to emphasise the close connection between Freemasonry and religion, not in the sense of Masons being slaves to religion, but rather as an act of respect towards it.'

37 This had not always been the case. When Bro. Alexander Stuart became the first recorded Master of the Lodge of Aberdeen his lodge 'worked' only two ceremonies. They had a ceremony of Initiation, where the

Apprentice was brought into the lodge and entered on its books, and a ceremony of accepting the duly qualified Apprentice as a Fellow of The Craft of Masonry. This would take place after he had completed his apprenticeship, made his masterpiece to demonstrate his mastery of stone-carving and was accepted by the lodge as a Fellow Craftsman. This ceremony gave him the freedom to take on work in his own right and to take apprentices. When he became a Craftsman he was given the Mason's Word, a secret password that would enable him to identify himself as a qualified Mason wherever he chose to travel and work.

No Fellowcraft of that early Lodge of Aberdeen had to make a public statement supporting the Galilean heresy. They probably all believed that the Earth was the centre of the universe, and the idea of the Earth revolving round the Sun would have seemed impossible to them. And yet, somehow, they laid down the intellectual seeds that flowered into the immense power of physical explanation which modern science commands.

38 Lomas (2007), pp. 295–6.
39 Lomas (2011).
40 See Barker-Cryer (2006).
41 Stevenson (1990), pp. 125–6.
42 Lomas (2005), pp. 69–71.
43 *Ibid*, pp. 339–45.
44 I lost touch with Mr Roberts when I left school. He moved to Birmingham, but some forty years later, when I was speaking at the Edinburgh Book Festival he turned up at a book-signing and introduced himself. By then he was a successful academic at Glasgow University. I was delighted to find him again and have since kept in touch. He told me that when he took his first job teaching at Heys Road Boys school in North Manchester he struggled with English spelling, for he spoke English only as a second language. Of all the teachers at that school I was lucky to be taken under the wing of the one man who shared my problems with reading English and so helped me learn to read. He also gave up many afternoons after school to help me improve the Welsh that I had learned from my *Nain* and her sistren in Mold.

Just a few years ago, when Dr Roberts and I met for dinner in a North Wales restaurant he told me how surprised he had been as a young teacher to find what appeared to him to be 'a bright, interested and intelligent boy in a class of dull 11-plus failures'. He then went on to add that when he saw my first written work he realised that I was totally unable to spell.

45 Modern society equates the ability to spell with intelligence. Everybody knows that if you can't recite the alphabet and can't spell, it's because you're stupid. All intelligent people know the alphabet – it's obvious. But then most people are blissfully unaware that, at the briefest roll call, Leonardo de Vinci, Albert Einstein, Charles Rennie Macintosh and I never mastered the alphabet. And we are not alone.

Perhaps you suspect I have just cobbled together a list of perverse and awkward people who went out of their way to be difficult and pretended not to know the alphabet as individual acts of defiance. I have to admit you have a superficial case. Certainly Leonardo was disposed to be difficult. He had some odd habits, such as designing weapons of mass destruction for his rich patrons, cutting up rotting corpses for fun and driving women to smile enigmatic smiles before he painted them. Einstein, also, was considered too dim and perverse to go to university, had a roving eye for pretty girls and was working as a lowest of low-grade civil servant when he took it into his head to solve a question of physics which had defeated Newton, before going on to invent the atom bomb. Macintosh was a solitary, morose man with a withered leg, who always found other people difficult to understand. Reading was so difficult for him that he invented his own font to help him make sense of printed material. But he also designed some of the most stunning buildings of the twentieth century, and his drawings and interior design have been turned into an instantly recognisable style of jewellery. So did these gifted and talented misfits pretend not to understand the alphabet just to annoy the less creative people around them? I somehow doubt it.

46 See Lomas (2009A).

47 Farmelo, ed. (2003), pp. xi–xii.

48 http://202.38.126.65/navigate/math/history/Mathematicians/Wallis. html (accessed February 2011).

49 http://www.newton.ac.uk/newtlife.html (accessed February 2011).

50 Hannah (1952), pp. 18–19.

51 *Ibid.*, p. 66.

52 Hannah eventually moved to Canada and joined the Roman Catholic Church.

53 Knight (1984), p. ix.

54 It took another twelve years before I found out why I had been expected to know all about Hiram Abif, his role in the construction of King Solomon's Temple and the violent and cruel manner of his death. Had I taken my Masonic degrees in Scotland I would have taken an additional degree between the Fellowcraft and the Master Mason, and everything would have been much clearer. However, had that been the case, I might never have felt the need to research the matter for myself, and so my experience of Freemasonry might have been quite different.

55 The saltire cross is formed by two lines, each at angle of 45° to the horizontal: it looks like an X. The thigh bones and the skull created the traditional symbol of the skull and crossbones, which every childhood fan of pirate stories knows well.

56 It was the custom of Ryburn Lodge to send the Candidate out of the lodge at the end of the ceremony to allow him to dress before the lodge finished. This meant that he never saw the lodge closed fully in the Second Degree until he attended another Second Degree ceremony.

57 Lomas and Knight (1996), p. 4.

58 An interesting spin-off from the Bikini test was that the name was adopted for a new kind of swimwear. The term 'bikini' arose when the French swimsuit-maker Jacques Heim designed a small bathing suit which he called the Atom. Three weeks later, Louis Réard, a mechanical engineer, came out with a smaller two-piece outfit and called it after the US atomic testing site with the slogan 'Bikini – smaller than the smallest bathing suit in the world'. He said he thought the shape of the bathing-suit bottom was similar in shape to Bikini Atoll. As an undergraduate I took an interest in both the atoll and what filled the bathing suit.

59 Letter to the Editor, *Pittsburgh Post-Gazette*, 29 December 1934.

60 Lomas and Knight (1996), p. 17.

61 *Ibid.*, pp. 78–9.

62 Although it wasn't until I was made a Masonic Knight Templar, at the Preceptory of St George Aboyne in Aberdeen, that I was able to access enough data to fully understand the role of Rosslyn and the Sinclair family in early Freemasonry. I eventually wrote the story in Lomas (2007).

63 Grand Lodge of Antient Free and Accepted Masons (1997), p. 86.

64 French (1979), p. 314.

65 If a rope be suspended loosely by its two ends, the curve into which it falls is called a catenarian curve; this shape, inverted, forms the catenarian arch, which is said to be the strongest of all arches. As the form of a Craft Lodge is an oblong square, that of a Royal Arch Chapter is a catenarian arch.

66 A Platonic solid is a three-dimensional shape of which each face is the same regular polygon, with the same number of polygons meeting at each vertex (corner). The Platonic solids are convex polyhedra with equivalent faces composed of congruent convex regular polygons. There are exactly five such solids – the cube, dodecahedron, icosahedron, octahedron and tetrahedron – as Euclid proved in the last proposition of the *Elements*.

67 Di Bernardo (1989), pp. 39–40.

68 *Ibid.*, p. 40.

69 *Ibid.*, p. 40.

70 Wilmshurst (1904), p. 5.

71 *Ibid.*, p. 6.

72 Feynman (1985), p. 82.

73 Tipler (1995), p. ix.

74 *Ibid.*, pp. x–xi.

75 *Ibid.*, pp. xiv–xv.

76 Wilmshurst (2010), p.6.

77 Wilmshurst (1925); see http://www.brad.ac.uk/webofhiram/?section=walter_leslie_wilmshurst&page=Secrets.html (accessed February 2011).

78 Wilmshurst (1924); see http://www.brad.ac.uk/webofhiram/?section=walter_leslie_wilmshurst&page=Cosmic.html (accessed February 2011).

79 James (1983), p. 276.

80 *Ibid.*, p. 277.

81 Normally the audio nerves in my head conduct electrical signals only when I am hit by a wave of sound. However, a strong electrical field will also trigger them in a different and strange way. The nerve that connects my left ear to my brain and the nerve which connects my right ear to my brain are about the same length; but they conduct electricity in one direction only, from dendrite to axon (or, if you like, from ear to brain). I judge the direction of a sound by 'hearing' the different arrival times of the same sound at my two ears. When these two nerves are triggered by an electric field coming from the side of my head, then the

two nerves conduct in opposite directions, so one pulse will be slowed down more than the other. The result of this time delay is that the 'zizzing' sound seems to come from about 5° to one side of the direction of the lightning flash. Believe me, it is a scary experience!

82 Lomas (2005), p. 21.

83 *Ibid.*, p. 251.

84 http://www.newadvent.org/cathen/14153a.htm (accessed Feb 2011).

85 Russell (1947), p. 4, or see http://www.cscs.umich.edu/~crshalizi/Russell/what_is_the_soul.html (accessed Feb 2011).

86 Dawkins (2006), p. 14.

87 Hoyle (1957), pp. 154–5.

88 Lomas, (2009).

89 Hoyle (1957), pp. 152–3.

90 Anti-matter is used in positronic emission tomography to produce a three-dimensional image of a patient's insides.

91 Lomas, Hampshire and Tomlinson (1972).

92 Physicist Euan Squires from Durham University summarises this philosophical issue in Squires (1986), p. 62. Consider an isolated system, which may be as complicated as we desire, but which must not contain any conscious mind. According to our assumption, such a system is described by a wave function which changes with time according to the rules of quantum theory. A conscious observer now makes a measurement of some property of this system: e.g. of the position of a particle. When the result of this measurement enters the mind of the observer, then the wave function reduces to the form corresponding to the particular value of the measured quantity. Note that it is not enough for the conscious observer simply to be aware only of the part of the wave function corresponding to the observed value. If this was all that happened, then we could not be sure that a different observer would see the same value of the observed quantity. We require that the act of conscious observation actually changes the wave function.

93 The quantum coupling coefficient is an arbitrary constant that has to be introduced into quantum electrodynamic calculations to make them work out in a way which matches reality. Feynman's rules, often in the form of Feynman diagrams, are used to calculate the transitions between electrons and photons when they interact in controlled ways, often producing intermediate virtual particles, before arriving at a final

desired state. Unless a compensating factor is introduced into these calculations, involving a coupling coefficient which allows for an interaction between the fundamental electromagnetic and nuclear forces, then the results of the calculation become infinite, and hence meaningless. However, once this arbitrary coupling coefficient is introduced, the calculations work to a high degree of accuracy. There is no theory as to why the coupling coefficient should take the value 137.05587, except that, when that value is used, the sums work out properly.

94 Farmelo (2010), p. 402.

95 *Ibid.*, p. 402.

96 Burbidge *et al.*(1957), or see http://rmp.aps.org/abstract/RMP/v29/i4/p547_1 (accessed February 2011).

97 Hoyle (1983).

98 Hoyle (1999).

99 Dawkins, ed. (2008), p. 67.

100 Hoyle (1999), pp. 139–40.

101 Hoyle and Wickramasinghe (1993), p. 167.

102 Alleyne (2010), or see http://www.telegraph.co.uk/science/7745868/Scientist-Craig-Venter-creates-life-for-first-time-in-laboratory-sparking-debate-about-playing-god.html (accessed February 2011).

103 Life is different from non-life in its ability to replicate itself and organ-ise random atoms into co-ordinated molecules. This arises from the enzyme's ability to act as a template to form accurate copies of proteins. Each enzyme has an internal cavity which acts as a miniature trawl net for elemental atoms. Atoms are held in preferred positions, so that the whole collection is forced into a distinct shape. In fact the separate atoms are forced to fit together in the only way out of millions of others that will make a new molecule of protein. And as the separate atoms merge into a molecule within the active cavity, they change their shape and no longer fit the cavity. The new molecule is ejected from the mould, leaving the cavity free to create more new molecules. Enzymes are therefore highly effective nano-factories for the manufacture of proteins and are at the root of DNA's ability to reproduce cells.

    All enzymes have a precise match between their active cavity and the shape of the chemicals whose reaction they facilitate. To make all the proteins required for a living organism requires a range of different and specific enzymes. The information needed to engineer the correct sequence of enzymes is contained in a four-bit code carried within the double-helix structure of DNA. This information is duplicated by unwinding the double helix into separate strands. Each one attracts fragments of previously fabricated amino acid strings, forming an exact copy of the original DNA. In this way it produces two new living molecules, where only one existed before. It is a complex system of reproduction involving vast amounts of accurate engineering of individual elemental atoms to produce successful organisms. For example, the simplest type of bacterium, such as the one built by the Venter Institute, needed 1.08 million chromosomes to be linked in the correct sequence to create its genome. (http://www.jcvi.org/cms/press/press-releases/full-text/article first-self-replicating-synthetic-bacterial-cell-constructed-by-j-craig-venter-institute-researcher/ (accessed February 2011).)

104 If one thinks there was a time before which life did not exist, a conundrum arises in understanding its origin. Which came first, the blueprint for an enzyme or the enzyme itself? If one says DNA came first, the problem is that DNA is inactive. If one says the enzyme came first, enzymes apparently cannot copy themselves. The favoured answer among biologists is to say that an intermediate blueprint came first, a blueprint expressed by RNA not by DNA. In recent years RNA has been shown to possess a limited degree of activity of its own, although whether the activity is diverse enough to be able to maintain a replicative system still remains a question. The problem is that the bond strengths, whether in RNA or proteins, are in the region of 4 eV: much too strong to be broken thermally. Thus a failure to find a working system at the first joining of atoms stops there. Without enzymes to break the bonds a second trial cannot be made, except by flooding the material with so much energy that everything is smashed back into the constituent atoms. But such extreme violence cannot lead anywhere, since floods of energy would also destroy anything useful that might arise. There is but one way out of this logical impasse, which is to make trials – not repeatedly on a limited sample of material, as in Darwin's 'warm little pond', but to make just one trial on a breathtakingly large number of samples (Hoyle and Wickramasinghe (1997), p. 50).

This is the crux of the problem. When the atoms of life bond together they stick so hard it takes enormous amounts of energy to split them apart again. The enzyme works by using this sticky property, first to capture free atoms of the right species and hold them within a template. When the full complement of atoms is captured, each held by strong atomic bonds to the atoms making up the cavity within the enzyme, their mutual attraction is now stronger than the bonds holding them to the enzyme. They snap into a new protein molecule, which then is forced out of the cavity by the same atomic forces which previously attracted the individual atoms in. It is a magnificent piece of atomic-scale engineering.

Without the preformed template of the enzyme the chance of the right atoms coming together in exactly the right configuration is vanishingly small. And there is no second chance of getting it right with that particular set of atoms. The enzyme makes creating proteins simple, so if enzymes formed easily in the environment of the early Earth, then the production of proteins would be inevitable.

105 An extreme position would be to say that . . . the chain of amino acids be unique for each enzyme, demanding $f = 1$. This appears to be close to the truth in some cases. The protein histone-4 is found in both plants and animals and it has essentially the same amino acid structure in every organism. Little or no variants have been permitted throughout biological evolution. Human DNA has some 30 distinct genes coding for histone-4. Variants are found among the 30 but they are all of the kind that lead to the same chain of amino acids (same-sense mutations). Other proteins are not as restrictive as histone-4, however. But every enzyme that has been examined in detail has been found to vary among plants and animals only to a moderate degree . . . about one third of the amino acids in a typical enzyme . . . must occupy each of about 100 positions in a chain of 300. The remaining 200 positions are by no means free choices. Each of them can be occupied by three or four among the bag of 20 amino acids, not by any member of the bag. Arguing thus leads to $f = 4^{200} = 10^{120}$ (to sufficient accuracy), and $(10^{390}/f) = 10^{270}$ trials are needed to ensure the working outcome was formed for a single enzyme. (Hoyle and Wickramasinghe (1997), p. 54.)

106 http://lunarscience.arc.nasa.gov/articles/the-solar-systems-big-bang (accessed February 2011).

107 Mitchell and Williams (2008), p. 74.

108 *Ibid.*, p. 112.

109 *Ibid.*, p. 84.

110 This comes about because the position of any object described by quantum theory is calculated using a mathematical function called the Schrödinger wave function. There are many circumstance when this Schrödinger equation comes up with solutions which say that the object is in more than one place at some fixed time.

111 Penrose (1989), pp. 331–2.

112 Esoteric Freemasonry sets out to train individuals to become psychoactive using ritual, myth and symbols.

113 Mitchell and Williams (2008), p. 119.

114 Wheeler, in Hoyle (1993), p. 70.

115 Wilmshurst (1928).

116 Quoted in Jammer (1999), p. 49.

117 Quoted in Infeld (2007), p. 196.

118 Quoted in Gribbin (1984), p. 211.

119 Quoted in Pagels (1982), p. 73.

120 Brian (2000), p. 69.

121 Acceptance Speech for 1918 Nobel Prize, quoted in Pickover (2008), p. 417.

122 Hoyle (1993), p. 83.

123 The Copenhagen Interpretation says there is no reality, and all physics can do is estimate probability. It amounts to an instruction to shut up and do the calculations! For a fuller discussion of the Copenhagen Interpretation, see Appendix I.

124 Hoyle (1983), pp. 198–9.

125 *Ibid.*, pp. 201–2.

126 Wheeler with Ford (1998), p. 337.

127 *Ibid.*, p. 338.

128 Wheeler (1986).

129 http://news.bbc.co.uk/1/hi/science_and_environment/10132762.stm (accessed Feb 2011).

130 Physicist Roger Penrose summed up this problem.

> We need merely suppose that the universe's initial state – what we call the Big Bang – had, for some reason, an extraordinarily tiny entropy.

The appropriate continuity of entropy would then imply a relatively gradual increase of the universe's entropy from then on (in the normal time-direction), giving us some kind of theoretical justification of the Second Law [of Thermodynamics]. So the key issue is indeed the special-ness of the Big Bang, and the extraordinary nature of this special initial state.

He goes on:

Once we accept that such an extraordinarily special state did indeed originate the universe that we know, then the Second Law, in the form that we observe it, is a natural consequence . . . One further point to bear in mind is the following. If we do not assume . . . that the universe originated in some extraordinarily special initial state, or something else of this general nature, then . . . no matter how curious and non-intuitive it may seem, the production of life would be far less probable to come about by natural means – be it by natural selection or by any other seemingly 'natural' process – than by a 'miraculous' creation simply out of random collisions of the constituent particles! (Penrose (2010), pp. 51–2.)

Penrose sees problems with Big Bang theory that lead him to propose alterna-tive explanations which 'have strong echoes of the old steady-state model!', about which he says:

In the 1950s, a popular theory of the universe was one referred to as the steady-state model, a proposal first put forward by Thomas Gold and Hermann Bondi in 1948, and taken up in more detail by Fred Hoyle, who were all at Cambridge University at the time. The theory required there to be a continual creation of material throughout space, at an extremely low rate. This material would have to be in the form of hydrogen molecules – each being a pair consisting of one proton and one electron, created out of the vacuum – at the extremely tiny rate of about one such atom per cubic metre per thousand million years. This would have to be at just the right rate to replenish the reduction of the density of material due to the expansion of the universe. (*Ibid.*, p. 68.)

Penrose admitted a long-standing affection for this theory.

I got to know all three of the steady-state theory's originators, and I found this model to be appealing and the arguments fairly persuasive. However, towards the end of my time at Cambridge, detailed counts of distant galaxies carried out at the Mullard Radio Observatory by [Sir] Martin Ryle (also in Cambridge) were beginning to provide clear observational evidence against the steady-state model. But the real death-blow was the accidental observation by the Americans Arno Penzias and Robert W. Wilson, in 1964, of microwave electromagnetic radiation, coming from all directions in space. Such radiation had in fact been predicted, in the later 1940s by George Gamow, and by Robert Dicke on the basis of what was then the more conventional 'Big-Bang theory' . . . After Penzias and Wilson had convinced themselves that the radiation they were observing (of around 2.725 K) was genuine, and must actually be coming from deep space, they consulted Dicke, who was quick to point out that their puzzling observations could be explained as what he and Gamow had previously predicted. This radiation has gone under various different names ('relic radiation', '3-degree background', etc.); nowadays it is commonly referred to simply as the 'CMB'. (*Ibid.*, p. 69.)

131 St Augustine of Hippo would have been proud of that answer, as it restates his view that God is outside space and time, but I am not satisfied with it.

132 Sandage and Perelmuter (1990).

133 Hoyle, Burbidge and Narlikar (2000), pp. 229–38.

134 Eales and Rawlings (1996).

135 Hoyle, Burbidge and Narlikar (2000), p. 65.

136 *Ibid.*, p. 83.

137 *Ibid.*, p. 88.

138 See Weinberg (1977).

139 Chown (1993), p. 138.

140 Newell, in Hoyle (1993), p. 82.

141 http://www.universetoday.com/2010/05/26/galaxies-like-grains-of-sand-in-new-herschel-image/ (accessed Feb 2011).

142 Wheeler (1986).

143 See Barrow, Tipler and Wheeler (1988).

144 Shimony (1963).

145 Mathematicians Philip Davis and Reuben Hersh point out, 'The ruler and compass are built into the axioms at the foundation of Euclidean geometry. Euclidean geometry can be defined as the science of ruler-and-compass constructions' (Davis and Hersh (1981), p. 13).

146 This is a popular term used to describe the Masonic science of teaching meaning from the contemplation and manipulation of symbols. For a fuller explanation of how it works, see Lomas (2011).

147 See Lomas (2009B).

148 Why this should be nobody knows, but all physicists accept the mysterious truth of the perfect equality that enables them to write down and manipulate the laws of nature.

149 Davies (2007), p. 17.

150 See Lomas (2010).

151 Penrose (2004), p. 12.

152 See Lomas (2011).

153 Feynman, ed. Robbins (1999), p. 15.

154 Feynman (1965), p. 40.

155 Penrose (1994), p. 50.

156 Feynman (1965), p. 58.

157 *Ibid.*, p. 34.

158 See Appendix I for an explanation of Fermi's argument about the likely spread of intelligent life in the universe.

159 In 1935, along with Boris Podolsky and Nathan Rosen, Einstein wrote a paper called 'Can Quantum-Mechanical Description of Physical Reality Be Considered Complete?'

Here is a brief summary of the thought experiment they proposed. Imagine that a neutral pion (a common subatomic neutral particle), which has no spin, decays into a pair of photons (a particle of light). As the two photons were created together they must be described by a single two-particle wave function, and according to quantum theory their spins must cancel each other out. Even when separated, the two photons are still described by the same wave function, and a measurement of the spin of one will immediately fix the spin of the other photon, no matter how far apart they are. Photons can spin in different direction about any axis you choose to measure (remember they are tiny wave packets, not little golf balls). Only when you decide which axis about which to measure the spin does it fix the direction of that spin.

Before that choice is made and the observation carried out, all spins are possible. But, once this is carried out on one particle, the other particle immediately takes up the opposite spin in that plane, no matter how far apart the photons are.

160 It is an inference from quantum theory that events that are separated in space and that are without possibility of connection through interaction are correlated, in a way that can be shown to be incapable of a detailed causal explanation, through the propagation of effects at speeds not greater than that of light. Thus quantum theory is not compatible with Einstein's relativity, in which it is essential that such correlations be explainable by signals propagated at speeds not faster than that of light. All these evidently imply a breakdown of the general order that had prevailed before the advent of quantum theory. (Bohm, (1980), p. 164.)

161 Squires (1986), p. 85.

162 Bell (1966). His formula, known as Bell's Inequality, has been checked by experiment many times, and every experiment confirms the effect is real (e.g. Aspect, Grangier and Roger (1981)).

163 Einstein could never accept that the theory which later developed from his ideas could be anything but provisional as a description of the physical world. His aversion to the probabilistic aspect of the theory is well known, and is encapsulated in his reply to one of Max Born's letters in 1926 (quoted in Pais (1982), p. 443).

164 Penrose (1989), p. 361.

165 Penrose points out that Niels Bohr seems to have regarded the quantum state of a system as having no physical reality. Such a picture was abhorrent to Einstein, who believed that there was an objective physical world, even at the minutest scale of quantum phenomena. Einstein attempted and failed to find any inherent contradictions in the quantum picture of things (Penrose (1989), p. 362).

166 Penrose (1989), p. 362.

167 Holroyd (1991), p. 81.

168 Feynman (1998), pp. 33-4.

169 Krishnamurti and Bohm (1985).

170 Osborne, Pinsky and Bailey, http://lsda.jsc.nasa.gov/books/apollo/S4CH2.htm (accessed February 2011).

171 The EPR paradox and experimental tests of the Bell Inequality show that entangled particles remain correlated at any distance, and that

when deferred-decision experiments are conducted on them the particles are able to communicate the outcome of the measurement to their entangled partner particle instantly.

172 http://physicsworld.com/cws/article/news/45152 (accessed February 2011).

173 Mitchell and Williams (2008), p. 65.

174 Holroyd (1991), p. 87.

175 Quoted in Jammer (1999), p. 47.

176 *Ibid.*, p. 48.

177 Heisenberg (1958), p. 135.

178 Schrödinger (1967), pp. 138–9

179 Feynman (1988), pp. 243–4.

180 Hoyle (1983), pp. 243–4.

181 Hawking (1985), Letter to the Editors, *American Scientist*, vol. 73, no. 12.

182 Armstrong (2004), pp. 80–1.

183 Hoyle (1983), pp. 248–9.

184 Wilmshurst (1927).

185 Wilmshurst (1929).

186 Wilmshurst teaches that the East of the Lodge represents spirituality, the highest and most sacred mode of consciousness. Often this is little developed, but is still latent, to become active in moments of stress or deep emotion. The West, its polar opposite, represents normal, rational understanding, the consciousness we employ in everyday affairs. It is material-mindedness or common sense.

187 It occurred to me that it can also be viewed as a metaphor for the different types of knowledge that have to be studied in order to approach truth in the round. I was reminded of the patriarch Enoch who, in the 13th Degree of the Ancient and Accepted Rite, was said to have met with the archangel Uriel, whose specialist knowledge, and responsibility, was the movement of the heavens. Uriel was also said to have instructed the prophet Ezra about the secrets of the universe and warned Noah about the flood. If I was going to have to choose a guardian angel, then Uriel seemed a good choice. Uriel would, of course, represent the logic and science of the Senior Warden.

188 Before conducting a ceremony the lodge sits in silence with lights lowered. This dark silence is to prepare the individual minds of the

brethren to merge into the corporate mind of the Perfect Lodge. After the ceremony we again sit in dark silence, to allow us time to untangle our individual minds from the group mind of the lodge and to prepare us to separate and go our different ways.

189 The original idea of a lodge was a small community devoting itself in privacy to corporate work of a philosophical nature. It was for the intellectual development and spiritual perfecting of its members. Its real purpose is to provide a model of the inner workings of the human mind and so provide a group to assist nominal Initiates realise their full potential as they progressively learn to know themselves.

The strength and worth of a lodge does not depend upon numbers and popular attractions. It rests on the quality of the corporate life of its members. It depends on their united and consistent co-operation towards a common ideal. Its success relies on their ability to form a group-consciousness.

The Craft is not a monastic community, it is a discipline of 'the secret' that is adapted to people who live in the real world, and who discharge domestic and secular duties. It does not call upon you to follow any uniform rule of life, such as is followed in an enclosed order. It leaves you to live your life in your own way but helps you acquire a unique way to harmonise your outward and inward lives.

It does, however, make definite provision in three respects. These guidelines constitute a rule of life.

1. It emphasises continual obedience to Moral Law.
2. It calls for daily progress in Masonic Science by the use of some form of helpful study, reflection or meditative practice, adapted to your taste and temperament.
3. It provides the symbolism of the working-tools and the tracing boards for daily contemplation and reflection.

190 To recapitulate the purpose of each degree – the First-Degree tracing board helps you work on emotional control, the Second assists in developing the mind, the Third teaches about controlling the Ego. The Mark tracing board helps you to realise that for a lodge to be properly formed it also needs unusually shaped living stones to be complete and strong. The Royal Arch tracing board illustrates how the way to the Centre is hidden within your own soul, while the tracing board of the

Centre illustrates the Masonic Plan for the creation of a perfected Temple of Humanity.

191 Relief is usually interpreted as the practice of charity to the whole of society.

192 Annealing is a type of heat treatment which changes a material, making it stronger, harder and less brittle. It works by heating the metal above its recrystallisation temperature, then holding it at a suitable intermediate temperature before cooling it. The Romans used to make short swords which were strong and durable.

193 Davies (1995), pp. 51–2.

194 Wheeler with Ford (1998), p. 337.

195 *Ibid.*, p. 338.

196 Black (2007), p. 398.

197 See Lomas and Knight (2000).

198 See Lomas and Knight (2003).

199 See Gauquelin (1994).

200 See McClelland (1961).

201 Lomas (2009C), Appendix 8.

202 *Ibid.*, p. 268.

203 *Ibid.*, p. 273.

204 Preston (1795), p. 224; see http://www.robertlomas.com/preston/padlock/index.html (accessed Feb 2011).

205 Leadbeater (1925), pp. 145–7.

206 I have written about this in Lomas (2009B), pp. 109–12.

207 Hodson (1976), pp. 46–7.

208 *Ibid.*, p. 269.

209 *Ibid.*, pp. 212–13.

210 Leadbeater (1925), p. 169.

211 Hodson (1976), p. 97.

212 Wheeler with Ford (1998), p. 341.

213 It is a rule of relativistic physics that nothing can exceed the speed of light. Such a cosmic speed limit makes it highly unlikely that we will ever communicate successfully with alien intelligences, because Fermi's reasoning shows that if any exist they must be an extremely long way off.

214 A new-born baby in the early days of its life has three times as many separate brain cells as there are people alive in the whole world. And by

the time its brain is fully grown there are 15,000 synapses per neuron, making the average number of neurons in the brain about 100 billion (1×10^{10}).

If each neuron has 15,000 (1.5×10^4) connections, this gives the number of possible separate interconnections as 100 billion raised to the power of 15,000, or about (1×10^{40}), that is 10,000,000,000,000,000, 000,000,000,000,000,000,000,000,000,000. And with every connection being made up of at least 10^{10} atoms, and each atom having around at least 20 subatomic particles, such as protons, neutrons and electrons, that makes at least 10,000,000,000,000,000,000,000,000,000,000,000, 000,000,000,000,000,000,000,000 possible entangled halves of a linked pair in every human brain.

215 http://physicsworld.com/cws/article/news/45152 (accessed February 2011).

216 If space–time is quantised, just as everything else in nature is, the most likely shape of those particles of space–time would be tiny spheres with a diameter of about a Planck length (the shortest length that can be shown to exist in quantum theory: about 1.6×10^{-35} metres). This would mean the wavelength of most subatomic particles would be far longer than the diameter of any individual sphere, and the wave functions of all everyday particles would sprawl across many granules of space–time. For all stable particles, space–time would appear continuous, as their wave functions would be orders of magnitude longer than the diameter of the granules of space–time. This idea is completely compatible with the theory of general relativity, as the space–time-granules could move and bend space–time to produce the effects of gravity for all objects larger than the size of a hydrogen atom.

217 http://plus.maths.org/issue23/features/kissing/ (accessed Feb 2011).

218 http://scienceworld.wolfram.com/physics/Michelson-Morley Experiment.html/ (accessed Feb 2011).

219 http://www.phys.unsw.edu.au/einsteinlight/ (accessed Feb 2011).

220 The paradox of instantaneous communication had worried Dirac so much he had proposed an alternative, which has been largely ignored. As his biographer, Graham Farmelo, explains:

> [Dirac] reintroduced a concept that most scientists believed Einstein had slain: the ether. Dirac's ether was quite different from the

nineteenth-century version: in his view, all velocities of the ether are equally likely at every point in space–time. Because this ether does not have a definite velocity with respect to other matter, it does not contradict Einstein's theory of relativity. Dirac's imagination slipped through this loophole and reinvented the ether as a background quantum agitation in the vacuum . . . The press were more interested than scientists in the idea, which appeared to go nowhere: the logic was impeccable but it seemed to have no connection with nature. (Farmelo (2010), p. 344.)

221 http://physics.about.com/od/glossary/g/wormhole.htm (accessed Feb 2011).

222 http://magic.mppmu.mpg.de/ (accessed Feb 2011).

223 http://www.newscientist.com/article/mg20327210.900-late-light-reveals-what-space-is-made-of.html (accessed Feb 2011).

224 *MAGIC Collaboration* (2008).

225 http://nobelprize.org/nobel_prizes/physics/laureates/1938/fermi-bio.html# (accessed February 2011).

226 http://www.fermisparadox.com/ (accessed February 2011).

227 Farmelo, ed. (2003), pp. 46–67.

228 http://www.fermisparadox.com/Fermi-paradox.htm (accessed February 2011).

229 Wickramasinghe (2005), pp. 109–11.

230 Hoyle and Wickramasinghe (1979).

231 http://map.gsfc.nasa.gov/ (accessed February 2011).

232 Mitchell and Williams (2008), p. 54.

233 String theory requires reality to have a property called supersymmetry. A supersymmetric Standard Model with string theory boundary conditions contains Higgs bosons and predicts they are what cause particles to have mass.

234 http://www.lhc.ac.uk/About+us/What+is+the+LHC/Detector+experiments/14438.aspx (accessed February 2011).

235 Smolin (2008), p. 7.

236 Gordin (2007).

237 Einstein, Podosky and Rosen (1935).

238 Unitarian Universalism is a theologically diverse religion in which members support one another in our search for truth and meaning. It

has historic roots in the Jewish and Christian traditions, but today individual Unitarian Universalists may identify as atheist, agnostic, Buddhist, Humanist, pagan, or with other philosophical or religious traditions.

239 Wheeler with Ford (1998), p. 250.

240 *Ibid.*, p. 124.

241 *Ibid.*, p. 124.

242 You can imagine what effect this has on accuracy. Think of trying to read the tiny dots of Braille while wearing a welder's thick protective gloves: you would need the touch sensitivity of the princess who felt the pea through twenty mattresses to hope to make sense of the text. In addition, the hard surface of your clumsy gloved fingertips could destroy the fragile paper impressions and the message they carried.

243 Davies (2007), p. 295.

244 Weinberg (1983), pp. 102–19.

245 Penrose (2004), pp. 12–17.

246 See Cameron, P.J., 'Gödel's Theorem', http://www.maths.qmul.ac.uk/~pjc/preprints/goedel.pdf (accessed February 2011); see also Penrose (1989).

247 Davies (2007), p. 295.

248 Stephen Hawking, quoted in Deutsch (1997), pp. 177–8.

249 Darwin (2001), p. 203.

250 Jönsson (1961).

251 Merli *et al.* (1976).

252 Tonomura *et al.* (1989).

253 Dirac (1930).

254 Alley *et al.* (1984).

255 Hellmuth, Walther and Zajon (1985).

256 Wheeler (1986).

257 Lomas and Knight (2000), pp. 185–9.

258 Lomas (2009C), pp. 266–8.

INDEX